PSYCHOLINGUISTICS

AMSTERDAM STUDIES IN THE THEORY AND
HISTORY OF LINGUISTIC SCIENCE

General Editor
E.F. KONRAD KOERNER
(University of Ottawa)

Series IV - CURRENT ISSUES IN LINGUISTIC THEORY

Volume 86

Joseph F. Kess

Psycholinguistics
Psychology, Linguistics, and the Study of Natural Language

PSYCHOLINGUISTICS
PSYCHOLOGY, LINGUISTICS, AND
THE STUDY OF NATURAL LANGUAGE

JOSEPH F. KESS
University of Victoria
Victoria, B.C., Canada

FJ

JOHN BENJAMINS PUBLISHING COMPANY
AMSTERDAM/PHILADELPHIA

1992

Library of Congress Cataloging-in-Publication Data

Kess, Joseph F.
    Psycholinguistics : psychology, linguistics, and the study of natural language / Joseph
F. Kess.
        p.   cm. -- (Amsterdam studies in the theory and history of linguistic science.
Series IV, Current issues in linguistic theory, ISSN 0304-0763; v. 86)
Includes bibliographical references and index.
1. Psycholinguistics. I. Title. II. Series.
P37.K48   1991
401'.9--dc20   91-37929
ISBN 90 272 3583 X (Eur.)/1-55619-141-3 (US)(hb.; alk. paper)   CIP
ISBN 90 272 3584 8 (Eur.)/1-55619-142-1 (US)(pb.; alk. paper)

Contents

Preface

This textbook is intended to serve as an introduction to the discipline of psycholinguistics for graduate students and undergraduate students at the senior levels. Ten chapters focus on the nature of psycholinguistic inquiry, its history, studies in phonology, morphology, syntax, discourse, semantics, biological correlates, language and cognition, and first language acquisition by children. The text is directed at filling the reading needs of courses in both departments of linguistics and psychology, presenting an overview of how these two disciplines have converged at various points in a search for the answers as to how natural language works.

Inquiry into the psychology of language is an ongoing activity, with a stimulating history and an exciting future. The book presents an interdisciplinary view of psycholinguistics, suggesting that inquiry into pertinent questions is neither the exclusive prerogative nor the accomplishment of a single field or academic discipline. The book also assumes that a unified approach to research in the psychology of language and cognition is not only realistic but necessary. Thus, our approach is not based on one current model, but is an integrated history of the development of ideas, and their subsequent successes, in psycholinguistics. The presentation attempts to show where we came from and why we are where we are now. It is as important to know how and why science is done, as it is to know the facts that arise from some particular period of scientific endeavor.

The textbook charts the modern re-convergence of disciplines, particularly psychology and linguistics, as they search for satisfying answers to how natural language is learned, produced, comprehended, stored, and recalled. In general, the textbook presents a unified view of psycholinguistics, in a sense parallel to the convergence of research interests one now sees in the superordinate activity labelled **cognitive science**. The rise of cognitive science with its interdisciplinary commitments to understanding the structures and relationship of language and cognition simply continues many of the research interests and developments in the psycholinguistics of recent decades.

Psycholinguistics may be an inquiry into the psychology of language, but the facts of language are what generates theories about why human language is learned, produced, and processed the way it is. Thus, you can expect a wide array of examples from the languages of the world, intended to provide a feeling for what the nature and range of human languages are like. And you can also expect a broad, but fair, coverage of the **many** topics that have taken the interest of psycholinguists over the past few decades. I have attempted to integrate current topics of intense debate, such as modularity vs. interactionism, the role of parsing strategies in sentence comprehension, and accessing the mental lexicon in word recognition, as well as earlier topics, such as sound symbolism and linguistic relativity, that attracted considerable energy not so long ago.

The single greatest help in preparing this textbook has been Andrea Giles, whose industriousness and meticulous attention to detail simply has no comparison. I am equally grateful to Paul Hopkins for his diligence and scholarly care in helping me put the finishing touches on this book. And I should also thank Konrad Koerner, for introducing this book to John Benjamins Publishers; without his unerring eye for detail and bold entrepreneurial style the *CILT* series would likely not exist. I have been particularly fortunate to have colleagues whose patience matches their expertise. Allow me to acknowledge those understanding scholars, psychologists and linguists alike, who have read and commented on part or all of the book: Pam Asquith, Craig Dickson, Steve Eady, John Esling, Bill Frawley, Ron Hoppe, Tom Hukari, Walter Kintsch, P. G. Patel, Gary Prideaux, Otfried Spreen, and Teun van Dijk. Thanks are due to Craig Dickson for producing the sound spectrographs in Chapter 3 in the phonetics laboratory in the Department of Linguistics at the University of Victoria. Special thanks go to Mike Keating, in Computing and Systems Services at the University of Victoria, for cheerfully and effectively leading me through the world of font types and mainframe mysteries; it was he who turned the manuscript into a camera-ready art form. Lastly, I wish to acknowledge the research grant (#3-48161) recently provided by SSHRCC, the Social Sciences and Humanities Research Council of Canada, which prompted me to consolidate my final thoughts on the developing history of Western psycholinguistics before attempting to survey the historical development of Japanese psycholinguistics.

The book is dedicated to my late father, Joseph Kess, *ta prav slovenec*, who knew the value of education in the New World, to his grandson Tony, who will carry on for him, and most especially to my wife Anita, who brings such joy to my life and makes it all worth doing.

Chapter 1

Introduction

Introductory Comments

Language is all-pervasive in our lives, and its function is that of commmunication. Basically, this is carried out by two related but separate activities, the activities of speaking and listening. Though we take them for granted, and rarely stop to analyze them, on closer inspection we quickly realize that they are complicated skills. We will be taking these activities apart in greater detail to find their structure and their function, and we will do this under three headings: comprehension, production, and acquisition. **Comprehension** inquires into what people do when they listen to speech and understand it, when they store it, and when they remember it. **Production**, on the other hand, deals with why and how people say what they do say. Lastly, **Acquisition** deals with how this complex of activities develops and matures in very young children as they acquire their native language. This last area, the study of child language and developmental psycholinguistics, is a vast one, and we will only touch the surface of what acquiring one's first language must entail. It is obvious, however, that an understanding of the production and processing of natural language reflects on what children must acquire in the course of their linguistic and cognitive development, just as the way in which this occurs provides insights into the abilities that we exhibit as adult native speakers of a language.

As the very interdisciplinary name suggests, **psycholinguistics** is that field of study concerned with psychological aspects of language studies. Like most fields, its practitioners may concentrate on one of two aspects, the theoretical side or the practical, applied side. The theoretical focus attempts to provide a linguistically and psychologically valid theory of language which can explain the nature of language and its acquisition. The practical or applied focus has traditionally attempted to apply linguistic and psychological knowledge to problems like reading, bilingualism, second language learning and teaching, speech pathology, and so forth. More recently, it has also attempted to contribute to a wide range of work, including the formulation of comprehensible legal language, information transferral in doctor/patient discourse, and even man-machine communication protocols. Since language is so central to human behavior, the fact of studying language behavior puts us into a complex web of relationships with many other disciplines. Some of these are immediately obvious, as for example, the interdisciplinary relationship between linguistics and psychology. In fact, when one looks back, psychological interests in the nature of language are isomorphic with the very origins of psychology as a discipline. Wilhelm Wundt himself, the father of modern experimental psychology according to many, shared a chair in philosophy with a philologist (these were the linguists of the previous century) at the University of Leipzig (see Kess 1983). Very simply, the ultimate aims of modern psychology and linguistics are not so very different in respect to understanding human language, and this recent convergence recalls for us the beginnings of both sciences when their mutual interests were very similar indeed.

Modern psycholinguistics also has fairly obvious relationships with philosophy, anthropology, sociology, communications engineering, and more recently, artificial intelligence and programming "smart computers" to respond to human language through spoken discourse rather than by feeding in that artificially prepared piece of text known as a computer program. There may be less obvious relationships with psychiatry, political science, journalism, rhetoric, literary and stylistic analysis, aesthetics, and whatever else there is, but psycholinguistics is right there at the center of things. In sum, the study of language touches all of the social sciences and certainly all of the humanities. This is because language is the singularly characteristic behavior of the human species, and is in fact the chief means of communication between members of this species.

Language makes possible a precision and abstractness which in turn makes possible the elaborate system of organization we call "human culture". Thus, whatever we learn about language also tells us much of value and insight about these other areas. Because of this centrality, it is not surprising, then, that psycholinguistics looks not only into the relationship between language and cognitive processes, but also into the relationship of language to the biological considerations that must have governed language development in the species phylogenetically, as well as its development in new members of the species ontogenetically. Equally unsurprising is our interest in the sociocultural considerations that govern language use in human societies.

As a practicing science, psycholinguistics represents a miscellany of theoretical and experimental approaches to various aspects of human language and related human behavior. Here one must remember that the practice of science depends to some degree on the theoretical model selected as one's entry point in the search for knowledge. In the case of language, this choice in turn selects not only the aspects of language behavior you will look at, but also which questions to ask and perhaps even how to proceed. One cannot stress enough the importance of the role of a scientific or theoretical model in the development of a discipline. The history of psycholinguistics is also tied to the history of ideas in the scientific pursuit of language. The constellation of ideas that characterizes an age or period is important to an understanding of the past as well as the present, and ideas about language are no exception to this rule. In the 1960s, Thomas Kuhn, a physicist turned philosopher, published an insightful little book which asserted that scientific progress is not linear, pointed, and absolutely cumulative (see Kuhn 1962/1970). Instead, the development of science is characterized more by revolution than evolution. Thus, one moves from the physics of Newton to that of Einstein, from the astronomy of Ptolemy to that of Kepler and Copernicus, from the chemistry of Priestley to that of Lavoisier, from the taxonomy of specifics in the social sciences like linguistics and anthropology to a quest for universals. Many may not agree with Kuhn's attempt to relativize science, but the suggestion that prominent figures establish a new way of looking at a problem, a new **paradigm** in Kuhn's terms, is undeniable. Important new questions are posed which require answers, and the new scientific paradigm makes serious, hopefully successful, attempts to answer those questions. That particular field of science thus progresses until the next revolutionary figure, and set of ideas, comes about, turning the focus of attention in yet another direction.

When there is too much variety in approaches and not enough unity to the field, the emergence of a unifying theme does much to further the development of a discipline. For example, Ervin-Tripp and Slobin's (1966) overview of psycholinguistics in the *Annual Review of Psychology* described exactly such a period in earlier psycholinguistic research. Their observation was that psycholinguistics was a field in search of a definition, just as Rubenstein and Aborn (1960) had earlier observed that psycholinguistics was in need of some unifying direction, or, as they put it, "helmsmanship". The field of psycholinguistics was ready for a unifying focal point, and the situation they described changed very dramatically in the mid-60s and 70s, when there was great unity in the model and goals seen in psycholinguistics because of its heavy reliance on generative linguistic theory for both a working model of natural language as well as the goals of a theory of language.

Now we seem to have a great deal of variety again, as a more eclectic psycholinguistics has successfully moved off into independent directions in the study of language behavior and is only reflective of developments in linguistic theory, rather than dependent upon them for direction. The goal of course is still to find the most informative explanation of language behavior, and this objective is unchanged. Of course, linguists in general are also most interested in finding the most informative theory of language. Where a previous generation of linguists would have found the formulation of linguistic rules to explain language sufficient as a scientific pursuit, a growing number of linguists would also demand that their work meet cognitive and learnability criteria.

Most linguists in the Chomskyan tradition of the past thirty years have also suggested language is a special faculty apart from other higher faculties, genetically inherited as a special species-specific endowment within the species. Thus for many, it has become even more compelling to ascertain whether and to what degree a theory of language behavior may be co-extensive with a theory of human cognition or human behavior. This is not an entirely novel preoccupation, and in the recent past the quest has taken many forms, ranging from explanatory models which attempt to achieve partial to complete overlap of the two. For example, even in the linguistic period known as structuralism, one had grand attempts at relating human behavior and human language by one set of explanatory principles. Among these may certainly be counted structural linguist Pike's (1967) three-volume

description of human activity in terms of particle, wave, and field, as
well as anthropologist Birdwhistell's (1970) description of kinesic gestures and movement by the etic/emic terms borrowed from structural
linguistics. In psychology, the manifestations of behaviorism expected
that the same operational principles which explained learning in organisms like pigeons and poodles would also demonstrate that human language is the product of experience and reinforcement.

In their turn, many modern cognitive psychologists have viewed
the relationship of language and cognition in a way that allows for, and
perhaps requires, parallel or isomorphic explanations. Certainly the
current meeting of psychology, linguistics, and psycholinguistics
(together with philosophy and artificial intelligence concerns in computer science) in the new discipline of **cognitive science** is the most compelling contemporary example of the drive to have our descriptions of linguistic and cognitive behavior meet around a common and mutually
important focal point. This interdiscipinary collegiality in the face of
common problems is particularly evident at the intersection of cognition and language, where different theoretical paradigms must be
brought together in focussing on a common set of scientific problems.
Indeed, if the resolution of the problems inherent in understanding natural language processing is to be a realistic one, the answer shall most
certainly be found in a paradigm which unites the various disciplines
rather than further dividing them. Although we may not be ultimately
correct in our current explanations of the degree of overlap between
language and cognition, we are at least striving to understand language behavior and to tie aspects of linguistic performance to cognitive
strategies of a more general nature.

Certainly from the point of view of the psycholinguist, there are
many instances in which it is all too evident that there is nothing in a
theory of grammar alone that would predict a particular outcome in
language behavior, and that there are explanations which must be
sought in the cognitive or physiological underpinnings for language production and processing. In the opposite direction, there have been
many instances in which psychological claims about language have
been either unaware of certain fundamental features of language structure (see Skinner 1957) or experimentation has gone off in search of
issues having little to do with the nature of linguistic abilities. As an
example of the latter, we might cite the early focus on the learning of
paired associates, reflected in the very choice of the first name for the
Journal of Verbal Learning and Verbal Behavior; its new name is the
Journal of Memory and Language, reflecting more current concerns to
do with cognition and language. Psycholinguistics must attempt to
provide a comprehensive and unified theory of language and language
behavior, accounting for how natural language constrains us into the
set of processing and production strategies that characterize real-time
language use.

Linguistic strategies come in all sizes and shapes, and for us the
first step must be to isolate factors that can be controlled and manipulated in experimental investigation. Psycholinguistics must make and
then experimentally examine testable predictions to maintain its claim

to scientific status. Now it would be easier if we could simply do one
grand experiment that would establish the one general and sovereign
principle from which all the petty details of a theory of language could
be deduced. But the reality is that we chip away at this formidable
mountain of a task one experimental piece at a time. The results from
this scientific activity over the past thirty years, under the rubric titled
psycholinguistic theory and research, is what forms the basis of the discipline that this textbook attempts to survey. We will pay attention to
the best of what we have learned in that time span, as we survey the
results of psycholinguistic research. Sometimes 'best' translates as
'most provocative' or 'most stimulating' too, and one should not expect
the following pages to just list and explain 'facts', for much of what we
wish to know of language behavior must first be stated as important
questions which require us to think out the plausible reasons for why
human language is the way it is. Only then can we begin to attack the
problem by planning out our methodology and the frame of reference
that it will operate within.

Comprehension

Let us return to considering the domain of psycholinguistics as
defined by the activities of comprehension, production, and acquisition,
and look at what each of these areas requires in the way of explanation. Comprehension asks what do people do when they listen to
speech? When they understand it? when they store it? when they
remember it? The fact is that language comprehension is an active,
dynamic process, not a passive one. The hearer takes as input the
speech he or she hears, plus other linguistic and extralinguistic information, and constructs the most likely interpretation for the linguistic
signal being processed. Not only does the hearer have a knowledge of
the structure of the language available to do this with, but he or she
also has access to other relatively structured kinds of extralinguistic
information. Among other things, as part of the ongoing thematic
structure, the speaker is aware of the preceding linguistic context and
the topic under discussion. The speaker is also aware of the roles of
the various events and participants in the narrative and the way in
which the conversational partner relates to the discussion of that narrative.

There is also a vast but well-organized inventory of general knowledge that one can refer to. For example, an unstated fact that most of
us know about eating in restaurants is that at the end of the meal a
bill will come; similarly, we know that if we order wine, it will come in
a glass, and not a paper cup. One is reminded of how organized our
underlying knowledge of such experiences is when we try to programme computers to understand even limited scripts like the restaurant scenario. Such well-known background "facts" would have to be
made explicit to a computer to enable it to process a piece of text dealing with a restaurant scenario, for it has no way of knowing what we

simply assume; it simply does not have such a well-organized inventory of general knowledge unless we provide it. In addition, inferences are constantly being made on what is overtly said, as well as from what is implied, understood, or generally known. And lastly, the hearer also has some expectations that arise from the conversation, certainly expectations that include some idea about what the other participants know in relation to the discussion and what they too may expect from the conversation. It is all too obvious that comprehension is an active process, not a passive act in which the hearer's mind is entirely blank and waiting to be written upon by the speaker.

The final goal, of course, is to understand the message, and as this activity unfolds, the hearer must perform multi-level analyses on the incoming speech. The hearer must undertake a phonological analysis, that is, construct an appropriate phonological segmentation of the incoming signal. For example, was that sound in the word I just heard an /r/ or a /w/? Although both sounds involve rounding of the lips in their production by the speaker, we ask ourselves if there are other acoustic cues we should pay attention to in analyzing the speech signal coming from the speaker. After all, deciding on this phonetic feature really decides on whether the word we just heard was *red* or *wed*. The hearer must also carry out a grammatical analysis of input, on both morphological (word-building) and syntactic (sentence-building) levels. For example, he or she knows to segment the plural ending from the words *bees, trees, knees, keys,* but not on *cheese.* One must also process sentences like *John is eager to please* and *John is easy to please* to reflect the fact that *John* is the logical subject of both *eager* and *please* in the first sentence. In the second sentence, there is an unspecified noun phrase (NP) subject of *easy,* while *John* is the object NP of *please.* The analysis of some ambiguous sentences like *Visiting relatives can be a nuisance* and *The peasants are revolting* requires an interaction between the two levels, for one must decide which interpretation of the ambiguity is correct before assigning a syntactic analysis, and this defines the analytic treatment of the *-ing* words.

Lexical assignment is also necessary, such that lexical items are looked up in our mental dictionaries and their various meanings are scanned and evaluated for their appropriateness (or inappropriateness) in the sentence being processed. For example, consider how one makes judgments about the metaphoric or innovative meanings of the first verbs in sentence pairs like *Fred elapsed for an hour/Fred slept for an hour* and *Kissinger persuaded sincerity/Kissinger persuaded Egypt.* Continuing this active process on the part of the hearer, note that the hearer must also assign the appropriate semantic case roles to the various participants and events in the sentence. For example, the subjects of the sentences *The key opened the door/The boy opened the door/The door opened* differ in being the underlying instrument, agent, and acted-upon patient in their semantic case roles, even though all three appear as subject. This knowledge is reflected in the fact that we know a sentence like *The boy opened the door with a key* can be constructed from such case roles, while a sentence like **The key opened the door with the boy* is not grammatical under normal language circumstances. And as if this were not enough, hearers must also process the underlying speech act intent of the speaker, for example, realizing that the utterance *Can you open the door?* is not a question, but really a command to go and open the door.

All of these considerations must be taken into account not only for single sentences, but since sentences normally fit into larger thematic structures, for the discourse as a whole. In doing do, there are of course heuristic short-cuts which hearers employ in their comprehension of sentences. On the basis of our past linguistic experience, we typically make educated guesses or predictions that a certain type of structure is involved or that certain kinds of constituents should appear at certain places. For example, we know from experience that the article *the* signals a following NP, containing a possible adjective but ultimately a noun as head of a coming noun phrase. Similarly, we know that a preposition signals a coming NP object and that a transitive verb signals a coming NP direct object. As a last example, we also know that a relative pronoun like *who* or *that* signals a coming embedded clause. Contrast *John paid the man who came with the package* with *John paid the man with the package he had set aside on the shelf for just such an occasion.* The *who* in the first sentence immediately alerts the hearer to the fact that a relative clause is coming up next, and that the object of the main clause is the same as the subject of the embedded clause. That is, the man John paid is the same one that came with the package. In the second sentence, no such clue exists and one must backtrack with information taken from the latter part of the sentence to analyze where the phrase *with the package* belongs.

Many of these cues are language-specific, just as these above examples were cited for English because of our familiarity with the structure of the English language. But there may also be general strategies, like the one which leads us to anticipate the completion of a sentence at the earliest possible point. For example, sentences like *Galileo anticipated the answer eventually found in this century/The man expected to win the election died/The horse raced past the barn fell* typically fool us into wanting to make the sentences end at *answer/election/barn*, respectively. English as a SVO (Subject-Verb-Object) language leads us in this direction, plus the more general processing strategy that the sentence will end at the earliest possible logical point. It is only in *garden path* sentences like these where the strategy does not work that we are even aware of the existence of our expectation of early closure.

Production

In the study of production, we wish to know why and how people say what they do say. We should note that comprehension and production are not mirror images in terms of the processes involved, though they may prove to be closely related. In production, a speaker has a message to communicate, and the message is encoded. The hearer only has incoming speech, and not the underlying intention which generated that particular utterance, so the signal must be decoded and the intended message reconstructed. A good example of how this can be so is ambiguity, for an ambiguous sentence is often a problem for the hearer who is trying to comprehend the message; it is not a problem for the speaker who knows what he or she wants to say as the utterance is produced. The strategies for comprehension and production may not be the same, but it is conceivable that the units that both make use of are either similar or related.

If we ask what a speaker does when an utterance is produced, we note that he or she must first settle upon the propositional content, or the ideas to be conveyed. Thus, the message must be represented semantically in terms of a set of elemental propositions which contain predicates with arguments attached. For example, assuming the message behind the utterance *John sent Mary a package* is transparent, we can note how the message is coded in English by a proposition having the verb *sent* as its predicate with related arguments *John, Mary, package*. The arguments placed in certain syntactic orderings like the one in our sentence above establish *John* as agent, *Mary* as beneficiary or recipient, and *package* as the acted-upon patient. These facts, established by linguistic devices like word order, affixed endings like the past tense on the verb, and so forth, constitute the ideational content to be conveyed in this act of information transferral.

But there is also an activity side to language in the sense that we use language to perform functions, as an activity in which we use words to get people to do things for us. In this sense, the speaker must also decide upon the speech act format that this utterance will employ, and for what purpose. Thus, in production I may decide that the speech act I wish to perform is that of a command, but that I will do this in an indirect, perhaps more polite way, by uttering *Can you close the door?*, rather than *Close the door!*. Thus, in production the speaker must not only decide upon the ideational content or information to be conveyed, but also what particular act this utterance is performing. Is it a command, an assertion, or a promise? And how shall that speech be formatted? Will it be an indirect speech act like *Can you close the door?*, an utterance which is really a command, even though it looks like a question.

Then, too, the speaker must also be aware of the unfolding thematic structure of the interaction, fitting the contribution in at the appropriate point, and with the appropriate relationship, in an attempt to maintain coherence in the exchange. He or she also has access to a vast store of general knowledge, presumably shared by the conversational partner, as well as access to the expectations generated by the developing conversation. Again, these are also presumably largely shared with the partner(s), and he or she must fit the contributions into their mutual understanding of the thematic development of the discourse, and the expectations that are derived from the conversation.

Once this basic two-part framework of **propositional content** and **speech act** purpose has been established--that is, once a semantic proposition and a speech act format have been decided upon--the utterance must be converted into a grammatical representation. Typically this is a matter of language-specific rules, making use of grammatical strictures like the fact that English exhibits a Subject-Verb-Object (SVO) order, while Japanese is an Subject-Object-Verb (SOV) language. A semantic representation must also incorporate lexical items, or at least the meanings of lexical items. Morphophonemic rules must assign actual phonological shapes to grammatical morphemes like tense, number, and case. Irregularities must also be taken care of, so that one selects appropriate forms not only for the regular past and plural forms in *missed* and *roses*, but also for the irregular forms in *broke* and *mice*. And phonological rules must then convert the phonological sequence into the appropriate phonetic representation of the sound in that particular position in the word; for example, the /r/ in *red* is produced with an accompanying rounding of the lips in a way that the /r/ in *hair* is not. Moreover, during the entire production process, there is constant feedback with self-monitoring always taking place, such that the speaker can alter, re-route, or even re-start the processes at whichever stage is reached. Obviously, we do not work out all the niceties of the sentence before beginning it, but are instead actively and creatively building it as we go.

We are also interested in the the nature of the constituent structure assigned by the speaker in production, and to what degree this is the same as the structural analysis employed by the hearer in comprehension. The units may turn out to not always be consistent with the structures and units proposed by the linguist in a description of the language, but one assumption will certainly be the same. This is the the need to state the rules speakers use in production, as well as in comprehension. The structure of language is usually stated in the form of a system of rules, with such rules set out as explicit statements that specify what will occur and in which order. A complete inventory of such rules is a description of the language, or its grammar. Typically we know such rules only implicitly, but this does not make the rules any less real. In addition to clearly specifying the structural rules of language, we would also like to state the rules that speakers and hearers employ in their comprehension and production of natural language. The creation of such an inventory of observations, principles, and rules is really what constitutes the essence of the discipline of psycholinguistics.

Acquisition

How is the complex set of activities described above acquired by children learning their first language? Since we are primarily interested in comprehension and production processes by adults, we can only undertake a brief review of this important area of psycholinguistics. Concentrating on the areas of adult production and comprehension will take up an entire textbook; doing justice to developmental aspects of first language acquisition would require yet another textbook. However, there is an inescapable relationship between the capacity for human language and the way in which it is acquired is related to the final product that we adults all share in as **competent** speakers of the language. Here **competence** refers to the general set of linguistic abilities that native speakers of a language share as speakers of that language. In fact, we may note that, barring a physical or mental deficit that specifically impairs such linguistic abilities, all human communities are composed of adult speaker/hearers who speak natural languages with more or less the same set of competence abilities.

Very simply, there are no human societies where we fail to find a language, and no human community in which the typical speaker/hearer fails to have the linguistic abilities to produce and understand the human language that community employs. If this is the case, we might well ask what it is in the human endowment that makes all children capable of acquiring language with such relative ease and success at such an early age, as they become fully functioning members of a human culture. What similarities are there right across languages that makes it an absolute certainty that human beings acquire a first language with such ease and along similar pathways of development?

It must be obvious that much of what we might have to say about such basic acquisition questions has a serious impact upon what we can expect to say in the matter of how and why adults produce and process language the way they do. Thus, it should not be surprising that we will pay some attention to the biological foundations of language, questions of language origins and development, and what we know of the physiological, as well as cognitive, underpinnings for human language. Many questions of language acquisition are inextricably tied up with the very capacity for language itself, and the fulfillment of this capacity in adults is obviously related to the pattern of acquisition by children as they realize this genetically programmed set of abilities.

Summary

The discipline of **psycholinguistics** seeks to provide a comprehensive and unified theory of language and language behavior which accounts for how natural language constrains us into the set of processing and production strategies that characterize real-time language use. Psycholinguistics also attempts to formulate a linguistically and psychologically valid theory of language which can explain the nature of language and its acquisition by children acquiring their first language.

Psycholinguistic inquiry usually falls under one of three headings: comprehension, production, and acquisition. **Comprehension** involves what listeners do when they listen to speech and understand it, when they store it, and when they remember it. Comprehension studies may also examine what readers do when they read text for understanding, storage, or recall. **Production** deals with why and how people say what they do say. Speakers have both information and intentions to communicate, and production studies are interested in how messages are encoded to achieve this. Lastly, **Acquisition** deals with how this complex set of productive and processual abilities develops and matures in very young children as they acquire their native language. An understanding of the production and processing of natural language by adults is, of course, a necessary prerequisite for setting the parameters of what children must acquire in the course of their linguistic and cognitive development.

As a scientific discipline, psycholinguistics makes and experimentally examines testable predictions about linguistic and cognitive behavior in the areas of language comprehension, production, and acquisition. This textbook surveys the results of this scientific activity over the past forty years, attempting to provide an informative and even-handed overview of the major trends in psycholinguistic theory and research over that period.

Chapter 2

A History of Psycholinguistics

Early Signposts: Syntactics, Semantics, and Pragmatics

Disciplines erect signposts for their convenience as well as guidance, and in this chapter we will survey the major developments in the psychology of language by reviewing the influential ideas, and their proponents, which have contributed to the way in which psycholinguistic studies have evolved since the turn of the century.[1] An early set of signposts for the study of signs and symbols, as well as language and thought relationships, was established by Morris' (1938) contribution to the *International Encyclopedia of Unified Science*. Morris' logical positivistic division of the study of signs and symbols listed the following fields of activity:

1. syntactics = the relationship of signs to signs
2. semantics = the relationship of signs to their meanings
3. pragmatics = the relationship of signs to the people who use them

In explaining a linguistically-based approach to psycholinguistics some thirty years later, Miller (1964b) also used this logico-philosophical frame of reference. He noted that the effect of such a scheme is to divide the field into problems of structure, of comprehension, and of belief, and that such a division of efforts provides its own hierarchy of activities for the relevant disciplines of linguistics, psychology, and philosophy.

1. syntactics or problems of structure: at the lowest level it is necessary to understand the syntactic structure of a language
2. semantics or problems of comprehension: it then becomes possible to understand its semantic content
3. pragmatics or problems of belief: once both structural analysis and semantic comprehension are achieved, then an understanding of pragmatic acceptance or rejection, and belief or disbelief, is possible

Miller's (1964b) observation that this division corresponds roughly to the order in which the study of language has progressed was accurate for its time, as well as a predictor for the future, though not quite in the way that Miller had envisioned. It is still true, as he suggested, that syntactics is the best known, semantics the next best, and pragmatics the least, though it too is receiving increasing attention (note, for example, the recent appearance of several journals in pragmatics,

---

[1] This chapter is a considerably revised version of an article which originally appeared under the title "On the Developing History of Psycholinguistics" (*Language Sciences* 13:1.1-20, 1990).

an international organization, and the recent international congresses [Antwerp, 1987; Barcelona, 1990] in pragmatics). But it was still true that when he wrote, the three fields could be apportioned between the disciplines as follows:

1.   psychology's interests traditionally in pragmatics, with the psychologist try-
        ing to understand the ways in which humans acquire, understand, and
        exploit the linguistic system
2.   semantics traditionally the interest of philosophy and later of anthropology
3.   syntactics traditionally the interest of linguistics, with its analysis of the
        formal relationship of signs to one another, in abstraction from the relation-
        ship of signs to objects or to their users

But when Miller wrote, he was attempting to demonstrate the importance of theoretical insights derived from linguistics to psycholinguistics. We no longer make such severe distinctions between theories of language and theories of language users, nor do we now see the fields as neatly broken into linguists just doing syntactic analysis and psychologists describing how humans acquire and use that and related systems. Changes have occurred in the definitions of what semantics and pragmatics mean, and changes have also occurred in zones of interest. Psychologists are more aware of problems of structure and meaning in their research plans, as are linguists now aware of also constructing theories of language users and language acquirers.

Miller's (1964a, b) comments are best understood in the context of the Linguistic Period in psycholinguistics. Such comments acted as a prompt to psychology in noting that in order to construct a theory of language user, one first had to understand how the user deals with syntactic and semantic aspects of language, with the realities of structure and meaning derived from language. Many now take such assumptions for granted, and new signposts have been erected giving directions to where we should go and why. For this reason, it is worth reviewing the recent history of psycholinguistics for the theoretical ideas which defined the field of interests from the 1950s to the 1980s, both from the perspective of methodological commitments which motivated research as well as for the ideas which proponents of each new *paradigm* rebelled against.

An Historical Overview

The term **psycholinguistics** suggests that this is a field which depends in some crucial way on the theories and intellectual interchange of both psychology AND linguistics. There have been two major periods in which psycholinguistic interests have flourished, once around the turn of the century, primarily in Europe, and once in the 1950s and 1960s, primarily in America (Blumenthal 1987, Reber 1987). Blumenthal (1970, 1974) has painted Leipzig's Wilhelm Wundt as the influential "master psycholinguist" during that first period, one who was prepared to demonstrate that language could be explained on the basis of psychological principles. It was a period when linguistics was prepared to exchange its older, Romanticist evaluation of language on cultural and aesthetic principles, for a more modern, 'scientific' approach to language. Wilhelm Wundt, and the new psychology, offered this with the rigor and and enthusiasm that only a new scientific discipline can offer. Many younger linguists were keen to import this new rigor and scientific vision to linguistic theory and research, and for a time psychological concerns were directly reflected in the emerging field of linguistics. For example, all linguists know Leonard Bloomfield as the prototypical structuralist, often quoting his 1933 book as the classic text of the structuralist period in linguistics. But his little-known first book of 1914 pays careful homage to Wundtian psychology. Faced by the decline in the power of German intellectual life after the devastating first war and an equally weakened Wundtian cognitive psychology, his later book parallels the aspirations of the powerfully emerging behaviorism, but psychological theory no longer guides linguistic theory (see Kess 1983).

Curiously, there was to be another period of intellectual unity, equally fertile, equally enthusiastic, and equally brief (see Reber 1987, and McCauley 1987). This was the period after the 1960s, when linguistic theory fueled the engines of psycholinguistic enterprise. Specifically, this was the type of linguistics founded on the theoretical pattern of transformational generative grammar, as proposed by Noam Chomsky. But this unity of purpose also faded after several decades of experimentation based on Chomskyan theory, leaving us now with a more balanced, and certainly a more eclectic view of what psycholinguistic theory should pursue in attempting to offer explanations for natural language. We will only pay attention to the history of psycholinguistics since that second period in the 1950s. The major reason for doing this is because this recent history reflects the changing roles of linguistics and psychology vis-a-vis one another in the contemporary discipline of psycholinguistics. It also represents a time when these two mature disciplines collaborate in meaningful and productive ways to approach the problems of the psychology of language.

Updating Maclay's useful (1973) classification of developmental steps in modern psycholinguistics, we can trace the field's progression in four major periods (see also Kess 1990).

Four Major Periods:

1. Formative
2. Linguistic
3. Cognitive
4. Psycholinguistic Theory, Psychological Reality, and Cognitive Science

The Four Major Periods

Formative Period . The first formal contacts were established at a Social Science Research Council Summer meeting at Cornell in 1951, and a Committee on Linguistics and Psychology was formed with Charles Osgood as chairman. A second summer seminar was held at Indiana University in conjunction with the Linguistic Institute of 1953; the intellectual directions of such exchanges are chronicled in Osgood and Sebeok's (1954) *Psycholinguistics*, one of the first uses of the new hyphenated label (the term **psycholinguistics** was unknown in Wundt's time!). The Committee sponsored a number of smaller meetings on a variety of topics like language universals (see Greenberg 1963/1966) and encouraged research like Carroll's Southwest Project in Comparative Psycholinguistics investigating the Linguistic Relativity Hypothesis which had attracted renewed attention through the writings of Benjamin Lee Whorf (see, for example, Carroll and Casagrande 1958, and Maclay 1958).

This period boasted a symmetrical relationship between linguistics and psychology, because both were committed to an operationalist philosophy: **structuralism** was the prevailing paradigm in linguistics and **behaviorism** was predominant in psychology. An operationalist approach in philosophy of science terms derives theoretical constructs from observable data by using a set of verifiable operations which are highly explicit. Thus, structuralism in linguistics defined units like phoneme and morpheme in terms of operational procedures. For example, one used concepts like **minimal contrast** or **complementary distribution** to define a given phoneme or morpheme. These operational procedures were called **discovery procedures** and were used in interview situations like **field work** to "discover" the structure of an unknown, or even familiar, language. Similarly, behaviorism in psychology gave primacy to observable data, and devoted its theoretical efforts to the elaboration of operational methods which guaranteed that any explanatory device (like **drive** or **habit strength**) was anchored in the real world. Behaviorist methodology thus came to focus upon rigorous experimental design and statistical analysis of data. We should note that the emphasis on good experimental design before a given psychological investigation and a thorough statistical analysis of the resultant data continues to be the hallmark of mainstream psychology, regardless of which particular paradigm holds sway in the discipline.

One of the earliest and strongest statements on behaviorism and its perception of how language should be approached comes from John B. Watson (1924:6).

> In his first efforts to get uniformity in subject matter and in methods the behaviorist began his own formulation of the problem of psychology by sweeping aside all mediaeval conceptions. He dropped from his scientific vocabulary all subjective terms such as sensation, perception, image, desire, purpose, and even thinking and emotion as they were subjectively defined.

> The behaviorist asks: Why don't we make what we can *observe* the real field of psychology? Let us limit ourselves to things that can be observed, and formulate laws concerning only those things. Now what can we observe? Well, we can observe *behavior--what the organism does or says.* And let me make this fundamental point at once: that *saying* is doing--that is, *behaving.* Speaking overtly to ourselves (thinking) is just as objective a type of behavior as baseball.

Now the Hullean psychology that made common cause with linguistics in the Formative Period was not of this extreme behavioristic bent, though B. F. Skinner's contemporaneous work (1957) was an extension of the same underlying philosophy into what has been termed Radical Behaviorism. Psychologists like Charles E. Osgood postulated models of stimulus-response relationships that posited internal, and thus unobservable, mediational variables that earned them the designation of Neo-Behaviorism; it was this group that was more active in psycholinguistics research.

There was a third partner in this Formative Period; Information Theory, derived from communications engineers, served largely as a source of ideas and models. For example, Shannon and Weaver (1949), communications engineers with Bell Telephone, defined a "communication" unit as follows:

Source->Transmitter/encoder->Channel->Receiver/decoder->Destination

The channel might be subject to interferences, or "noise", a prime concern for communications engineering at the time, and thus there was emphasis on decoding and encoding processes on opposite ends of the channel, plus attention to the possible interference properties the channel might be subject to. Information Theory, and by extension, psycholinguistics, made use of this mechanical metaphor of language for a brief period in the 1950s. As an example of how psycholinguistics for a time spoke in terms of investigating "communicating units" who produce/encode and receive/decode messages, one notes that Osgood and Sebeok (1954:4) state that "psycholinguistics deals directly with the processes of encoding and decoding as they relate states of messages to states of communicators".

Though there was room for disagreement as to who did what in psycholinguistics, none arose because of the obvious split in the division of labor. Linguists took the states of messages as their area of research inquiry, and psychologists took the states of communicators, and by default, the encoding and decoding processes, perhaps because of the natural affinity between behaviorism and information theory. The striking characteristic of this period in psycholinguistics is its diversity, and if one asked what psycholinguistics does, the answer seemed to be "Everything!". Saporta (1961), a popular book of readings in the new paradigm, had essentially a juxtaposition of the two disciplines, with little effort at integrating linguistics and psychology.

The first overview of psycholinguistics that appears in the *Annual Review of Psychology* (Rubenstein and Aborn 1960) thus notes "little helmsmanship" in the field, and is largely an account of traditional psychological endeavors. There is little mention of linguistics, except for a paragraph just mentioning linguists Noam Chomsky and his mentor Zellig Harris. The time seems ripe for the introduction of a new and unifying paradigm in the Kuhnian sense we discussed in the introductory chapter. And this is just what happened for a time. It is interesting to compare the evolution of the field as characterized by later reviews in the *Annual Review of Psychology*. Ervin-Tripp and Slobin (1966) and Fillenbaum (1971a) very much reflect the centering focus of linguistic theory in Chomskyan terms. But time takes its toll, and it is equally worthy of note that later reviews by Johnson-Laird (1974) and Danks and Glucksberg (1980) do not cite a single paper by Chomsky, though much of the experimental work reflects his ideas. And those ideas still have a certain influence; as the current review by Foss (1988) observes, the hegemony of syntactic theory may be long past in both linguistics and psycholinguistics, but both fields continue to be profoundly affected by Chomskyan claims. It was during the Linguistic Period that psycholinguistics experienced its second historical period of total theoretical unity, and so it is worth surveying this period in somewhat more detail to understand its aims, as well as gauge the reasons for the reactions which followed in the history of the discipline.

Linguistic Period . The rise of transformational generative grammar in linguistics is followed by its theoretical domination of psycholinguistic research, particularly from 1960 to 1969. Chomskyan criticisms of behaviorism, coupled with the basic tenets of generative grammar, come to dictate the shape of psycholinguistic research. Chomsky (1957, 1959) had destroyed the two cornerstones of psycholinguistic research which had served the formative period, by arguing that an operationalist philosophy cannot provide adequate grammars of natural languages. He further argued that a deductive approach is required, and that linguistic theory has as its proper domain the competence of speakers, and not their performance (Chomsky 1965). Thus, the previous division of labor was called into question, as well as the theoretical cornerstones upon which research activity had been based. In linguistics, this was a shift in paradigm, but in psycholinguistics this was really the introduction of one where there was none. For a psycholinguistics based on what generative grammarians thought to be crucial to an understanding of language, the starting point was the study of competence, with the study of performance a secondary activity, if indeed even that important. It was generally agreed that an understanding of competence would be crucial to understanding the nature of actual performance. Thus, the centrality of grammar was taken as a basic assumption, with the sentence emerging as the prime unit in this quest to understand grammar. Not surprisingly, most psycholinguistic experiments during this period dealt with the understanding and use of sentences, because the sentence played such an important role in defining the data and dimensions of transformational generative grammar.

Much of this orientation came through George A. Miller, whose writings and experiments served as bridge between linguistic theory and psychological experimentation in the earliest years (for example, 1964a, b). Some of the early titles of papers are suggestive of the centrality of grammar commitment; for example, (Miller 1962) "Some Psychological Studies of Grammar" and (Miller and Isard 1963) "Some Perceptual Consequences of Linguistic Rules". Some of these early experiments hinted that production or perception of sentences could be isomorphic to the derivation of that sentence by the grammar. Assuming that these were linguistic rules of the type postulated for grammatical descriptions, psycholinguistic studies in the 1960s tested whether the linguistic formulations embodied in transformational grammar were involved in language comprehension. They tested whether the number and complexity of mental operations performed during processing was a function of the number and complexity of formal transformations seen in the grammatical derivation of that sentence. This notion, known as the **Derivational Theory of Complexity**, never received sufficient support to warrant its continuing presence as even a working hypothesis, but much of the information which experimental results demonstrated along the way was even more informative, and showed that there was much more to be learned from psycholinguistic research than just this weak hypothesis. The originator of transformational generative grammar, Noam Chomsky, had rejected this idea early on, and linguistics waxed hot and cold on how the grammar might be related to the actual derivation of sentences by the speaker and its interpretation by the listener. This ambivalence has been true until this last period we are now in (**Psycholinguistic Theory, Psychological Reality, and Cognitive Science**), when the notion of **psychological reality** has found acceptance in linguistic theory and cognitive science easily, and typically without ever being called that.

Because of generative grammar's pursuit of linguistic universals, and explanations for instead of taxonomies of data, there was soon considerable interest in language acquisition as well (see Smith and Miller 1966). McNeill's writings (1964, 1970) in developmental psycholinguistics wholly accepted the transformational approach, suggesting that the child enters the process of language learning with an innate predisposition for the general form of linguistic rules, and possibly even certain linguistic categories. Lenneberg's (1967) work on the biological foundations of language most fully developed the argument for innateness, fully chronicling the argument with evidence from other sciences, but relying for its original impetus from Chomsky's theoretical notions in generative grammar. The basic argument is that the capacity for language acquisition is species-specific and is a genetically determined attribute of humans and humans alone. Consequently, the field of developmental psycholinguistics and child language studies boomed with a richness and vigor which is still with us, as researchers attempted to discover what it was that children could be expected to master in natural language and how they went about achieving this as they passed from stage to stage until linguistic maturity.

But this Linguistic Period slowly gave way to a richer, more inter-disciplinary commitment in psycholinguistics. For one thing, the rapid pace with which formalizations changed in linguistic theory placed a heavy burden on even committed psychologists (and linguists too!) try-ing to keep track. There was also some fragmentation in the aims of transformational grammar, and in the formalisms that it employed, leading to a decline in the uniformity and optimism which marked ear-lier work (see Reber 1987). Other problems confronted linguistic theo-ry in the form of the role of performance facts, data from language acquisition studies, and where to place and what to include in seman-tics vis-a-vis syntax in a comprehensive grammatical theory. Not sur-prisingly, a third period arises, largely prompted by psychologists and philosophers of language. This does not mean that the Linguistic Peri-od ends abruptly, nor that linguistic theory ceases to have an influence. But it does imply a rejection of the direction of traffic from about 1970 on, with linguistics no longer supplying psycholinguistic units, models, and methodologies almost exclusively (see Kess 1976a, b).

Cognitive Period . First of all, one should note that *cognitive* in this sense does not have quite the same meaning as in an earlier *cognitive psychology*, though there was indeed similarity between Gestalt cogni-tive psychology and transformational grammar in their rejection of behaviorism (see Neisser 1967). The crucial difference here rests more in the area of language acquisition and what the so-called "intrinsic capacity" to learn language really means. J. A. Fodor (1966) had already noted that perhaps what is brought to bear is a set of general learning principles, and Lenneberg (1967) had also seen language in the broader sense of general biological and cognitive foundations.

The major premise that underlies a cognitive approach is the dependence of language upon human cognition, the notion that lan-guage is but one of several outcomes of more fundamental cognitive processes. Chomsky had himself paved the way with his (1968) com-ment that linguistics is a field concerned with human cognition, and that linguists are really cognitive psychologists. Perhaps the best early representatives of the cognitive approach are Bever (1970) and Slobin (1973) on the cognitive basis for linguistic structures. They reject the centrality and independence of grammar, arguing that the cognitive capacity described in grammatical accounts of competence is only one manifestation of human language and is in no way prior to or indepen-dent of other cognitive and behavioral systems involved in the acquisi-tion and use of language. Linguistic structures are not learned inde-pendently of semantic concepts and discourse functions, and more importantly, cognitive principles must be assumed to govern the acqui-sition of linguistic structures. The acquisition of language was explained as a result of the interaction between the linguistic and other behavioral systems, such that the nature of linguistic systems is ulti-mately a product of more basic cognitive structures. Some even went so far as to suggest that perhaps transformational grammar itself was just a theory about having linguistic intuitions, with the implication that this type of language behavior is no more closely related to the ultimate nature of language than other linguistic aspects of learning, perceiving, and speaking.

Thus, although linguistic theory continued to play a role in psycholinguistic theory and practice, the role is not quite the same as before. For the best contemporaneous assessment of what was learned from linguistic input, see Fodor, Bever and Garrett's (1974) summation of psycholinguistic achievements based on linguistic theory (see also Kess 1976a). Very simply, Fodor, Bever, and Garrett's review of experiments which set out to investigate the psychological reality of grammatical structure and operations postulated by linguists have a simple conclusion. Their review of this line of experimentation re-confirms the reality of the taxonomy of sentences (the sentence family and intersentential distances) implied in transformational syntax, but not the psychological reality of transformations. In fact, their observation is that the larger pattern of experimental findings on generative grammar suggest that "experiments which undertake to demonstrate the psychological reality of the structural descriptions characteristically have better luck than those which undertake to demonstrate the psychological reality of the operations involved in grammatical derivations" (Fodor, Bever, and Garrett 1974:241). Thus, structural descriptions and units like the sentence constituent specified therein, do appear to have some psychological status in organizational and memory tasks, but evidence for the claim that transformational processes, as set out by linguists' descriptions of the language, might play a role in the comprehension, storage, or recall was far weaker in comparison. Interestingly, Fodor, Bever, and Garrett concluded that work on the psychological reality of syntactic structures may be "concerned less and less with the vindication of independently motivated linguistic analyses where the linguistic arguments are equivocal" (p. 512) and that "it may well be that only direct experimentation on psychological reality will ultimately choose between competing syntactic theories" (p. 512).

Up to this point, we have charted the historical progression of issues in psycholinguistics, in order to be able to look back to see where we were and how we arrived at where we are presently. For a contrastive summary of these three main orientations of the behaviorist (association), cognitive (process), and generative (content) positions in respect to the major issues in psycholinguistics, see Reber (1973). But the fourth and current period is more difficult to characterize, for it is one which we are presently in the middle of, and its final conclusions and contributions we have yet to see realized.

Psycholinguistic Theory, Psychological Reality, and Cognitive Science .
Psycholinguistics is in a state of transition, and there is no longer any one single prevailing school of thought in the discipline (see Rieber and Voyat 1981). Nor is there one in psychology or linguistics. Instead, one sees a tremendous amount of interdisciplinary activity, with researchers very much aware of developments in adjacent fields, often even contributing to those developments. More importantly, perhaps, scholars can no longer afford to ignore scientific answers in other fields which impinge on research problems in their own fields and the expla-

nations they offer for them. For if **cognitive science** is truly the scientific understanding of how the human mind works (Johnson-Laird 1983), then the demand for psychological reality in psycholinguistic theory is no longer novel or trivial. But the acceptance of this criterion as one which was necessary for a realistic and well-formulated theory of language (see Halle, Bresnan, and Miller 1978) is more a feature of the last decade than of the previous three periods. It is implicit in the collaborative participation of linguistics, psychology, and psycholinguistics in the development of cognitive science, one of the more noteworthy events of the last decade. Basically, the linguistic approach here is now one which takes information processing constraints into account. "Correctness" of a grammatical theory is no longer being argued here, for grammatical theories can all be internally "correct"; it is a question of usefulness or compatibility of a system of grammatical description that is attuned to the problems, as well as the results, of psycholinguistic research. For example, the treatment of such grammatical phenomena as the derivation of truncated passives or the ordering of center-, left-, and right-embeddings may be independently treated in a grammatical description, that is, independent from the way they operate for language users in terms of processual strategies. And many linguists might insist that this is rightly so, and that this is all that linguistic theories should account for, that is, linguistic structures and putative operations that linguists might claim to occur. "Psychological reality" is a term we should reserve only for grammars which have relevance to language processing and which are in turn constrained by language processing factors. The problem of psychological validity is thus only a problem for those linguists who wish to make psychological claims about their theories and resultant grammars; many of course do not wish to, many do so explicitly and some do implicitly. But certainly psychological reality is a desideratum for any linguistic theory which truly wishes explanatory power about the nature of language beyond the linguistic system itself. And it is certainly a requisite for any psycholinguistic theory that is worthy of the name. Such realistic theories of language thus describe our language knowledge and linguistic abilities in a way that incorporates performance abilities that are crucial to information processing tasks.

One example of such an attempt to integrate linguistic and psycholinguistic information into a single theory of language is found in the lexical-functional theory of grammar (Bresnan 1981, Bresnan and Kaplan 1982, Kaplan and Bresnan 1982), also known by LFG as the acronym for Lexical Functional Grammar. Unlike many theories of grammatical description, it does concern itself very directly with the relationship between an adequate grammatical theory and language processing considerations. And in the innovative paper in the Halle, Bresnan, and Miller volume mentioned above, Bresnan (1978) makes claims that her grammmatical postulates are not only meant to be, but are, psychologically real. As a representative model of linguistic knowledge compatible with real language processing, this theory actually does make a claim that a competence grammar of this sort is directly incorporated into a language processing model. Lexical-functional grammars simply store grammatical information directly in the lexical entry, assuming that it is easier to retrieve lexical information from memory rather than grammatical permutations like transformational rules which change the syntactic format of sentences. It is also sensitive to the well-established fact that we remember the semantic gist of sentences and discourse rather than their actual syntactic format.

This approach also avoids the problems that transformational grammar suffered when it was applied as a model of sentence processing and storage under the experimental paradigm known as the **derivational theory of complexity**. In a lexical-functional theory of grammar, it is assumed that grammatical information needed to relate or differentiate sentence types is stored in the lexical entry itself. Thus, we no longer have a hierarchy of sentences with the active sentence serving as a starting point in processual terms, and with other sentences like passives or truncated passives ranked as being more difficult, and in that order. A truncated passive sentence like *The dog was bitten* is not more complex than a full passive like *The dog was bitten by the cat* in this model, though this was the order of derivation in some previous generative frameworks. Such a theoretical appproach clearly acknowledges the fact that linguists are responding to the need to present our linguistic knowledge of structure in a way that also reflects the way in which speaker-hearers of a language process those structures in real-time performance tasks like understanding, storing, and recalling those structures. The evaluative metric for an adequate description of a linguistic fact is no longer driven exclusively by purely internal criteria like simplicity and elegance of description.

If one accepts Winograd's (1983) clever portrayal of paradigm shifts in linguistics as a series of metaphors borrowed from the successful paradigms in the hard sciences, it is easy to see how the shift from the previous periods came to coincide with research directions in sister disciplines. It is also easier to see why we are presently involved in a transition period of intellectual growth and re-orientation toward issues in cognitive science. In the previous century, Darwinian evolutionary theory matched with "linguistics as biology", with much attention paid to language change and delineating families of languages. In this century, the taxonomic orientation of structuralism was really "language as chemistry", where one discovered the units of language structure, as for example, the phonemic units that constitute the phonology of a language. In the fifties, Chomsky's generative grammar, as first laid out (1957) in *Syntactic Structures*, was really a shift to a view of "language as mathematics". The mode of inquiry was deductive, as was mathematical inquiry, although the goal was an understanding of competence, the abstract characterization of the knowledge that native speakers have that makes them native speakers of a language. This knowledge, albeit knowledge of language structures and language operations, was viewed as a mathematical object which could be described by a set of rules; such a set of rewrite rules attempted to realize the explicitness requirement that generative grammar prided itself on.

But now the models and metaphors come from elsewhere. A new focus of interest has emerged, one which has now put linguistics and psycholinguistics in league with the powerful influence of those mechanical devices that are having their effect on all fields of knowledge. The eighties now enjoy a fourth paradigm, the computational paradigm, obviously catalyzed by the use of computers as models of language processing functions. Language is now seen as a symbolic process, often leading to decisions, based on knowledge, and not as the ultimate and only interesting knowledge set. Human minds using natural language, as well as computers using programmatic "languages", manipulate symbols and make decisions on the basis of stored and inferred knowledge. It is inevitable that psycholinguistics, and linguistic theory, would have to become involved in a larger field of inquiry, that is, the nature of knowledge, the structure of mental representations, and how these are used in mental processes like reasoning and decison-making.

Chomskyan notions had in a way already set the stage for this new focus of interest in linguistics, not so much by the (1968) observation that linguists were really cognitive psychologists, but by the very nature of what the description of competence entailed. Generative grammar had attempted to characterize speakers' knowledge of their language, and this to a large degree entails understanding the cognitive processes underlying the language facility. Indeed, it is typical of the times that names previously associated with formal syntax or semantics now are committed to problems of conceptual representation and the structure of human cognitive systems. For example, in discussing semantics and cognition, Jackendoff (1983) admits that the problems of semantics in linguistics is really a problem of conceptual representation, common to all forms of cognition. Similarly, in formulating the "cognitive grammar" approach to analyzing syntactic and semantic structure, Langacker (1986) espouses the basic premise that language is not a self-contained system separate from general cognitive systems, and that the findings of linguistics and cognitive psychology should be integrated.

In turn, psychologists are once again interested in the role of linguistic structures in language processing. An excellent example of this can be seen in recent texts like Carlson and Tanenhaus (1989a) and Marslen-Wilson (1989a). Psychology and linguistics once again interact, and in a real way, as joint papers are authored by a linguist and a psychologist, and even single-authored papers exhibit research goals and a breadth of knowledge not confined to a single discipline (see Kess 1991a, b). Psychology in the 1970s began to be disenchanted by linguistic theory, given its limited applicability to dealing with how we actually produce or comprehend language, and psychological investigations of language processing made less and less reference to linguistic theory. Carlson and Tanenhaus (1989b) claim that psycholinguistics is currently more vibrant than it has been since the 1960s, and that this is accompanied by a renewal of interest in the role of linguistic structure in language behavior. But linguistic theory, at least as we have known it in its recent forms, does not occupy the center-stage in this new refurbishing of the old partnership, and for a number of reasons. There is robust evidence for the role of surface structure in processing, but not for transformations. Computational models of language are unnecessarily complicated by transformations, and increasingly look to other more workable devices as serious competitors within linguistics minimize or eliminate transformations altogether. The interaction of linguistic structure and language processing may be the focal topic of psycholinguistic research, but that interaction is now subject to the double, and equally important, rigors of linguistic analysis and psychological experimentation.

It is also worth noting that while psychology and linguistics may be converging again, this does not mean they subscribe to same philosophy of science. One of the current questions is whether the language processing system is modular or interactive, and much recent research probes the degree of **modularity** or **interaction** in the system. Modularity suggests that the processing system is composed of a series of modules, each handling some specific type of information without reference to the activities of other such modules. In sharp contrast, an interactive explanation of processing rests on the assumption that the levels of language knowledge are not cut off from one another, and that there is an active exchange of information. Given their traditional preoccupation with levels of language knowledge, linguists have favored the modularity hypothesis, while psychologists have been more attracted to interactive explanations of language and learning principles. The two disciplines may once again be more compatible, but they also tend to confront the major issues from different perspectives.

We might conclude this chapter by noting that the current information processing view of language now sets our goals as understanding how mental representations operate, in tasks like acquisition of knowledge from discourse by direct extraction or by inference, and then its storage, recall, cross-classification, or whatever human language users do in the processes of reasoning and decision-making. Indeed, the generative, cognitive, and computational paradigms were all cognitive paradigms in their commitment to studying the structure of the knowledge possessed by humans who use language. The major difference now is how knowledge about mental processes and representation involved in language use shall be accessed and represented, and the degree of commitment to incorporating the research findings from other disciplines into psycholinguistics. This means that psycholinguistics no longer just takes into account findings from psychology and linguistics in its role as the final superordinate, or umbrella, interdisciplinary category for theory, research, and the findings of such research. Instead, one now sees psycholinguistics itself as also being subsumed under the larger scheme of research, in that truly broad interdisciplinary activity that has come to be labelled as *cognitive science*. The contributory disciplines in this new discipline are variously agreed upon as being cognitive psychology, linguistics, artificial intelligence, neuroscience, and philosophy (see, for example, Stillings et al. 1987), but with obvious inclusion for overlap areas of inquiry like psycholinguistics and cognitive anthropology. In many ways, the overwhelming multidisciplinary commitment to the goals of cognitive science has effectively meant that the psychological reality of theories about natural language must be matched with information about natural language processing, and that this is now an actively desired goal. This is indeed an exciting time for research, with the ultimate promise an exacting and realistic science of the human mind and all that it is capable of, including language.

Summary

The progression of modern psycholinguistics can be traced in four major periods: the Formative Period, the Linguistic Period, the Cognitive Period, and the current Cognitive Science Period.

In the Formative Period, both linguistics and psychology were committed to an operationalist philosophy which derived theoretical constructs from observable data by using a set of highly explicit and verifiable operations. Structuralism was the prevailing paradigm in linguistics and defined units like the phoneme and the morpheme in terms of operational procedures. Behaviorism was predominant in psychology and also gave primacy to observable data, methodologically focussing upon rigorous experimental design and statistical analysis of data.

The Linguistic Period is characterized by the rise of transformational generative grammar in linguistics, followed by its theoretical domination of psycholinguistic research. Noam Chomsky, the originator of transformational generative grammar, successfully argued that behaviorism, structuralism, and information theory, the scientific perspectives which had oriented psycholinguistic research in the Formative Period could not provide an adequate explanation of natural language if it was based on an operationalist philosophy. He further argued that a deductive approach was required, and that linguistic theory has as its proper domain the underlying competence of speakers, and not their actual performance. By extension, psycholinguistics also took as its starting point the study of competence, with the study of performance a secondary activity. The centrality of grammar was taken as a basic assumption, with the sentence emerging as the primary unit in most psycholinguistic experiments during this period. Psycholinguistic studies in the 1960s tested whether the number and complexity of mental operations performed during processing was a function of the number and complexity of formal transformations seen in the grammatical derivation of that sentence, as postulated by linguists.

Because generative grammar was inherently interested in the nature of human language, there was also considerable interest in language acquisition as well as in linguistic universals. It was commonly held that the capacity for language acquisition is species-specific and is a genetically determined attribute of humans and humans alone.

The Cognitive Period questioned what the intrinsic capacity to learn language really means, and whether what is really brought to bear is a set of general learning principles. The major premise that underlies a cognitive approach is the dependence of language upon human cognition, the notion that language is but one of several outcomes of more fundamental cognitive processes. The centrality and independence of grammar was rejected, in favor of a view that the cognitive capacity described in grammatical accounts of competence is only one manifestation of human language, and is in no way prior to or independent of other cognitive and behavioral systems involved in the acquisition and use of language. Linguistic structures are not learned independently of semantic concepts and discourse functions, and more importantly, cognitive principles must be assumed to govern the acquisition of linguistic structures. Thus, although linguistic theory continued to play a role in psycholinguistic theory and practice, the role was not as directive as before.

Psychology in the 1970s also began to be disenchanted by linguistic theory, given its limited applicability to dealing with how we actually produce or comprehend language, and psychological investigations of language processing made less reference to linguistic theory. There was robust evidence for the role of surface structure in processing, but not for transformations. The **Derivational Theory of Complexity**, suggesting that the number and complexity of mental operations performed during processing was a function of the number and complexity of transformations, never received sufficient support to continue as a working hypothesis. Instead, much of the information gleaned from experimental results along the way was extremely informative about natural language processing, and showed that there was much more to be learned from psycholinguistic research than just this weak hypothesis.

The last and most current period in psycholinguistics is one matched by the development of Cognitive Science as an interdisciplinary activity. Psycholinguistics is now involved in a larger field of inquiry, that is, the nature of knowledge, the structure of mental representations, and how these are used in mental processes like reasoning and decison-making. Current psycholinguistic theory also reflects a considerable theoretical variety in both psychology and linguistics, but there is nonetheless a tremendous amount of truly interdisciplinary activity. More than ever before, researchers are very much aware of developments in adjacent fields, exhibiting research goals and a breadth of knowledge not confined to a single discipline. Linguists and psychologists can no longer afford to ignore scientific answers in the other field which impinge on research problems in their own field and the explanations they offer for them.

The linguistic approach which one sees increasingly is one which takes information processing constraints into account. "Correctness" of a grammatical theory is no longer as vehemently argued, for grammatical theories can all be internally "correct"; it becomes more a question of compatibility of a system of grammatical description that is attuned to the problems, as well as the results, of psycholinguistic research. Language is now increasingly seen as a symbolic process, often leading to decisions based on knowledge, and not as the ultimate and only interesting knowledge set.

In turn, psychologists are once again interested in the role of linguistic structures in language processing. Some claim that psycholinguistics now is more vibrant than it has been since the 1960s. The interaction of linguistic structure and language processing may be the focal topic of psycholinguistic research, but that interaction is now subject to the double, and equally important, rigors of linguistic analysis and psychological experimentation. Although psychology and linguistics are once again equal partners in the psycholinguistic enterprise, they do not always subscribe to same philosophy of science. One of the current questions is whether the language processing system is modular or interactive, and much recent research probes the degree of modularity or interaction in the system. Linguists generally have favored the modularity hypothesis, while psychologists have been more attracted to interactive explanations of language and learning principles. This is an exciting time for psycholinguistic research, with its potential for contributing to an exacting and realistic science of the human mind, a cognitive science.

Chapter 3

Speech Perception and Production

Articulatory Phonetics vs. Acoustic Phonetics

Words and sentences are ultimately made up of sounds, and when we hear an utterance, we try to discern which sounds have been strung together to construct that utterance. For example, the word *pit* differs from *bit* in its initial consonant, and we pay attention to certain phonetic features in making this discrimination. In turn, the word *pit* differs from *pat* in its vowel, and we pay attention to other kinds of phonetic features in discriminating between vowel sounds. Such phonetic characteristics have been studied from two vantage points, that of **articulatory phonetics** and that of **acoustic phonetics**.

Articulatory Phonetics

Articulatory phonetics is the study of speech sounds based on their articulatory properties, that is, how the speech sounds are produced. Speech sounds are usually broken into two major types, consonants and vowels, because of basic differences in how they are produced. The system used to describe consonants typically lists characteristics like the place of articulation (where in the vocal tract the sound was made), the manner of articulation (how the sound was made), and voicing (whether the vocal chords were vibrating and making noise at the same time we made the sound). The sounds /p/ and /b/ would thus be labelled as bilabial stops, because the airstream is temporarily "stopped" by closing the lips. But in making the /b/, there is accompanying vibration in the vocal chords, whereas this does not happen when articulating the /p/. And so we would term the /b/ a *voiced bilabial stop* and /p/ a *voiceless bilabial stop*. Slashes like /.../ indicate that this is a **phonemic transcription** of the sound, meaning that we are paying attention to the articulatory characteristics of a systematically relevant sound in some particular language. Our English examples so far, the words *pit*, *bit*, and *pat* would be transcribed as /pɪt/, /bɪt/, and /pæt/, respectively. A whole sentence like *The cat hissed* would look like /ðə kæt hɪst/.

Vowels require a different classification based on tongue height (which part of the tongue is high, mid, or low in the mouth?) and tongue position (is it the front, central, or back part of the tongue that is high, mid, or low in the mouth?). For example, the /i/ in *machine* would be labelled as a high front vowel because the front part of the tongue is high in the mouth. In contrast, the /æ/ in *hat* is a low front vowel because the front part of the tongue is low in the mouth. The /o/ in *goat* is labelled as a mid back vowel because the back part of the tongue is at mid height in the back of the mouth. In addition, several language-specific features like rounding or tenseness can be used to refine the description of vowels even further. For example, /i/ can be further specified as a high front unrounded tense vowel. Contrast how the /i/ in *heat* is accompanied by a **tensing** of the tongue muscles, whereas this posture is relaxed when producing the /ɪ/ of *hit*. Contrast now how you produce the vowel /u/, as in *moon*; it is accompanied by **rounding** of the lips. But this feature is not present in the production of either /i/ or /ɪ/.

Every language has a small set of relevant sounds it makes use of, and these are called the **phonemes** of the language. This set constitutes the phonemic structure of the language, meaning that this is the inventory of speech sounds which operate systematically in the language. Thus, when we hear words like *light* or *full*, we perceive words as being composed of these sounds, and tend to ignore any smaller differences. For example, we perceive the initial /l/ in *light* and the final /l/ in *full* as being the same /l/. We do not pay attention to the small differences they exhibit; instead we focus on what the possible phoneme might be, for a different phoneme would mean a different word. For example, an initial /s/ would mean the word was *sight*, an initial /b/ would signal *bite*, an initial /h/ would signal *height*, and so on.

If we wished, we **could** look at speech sounds in a language in even greater detail, without reference to how they might be organized in that language. This would be a phonetic description, and is more detailed than the phonemic description we noted in the preceding paragraph. When you look closely, the English phoneme /l/ is objectively diferent in initial and final positions in the words *light* and *full*. And we could show this difference by using phonetic symbols like [l] and [ɫ] to represent finer articulatory details which are usually below our level of conscious attention. Square brackets like [...] indicate that this is a **phonetic transcription** of the sounds, and that we are paying attention to finer specifications of articulatory detail in our description of the sound(s) in question.

We could also describe the type and range of possible speech sounds found in the languages of the world by using just such articulatory properties. We might wish to say, for example, that the contrast of labial stop consonants like [p] with non-labial stops like [t] or [k] is a fairly common feature in many languages of the world. Or that a contrast of stop consonants like [p t k] with nasal consonants like [m n ŋ] is also fairly common. For example, English has *pad* vs. *cad*, as well as *pad* vs. *mad*. Articulatory phonetics can thus also focus on the detailed study of raw speech sounds in human language, without reference to how they might be organized in some specific language.

Phonetic Feature Specifications

Lastly, we might wish to more fully specify the phonological identity of a sound by listing all of its possible identifying characteristics, or its **distinctive features**. For example, we could list the features that make [p] distinguishable from every other speech sound as follows. Such features would be listed as plus (+) or minus (-), depending on whether the feature is present (+) or absent (-) for a given sound.

DISTINCTIVE FEATURES

1. [-sonorant]: meaning that it is produced by totally obstructing the passage of the exiting airstream at some point in the vocal tract
2. [+consonantal]: meaning that it is a consonant or consonant-like
3. [-continuant]: meaning that the sound is executed as a continuous sound since the stream of air continues without interruption
4. [-voiced]: meaning that there is no vibration by the vocal cords at the time the sound is being produced
5. [-nasal]: meaning that the air is released through the mouth and not through the nasal passage
6. [+anterior]: meaning that it is made in the front half of the mouth
7. [-coronal]: meaning that it is not made by raising the tongue toward the top of the mouth

The phonetic feature specifications for very similar sounds reflect the fact that most of their distinctive features are the same, except for the one or more distinguishing characteristics which set them apart. For example, [b] would be similar to [p], except for being *+voice*; [n] would be different in being *+voiced*, *+coronal*, *sonorant*, and *+nasal*. This use of a large feature set allows us to specify more fully the complete phonetic identity of any given sound, as well as allowing us to call attention to similarities and differences between sounds or groups of sounds. For example, the stops [p t k] constitute a grouping distinct from the stops [b d g] by the single feature of *-voiced*. Or the stops [p t k b d g] constitute a grouping distinct from the nasals [m n ŋ] by the feature of *-nasal*. The concept of distinctive features to describe sounds makes use of a set of properties far larger in number than typical phonetic descriptions, but still is based on articulatory considerations.

Acoustic Phonetics

The science of acoustic phonetics examines the acoustic properties of sounds by studying the physical features of variation in air pressure produced by vocal tract movements. Psycholinguistic studies of speech perception make use of this information to understand the characteristics of speech sounds in the continuous train of sound waves which constitute the speech signal. A machine called the **sound spectrograph** has been an invaluable instrument in studying these properties of sounds, for it allows a visual representation, literally in black and white, of the acoustic features that characterize the speech signal. As you can see in the example of a spectrogram in Figure 1, the physical properties of the speech signal are converted into shades of black over the white paper to represent variations in those physical properties of sound which can be detected by the human ear. We pay attention to variations in frequency, intensity or amplitude, and duration over time. Frequency refers to the fact that when the vibrations are regularly spaced in time, we hear a musical tone of a definite pitch; the more rapid the vibrations (that is, the higher the frequency), the higher the pitch. When the vibrations are irregularly spaced in time, we hear "noise" instead of a musical tone. Intensity refers to the amount of energy present at the frequency, that is, its "loudness" or "volume". Such properties can be graphically presented, as can be seen in the spectrogram of the sentence *The cat hissed* in Figure 1.

The sound spectrograph has also been extremely useful in studying speech perception, for it allows us to manipulate these features. That is, by varying acoustic features and feeding these into a speech synthesizer that can "read" such information, we can artificially produce speech. This means we can test how human listeners react to minute variations in the speech signal we give them.

Figure 1: A Sound Spectrogram

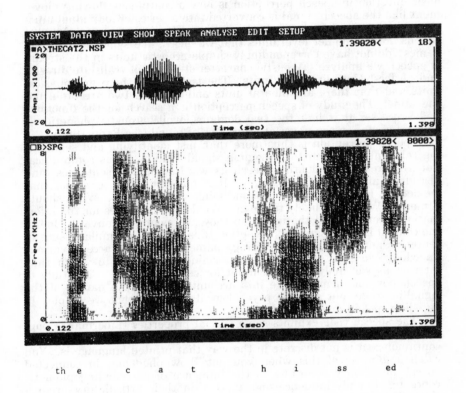

Speech Perception

Speech perception studies how we perceive messages in the acoustic signals produced by the speech organs of other human beings. The basic question in speech perception is how a continuous flowing movement like the speech signal is converted into a series of individual units that we call the sounds of the language. This is not as simple as it sounds, for the higher level units that we 'hear', like syllables and phonemes, do not have correpondingly simple acoustic units in the stream of speech we analyze. Acoustic characteristics do not translate directly and perfectly into linguistic units. The fact is that there are physical units and that there are mental units and that the two are often not the same. The study of speech perception is a search for the functions and processes that link the two domains, while acoustic phonetics is only interested in the physical properties of sound (see Repp 1988).

Speech perception is thus more than just identifying and segmenting relevant sounds in the incoming signal. Language as communication requires us to identify speech as words, phrases, sentences, and discourse--ultimately as messages. It is not just sound as sound that we decode, but rather what that incoming speech means. What should it mean? What is it likely to mean? We decode messages for the informational content and the intention they are meant to convey. One of the central issues in speech perception thus touches on similar issues in sentence and discourse processing, namely, how we access various knowledge sources and how we determine the extent to which they interact as we analyze speech input for comprehension. The study of speech perception must take into account not only the nature of the signalling code, but also the psychological processes that we employ in decoding spoken messages.

The speech code exhibits some special properties (Liberman, Cooper, Shankweiler and Studdert-Kennedy 1967). For one thing, speech is continuous; it is not discrete in the way that printed language is. You catch a glimpse of this when you note how phonemes in connected speech often vary according to the influence of surrounding phonetic contexts. Sounds influence one another in their articulatory production. This happens within words, as when the /i/ following the /k/ in *keen* causes it to be made further front in the mouth than the /k/ in *coon*. Or when the /k/ anticipates the following /w/ and becomes rounded in the /kw-/ of *queen*; compare *queen* with *keen*. Acoustic studies have shown us that a single acoustic cue carries information about successive sound segments, and this **parallel transmission** presents us with overlapping information about several sounds at the same time.

Secondly, there is seldom a one-to-one correspondence between the units of perception and the acoustic signal, in the sense that a specific phonetic unit would always correlate with some acoustic cue. Instead, a phonetic segment may match up with several acoustic correlates; the same acoustic feature may be perceived differently in different linguistic environments, and conversely, different features may at times be perceived as the same. The only exceptions to this seem to be fricatives and stressed vowels, which can be isolated in slow speech. Very simply, there does not appear to be a unique and absolute physical-psychological equivalence between acoustic cues and perceived phonemes.

The speed of speech input is certainly greater than our ability to perceive other noises and signals. For example, Liberman (1970) estimates that speech is decoded at a rate of about 25 to 30 phonetic segments per second. This rate would overreach the resolving power of the human ear, except for the fact that the speech code simultaneously transmits information about successive segments on the same acoustic cue. Parallel transmission reduces the number of acoustic segments that have to be perceived per unit time, and this is of course a great advantage. But it is not without its costs, for the relationship between acoustic signal and perceived phoneme becomes a complexly coded one. Sentence organization, by the way, is also characterized by parallel transmission; sentences come in a highly encoded form, allowing us to deliver the message rapidly (Liberman 1970). For example, the fact that there was more than one dog is shown more than once in *The three dogs were running along the river when we caught them.* Plurality is shown by *three*, *dog-s*, the plural past tense form of *were*, and the pronoun *them*.

Listeners segment the incoming speech into phonological units even though the acoustic signal does not manifest obvious physical boundaries. Phonemes are encoded in such a way that a single acoustic cue will carry information about successive phonemic segments. This smearing of the acoustic properties of adjacent sounds makes for a complex relation between perceived phoneme and acoustic cue, but creates the advantage of reducing the rate at which discrete sounds can be perceived (Liberman et al. 1967). Humans take more than a second to decode a noise signal consisting of only 4 non-speech sounds, and cannot determine the order of the units unless the presentation is slowed to 1.5 seconds; if these are played at the rate of normal speech, one only hears a blur.

The factors which aid us in efficiently analyzing the speech signal can be seen by examining speech perception in four stages: the **auditory stage**, the **phonetic stage**, the **phonological stage**, and the **lexical, syntactic, and semantic stage** (Studdert-Kennedy 1974, 1976). The stages are interdependent, with the higher level stages often influencing decisions about the lower ones. The acoustic information in the **auditory stage** is an exact match with the acoustic stimulus, but the units found at the other stages are really abstractions, since they are units derived from our decisions as to what the sound must be. This interaction between perception and identification--translating the physical properties of acoustic cues into psychological decisions about perceived phonemes--is the essence of the task we call speech perception.

Stages in Speech Perception

Auditory Stage

The auditory stage is based directly on the physical input, and is the initial point at which we take in the raw speech signal, with its acoustic attributes of frequency, intensity, and time span. Vowels exhibit fairly constant acoustic cues, but not all consonants do. For example, there is simply no single acoustic signal which is always and invariably /g/; the acoustic cues for /g/ in /gi/ are different from the acoustic cues associated with /gu/. So far there is no successful way of uniquely identifying acoustic properties of the speech wave and matching them with the units of perceptual analysis. Since the vowels often contain information about neighboring linguistic segments, you cannot cut the sound pattern up to get a piece that will just produce the /g/. As you can see by contrasting Figures 2A and 2B, there is no single pattern associated with stops like /b d g/ in the syllables /bi-bu di-du gi-gu/. Information about consonants, except for the fricatives, is very dependent upon information carried by the vowel.

Figure 2A: Context-dependent Acoustic Cues in Syllables /bi-di-gi/

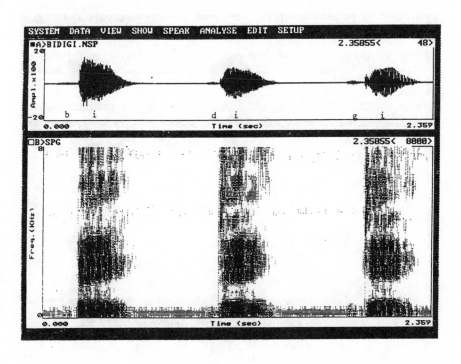

b   i   d   i   g   i

**Figure 2B: Context-dependent Acoustic Cues in
Syllables /bu-du-gu/**

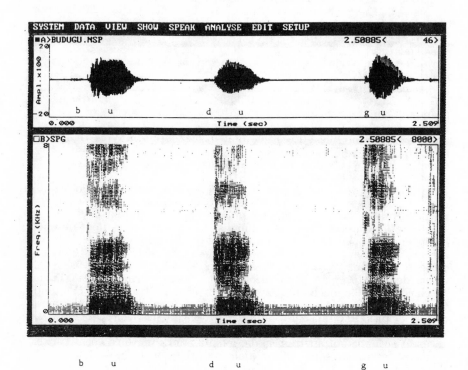

        b   u   d   u   g   u

But this fact of context-conditioned variation goes both ways. There is now evidence that missing vowels can be accurately recovered in cases where the vowel portion of the syllable has been silenced (see Rakerd and Verbrugge 1987). This suggests that some vowel information must also be conveyed by consonantal onset and offset, the initial and final portions of the syllable filled by the consonants surrounding the vowel. There are reports of accurate recognition when 50 to 65% of the CVC^2 is deleted, and even when as much as 90% of the syllable is deleted; errors in vowel recognition show confusions with the closest vowel categories (summarized in Diehl et al. 1987). Some degree of parallel transmission may thus be the rule for both vowels and consonants, so that listeners perceive phonetic segments in a way that makes use of this overlap in acoustic characteristics. This may account for the consistent finding that syllables are identified more rapidly than individual phonemes under most conditions (Norris and Cutler 1988). Although the phoneme is the smallest unit that speech can be analyzed into, the more accessible unit in perception may be the syllable. That is, a minimal utterance is normally a syllable consisting of a vowel nucleus, which may be framed by one or more consonants.

Speech Recognition and Speech Synthesis by Machines . So far it has not yet been easy to segment speech into independently defined units that are free of the effects of surrounding phonetic context or the larger sentential context. The same linguistic segment shows up differently depending upon the immediate phonetic environment, the rate of speech, and even the individual speaker's characteristics. Complex coding is the main reason that we have not yet perfected speech recognition devices to equal print recognition devices. Print recognition is an easier task for mechanical devices, for print is straightforward, and without parallel transmission problems. Listeners also learn to ignore minor factors like absolute differences in pitches, foreign accents, speech deficits, idiosyncratic properties like nasality, and even differences in acoustic output from male, female, and children's vocal tracts. Although we derive some information from these factors, we largely filter them out in making decisions about the identity of the speech sounds which constitute the speech signal. Human listeners are able to ignore and compensate for such speaker differences, but this remains a problem for speech recognition devices.

But some progress has been made in this area. Poor success rates in reading the spectrograms of unfamiliar utterances were previously the norm (Liberman 1970), but current reports quote more successful and consistent analysis of the visual information presented by spectrograms (Pisoni 1985). From a speech technology point of view, this now makes the speech spectrogram and its computer analogues more than just a convenient visual representation. Speech recognition devices need a reliable inventory of the feature packages that uniquely identify the acoustic correlates of speech sounds, because machines cannot

---

[2] C is the typical abbreviation for **Consonant**, and **V** is the typical abbreviation for **Vowel**. Thus, **CVC** stands for **Consonant-Vowel-Consonant**.

make decisions about sounds by referring to higher levels of language
or general world knowledge. Voice-activated speech recognition devices
and mechanical voices that answer your questions are among the 'hot-
test' commercial topics lately, and much recent work has been prompted by the demands of voice-activated computers. The success of this
enterprise ultimately depends upon the joint research results coming
from studies in speech perception and acoustic phonetics.

Phonetic Stage

The phonetic stage reflects what we decide to call the sound, based
on various types of knowledge. As Studdert-Kennedy (1974:16)
observes, "phonetic perception in a high wind is governed as much by
situational and higher linguistic factors as by the acoustic signal".
After examining the speech signal for acoustic cues, we then assign a
name like /s/ or /p/ or /i/ to that acoustic pattern.

Speech perception makes use of both context-dependent and
context-independent acoustic cues in deciding how to categorize the
sound. Context-dependent cues are those that we noted above, cues
that derive from preceding or following segments. They are in fact
more common than context-independent features, which occur regardless of the preceding or following environment. For example, /s/, with
its unmistakable hiss, is a sound with reliable, content-independent
cues in the speech stream. Another example can be seen the way that
the nasals /m n ŋ/ exhibit a single bar of low-frequency energy, along
with a complete lack of high-frequency energy, in proximity to vowels.
The arrows in Figure 3 show these features for the syllables /ɪm ɪn ɪŋ/.
But acoustic cues have a fairly short life in the phonetic memory, for
we quickly discard the actual cues as we name the sound as belonging
to a category. For example, when we name a sound as /k/, we are
actually saying that this particular sound belongs to a category of
acoustic patterns that we label generally as /k/.

Figure 3: Context-independent Acoustic Cues

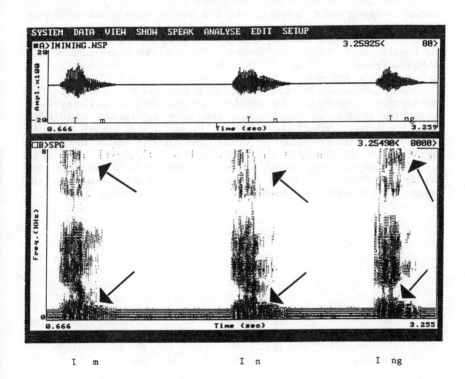

I   m   I   n   I   ng

Categorical Nature of Speech Perception. **Categorical perception** means a stimulus is always perceived as a member of a particular category; discrimination is good **between** different categories, but poor among stimuli **within** the same category. This is typical in the perception of speech, but not typical for many other types of stimuli like musical tones or colors which can be interpreted as gradual shifts (see Eimas 1963). We quickly judge where a sound unit fits in terms of its category membership and name it accordingly. As an example, move the tongue tip in stages back from the place where you articulate the /s/ to the place where you articulate the /ʃ/. Note how you will "name" each particular sound you articulate along the way as either an /s/ or a /ʃ/; there is never an inbetween 'sound', it is either an /s/ or a /ʃ/; The spectogram in Figure 4 shows six different articulations as the speaker moved the tongue tip from the alveolar ridge behind the teeth back along the palate. All six look different, but the first three are called /s/ and the last three are called /ʃ/ without hesitation, because the sounds are perceived as belonging to one or the other category. Our goal in analyzing the incoming speech signal, of course, is to identify the particular speech sound, because this is how sounds function in the language; they contrast one word from another, as in *sip/ship*.

Figure 4: Categorical Nature of Speech Perception

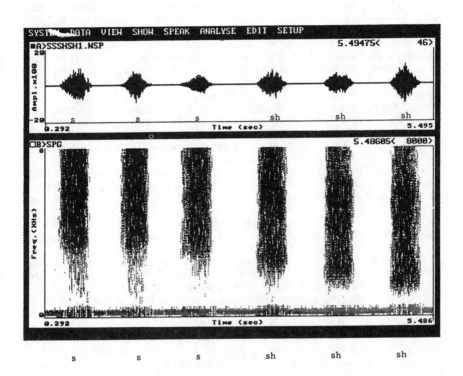

This is why we initially experience difficulty in hearing another language the way that native speakers seem to. For example, to native speakers of English the difference between /k q/ in languages like Arabic or Haida seems to be an overly fine distinction at first. But we in turn marvel at how the "simple" distinction between /l r/ can be missed by speakers of Thai, Japanese, Korean, and Cantonese when they speak English. The /l r/ pair is used categorically by English speakers, but is not so used in Japanese. At first they show poor discrimination all along the continuum between /l/ and /r/, with no peak at the category boundary, just as we might with the /k q/ pair in Arabic. Native speakers learn to focus on sound differences that are phonemic in their own language, but to ignore other differences, even though those differences may be phonemic in other languages. The ability to make phonemic discriminations in a language is learned and is firmly fixed by exclusive exposure to that language. We can of course learn another perceptual set, as we must in learning another language, but the acquisition of a second language as an adult is often influenced by our habits in the native language.

An excellent example of categorical perception is offered by **voice onset time** studies which illustrate the differences between auditory memory and phonetic memory. Voicing typically starts as soon as the lips are released for a /b/, but does not begin until about 60 milliseconds for /p/. Instrumental equipment allows us to make minute changes in the speech stimulus given to subjects, and we can study how subjects respond to such differences in speech signal. In the case of voice onset, we can vary the time in milliseconds between the instant the sound is released and when the vocal cords begin to vibrate. The experimental question, of course, is just when do human subjects decide when to stop calling it a /b/ and start calling it a /p/? And do subjects notice the differences we created within the continuum of acoustic stimuli the subject labels /b/ or /p/?

The results are that between-category discrimination is good, but within-category discrimination ability is poor. Two sounds labelled as /b/, within the continuum below 60 milliseconds of voice onset, are not discriminated; nor are two sounds above that point, and both are labelled as /p/. But one sound taken from below the boundary, say, below 40 milliseconds, and another taken at 80 milliseconds, are easily discriminated as different, and are labelled differently as /b/ and /p/.

After the information from acoustic cues has been extracted, we put the acoustic stimuli into categories. The sound then becomes an occurrence of either /b/ or /p/, and there is no inbetween. The results of such experiments tell us that we perceive in categorical fashion, and that once we have decided which category the sound fits into, we keep only that name (a name like /p/) in the phonetic memory. The actual acoustic cues we heard in the auditory stage are quickly discarded.

Categorical Perception by Infants . Infants appear to discriminate among many phonetic stimuli, like voice onset time, place of articulation for stop consonants, and so forth, in what looks like categorical perception. That is, they appear to discriminate between two phonetic stimuli which lie across a perceptual boundary like the /p-b/ voicing boundary, but do not pay attention to differences contained within each boundary. Children may begin life prepared to discriminate sound differences which are potentially phonemic in human languages. Such plasticity must aid in the language learning task, for the predisposition to segment sounds into functionally useful categories is matched by the fact that each language makes use of some small set of phonetic contrasts as the basis of its phonological system. Some would argue that infants are genetically programmed to pay attention to differences that are likely to be categorical in natural languages. Not all would agree, for there has been some evidence for strong parallels in the way that infants perceive certain non-speech sound contrasts, and there has has even been evidence that chinchillas and rhesus monkeys react to certain sounds in a way that suggests perceptual categories. However, this does not rule out the possibility that the development of speech perception in humans is an innately guided learning process, and this explanation is not contradicted by the course of language mastery in the first year of life (see Jusczyk and Bertoncini 1988).

The effect of the child's experience in a first language is to lose the ability to discriminate categorical differences in languages other than the one the child is acquiring (see Eimas 1985). Various measures have shown that infants can discriminate consonantal contrasts of another language as well as native-speaking adults of that language. For example, North American infants 6 to 8 months old discriminated two Hindi consonantal contrasts as well as native-speaking Hindi adults could. But older English-speaking children and adults were very poor in their abilities to discriminate (Werker et al. 1981). Further work not only confirms that infants discriminate non-native speech sounds into categories without prior experience, but that this ability declines within the first year of life. Werker and Tees (1984) investigated the discriminative abilities for North American infants on stop contrasts used in Thompson, an Amerindian language in British Columbia, and in Hindi, an Indo-European language from India. The Thompson contrast was the opposition of velar and uvular glottalized stops (/k'-q'/) common to the Salish language family; the Hindi contrast was the opposition between dental and retroflex stops (/t-ʈ/) so common in the languages of India. English infants aged 6 to 8 months did about as well as native speakers of those languages; the ability declines, however, so that at 8 to 10 months fewer infants perceived the contrasts. By 10 to 12 months of age, the infants perform as poorly as English-speaking adults, so that few infants at this age perceive the contrasts. Native Hindi or Thompson infants continued to discriminate the relevant contrasts at 12 months of age, demonstrating that specific language experience maintains the ability to discriminate those contrasts a given language employs. The Hindi and Salish infants who continued on in a Hindi- or Salish-speaking environment retained at 12 months the capacity to perceive those linguistic contrasts found in their native languages. But the infants from an English-speaking background lose the ability to perceive such contrasts, and by 12 months do not fare very well.

These results suggest that infants are attuned to a variety of possible phonetic contrasts that natural languages might make use of, but that this early ability is lost by 12 months of age. Such plasticity is lost as the infant tunes out all contrasts not used in the language that is now becoming his or her native language. This is also the age when the first words are emerging, and language-specific phonological contrasts are central to the acquisition of vocabulary words. Language is founded on the principle of **duality**, whereby a limited set of phonemes create an enormous inventory of words with contrasting meanings. The child must now focus upon a specific set of phonological contrasts, if the foundational framework of word contrasts is to be achieved.

Phonological Stage

The third stage in speech perception is the phonological stage, where the phonetic segment is converted into a phonemic unit of the language we are hearing. Here we discard phonetic facts like the initial /p/ in *pickle* being aspirated, the pre-consonantal /p/ in *apt* being unreleased, or the /p/ in *spit* being unaspirated because of the /s/. Some features we re-interpret; for example, perceiving nasalization on the vowel (but no [n] following the vowel) in someone's pronunciation of *can't*, we realize it must stand for the /n/, and so we call it an /n/.

We also consult our knowledge of **phonotactics**, the sequencing rules about which phonetic segments can go together. Hearers typically adjust the input to fit these rules, and such rules often take precedence over the actual phonetic cues themselves. For example, even if nonsense words like *nganga* or *fways* are said with English sounds, they are hard to indentify accurately, because English prohibits /ŋ/ in initial position and /fw-/clusters. But the non-words *manga* and *kwice* are easily recognized, because they follow phonotactic rules and could be words.

Redundancy is an important factor here, and language typically operates at a high rate of redundancy. Morse Code, for example, piggybacks on the redundancy of natural language to create a maximally efficient system. Simple values are assigned to common letters like T, E, and I, but more complicated patterns to the less common Q and X.

1.   T   -
2.   E   .
3.   I   ..
4.   Q   --.-
5.   X   -..-

Morse Code reflects the redundancy of letters in the written form of the language, but that redundancy rests on the frequency of phonemes in the spoken language. Some phonemes are more common than others; Mines, Hanson, and Shoup (1978) found that 10 phonemes (/ə n t ɪ s r i l d ɛ/) accounted for 47% of their sample of conversational English. The total ratio of consonants to vowels was about

2-to-1; vowels accounted for 38% of the data, consonants for 58%, and retroflex and syllabic elements for the remaining 4%.

Such redundancy may reflect the absolute frequency of a given phoneme; for example, /ə/ occurs in many words in stressed or unstressed position, as well as in commonly appearing words like a/the/but. Redundancy may also arise from the frequency of the words that a given phoneme occurs in; for example, /ð/ does not occur in many words, but those words are the very common the, this, that, these, those, then, there, they. Knowing what the most commonly occurring speech sounds are is a definite advantage in trying to decide what's what in the speech stream coming at us. If these distributions are fairly characteristic of conversational English regardless of age, sex, dialect, or level of education, then we have a ready-made table of frequencies to apply to the incoming signal.

Lexical, Syntactic, and Semantic Stage

This stage reflects the contribution of higher orders of knowledge, including a knowledge of the structure of words, sentences, and discourse, as well as properties derived from our general knowledge of situational and pragmatic constraints. One of the major tasks in modern psycholinguistics is to describe the levels of processing that take place, and to indicate how these levels interact with one another to help the listener figure out what the speaker said. Many findings have been supportive of **top-down** processes which help listeners draw inferences or make guesses about the likely value of the speech signal when it has been incompletely heard or erroneously presented. Top-down models assume that comprehension integrates information from the lexical, syntactic, and semantic levels, and there has been considerable support for the influence of higher levels of analysis on the information derived from **bottom-up** analysis of the actual data. This may be best illustrated by looking at some of the results for speech perception when speech sounds are in the context of stretches of continuous speech.

Continuous Speech. Numerous experimental results show the role of higher level constraints in conditioning our perception of continuous speech. An early study by Miller, Heise, and Lichten (1951) tested subjects' abilities to identify units under white noise conditions. For example, some subjects received words which appeared in isolation, while other subjects received words in the context of sentences. At all levels of noise, subjects identified words embedded in sentences more accurately; for example, when speech and noise levels were equal, the difference was a 70% vs. 40% accuracy rate. A similar experiment by Miller and Isard (1963) tested subjects' abilities under noise conditions by varying the grammaticality of the input 'sentence'. Subjects always heard the grammatical sentences like (1) best; next best were 'sentences' like (2) and worst were 'sentences' like (3).

1. Grammatically well-formed sentences: *Accidents kill motorists on the highway.*
2. Grammatically possible but semantically odd sentences: *Accidents carry honey between the house.*
3. Ungrammatical strings with neither structure nor semantic coherence to them: *Around accidents country honey the shoot.*

In fact, conversations are quite unintelligible without employing syntactic and semantic expectations to help make sense of the acoustic signal. Pollack and Pickett (1964) played single words excised from tapes of real conversations, and found the recognition rate only 47%. The recognition rate for excised words was not much higher when the passages were read at a slower than conversational rate. But when the words were put back into longer stretches, they became more intelligible. And as the stretch of excised speech was increased, so also was the recognition rate increased.

Contextual expectations may determine what we actually do perceive, as we fill in the blanks with what is expected. A compelling example of this is the **phonemic restoration** effect (Warren 1970), where listeners hear utterances as intact when they are not. Subjects actually received *The state governors met with their respective legi*latures convening in the capital city*; 120 milliseconds had been excised at the /*/ and replaced with a cough or by a burst of 1000 Hz tone. Subjects do not report the cough or tone as replacing a sound in the sentence they are given. And they are poor at locating the cough or tone, typically placing it somewhere else in the sentence, usually a few phonemes earlier than its actual position. The same illusion can be created with a buzz or a tone, or even when a larger stretch is excised, as in *le***lature*. However, the illusion disappears with silence, which is easily noticed and easily located (Warren and Obusek 1971), probably because phonemic pauses in English signal where the boundaries are to be drawn in similar utterances (contrast the pairs *why choose/white shoes* or *I scream/ice cream*).

The organization of the mental lexicon is also reflected in phonemic restoration. How unique is the possible lexical item? Can only one word be formed? Samuel (1987) found more perceptual restoration for stimuli that were multiply restorable, than for lexically unique ones. For example, the segment **egion* can be restored as either *legion/region*, but **esion* can only be *lesion*. Secondly, the sooner the lexical uniqueness of the word becomes available, the more quickly all other alternatives are eliminated. For example, words like *dor-mitory* exhibit unique first syllables and are good candidates for strong restoration effects. Very simply, lexically ambiguous stimuli (like **egion*) give rise to more perceptual restoration than lexically unique stimuli (like **esion*) because there are more possible words that could match the stimulus with the phoneme missing. But lexically unique stimuli also have their effect in inducing a strong bias to report the stimuli as intact, especially if the unique information appears early in the stimulus (as in *dor-******* > *dor-mitory*).

Semantic expectations may also condition the replacement, even if the crucial contextual feature appears several words after the target point (Warren and Warren 1970). Subjects will report hearing *wheel, heel, peel,* or *meal,* depending on whether the rest of the sentence contains the word *axle, shoe, orange,* or *table.* Listeners access their knowledge of the language structure, as well as general knowledge, to decide about what the message must really be. In this case, listeners know that the slot in question is one filled by a noun, in accord with the structure of the language, and they use this fact together with their knowledge that oranges have peels, that shoes have heels, and so on. In another study, even experimenters and graduate students familiar with the experimental design still 'heard' a sound that was consistent with the context. For example, though they knew that an /s/ had been excised from *sandwagon,* they reported hearing the sentence as *It is common for people to jump on the bandwagon when a political movement becomes popular* (Warren and Sherman 1974).

These findings are supportive of **top-down processes** in speech perception, which aid comprehension by integrating information from higher levels of analysis, like the lexical, syntactic, and semantic levels. Such top-down hypothesizing can restore missing sounds or correct mistaken ones, as the above examples show. Such strategies help us cope with a noisy environment in which we try to capture what people are saying to us, through a haze of coughs, music, passing cars, and general background din.

But our analysis always begins with **bottom-up processes** in speech perception, taking into account the phonetic information contained in the speech signal as the rich starting point for our analysis. While there has been considerable support for the influence of lexical, syntactic, and semantic information on the information derived from bottom-up analysis, the type of influence depends upon the processing task at hand and the types of units involved. Samuel's (1981) refinement of the phonemic restoration task addressed just this issue of how much we rely on bottom-up acoustic information, as opposed to how much we use higher level information information in making decisions about what we are hearing. He compared how well subjects could discriminate in conditions when noise was **added** to the phoneme and when noise **replaced** the phoneme. With such measures of discriminability vs. bias in the restoration findings, Samuel found support for bottom-up analysis. For example, restoration was related to the phone class of the sound to be restored and its acoustic similarity to the replaced sound. But increasing the role of top-down expectations increased restoration and reduced discriminability between superimposed and replaced sounds. For example, sounds were better restored in real words than non-words, priming the words resulted in even more restoration, and sentence context elicited reports of utterances as intact. His results confirm that higher levels do have a biasing effect on how well information derived from bottom-up analysis is attended to, but reminds us that the bottom-up analysis of actual acoustic properties is the base point for our analysis of the speech signal. This is especially reflected in our dependence on the acoustic signal when top-down influences are weak, but even a full sentence context does not destroy our ability to discriminate that acoustic signal. Speech perception is ultimately dependent upon the interaction of top-down expectations which derive from the listener's knowledge and and the bottom-up information contained in the acoustic characteristics of the signal.

Syllables, Rhythm, and Stress-Patterning . Continuous speech displays a rhythm, with accented syllables coming at spaced intervals; the rhythm of rising and falling pitches is tied to stress-patterning and together they convey information about the phonological content of the speech signal. Languages are sometimes characterized as **stress-timed** or **syllable-timed**, on the basis of the subjective impressions they give to listeners. 'Syllable-timed' suggests that syllables come at equal intervals, taking the same relative length of time, as in French, Spanish, Telegu, Japanese, and Yoruba. In Japanese *tokoro-dokoro* 'here and there', each syllable seems to take an equal amount of time, rather like *to-ko-ro-do-ko-ro*. 'Stress-timed' languages like English, Russian, and Arabic seem to have stressed syllables coming at regular intervals. For example, in an English sequence like *hickory-dickory-dock*, it is the heaviest stress that we notice most, rather like *HIckory-DIckory-DOCK*.

Things are not really that simple, for there is a tendency for stresses to recur regularly in most languages. Dauer (1983) has proposed a continuum by which we can order languages according to differences in syllable structure, vowel reduction, and the phonetic influence of stress. Thus, both English and Japanese are stress-timed, but at opposite ends of the continuum if we consider how they use syllabic rhythm and stress-patterning.

Japanese--->French--->Spanish--->Greek-->Portuguese--->English

First, there is considerable variation in syllable length in English, as well as many different kinds of syllables. Japanese usually has V and CV syllables. Secondly, English uses a restricted set of vowels in unstressed syllables, typically /ə/ or /ɪ/. Vowel reduction to /ə/ or /ɪ/ in English unstressed syllables is typical, and such reduced vowels also appear in unstressed function words and morphological endings. They carry little semantic information, and thus appear subjectively shorter than full vowels in stressed syllables. Languages like Japanese do not regularly have reduced variants of vowels in unstressed position. Third, most stress-timed languages have a word stress, often a somewhat unpredictable free stress, realized by changes in length, pitch, contour, loudness, and quality. This makes stressed syllables even more prominent than unstressed syllables, giving that clearly discernible beat you noticed in *HIckory-DIckory-DOCK*.

Listeners are sensitive to such syllable rhythms, for vowels are the carriers of sonority and primary acoustic cues in the syllable. It is not as critical to process all segments, for the stress patterns provide information about the phonological identity of the word. Stressed syllables last about 200 to 350 milliseconds, transmitting information on 1 to 6 phonemes; unstressed syllables only last 100 milliseconds or less. If stress comes at regularly spaced intervals, listeners can expect where the syllables with the heaviest stress will come and make use of that informative syllable peak. In English, such stressed syllables carry much information, because it is often the root of the lexical item that is stressed; and any of the vowels or diphthongs may occur, whereas in contrast, unstressed syllables typically have /ə/ or /ɪ/. Such information is central to identifying word roots, a crucial factor in successfully searching the lexicon for the likely word. An effective strategy, then, is to pay attention to the stressed syllables, for this is a reliably informative piece of the acoustic signal (see Grosjean and Gee 1987).

Establishing word boundaries in continuous speech may also rely on such information about full vowels and stress placement. Open class words in English either are or begin with stressed syllables about 85% of the time. Knowing this, we can postulate a strategy which operates as follows: Since a strong syllable in continuous speech is likely to be the beginning of an English word, start lexical access procedures each time a stressed syllable is encountered. That is, it is likely that when you hear a strong syllable you have just crossed a word boundary and initiated a new word--so use that stressed syllable to begin looking up a potential new word in your mental dictionary! To see how this strategy might work, consider the stressed syllables in *Humpty Dumpty sat on a wall.* If you predicted that **Hump-, Dump-,** sat and **wall** would begin new content words in this utterance, you would have been quite successful (see Cutler 1989).

Findings from the Non-continuous Speech of Nonsense Syllables . Early experimental work investigated the identification of speech sounds in nonsense syllables, and the results illustrate the interlocking organization of the phonological system. The results demonstrated that features smaller than the phoneme also play a role in perception, because they are confused in an orderly fashion under noise conditions. Recall that we described each speech sound as a package of features; for example, /p/ was said to be labial (at the lips), oral (airstream proceeds out the oral cavity), and voiceless (no vibration in the vocal cords). Errors do not have a random distribution, but usually differ by one such distinctive feature or two.

Miller and Nicely (1955) had subjects try to identify CV syllables, consisting of the vowel /a/ preceded by stops, fricatives, or nasals. But the identifications were made under 7 levels of white noise, from very loud to very soft. Not unexpectedly, the louder the noise, the more the errors. But the errors fell into some interesting patterns at the the intermediate ranges of noise. The consonants most likely to be confused shared some articulatory feature; for example, pairs or triplets like the following were likely to be confused: /m-n/, /f-θ/, /v-ð/, /p-t-k/, /b-d-g/, /s-ʃ/, and /s-ʒ/. Consonants which were least likely to be confused differed in basic primary features like voicing (/p-b/) or nasality (/p-m/, /b-m/). Noise seemed to obliterate place of articulation features first, then manner of articulation, and least of all voicing or nasality.

Wickelgren (1966) also showed that such errors are not random in an experiment which had subjects recall lists of six nonsense syllables. The syllables were of the CV form /ba, ka, ta, sa, ra, ma/. The errors in recall tended to maintain distinctive feature similarities; for example, /pa/ was recalled for /ba/ (a difference in voicing), /va/ for /ba/ (a difference in place and manner of articulation), or /ga/ for /ba/ (a difference in place of articulation). The point is that consonants are related to one another in sub-groups defined by a feature or two, and this accounts for the systematicity of the errors. Otherwise, accuracy in perception or recall in such experiments would have been more random.

Speech Errors and Speech Production

Speech production involves how a speaker translates information and intentions into the language formats available in a language like English or Japanese. It is an ordered activity, with units and rules which order those units. However, we know less about production than we do about perception, largely because production rules are not as easily accessed by experimental techniques as is comprehension. The actual production of real-time speech is filled with pauses and hesitations, corrections, repeats and replacements, and even slips of the tongue. Speech errors are not just eccentricities, however, but reflect those rules in a way which is far from random and without explanation. As Fromkin (1971) has said, anomalous utterances are really quite non-anomalous in nature. As a result, speech errors have been a primary source of data in speech production, because they allow us some insight into the actual process which takes us from concept to realization of the message. Since errors result from misapplication of linguistic rules, they also serve as a testing ground for whether the theoretical concepts linguists propose are matched in the way units are altered, exchanged, or lost.

The match between what we wish to say and what we actually do say is rarely a perfect one. Whenever we speak, we often produce errors as we turn our ideas into speech. We may pause and hesitate as we speak, leaving that pause empty with silence or filling it with inserts like *uh*. Or we may put in the wrong word, giving a semantically related but incorrect lexical item; for example, we say *Jack was there yesterday* when we meant to say *Jack was there today*. Or a phrase like *slip of the tongue* comes out as *tip of the slung*. The nature and range of errors in speech production gives some idea of the units we use in producing language, as well how and to where they can be moved around.

Speech errors may increase when situational considerations cause anxiety; for example, an important interview may elicit more than than usual hesitation and pausing as we search for just the right words. Some speech errors may also fulfill other functions; for example, in English if a speaker has lost the train of thought and pauses during a conversation, he or she typically mumbles an *uh*. This *uh* signifies that the one holding the floor is maintaining the speaking turn in the conversation; otherwise, the silence during such pauses is so awkward for English speakers that a listener will usually jump in to fill the silence. The Japanese filler *eto* and the Spanish *este* do much the same in those languages. Lastly, there are individual variations in the type and rate of speech error production in a given language. For example, one speaker may exhibit the occasional pause, another a moderate use of "uh" or "er" or "uhm", and another an ever-present *you know*. Not all of us exhibit the same speech errors.

Pausing and Hesitations

The impression of speed in speech production seems to be determined by the amount of pausing. When one speeds up, it is by eliminating pauses; "fast" speakers do not hesitate a lot, but "slow" speakers do. Most speakers pause 40% to 50% of the time, with a large amount of the time spent simply not speaking. As a matter of fact, two-thirds of speech production in spoken language comes in chunks of less than six words (Goldman-Eisler 1968). Although speech is linear and serial, it does not fill time continously; there are frequent breaks instead of flowing continuity. Pausing is as much a part of speech as is vocal utterance itself, and the rate of speech production emerges as a function of the proportion of time taken up by breaks and pauses. What seems to be an increase in the speed of talking is often just a variation in the amount of pausing; the type and duration of pauses are, however, variable and subject to individual differences.

Goldman-Eisler reports that when speech is natural and most unprepared, 50% of speech is broken into phrases of less than 3 words, and phrases of more than ten words constitute only 10% of fluent, unprepared speech. Even when speakers are allowed to practice six times, pause-free phrases of more than ten words occur 15% of the time. 35% of what they say occurs in phrases of less than 3 words, and 65% of speech comes in phrases of less than 6 words. Pauses do diminish with learning, since practice means more skill. Well-learned sequences have greater continuity, for repetition leads to a closure of gaps through practice; recall that this is what you strive for in mastering *How much wood could a woodchuck chuck?* or *Peter Piper picked a peck of pickled peppers.*

Practice by pre-planning also has an effect on the frequency of hesitation and pausing in the discourse structure as a whole. Greene and Capella (1986) found that cognitive complexity increases at the choice points of ideational boundaries and is associated with a decrease in speech fluency. But this relationship is lessened when the structure of the discourse was prepared in advance. For example, subjects were provided with a four-point outline: a statement of the problem to be followed by its explanation, and then a statement of the solution followed by its explanation. This organized their monologues so that they never had to ponder a move, since they knew exactly which point came next. When this discourse outline was prepared in advance, there were fewer disfluencies; when not, the typical decrease in speech fluency at ideational boundaries appeared.

Constituent Size and Placement of Pauses . In spontaneous speech, 55% of pauses occur at grammatical junctures, while the rest occur at places which are not grammatical junctures and do not fit in with the grammatical structure of the utterance (Goldman-Eisler 1968). The greatest correlation with grammatical junctures takes place when reading texts; here pausing occurs almost entirely in terms of sentence structure, following the phrase boundaries. Pause and discontinuity in reading fulfill more of a function in reading aloud than in speaking; for example, the modulation of breath intake in reading is governed by the syntactic structure, whereas in speech it occurs at non-grammatical junctures over a third of the time.

The size of the constituent has an effect on where the pause is placed in reading passages. Grosjean, Grosjean, and Lane (1979) had subjects read passages at various rates and again found that pauses corresponded with the major structural breaks. But the size of the constituent determined which structural break the pause actually occured at. When the constituent is large, it is usually kept as a single unit, and pauses do not intrude as easily as when the constituent is small. For example, a sentence like (1) might have a **PAUSE** after *desperately*, putting the noun phrase, intransitive verb, and adverb of manner together. But in sentence (2), the **PAUSE** is more likely to come between the noun phrase and predicate break, after *batter.*

1.   *The batter swung desperately (***PAUSE***) at the curveball.*
2.   *The long-haired, slender, young batter (***PAUSE***) swung desperately at the curve ball.*

Nor are breath groups the explanation for where these pauses occur. We know this because Grosjean et al. also had their subjects refrain from taking a breath while reading the passages. Breath intake does not provide the explanation, because they obtained the same results in respect to where the pauses occurred. Constituents which are large in size are likely to be kept as single units, with the pauses outside their boundaries. But when the constituents are small, they may be grouped with other constituents to create a larger sequence and the pauses will likely occur at the boundaries of this larger sequence.

Will vs. Skill . Spontaneous speech reveals the relationship between the cognitive complexity and the actual production of the speech output conveying this set of thoughts. For example, pausing and hesitation phenomena are more frequent in demanding tasks like evaluating (as opposed to simply describing), as well as at choice points with the highest informational content. Goldman-Eisler (1968) illustrated how hesitancy in speech production is linked with cognitive complexity by having subjects examine captionless cartoons from the *New Yorker*. First, they simply described the cartoon once they understood it; next they had to formulate the point of the story as concisely as they could; and lastly, they were asked to repeat that output six times. Thus, we have seven occurrences of both the description and the interpretation, allowing us a scale from newly planned to well-practiced speech output. We can thus contrast verbal behavior elicited in the description of concrete events and the interpretation of the meaning abstracted from those concrete events. The organizational demands differed, and pause length increased considerably as subjects went from describing concrete events to interpreting their general meaning. Abstracting and generalizing produces about twice as much pausing as their description. Pausing also varies with spontaneity, declining after the first trial and gradually decreasing in subsequent repetitions.

These tasks primarily involve semantic choices in planning and execution. Syntactic complexity was not a major factor in speech disruption. Complex sentences do not exhibit considerably more hesitation phenomena than simple sentences, and there is largely an absence of a relationship between complexity in sentence structure and pausing. Goldman-Eisler suggests that the hierarchical structuring of sentences and embedding of clauses is a matter of linguistic skill. Cognitive complexity of the task and the planning involved in lexical and semantic operations, however, are volitional and are a matter of will. Hesitation phenomena in speech production often appear at such important cognitive points of transition when new or vital pieces of information appear in the output. Thus, more hesitations and pauses are found before content words than function words. Their appearance is reduced by practice or advance planning, for as uncertainty of choice is reduced, matters of will become more like matters of skill.

Slips of the Tongue

Many speech errors involve the substitution, metathesis, omission, or addition of segments (Fromkin 1971), and illustrate that units like distinctive features, phonetic segments, syllables, words, and even larger constituents exist in both planning and execution stages of speech production. Such **slips of the tongue** can occur either within or across word boundaries, but typically take place within the same phrase. And the resultant sequences do not violate the phonotactic rules of the language; they either look like 'words' (like *teep* in *teep a cape< ---keep a tape*) or already are 'words' (like *cape* in *teep a cape< ---keep a tape*). Slips of the tongue which occur in natural language always result in possible sequences (Cutler 1981), although impermissible consonant clusters have been reported in experimental tasks using tongue twisters (Butterworth and Whittaker 1980).

Many slips involve an **anticipation** of some following sound, as in sentence (1); errors which exhibit **perseveration** or carrying the influence of a sound forward, are not uncommon either (see sentence (2)).

1.   John dropped his cup of coffee--->John dropped his cuff of coffee
2.   John gave the boy--->John gave the goy

Metathesis involves a reversal of two elements, and this can be either between consonants, as in (1) below, or between vowels, as in (2). When consonants in clusters are exchanged, they keep their respective places in the new consonant clusters, as in examples (3) and (4). Sometimes, the whole cluster is exchanged, as in example (5). MacKay (1972) has reported that consonant cluster onsets are preserved intact more frequently than they are divided, and Cutler, Butterfield, and Williams (1987) add that word-initial clusters seem to be perceived as integral units. Part of the cluster may also be dropped, as in example (6), demonstrating that though clusters are very real phonotactic units, they are not indissoluble (Fromkin 1971).

1.   keep a tape--->teep a cape
2.   fish and tackle--->fash and tickle
3.   fish grotto--->frish gotto
4.   brake fluid--->blake fruid
5.   at the bottom of the pay scale--->at the bottom of the skay pale
6.   property that excludes--->property that excudes

Even phonetic features may be transposed, as in *glear plue sky* from *clear blue sky*. The [-voiced] feature from the /k/ and the [+voiced] feature from the /b/ have been reversed to produce the incorrect /g/ in *glear* and the /p/ in *plue* (Fromkin 1971). Some argue that such errors are rare, but there are more slips of the tongue with pairs of phonemes which share many phonetic features (like /p-t/ and /p-b/) than those that don't (like /p-d/). These production errors suggest an underlying plan which puts all the right pieces in the correct categories; but in actually producing the utterance, the actual tokens in a category may get confused or switched around as they come out.

Similar units interact at all levels better than dissimilars. In syllable-sized units, syllabic slots exchange with the same slots in other syllables: initial segments exchange with initial segments, vowel nuclei with other vowels, and final segments with final segments (Fromkin 1971). Fricatives are confused, as in *alsho sare* from *also share*. Across word boundaries, stressed syllables are exchanged with other stressed syllables, and not weak syllbles. At higher levels, nouns are exchanged for nouns and not verbs or adjectives.

Blends are speech errors in which two suitable words fall together. The words belong to the same part of speech class, and usually share semantic features, as in *It's a lot of brather* from *trouble/bother*. They are sometimes phonologically similar, as in *sparsity* from *scarcity/sparseness*, but need not be. Sometimes such words are made up consciously, and these blends are called **portmanteau words**. The author Lewis Carroll was fond of creating words like *snark* and *chortle*, and you see the same activity in modern journalism when it creates words like *snush* from *snow/slush* and *cinemagic* from *cinema/magic*. Blends illustrate how the mental lexicon is organized on the basis of characteristics like part of speech class and phonological as well as semantic features. We shall see more of this in the chapter on morphology and the mental lexicon, but we are reminded of this organizational structure when natural errors like blends occur.

Speech Errors and Higher Levels of Planning and Production

Analysis of speech errors also provides evidence for more than just the phonological level; they also illustrate the organization of larger units we make use of in planning on the morphological and syntactic levels. Sentence production may involve several ordered but independent stages, and speech errors can be found at the stages of word selection and phrase construction, as well as in the actual phonological coding of the utterance (Garrett 1975, 1988). For example, word exchanges and sound exchanges act differently. We have seen that sound exchanges usually span only a word or two; the words involved do not have to belong to the same part of speech class, and usually occur within the same phrase. Word exchanges, on the other hand, do involve words of the same part of speech class, and the exchange may jump over several words in the same phrase or even into the next clause.

Such characteristic differences in speech errors suggest that we access two different levels in production. Garrett (1988) proposes a model with syntactic (**Functional**) and phonological (**Positional**) levels. When a lexical item is selected at the **Functional** level, this also elicits the grammatical and semantic features of that word. The next stage, involving the **Positional** level, retrieves the actual phonological shape of the word. Thus we have two representational levels, both necessary but dealing with different types of linguistic information: the **Functional** level must first provide the functional information which consists of the grammatical and semantic attributes of a lexical item, and then the **Positional** level provides positional information of a phonological and prosodic nature.

The flow of spontaneous speech often exhibits repeats and replacements, and the relationship between them is systematic. Almost 90% of repeats are function words like articles, prepositions, conjunctions, and pronouns; the most corrected words are content words like nouns, verbs, adjectives, and adverbs. When a content word is repeated, so also is the function word or words preceding it; for example, *could have been *prevented* is corrected as *could have been prohibited*. But the opposite is not true for function words; the preceding words are not typically repeated when the function word is repeated because this would mean going back into another syntactic constituent. If an error in either function word or content word slips out, speakers only return to the beginning of **that** syntactic constituent to start again, thus keeping the phrase intact at the particular syntactic level it occurs (Maclay and Osgood 1959).

Certain types of interjections act as **editing terms** and are tied to the monitoring process for speech errors. Speakers often mark where they falter or go astray as speech plans are realized. Editing interjections fulfill a metalinguistic function by signalling this trouble spot to the listener, for they are tied to the nature of the mistake, as well as the type of self-repair that is likely to appear next (Levelt 1983). For example, in the sentence *Why not bring . . . oh . . . hot dogs*, the *oh* signals that the speaker is selecting a referent from a possible set (James 1974). Some terms will signal why a speaker is interrupting himself or herself: for example, *or rather* signals nuance-editing, as in a sentence like *I intend to lease, or rather, sublease*, while *I mean* exemplifies mistake editing, as in a sentence like *I love, I mean, despise broccoli* (DuBois 1974, cited in Clark and Clark 1977). The extremely common *uh* often signals something has been temporarily forgotten, but is being retrieved, as in *I saw . . . uh . . . twelve people at the party* (James 1974). But *uh* has a special status among editing terms, not only because of its frequency, but because it occurs at or close to the source of trouble in the interrupted stream of speech (Levelt 1983).

Errors in word selection illustrate our awareness of part of speech classes and how they fit into sentence frames. Our erroneous selections will always fit the appropriate syntactic slots because they come from the same part of speech class. Higher level groupings like content words and function words do not find themselves reversed, nor do part of speech classes like adverbs with adjectives. The words substituted are often closely related by semantic field; a common error is the exchange of antonyms, as in *I really like to--I mean, hate to--get up in the morning*. In pulling out the right choice from our mental dictionary, we get the right domain, but come out the wrong word, as in *This piece is too long, I mean, too short*. Or there is a more general semantic relationship, as in *sword* for *arrow*, *mother* for *wife*, or *listen* for *speak* (Garrett 1988). Some word substitutions are the result of interaction between phonetic and form class similarity, as in *mushroom* for *mustache*, *cabinet* for *catalog*, or *considered* for *consisted* (Garrett 1988). Or they may be the result of some situational influence, as when something in the immediate environment pulls us toward that word, and it pops out (see Cutler 1981). Grammatical pieces like prefixes and suffixes come out correctly, but the word choice is wrong. An example of this would be looking into a drawer full of typewriter ribbons, and saying *Where would we be without your ribbons?*, when we really meant to say *Where would we be without your rulers?*.

When words are exchanged within a sentence, they often come from the same part of speech class. In this case, the words need not be phonologically similar and the words exchanged can be separated by several intervening words, as in *He has a tennis for outdoor passion* from *He has a passion for outdoor tennis*. The resulting sentence is gramatically, though not necessarily semantically coherent. Any affixes in the original get re-assigned to make the morphology of the resulting sentence well-formed. For example, *The chairman was writing mentors to his memo* (from *The chairman was writing memos to his mentor*) switches the original plural -s on *memos* to the word that is moved. Some examples of **metathesis** on the sentence level do not exchange members of the same part of speech class, though they may involve members of larger groupings like content words. The grammatical pieces like prefixes and suffixes again come out correctly, though the word is wrongly placed. An example of this would be *Thin this slicely*, when we really meant to say *Slice this thinly*.

In general, stem forms and affixes behave differently in spontaneous speech errors, and suggests that the production system differentiates between the two morpheme types. For example, Garrett (1980) has documented that stem forms often exchange places, but affixes rarely do. On the other hand, affixes can shift position (as in *I'd forgot about-en that* from *I'd forgott-en about that*. In assessing speech errors from German and English, MacKay (1979) also observed that stems and affixes were separately encoded in speech errors in spontaneous speech production. But if verbs were exchanged in sentence frames, the verb stem showed inflectional changes appropriate to the new syntactic position. The other possibility, of course, is that the whole verb could have been moved over, complete with its original inflections, but this was not the case.

'Freudian Slips' and Psychological Explanations for Speech Errors

In contrast to purely linguistic explanations, psychological explanations have suggested that speech errors in some way reflect factors external to the linguistic structure of the utterance itself. The best known of these is Freud's claim that deeper meanings could be read into our speech errors, and that such *Freudian slips* arose from our hidden motives and anxieties. While hardly an explanation for most verbal slips, it is true that anxiety-producing situations will increase the incidence of speech errors. And such slips have even been induced by introducing the presence of such factors. Motley (1985) reports eliciting speech errors in a laboratory setting by providing an environmental stimulus that generated slips of the tongue in line with the hidden anxiety. For example, a provocatively dressed woman experimenter was assigned to monitor subjects' responses and did elicit slips of the tongue with sexual connotations (for example, *fast passion* from *past fashion* and *bare shoulders* for *share boulders*).

While such psychological explanations may not explain most verbal slips, they do make a valuable point in noting that multiple factors may cause a given speech error. For example, a word substitution like *Liszt's second Hungarian restaurant* from *Liszt's second Hungarian rhapsody* probably derives as much from the associative relationship between *Hungarian* and *restaurant,* as from the fact that the exchanged words both begin with /r/. In sum, however, linguistic explanations based on structural features have been more popular and more powerful in explaining speech errors than have psychological explanations (see Dell 1988).

Speech Production and Speech Perception Interface?

How are speech perception and speech production related? Theorists have debated whether perception and production share certain mechanisms for processing information about the physical aspects of speech, but there is little empirical evidence which bears directly on this relationship. Several proposals have suggested that the listener is actively involved in perceiving speech, so that in hearing and analyzing the speech signal we refer to properties and processes related to those we employ in speech production. The three best-known proponents of such an approach are the **motor theory of speech perception**, the **analysis by synthesis approach**, and the **auditory-motor theory of speech production**.

The classic motor theory of speech perception is the best known, and claims that speech perception is mediated by the motor codes used to produce speech. Encoding must occur below the level of neuromotor commands to the articulatory muscles, and we identify phonemes by reference to the way we use commands to produce those same articulations (Liberman, Cooper, Shankweiler and Studdert-Kennedy 1967; Meyer and Gordon 1984; Liberman and Mattingly 1985). This is like saying that because we know what we do when we produce speech, we also know how to analyze the incoming utterance because we know what the other person does to produce that utterance. The more recent **direct-realist** explanation of speech perception (see Fowler 1986) shares some fundamental similarities with the motor theory, in accepting that the correspondence between what speaker says and what hearer perceives is best explained in articulatory terms.

The analysis by synthesis model also explains speech perception by reference to the production side. The listener performs an analysis of the incoming speech signal by effectively creating a hypothetical synthesis, a phonetic model of production to match the acoustic input. This explanation also assumes a common level of overlap and is thus similar to the motor theory by postulating a common reference point for both perception and synthesis. In actual production, or synthesis, this phonetic construct would be sent to the articulatory mechanisms for realization as speech output, but in perception the phonetic construct is withheld and simply analyzed for cues that determine identification of segments in the speech train (see Stevens 1972). The auditory-motor theory of speech production claims conversely that the production of speech is guided by acoustic images (Ladefoged, De Clerk, Lindau, and Papcun 1972), but the results supporting it to date are also very indirect.

Support for a Production/Perception Interface

The classic motor theory of speech perception has rested largely on its theoretical attractiveness, but there has recently been some experimental support (see Meyer and Gordon 1984, 1985; Gordon and Meyer 1984). We know that some speech sounds are perceived categorically, but that unique and reliable acoustic cues are not present in these sounds to explain the categorical-perception phenomenon. Recall, for example, how subjects made categorical judgments for stops like /p/ and /b/ despite differences in voice onset time. Perhaps the auditory information is recast in articulatory all-or-none terms; for example, the motor command to activate the vocal cords is either given or it is not, and a sound is either voiced or it is not. Advocates of the motor theory have cited the effects of selective auditory adaptation on phonetic input where acoustic cues are context-dependent and not invariant. For example, a consonant sounds about the same regardless of which vowels accompany it. A motor theory would explain this by saying that the auditory signal is transformed into motor commands for the speech segment it contains; thus, regardless of which vowel follows labials like /p-b/, their production must involve a motor command to bring the lips together (see Gordon and Meyer 1984).

Criticisms and Conclusions on the Production-Perception Interface

The concept of a production/perception interface is not without its criticisms. Non-categorical perception for some speech sounds, like vowels, is a feature which cannot be overlooked. There are also reports of invariant acoustic cues; for example, samples of onsets by initial stop consonants allow reasonable accuracy in recognition by various speakers in different vowel contexts. Mutes disadvantaged from birth and normal individuals exhibit comparable speech-perception performance. And rhesus monkeys and chinchillas exhibit categorical perception of some human speech sounds. Obviously, subjects like chinchillas and mutes who are able to perceive speech categorically lack either the articulatory mechanisms or the training required to produce speech. Lastly, humans also exhibit categorical perception for some non-speech sounds. Obviously, normal people are limited in the extent to which their vocal tracts can produce the non-speech sounds that they perceive categorically, so something more must be at work here.

Critics thus claim that categorical perception may have a purely auditory basis, eliminating it as a source of support for the motor theory. Very simply, explanations like the motor theory cannot be justified solely on the grounds that the complexity of speech perception disappears when recast in terms of the motor system's greater simplicity (Gordon and Meyer 1984). The issue of whether the perceptual and production systems share some sensorimotor mechanisms for speech remains highly controversial, and we must conclude that important questions about how speech perception and production are related remain unanswered.

Sound Symbolism

One hears a good deal about sound symbolism in popular discussions, particularly in literary discussions, where sound symbolism is held out as an effect to be striven after. For example, sound symbolism is a popular device in poetry, where certain sound patterns are used for stylistic purposes in different languages. Keats used a sequence of lateral consonants to produce an impression of softness in *Endymion* (Book I, 157-58), as in *WiLd thyme, and vaLLey-LiLies whiter stiLL, Than Leda's Love, and cresses from the riLL.*

Literature notwithstanding, this evidence has been surveyed and re-surveyed many times, and the general conclusion one can draw is the same as that drawn thirty years ago by Roger Brown (1958a). Brown devoted a whole chapter to it ("Phonetic Symbolism and Metaphor") in his classic *Words and Things* and noted that while there is obviously a community, or language-specific, sound symbolism, the fact of a universal sound symbolism, one which operates across all human languages, is doubtful or at best difficult to show to exist. There are some similar tendencies, particularly among genetically related language groupings, but claiming that a given sound has the same universal value seems to be more than we can prove. Keats' literary device works only if we are instructed that that was what he was trying to achieve.

In surveying sound symbolism, it may be necessary to clarify the discussion by distinguishing between primary onomatopoeia, secondary onomatopoeia, and language-specific sound symbolism (see Ullman 1966).

Primary Onomatopoeia

The question here is simply "how is sound imitated by sound?". Primary Onomatopoeia is the direct imitation of sound by sound, for example, sounds of nature like dogs barking, sticks breaking, and machines whirring. But even sounds imitating sounds are relatively arbitrary. At first glance, you might think there are striking similarities in the world's languages, if you list examples like the following:

1.   /r/ in English *snore*, German *schnarchen*, Dutch *snorken*, Latin *stertere*, French *ronfler*, Spanish *roncar*, Russian *chrapet'*, and even Hungarian *horkolni*
2.   /s, ʃ, tʃ/ in English *whisper*, German *wispern* and *flustern*, Latin *susurrare*, Norwegian *hviske*, French *chuchoter*, Spanish *cuchicear*, Russian *sheptat'*, and even Hungarian *sugni, susogni, suttogni*

But upon closer inspection, one notes that, except for Hungarian, these languages all belong to the same Indo-European language family, and that one does not find the same words in Nootka, Cantonese, or Japanese. Nor is the Hungarian a clearly supportive example. The

Latin form *susurrare* 'to whisper' might just as easily have been cited for 'to snore'. And lastly, lots of Indo-European languages don't fit this supposedly onomatopoetic mold either; Slovenian, for example, does have a cognate with its Slavic relative, Russian, but everyday village talk uses *na tiho povedati*, literally 'to say softly' for 'to whisper'.

Secondary Onomatopoeia

A universal secondary onomatopoeia would expect that there are correspondences between individual speech sounds and non-auditory experiences like movement, size, emotive overtones, and so forth. A sound or sound configuation would always have a certain sameness of meaning in all languages. For example, does /i/ in all languages convey the impression of smallness in size? Or does /ə/ suggest unpleasantness in all languages, so that all speakers of all languages would feel that /ə/ is an appropriate sound for unpleasant things.

At first glance, it might seem that the phoneme /i/ sees such use as a synesthetic expression of 'smallness', if you list examples like the following.

1. adjectival examples like English *little, slim, wee, thin, teeny-weeny,* French *petit,* Italian *piccolo,* Latin *minor, minimus,* Rumanian *mic,* Greek *mikros,* and Hungarian *kis, kicsi, pici*
2. nouns like English *kid, chit, imp, slip, midge, tit, bit, chip, chink, jiffy, pin, pip, tip, whit*
3. diminutives like English *-ie, -kin, -ling*

But universals must be just that, and it is just as easy to find plenty of counter-examples like Russian *velikij/malen'kij,* exactly mirrored by its English gloss *big/small,* where the supposedly symbolic vowels reversed. As Ullmann (1966) has reminded us with such examples, we expect universals to be universals, not just selective choices from vocabulary lists.

Cross-linguistic Evaluative Similarities for Restricted Sets . If we reduce our search for universal sound symbolism to evaluative reactions for sound configurations as more or less appropriate for restricted sets of stimuli, some interesting findings do emerge. For example, there are some consistent results from experiments using visual stimuli to be matched with word pairs like *kraak/bloob* and *takete/uloomu.* Davis (1961) cross-culturally compared abstract drawings with nonsense words like *takete/uloomu,* and found that both Bantu and English children made similar choices. Typically, words like *takete* were matched with drawings with angular shapes and jagged edges, while *uloomu* was matched with rounded, flowing shapes. Similar experiments have been done at least a half-dozen times over the past sixty years, and they usually tend to confirm the suggestion that some widespread cross-cultural and cross-linguistic evaluative criterion is being applied here. But it seems to be applied for just this set of vocabulary, when a specific set of choices are applied to a limited set of stimuli for matching and evaluation. And such findings are really best understood as tendencies.

There are inherent problems with demonstrating universality in sound symbolism. For one thing, the phonemic inventories, and the allophonic variants of such phonemes, vary so much from language to language, that there is really no theoretical basis for universalistic comparison of sound symbolism on a phonemic level. But on a level of analysis where the unit of analysis is more gross, as for example, high vs. low vowels, we may find some tendencies (see Taylor and Taylor 1965). For example, high to mid front vowels like /i y e œ/ are associated with relative smallness and brightness, at least in European languages like English, French, German, Danish, and Russian. The low to mid back vowels like /a o u/ tend to be associated with largeness and darkness (Taylor and Taylor 1965). Of course, such secondary onomatopoetic associations are often simply the result of their appearing frequently in words which have such semantic reference points. And some of these generalities are also due to historical relationships or even drift, the fact that languages which are related are likely to show similar patterns of phonetic symbolism (Taylor and Taylor 1962). Lastly, historical borrowings of particular features of sound symbolism, like the use of phonetic hardness (e.g., glottalization) for dimunitive shifting in western North America (see Nichols 1971), also explain why some unrelated languages show such tendencies.

Language-specific Sound Symbolism

There is no question that language-specific sound symbolism exists, and in fact, is not uncommon. The differences seem to arise in the degree to which they make use of such mechanisms; for example, Korean has a very rich system of sound symbolism, but its typologically similar neighbor, Japanese, instead makes extensive use of the morphological device of word reduplication as onomatopoeia. Even English has phonesthemes of a limited type and variety. Jespersen (1922:400) once noted that *flow, flag, fleet, flutter, flicker, fling, flit, flurry, flirt, flip, flop, flux* use /fl-/ to show the connotation of movement, and Bolinger (1965:221-22) more recently observed that half of all English words beginning with /gl-/ have something to do with sight or visual impression, as in *glance, glare, gleam, glim, glint, glisten, gloom, glower.*

The Amerindian languages of northwestern America are known for large and complex consonant inventories, and the native Indian languages west of the Rockies use higher pitch and phonetic "hardness" in consonant symbolism to denote diminutiveness (see Nichols 1971). "Diminutiveness" here must be understood to mean concepts like light, bright, quick, cold, as well as small, as opposed to concepts like dark, heavy, slow, warm, or big. It takes a variety of manifestations, depending upon the language, as for example, a continuant to a non-continuant /c--->t/ or obstruents and sonorants to their glottalized counterparts (/k, m---> k', m'/. The Salish family is particularly fond of using glottalization; for example, Kalispel, a Salish language of northern Washington, Idaho, and Montana, glottalizes root consonants, also adding a prefix of a lateral fricative /ɬ/, as in *iləmixum* 'chief' to *ɬ-il'əm'ixum*. Consonantal shifts in showing dimunitiveness are also seen in speaking of small persons and animals, as well as in baby talk; other languages like Ahousaht, a Nootkan language of western Vancouver Island, just use a special diminutive suffix in baby talk (Kess and Kess 1986).

Korean also has a rich system of vowel and consonant shifts for sound symbolism; for example, there is a shift of initial stops in adjectival or adverbial expressions from the least forcefully articulated lenis member of a three-consonant series of voiceless stops and affricates to the aspirated or glottalized sounds. This consonant alternation changes the connotation of words by shifting from a lenis consonant to the aspirated or glottally tense counterpart, with the connotation shift an emphatic one, signalling a meaning shift in the speed or force of the movement. Kim (1977) notes that it is as if the original word with the lenis consonant was modified by an appropriate adverb with a gloss like 'very' or 'to a great extent'. This is a very productive consonantal alternation, so that such words with lenis consonants can be expected to have emphatic counterparts with either the aspirated or glottalized consonants, as for example, the Korean consonant alternation changes in *pəlttək* 'abruptly' to the aspirated /ph/ in *phəlttək* 'very abruptly or forcefully' or *kamahta* 'remote' to the glottally tense /kk-/ in *kkamahta* 'very remote'.

Language-specific sound symbolism obviously exists for the same reason that all other surface features of a language operate the way they do. In essence, the design features of languages are arbitrary in their appearance on the surface level, and users of a specific language learn a particular mechanism like "phonetic hardness" and consonantal shifts just as they learn other language-specific features like tone differences (the Chinese languages), plurality (English and most of the other Germanic languages), gender (the Romance languages), and syntactic subject in last position (the Philippine languages). It is hardly a universal feature of language design in the general sense, but it is a feature which can be and often is employed by languages in a language-specific fashion.

Summary

The phonetic characteristics of sound systems have been studied from two vantage points, that of articulatory phonetics and that of acoustic phonetics. Articulatory phonetics is the study of speech sounds based on their articulatory properties, that is, how the speech sounds are produced. Acoustic phonetics examines the acoustic properties of sounds by studying the physical features of variation in air pressure produced by vocal tract movements. Psycholinguistic studies of speech perception make use of this information to understand the characteristics of speech sounds in the continuous train of sound waves which constitute the speech signal.

The basic question in speech perception is how a continuous flowing movement like the speech signal is converted into a series of individual units that we call the sounds of the language. Acoustic characteristics, however, do not translate directly and uniquely into linguistic units, and listeners take into account not only the nature of the signalling code, but also resort to inferential processes in decoding spoken messages. For example, a phonetic segment may match up with several acoustic correlates; the same acoustic feature may be perceived differently in different linguistic environments, and conversely, different features may at times be perceived as the same. But a single acoustic cue often carries information about successive sound segments, and this **parallel transmission** presents us with overlapping information about several sounds at the same time. Parallel transmission is advantageous in reducing the number of acoustic segments that have to be perceived per unit time, but the relationship between acoustic signal and perceived phoneme becomes a complexly coded one.

The factors which aid us in efficiently analyzing the speech signal can be examined in four stages: the auditory stage, the phonetic stage, the phonological stage, and the contextual stage of lexical, syntactic, and semantic knowledge (Studdert-Kennedy 1974, 1976). The stages are interdependent, with the higher level stages often influencing decisions about the lower ones. This interaction between perception and identification--translating the physical properties of acoustic cues into psychological decisions about perceived phonemes--is the essence of the task we call speech perception.

The auditory stage is based directly on the physical input, and is the initial point at which we take in the raw speech signal, with its acoustic attributes of frequency, intensity, and time span. The phonetic stage then reflects what we decide to call the sound, based on various types of phonological knowledge. **Categorical perception** is typical in adult speech perception, meaning that a phonetic stimulus is always perceived as a member of a particular category; discrimination is good between different categories, but poor among stimuli within the same category. Some would argue that infants are genetically programmed to pay attention to differences that are likely to be categorical in natural languages, with this early ability lost by 12 months of age.

The phonological stage in speech perception then sees the phonetic segment converted into a phonemic unit of the language we are hearing. It is here that phonotactic knowledge of the sequencing rules about which phonetic segments can go together is consulted. Lastly, at the contextual stage of higher orders of knowledge, familiarity with the structure of words, sentences, and discourse, as well as the properties derived from our general knowledge of situational and pragmatic constraints, exert their effect on the likely values of the speech signal. Such influences support the contribution of **top-down** processes, but there is also considerable support for the influence of information derived from **bottom-up** analysis of the actual data.

Speech production means that a speaker translates information and intentions into the language formats available in an actual language like English or Japanese. The actual production of real-time speech is, however, filled with speech errors like pauses and hesitations, corrections, repeats and replacements, and slips of the tongue. Speech errors are in fact quite regular in the way that they reflect the rules of the language, and suggest that we access two different levels in production. These two levels are the syntactic or **functional** level which elicits the grammatical and semantic features of a word, and the phonological or **positional** level which retrieves the actual phonological shape of the word.

The issue of whether the perceptual and production systems share some sensorimotor mechanisms for speech remains highly controversial, and the important questions about how speech perception and production are related remain largely unanswered.

Studies of sound symbolism have distinguished between primary onomatopoeia, secondary onomatopeia, and language-specific sound symbolism. Primary onomatopoeia is the direct imitation of sound by sound, as for example, the sounds of nature being imitated by language. Secondary onomatopoeia implies that there are correspondences between individual speech sounds and non-auditory experiences like movement, size, and emotional values, so that a sound or sound configuration would always have the same symbolic meaning in all languages. There is, however, only evidence for language-specific sound symbolism; in essence, just as the design features of languages are arbitrary in their manifestation on the surface level, users of a specific language may learn a particular set of language-specific features to achieve the effects of sound symbolism.

Chapter 4

Morphology and the Mental Lexicon

Introductory Comments to the Study of Morphology

Morphology and the study of word formation processes have undergone a revival in both linguistics and in psycholinguistics. It had been a relatively neglected area in linguistics since the period when structuralists focussed on the observable aspects of this area of language. But the discipline has seen renewed interest in the processes of word formation as linguists (Bybee 1985) and psychologists (Henderson 1985) now pursue the critical questions of how morphology is acquired, how morphological classes are structured and how morphological paradigms are organized, and what determines the productivity of specific word formation patterns. Many linguists are expanding their database to include information on language processing and typological features to account for how morphological categories arise and how words are built.

Psycholinguistics has also committed itself to understanding how morphological structure and processes of word formation are related to the way in which words are identified. One of the first steps in processing for meaning is to search for the word in the mental lexicon, the mental dictionaries we carry about in our heads and that we make use of in comprehending spoken or written discourse. Morphological clues as to morpheme status are central to this process.

The **morpheme** is the basic unit in morphology and is typically defined as the minimal grammatical unit which has meaning. Morphemes are realized phonologically by one or more variants called **allomorphs**. For example, the morpheme *pay* always sounds the same wherever it appears, as in *pay-pays-paying-paid-payroll-payment*, but the negative morpheme which is prefixed to words like *impossible, intemperate, income tax* takes shapes like /ɪm-, ɪn-, ɪŋ-/ because of the following consonants. Morphemes like the latter are said to have allomorphs or variants.

Morphemes are either free or bound, and languages differ greatly in their morphological typology. Languages like English exhibit a large number of free morphemes, while Amerindian languages like Nootka or Haida exhibit much affixation. Free morphemes are those which can potentially stand alone, as was the case with the example *pay* above; the morphemes *-ment, -s, -ing* cannot, however, and are bound morphemes. Morphemes can also be cross-classified as to whether they are roots or affixes. The root is the basic bottom-line part of the word beyond which you cannot analyze any further; for example, *kind* is the root in *kindness, unkinder, unkindest, kinder, kindest, unkind, kindly, unkindly, kind, kindnesses, unkindnesses*.

Morphemes are often divided into two groups on the basis of what they do in the language. These two groups are content words and function words, also known sometimes as lexical classes and grammatical classes. Content words primarily carry meaning of the lexical type you might expect to find in a dictionary, while function words provide the grammatical framework of the language, showing what goes with what and in what way. Content words in English are nouns, verbs, adjectives, and adverbs; function words are the grammatical pieces like articles, conjunctions, prepositions, and pronouns. Function words are complemented in their job of showing how the grammar works by another group of grammatical morphemes called **inflections**. In English these are endings like the plural on nouns and the past tense on verbs. Grammatical morphemes signal structural relationships between words or phrases and thus frame the constituent structure of sentences. For example, articles like *the* signal a following noun, inflectional affixes like the possessive -s show the relationship between two nouns in phrases like *John's hat*, and both combine in *the boy's decision* to create a noun phrase from the underlying verb phrase *the boy decided*. In English the lexical morphemes are generally free, while grammatical morphemes are either bound (for example, past tense and plural) or free (for example, prepositions and articles).

Affixes are bound and can be of the prefix, infix, or suffix variety. Prefixes are added before the root (*im-possible*) and suffixes after the root (*pay-ment*). For an example of an infix, we have to go to Philippine languages like Tagalog, which an regularly forms its past tense in the active mood by inserting a -*um*- infix between the first consonant and vowel in verb roots like *kain, tawag, bili, sulat, hanap*, as in *kumain, tumawag, bumili, sumulat, humanap* 'ate, called, bought, wrote, looked for'.

Lexical classes containing content words are large in number, and open in the sense of constantly adding and deleting new members; grammatical classes are quite restricted in number and obviously much slower in adding or deleting new members to their numbers. With lexical classes the changes are observable on almost a daily basis, while in the case of grammatical classes one notices such changes in almost a historical sense. For example, think of how many new nouns you learned this year. But how many new prepositions or conjunctions did you acquire?

Grammatical Morphemes and Conceptual Structure

Morrow (1986) has reminded us that the semantic and pragmatic functions of the closed class of grammatical morphemes also needs to be fully integrated into a usable model of discourse processing. Too much attention has been paid to the semantic functions of open classes like nouns, verbs, adjectives, and adverbs, with a correspondingly exclusive focus on the grammatical functions of closed morpheme classes like function words and inflectional affixes. While it is true that content words in the open morpheme classes do express object and relational categories, the grammatical morphemes in their turn express a small set of conceptual distinctions that apply to most such object and relation categories. Since these grammatical morphemes are crucial to establishing how objects and relations are organized into situations, they are obviously crucial to the way in which we construct a mental model of the discourse which represents a given situation (see Johnson-Laird 1983; see also the section on **Mental Models** in the chapter on discourse). That such grammatical morphemes are both meaningful and central to establishing a mental model of a given situation can be easily illustrated by the following excerpt from Lewis Carroll's *Jabberwocky* poem. You may recall that *Twas brillig and the slithy toves did gyre and gimble in the wabe, all mimsy were the borogoves and the mome raths outgrabe.* You did not need any semantic or lexical content from the so-called content words to form the outline of a mental model in your mind. Like Alice found, the passage puts ideas into your head, and although you are not quite sure of what the ideas (the content words) are, you are reasonably sure of how they relate to one another. As Morrow concludes, the grammatical morphemes enable the content word slots to be filled in with specific units that specify the actual items in the mental model, but it is the grammatical morphemes which actually allow its construction.

It seems that though different languages will express such notions with different grammatical morphemes, such notions are likely to occur in the grammatical part of the language rather than in the content part (Slobin 1982). These grammatical notions are very general in that they can apply to many kinds of content; for example, spatial and temporal considerations intersect a variety of conceptual domains (Jackendoff 1983). Both verbal and nominal systems are concerned with temporality and spatiality, though verbs more typically with temporal dimensions and nouns with spatial ones. Such grammatical distinctions are best viewed as very broad conceptual categories of properties that are applied to the narrower, more specific piece of knowledge given by particular nouns and verbs. These grammatically expressed distinctions organize both our production and comprehension of discourse in offering a framework for the construction of mental models for the situations described in discourse. This grammatical-conceptual correspondence must exist in its current form because of the cognitive demands of communication via language. Such a correspondence facilitates comprehension by providing access to a small set of conceptual distinctions which organize a vast array of content into identifiable situations. For example, the small number of function words known as prepositions allow us to view any number of potential objects in relationship to any number of other potential objects by the pervasive but limited set of geometrical views allowed by *in/on/over/below/behind/ under/etc.*. Our mental models for the situations are really generalized frameworks which then simply 'fill in the blanks' with the specific semantic content provided by the lexical classes like nouns and verbs.

Inflectional Morphology and Derivational Morphology.

Affixes can perform one of two functions in a language that has them. They can serve to make up new words, in which case they are called **derivational affixes** because their function is to build (derive) new words. Or affixes can express the grammatical categories that a language exhibits, in which case they are called **inflectional affixes** because their function is to mark (inflect) words for the grammatical features a given language makes use of.

Before contrasting inflectional and derivational morphology, it may be useful to introduce one more distinction, roots vs. stems. Roots we have characterized as the basic unanalyzable part of the word. A stem, on the other hand, is what is left after all the inflectional affixes have been taken off. For example, in the word *characterized*, the ultimate root is *character*, but its stem is *characterize*.

Now go back to our list of examples based on the root *kind* from above. The only inflectional affixes are the plural marker -*es* and the adjectival inflections -*er*, -*est*. The stems left after taking these off are *kind, kindness, unkind, kindly, unkindly, kindliness, kindness, unkindness*. Since many words contain both a root and one or more derivational affixes, the distinction between roots and stems is a useful one to make in sorting out words and their various parts.

Inflectional Morphology

Inflectional affixes are usually found in sets of paradigmatic variations associated with a particular part of speech, like nouns. Inflections never change the part of speech class for the word, since they show the grammatical functions a word in a particular part of speech class is undergoing; thus, they can be potentially added to every word of that part of speech class. For example, in classical Latin and modern Serbo-Croatian nouns are inflected with endings for case, number, and gender. Modern French only has gender (masculine and feminine) and number, and English only has number, with the singular shown by zero and the plural ending shown by a final -*s* in the written form. Inflectional paradigms are highly structured set of endings which exhibit very regular patterns. For example, most English nouns take a plural and a regular one at that. Thus, such inflectional affixes are both systematic and productive, and you have no difficulty in assigning the phonologically correct plural as a final /s/ for a new word *wonk-wonks* or as a final /ɪz/ or /əz/ for *wudge-wudges*.

Inflections are limited in number; for example, English only has eight inflectional endings. There are two for nouns (plural and possessive), two for adjectives (comparative -*er* superlative -*est*), and four for verbs (past tense, past participle, the third person singular ending, and the progressive -*ing*). The allomorphs of an inflectional morpheme are also fairly regular, and usually phonologically conditioned. This means that there is some phonetic feature in their environment which explains their appearance; in the case of our nonsense words above, it was the last sound of the noun that conditioned your choices of the correct plural allomorph. To be specific, you will always choose an /ɪz/ or /əz/ after final /s z ʃ ʒ tʃ dʒ/, /z/ after all other final voiced consonants, and /s/ after all other final voiceless consonants. There are also instances of irregular inflections which defy explanation, other than the fact that this allomoph is the one which must appear with a given root; such irregular exceptions are said to be morphologically conditioned allomorphs, as is the case with *foot-feet*.

In English, German, and Dutch, inflectional affixes are always suffixes, but in other languages the grammatical categories can be shown by prefixes or infixes as well. For example, in Bantu languages, many grammatical features like number are shown by prefixes; past tenses are shown by infixes in verbs in Philippine languages like Tagalog. Grammatical processes can also be shown by reduplication, as when Philippine languages form their plurals by reduplicating the first consonant and vowel of the root, as in *kakain, tatawag, bibili, susulat, hahanap* 'will eat, will call, will buy, will write, will look for'. Finally, it has been noted that the existence of inflection in a language typically implies the existence of derivational processes as well (Greenberg 1963/1966).

Schemas in Irregular Inflectional Morphology . Most verbs in English form their past tense by adding an -*ed* suffix to the verb stem; traditionally, these are called the **weak verbs**. They typically have both their past tense and past participle formed in -*ed*, as in *walk-walked-have walked*. Many of the irregular verbs have a vowel and/or consonantal change, and may have the past and past participle the same (*tell-told-have told*) or different (*sing-sang-sung*), or even an -*en* suffix (*break-broke-have broken*). Such irregular verbs are called the **strong verbs**, and in general, have come down to Modern English from Old English, where they were more common. They have been slowly attracted to the increasingly common pattern of weak verbs over the centuries. A quick look at the King James Bible of 1611 shows a number of our modern weak verbs as still strong verbs then; for example, it gives the past tense of roosters crowing as *crew* instead of our modern *crowed*. The morphological irregularity of these forms should not be confused with their frequency; these irregular past tenses are often connected with the most common verbs in normal speech, and indeed, it is their very frequency that has kept them from entirely moving into the weak verb class.

Bybee and Slobin (1982) have investigated these irregular verbs in English with both children and adults, noting that speakers make generalized 'schemas' about the classes that such forms fall into. Such a schema will contain the phonological pattern of the irregular morphological class, and it is this schema that is used in organizing the lexicon. English speakers seem to have a prototype member for each irregular verb class, based on shared phonological properties of the class; speakers then employ this schema about the shape of a lexical item in a category rather than relying on rote memory or rule learning. Though such irregular verb patterns are learned by rote, and are then

stored in the mental lexicon as such, speakers apparently form generalizations about them which can be applied to novel instances.

Bybee and Moder (1983) further explored the two productive verb
classes exemplified by *sing-sang-sung* and *string-strung*. They
attempted to determine the specific shape of such classes, and were
particularly interested in learning how such classes are defined by
speakers. That is, which criteria are used in deciding that a set of
verbs actually forms a class? Such a question also entails a related
question regarding the productivity of the class; why are some irregular classes productive enough to attract new members?

The *string-strung* class is the most productive of the strong verbs
that survive in English, and has even attracted new members to itself
over the centuries. Within limits, both classes are still currently productive, as Bybee and Slobin (1982) showed in eliciting new past tense
forms from both children and adults. They explain subjects' willingness to produce new and 'regular' irregular forms in these two categories by postulating 'schemas' for the shape of lexical items in such categories. Such schemas were developed in semantic theory to define the
dimensions of natural classes of objects, with the natural class in this
instance containing linguistic objects, namely, lexical forms which
belong to past tense groupings. Rosch (1978) has explained such natural classes as clustering around a prototypical member, which has the
'best' cluster of attributes that characterize the class. Some members
of a class are more central to the class, in that they share more of the
relevant attributes that the focal point example exhibits; other members are somewhat more peripheral, because they have only one or several of the attributes. For example, robins seem more birdlike than
chickens or penguins, though both belong to the category of bird; four-
legged wooden chairs with straight backs and well-defined seats seem
more chairlike than a polyester covered bean-bag chair flopped on the
floor, though both might be on sale in the 'chair' section of the modern
furniture store you last visited. In natural classes, some members are
closer to the central cluster of attributes taken to characterize the
class, while others are more marginal; yet class membership includes
both, although a given class member might not exhibit the ideal attributes *in toto*. Nor do natural classes usually have a uniquely defined
set of properties that excludes all other categories. For example, fish
swim, birds fly, and mammals bear their young alive and suckle them;
but the fact that penguins and whales swim, while emus and ostriches
are earthbound throws us for a loop when we try to assign them to a
category. And the mighty platypus even has the zoologist up a billa-
bong!

Apparently linguistic objects also fall into natural classes as language users deal with this aspect of their environment. Speakers
make categorizations of linguistic objects in the same way that they
form categories of natural or cultural objects. In the case of the irregular strong verbs, the class is categorized by their form in respect to
phonological properties, and this is the basis for present and future
incorporation as members of the same morphological class. There is a
prototypical form as the focal point for this irregular morphological

class, in much the same way that Rosch has described prototypes in the organization of semantic classes. The prototype for this class is /sC(C) ɪ ŋ(k)/, and verbs like *string* and *stink* are close to that prototype. The closer phonologically a verb is to the prototype, the more easily it is absorbed into the class. Such irregular inflectional morphology tends to be treated according to phonological properties, with minimalization of list learning.

The psychological validity of such class definitions was demonstrated experimentally. Because this particular morphological class consists of verbs which bear a family resemblance to a prototype, as described above, the likelihood of obtaining a past tense for a verb is a reflection of how phonologically similar it is to the prototype. For example, given nonsense verbs like *sking-gling-spid-dob*, you will be most likely to form a past tense form in this class with *sking* and the least likely with *dob*. The chances of forming the the past tense of such nonsense verbs according to this irregular pattern, instead of by the regular *-ed* suffix, decreases as one moves away from the prototypical phonological pattern for the ideal member of the class. Try them for yourself, and notice the degree of acceptability for the competing, but possible, past tense options *skung-skinged, glung-glinged, spud-spidded, dub-dobbed*.

As Bybee and Moder (1983) found, this class of verbs does not have discrete boundaries with phonological features which are absolutely required in members of the morphological class; rather the class consists of members which are more or less close to the focal center of the class. It is this finding that explains how such classes grow and expand in a productive sense, and why the class can even grow to include verbs like *strike-struck* and even *dig-dug*. It is their relative similarity to the abstract prototype by which the class is best defined that explains how they were assigned membership in the class when they joined.

Derivational Morphology

Derivational affixes are larger in number than inflectional affixes, as well as less productive and less regular than inflectional morphology. Thus, while practically every noun, except for mass nouns like *confetti*, takes some inflectional affix for plurality, a limited number of nouns can co-occur with derivational affixes like *-ship, -dom, -ling, -let, -y/-ie, -eer/-er*. Try taking the endings off the following derived words, and see how they fit with the other nouns in the list: *friendship, kingdom, duckling, coverlet, baggy/doggie, auctioneer/batter*. Yet all of these roots will take a plural, and a phonologically regular one at that. English has more derivational affixes than inflectional. Derivational affixes in English can be either prefixes or suffixes, and can compound upon one another, as in *un-pre-meditated* and *kind-li-ness*. Inflectional affixes in English are never prefixes, nor can there be more than one inflectional suffix in a word.

Derivational affixes may keep the resultant word in the same part of speech class, as for example, *auction--->auctioneer*; but the meaning is usually changed, even if only slightly. But the addition of a derivational affix often causes a change in the part of speech class, as for example, nominalizers which convert verbs to nouns (*act--->action*) or adjectives to nouns (*eager--->eagerness*). The main function of derivational morphology is to make up new words, and in so doing, the end product is often different from the part of speech class of the original stem morpheme. And the meaning of the resultant word is somewhat changed.

We noted that in comparison to inflectional affixes, derivational affixes are highly irregular and selective in their appearance. It is often impossible to select the appropriate derivational suffix on basis of the root alone; for example, *refuse* becomes *refusal*, but *confuse* becomes *confusion*. Yet other suffixes like *-ness* seem quite productive. Exactly these issues of degrees of relatedness and productivity have attracted the attention of psycholinguists.

Degrees of Morphological Relationship . The descriptive criteria of phonetic similarity and semantic similarity are typically used to determine whether two forms are derivationally related. For example, the word pair *refuse-refusal* has both, while *class-classic* has the first, but not the second; *opaque-opacity* has semantic similarity, but phonetic similarity only in the first two sounds. A pressing question is whether the mental representation of such related words is treated as a stem plus an affix, or whether related words are learned and stored separately. There may even be some variability among speakers of the same language in terms of how they store lexical items in their mental dictionaries. One can use native speakers' judgments of such similarities, as Derwing (1976) did for adults on 115 word-pairs. His subjects rated pairs on a 5-point scale of semantic similarity and on a 7-point scale of phonetic similarity. The results provide a preliminary idea of how the mental representations of these must be stored. For example, *teach-teacher, dirt-dirty* are judged as phonetically similar, but *carpenter-wagon, ladder-lean* are judged as neither; *kitty-cat, wild-wilderness* are judged as semantically similar, but not phonetically similar, while *live-liver, ear-eerie* are judged as the opposite. Derwing also used a "comes from" test, in which subjects were required to indicate the degree of morphological relatedness on a 5-point scale. Not surprisingly, the results correlate highly with semantic similarity results, but less highly with phonetic results.

Productivity in Derivational Morphology . Some word formation patterns are more productive than others; for example, *X-ization* is more productive than *X-izement*, and *X-iveness* is more productive than *X-ivity* (Aronoff 1982). The more productive a pattern is, the less likely a speaker is able to distinguish potential words derived from that pattern from already existing words. However, speakers are acutely aware of the distinction between actual and potential words for the products of word formation patterns which are less productive. According to Aronoff, the feature of productivity interacts with the feature of frequency in determining how words are coined or scrapped from the language. Differences in productivity among word formation patterns are correlated with the willingness of native speakers to accept potential words as real words in the language. For example, in choosing between X-iveness and X-ivity in words like obsessiveness and obsessivity, subjects prefer the word resulting from the first pattern. Thus, there are more actual X-iveness words (like decisiveness) than X-ivity words (like objectivity), and the X-iveness words can be considered more productive than the latter. And the more productive a pattern is, the less likely a speaker is to be able to distinguish potential words, derived from that pattern, from real and already existing words. However, speakers do take note of the distinction between actual and potential for the products of word formation patterns which are less productive. Since hearers are more aware of such words, this awareness may be pressed into service in the coining of specialized or technical words. Less productive words have an automatic attention-getting appeal, and thus may be used for purposes of foregrounding. If reductive is a word in pottery, then reductivity is the logical choice for the technical term in the noun class; reductiveness would be an unlikely chioice because it would go unnoticed by hearers or readers, in that it fits the more productive, and thus less foregrounded, attention-getting pattern (Aronoff 1982:144). It is because the word formation pattern using -ivity are more remarkable that it is more likely to be used in the creation of lexical items which are assigned special meanings.

On the other hand, some patterns like X-ibility and X-ibleness are largely fossilized and no longer productive. The -ibleness pattern is a good example of a dead pattern, one which is no longer viable in being applied to the creation of new lexical items. Existing words containing this pattern may even be frequent, but it is not being applied to new lexicalizations, and can no longer be counted as part of the dynamic component in word building processes.

Developmental Productivity of Derivational Morphology. There is even productivity in a developmental sense. Derwing (1976) reports on the relative productivity of noun compounds (like birdhouse) and six suffixes: the agentive -er: runner; the instrumental -er: eraser; the diminutive -ie, -y: doggie, baggy; the adverbial -ly: quickly; and the adjectival -y: muddy. In testing children, adolescents, and adults, it was obvious that adults would score highest, and that the scores would decrease with age. One expects an increase in productivity with age. But the specifics are interesting. The agentive was the most productive for all, while the diminutive suffix exhibited the least productivity for all groups. The young children treated only the agentive -er, the adjectival -y, and the noun compounds as productive, suggesting that there may be a core of productive derivational processes which are in evidence even at earlier linguistic stages.

Historicity and Orthography Affect Derivational Knowledge . Some of the morphological knowledge we have interacts with and is affected by other kinds of knowledge we have, like the historical knowledge of where roots and affixes come from and the way in which they are spelled in their variant forms. For example, English has borrowed prodigiously from other languages in the last thousand years, and one source for a large number of borrowings is Latin. Even though most English speakers are unaware of the etymological origins of most words, Randall (1980) found relative acceptability of pseudo-words with *-ity* was higher when this suffix was affixed to a Latinate root (*obliquity*) than native non-Latinate words (*earthicity*). Subjects seemed sensitive to the historical origins for roots and affixes as they evaluated possible words, to the degree that Randall was willing to posit the feature of "classicality" as a unconscious factor in their morphological knowledge. She even suggested that this was the most salient parameter influencing word formation preferences for her subjects in this particular task.

Sometimes historical changes occur which make regular alternations irregular, and some trace is left in the way in which words are written. An interesting series of experiments combines both of these factors in looking at the results of the Great Vowel Shift in English. An analysis of the Vowel Shift Rules in English by Chomsky and Halle (1968) claimed that a deeper level of analysis, one which employs systematic phonemes, is necessary to explain the underlying regularities of sound structure in English. They consider the Vowel Shift to be "without doubt the pivotal process of Modern English phonology (1968:187)", and by extension, an important process in morphology. This shifting of vowels in English was largely the result of what has been termed the Great Vowel Shift in English which occurred between the 14th and 17th Centuries. In general, long vowels changed into the higher vowel immediately above (for example, Old English /hē/--->Modern English /hi/ 'he'), unless they were already high vowels; in this case they became diphthongs (for Example, Old English /fīr/--->Modern English /fayr/ 'fire'). Many short vowels were also affected. The writing system, however, did not change to keep pace with these phonological developments, and so the English orthographic system spells many words in a way better suited to Middle English vowel values. In the case of certain word pairs, the orthography represents one of the vowels correctly, but uses the same alphabet symbol to also show another vowel. This is true, for example, of the second 'i' in the words *divine-divinity*; *divinity* has the second 'i' correctly representing /ɪ/, but *divine* has it representing the post-Vowel Shift diphthong of /ay/.

Linguists of course wish to characterize any linguistic regularity that speakers exhibit, and such vowel shifts are common to a fair number of word pairs like the following:

1.   /aɪ--->ɪ/: derive-derivative, five-fifth, Bible-biblical, tyrant-tyrannical, divine-divinity, transcribe-transcription
2.   /i--->ɛ/: meter-metric, deep-depth, extreme-extremity, discrete-discretion, redeem-redemption
3.   /e--->æ/: grave-gravity, profane-profanity, sane-sanity, Spain-Spanish, nature-natural, explain-explanatory

Linguists could characterize this regularity of linguistic behavior by one of three possible avenues of analysis. We could just list by each instance, we could classify them into groups as above, or better still, we could perhaps find one rule to account for all of them. This last alternative was just what the Vowel Shift Rule in Chomsky and Halle successfully achieved as a descriptive device. But experiments testing the psychological validity of this descriptive rule have, however, found little support for speakers employing such a rule productively. MacKay (1978) did find that the time taken to produce derived nouns from verb roots varied with the complexity of the derivational process. Some derivations were more complex than others; for example, *decide--->decision* is more complicated than *intern--->internment*, because its derivation requires both the suffix *-ion*, a final consonantal change of /d--->ʒ/ in the root, and a vowel shift from /ay--->ɪ/. The vowel shift part of such word pairs does presents an extra step in the morphological task of word formation.

There was a suggestion that the traditional orthography had an advantage over employing more phonemically oriented alphabets for children at an early reading stage (C. Chomsky 1970), since the traditional orthography preserves derivational relationships in the way such words are presented. Based on Chomsky and Halle's (1968) *Sound Pattern of English*, she reasoned that if the conventional spelling of words in the traditional orthography corresponds to the important underlying representations of words and shows word relationships in the language, then the system is really an optimal one. For example, rather than decrying the poor phonetic fit of the English writing system by showing how /sen/ and /sænɪti/ fail to have their vowels neatly differentiated by the written symbols, she suggested that we should instead note the benefits of a system in which their morphological relatedness is shown. The derivational (and etymological) relationships of other roots are kept constant in the writing system, because of their identical origins at some abstract representational level. For example, in *anxious-anxiety* and *muscle-muscular*, one has a consonant shift (/-kʃ- to -gz-/) in the first and an addition of a consonant (/-s- to -sk-/) in the second example. But they maintain the same visual shapes of *anx-* and *musc-* in the orthography.

Her claim was that this arrangement permits reading to occur with more efficiency. There is no question that this is a feature of the English writing system because sound changes have left these irregularities. But whether it enables children to learn to read more efficiently is an experimental question. The vowel shift rules are not particularly productive, and are frozen in time as an artifact of a large number of borrowings from Latin. Moskowitz (1973) concluded that the vowel shift rules are learned quite late by children, and by deductive abstraction from the limited set of words they are exposed to in the written system of the language. That is, the source of children's knowledge of vowel shifting is in fact the spelling system of the language, and this knowledge stays in a psychological format which is reflective of that source. The Chomsky and Halle claims about vowel shifts seem to bear little resemblance to the functional grammars of native speakers.

Moskowitz did find that children have a definite knowledge about the vowel shift rule. When subjects were read a nonsense word and required to respond to each word by adding the suffix -ity and changing the vowel in one of three ways they had been taught, the vowel shift category was easiest for them to master. But her student subjects between the ages of 9 to 12 had obviously intuited this rule from their experience with learning to read and spell, as evidenced by such accompanying observations as "Oh, you just want me to make a long 'i' into a short 'i', right?" (1973:247). Children are explicitly taught in school that each vowel letter has a long and a short version, and these alternations pretty well replicate the vowel shift patterns in question here. It was also worthy of note that in a pre-test some adults did not know many of the real words in the experiment or failed to recognize them when paired with nonsense words, and that pre-junior-high school children do not have many of the Latinate words in their free speech vocabularies. The productivity of such processes is thus called into question, though it is obvious that a non-productive knowledge of such rules is present.

Jaeger (1984) has reviewed the past experimental data on Chomsky and Halle's (1968) Vowel Shift Rule, as well as posing her own experiment, concluding that subjects are behaving in accord with spelling rules and not the Vowel Shift Rule. She also observes that knowledge of such vowel alternations are real in English, but that these rules have their origins in the orthographic system. Literacy must be considered as a source of psychologically real knowledge, and in this case such alternations have either been brought to the conscious attention of children in their education or they have themselves intuited the presence of such alternations. Psychologists with an interest in reading are increasingly interested in morphemic structure and morphological processes, and with good reason. Aspects of the reading process involve word recognition strategies which may necessitate the search for roots, stems, or affixes in the lexical look-up task. Similarly, the task of spoken-word recognition reflects that fact that the pronunciation of many words depends upon whether a root or stem stands alone or has affixes attached, and if so, which affixes (contrast *serene-serenity* with *serene-sereneness*).

Morphological Structure, Word Recognition, and the Mental Lexicon

Word recognition and the structure of the mental lexicon has been a lively topic of late. The **mental lexicon** is your mental dictionary, that vast compendium of information about words and their relationships that you carry about in your head (see Emmorey and Fromkin 1988). Like the dictionary on your bookshelf, it too is organized along principles which reflect the phonological, orthographic, and semantic characteristics that words share. But in searching through the mental lexicon as we attempt to place a word, we note that the process of word recognition is sensitive to other characteristics as well, characteristics like word frequency and the effects of context. For example, read the following strings of letters and try to decide if they are words or not.

1. hit
2. hod

Chances are that *hit* was easier to recognize as a word, and the reason is simply that *hit* is more common than *hod*. This is the effect of word frequency. By the way, this method is called the **lexical decision** task and is one of the favorite ways of probing the dimensions of word recognition (not all, however, are impressed with the appropriateness of this task; see Henderson 1989).

Now read the following strings of letters and try to say the second word out loud as quickly as you can.

1. doctor horse
2. doctor nurse

Here you probably were able to say *nurse* out loud more quickly, as measured by milliseconds. The reason this time is that *doctor* preceded *nurse*, thus providing a context for the word recognition task. The **pronunication** task has been another favorite experimental method used to test word recognition procedures (see Garnham 1985 for an outline of experimental procedures).

Most work in lexical access and word recognition has been on the recognition of written words. For example, one of the most influential word recognition models, Morton's logogen model, dealt with the written word in reading tasks in its initial phases. Morton (1979) has proposed that each word is stored in the mental lexicon as a **logogen**, which includes the various phonological and semantic features that any realistic model of vocabulary storage and recall must be based on. In his theory of the mental lexicon, each logogen represents a corresponding word or morpheme. Logogens collect evidence for the occurrence of the word they represent by collecting evidence of stimulation for that word; this evidence may come from context or from the stimulus of the lexical item itself. If there is sufficient evidence to exceed a pre-set threshhold, the logogen fires like a synapse might. And everytime it fires, the threshhold is lowered, and kept lowered, so that it is easier to recognize a word which has been so primed. Such threshold variability accounts for the fact that common words are more easily recognized than infrequent words. The threshhold can also be lowered by related contextual information, or primed by the word itself or its semantic relatives. As we shall see, findings from repetition priming studies tend to support models like the logogen model, in that lowered threshholds from morphologically related words suggest that words are stored in interrelated networks of morphologically related lexical entries. The next question is how is this storage realized, by independent roots and affixes or by constellation-like groupings of whole-word lexical entries, and we shall examine this question in the following section on written-word recognition.

Research on spoken-word recognition is also receiving more and more attention. A processing model that accounts for both the multiple access and the multiple assessment that words undergo is Marslen-Wilson's (1989b) **cohort model** of spoken-word recognition. Multiple access means that we consider various possible words as candidates for the correct phonetic match to the phonetic input we are hearing. In the first 200 milliseconds of input, there is a class of potential word forms, a 'cohort', which is activated and which we assess against the acoustic input and the discourse context. Finally, there remains but one candidate that is consistent with the ascoustic input; word recognition means that we have correctly chosen from among the possible cohort, and matched the input with the correct lexical item. For example, imagine you hear as input the following phonetic stimulus: /dilɪ-/. So far this is not a word, but you know it will be as soon as a potential word boundary is reached. Is the word going to be *deliberate (adjective), deliberate (verb), deliberation, deliver, delivery, delineate, delineation, delimit, delirium, delirious,* or *delicious.* Successful word recognition means that you have correctly chosen from among this potential cohort. One of the key issues in spoken-word recognition studies, then, is ascertaining which cues you employ to achieve word recognition, as well as the cues you employ to decide on when a new word begins in the stream of speech input you are receiving. These topics we shall consider in the following section on spoken-word recognition.

Written-Word Recognition

The morphological characteristics of words appear to influence the visual word recognition process. The current experimental evidence suggests that morphological structure is important in lexical processing and in lexical access (see review contained in Caramazza, Laudanna and Romani, 1988). One of the major, and as yet undecided, problems is how the mental lexicon is organized and accessed. Are words represented in the mental dictionary in their root or stem shapes, that is, in a morphologically decomposed form. Are word stems and word roots stored separately from inflectional and derivational affixes? Are word roots stored separately from word stems? Is there a morphological parsing procedure by which a word is broken into its component pieces of root and its possible inflectional AND derivational affixes? Or is it the stem which is looked up? Or is it perhaps that words are stored as whole words, so that each possible word is stored independently in the mental dictionary? The evidence on the issues of storage and access is mixed.

Lima's (1987) results from eye movement data in reading tasks indicate that pseudo-prefixed words like *relish* receive longer fixations than prefixed words like *revive*. Recall that we asked whether words are stripped of their affixes before the lexical access search begins, or whether only stem morphemes are stored in the mental lexicon. In the case of these two words, the experimental task is constructed to assess whether the potential prefix *re-* is stripped off to look for the remaining stem. If the lexical access search goes through a process of stripping affixes to then look for the stem morpheme, one would expect there to be a cost associated with applying this process to pseudo-affixed words. The resulting "stem" left over from stripping the pseudo-affix *re-* from *relish* leaves the non-stem of *-lish*. This does not appear in the mental dictionary, and so there is a difference in reaction times for such cases, since the whole process has to be scrapped and re-initiated. Several previous studies had suggested that lexical decision times for pseudo-affixed words were not longer than for recognizably affixed real words. But Lima's recent data with real words suggests that in normal reading words are stripped of any letter pattern that could be a prefix, regardless of whether the remainder of the word is a a stem or not. It is for this reason that the pseduo-affixed words elicit longer eye fixation times; the lexical look-up process results in a unsuccessful search in the case of *-lish*, and the search must begin again.

Several experiments have reported this for experimentally constructed non-words, namely, that lexical access does depend upon having a morpheme stem address to look for. Caramazza, Laudanna and Romani (1988) looked at experimentally constructed non-words which were inflected for a pseudo-Italian verbal pattern, as in *cantevi, canzevi, cantovi, canzovi*. Their results show that non-words which can stand alone and which cannot be broken down morphologically were easier to process than those which looked like they could be segmented into pieces. The words that were the hardest to deal with were non-words which were exhaustively decomposable into morphemes. Their results suggest that the answer may be found in a model which is neither strictly whole-word nor stem-morpheme based, but the results do support the fact that lexical representations are morphologically decomposed. Caramazza et al. conclude that their results present strong evidence for a model of the lexicon in which the morphological structure of a lexical item is represented. This information plays a role in accessing lexical items, and the storage of written words appears to be realized in the mental dictionary in a way that reflects uninflected stem shapes. One can of course question whether results with non-words can inform us about real words and whether these findings on pseudo-inflections can also be applied to derivational affixes in word look-up procedures, but the evidence is compelling.

Some recent work by Andrews (1986) does shed some light on the derivational aspect of lexical search, as well as suggesting that morphological decomposition which occurs during visual word recognition may be an optional rather than an obligatory process. Suffixed words in her experiments were not accessed via their root morphemes, as you might have expected the derived words *booklet/drummer* to be accessed through their roots *book/drum*. But there was some evidence that compound words shift the lexical search process to a strategy whereby subjects do make use of information gained from breaking apart the morphemic constituents of the words, as in *sea-weed/rib-cage*. And when suffixed words appeared in the same list as compound words, the strategy was activated by the mere presence of compound words and was applied to the suffixed words as well.

One explanation is that this is a necessary strategy for compound words because there is no predictability of meaning for a compound word on the basis of its constituents. There is a somewhat greater predictability for the meaning of words created by adding derivational affixes. And, of course, inflectionally affixed words always have their meaning predictable from the stem of the word. For example, contrast the path by which you search for meaning in words like the following:

1.   compound words like *seaweed, ribcage*
2.   derivationally affixed words like *booklet, drummer*
3.   inflectionally affixed words like *dogs, eagle's, discussed*
4.   unaffixed words like *dog, eagle, discuss*

This was pretty well the explanation for results obtained from repetition priming experiments by Stanners, Neiser, Hernon, and Hall (1979), later replicated by Fowler, Napps, and Feldman (1985). Semantic priming in general refers to the finding that decisions about whether a string of letters is a word is faster if that string is preceded by a semantically related item. And repetition priming, or lexical priming, means repeated access to a lexical entry; these findings show that words are more rapidly classified if they have been presented previously in the experiment and that words shown under poor reading or listening conditions are also better recognized if they have been primed by having appeared previously. Both experiments found that inflected words prime the uninflected words as effectively as do the uninflected forms themselves. Derivationally related forms of the word, however, were less effective primes. One interpretation is that unaffixed stems and their inflected forms share the same lexical entry, and that even derived forms and the stem forms from which they are derived are closely situated, rather like neighbors, in their storage areas in the mental lexicon.

Fowler et al. did control for the effects of the fact that derivationally derived forms are often less formally close to their base word origins, and found that derived words could be just as effective primes as the unaffixed words themselves or their inflected forms. They even found that same effect for morphologically regular and irregular forms of the word, and they found this to be true both in reading and in listening behaviors. A possible interperetation of these findings is that stems and their inflected and derived morphological relatives, regular and irregular, all share the same lexical entry (Fowler et al. 1985:251). No matter what the final interpretation, it would appear that words which are closely related by morphological processes of word formation are stored in a way that recognizes this fact.

This explanation seems very straightforward when the roots are phonologically identical to their shapes when embedded in affixed words, as in *dog-dogs*. But it is not just identity of phonological shape that lexically organizes morphologically related forms into the same class with a common lexical representation. Identity of form is not a prerequisite, as Boyce, Browman and Goldstein (1987) have shown in their investigation of Welsh consonant mutations. As a member of the Celtic branch of our Indo-European language family, Welsh has the characteristic of consonant mutation, or lenition, in certain environments. The initial consonant of a word will change depending upon its environment, so that a word like *pont* 'bridge' may turn up as *bont* or *font* as well. Despite the fact that the phonological shapes of these variants differ, they are stored in a single abstract morphological category. Boyce et al. found that the particular phonological relationships among the forms generated by mutation processes do not affect their relationships during lexical access searches. The Welsh forms were considered as the same abstract morphological category, demonstrating that forms need not be easily pried apart in the concatenative sense of prefix plus root; neither do they need to share the same unmodified base form, nor do they even need to share the same initial consonants. Such variants are best explained by a 'shared entry' approach, not entirely unlike the notion of an abstract morphemic category with allomorphic variants often showing some modifications.

Feldman and Fowler (1987) report on work with the inflectional system of Serbo-Croatian, a South Slavic language of Yugoslavia. Serbo-Croatian exhibits a very rich system of inflections on nouns, verbs, and adjectives, just as Classical Latin and Greek had and all modern Slavic languages still have. Such languages use inflection as the primary way of showing grammatical information; thus, a grammatical ending like *-om* will show the noun to be an instrument, as when *ruka* 'hand' becomes *rukom* 'with the hand'. Feldman and Fowler investigated Serbo-Croatian nouns, which are marked for seven cases, two numbers, and three genders. In particular, they examined how nouns inflected for case in the singular number might be related in the mental lexicon when reading in this language. For example, masculine nouns have the nominative-accusative forms unmarked for inanimate nouns, and feminine nouns typically have a final *-a* in the nominative case, and are thus easily identified. A typical inflectional paradigm for masculine and feminine singular nouns looks like the following for *dinar* 'dinar, unit of currency' and *rupa* 'hole'. However, it should be noted that some of the case forms, like the vocative (*dinare* 'O dinar!') are practically a non-event, while the nominative form (*dinar* 'dinar' as sentence subject) is the most frequent in occurrence.

CASE	MASCULINE	FEMININE	GLOSS
Nominative	dinar	rupa	'dinar/hole' as subject
Genitive	dinara	rupe	'of the dinar/hole'
Dative	dinaru	rupi	'for the dinar/hole'
Accusative	dinar	rupu	'dinar/hole' as object
Instrumental	dinarom	rupom	'with the dinar/hole'
Locative	dinaru	rupi	'in the dinar/hole'
Vocative	dinare	rupo	'O dinar!/O hole!'

Previous experiments had indicated that the nominative singular case form of the noun has a special status as a base form or nucleus, around which the other case forms of the same noun cluster like satellites. It was found that decision tasks are quicker with the nominative form of the noun than with other cases like the dative, genitive, or instrumental cases. This finding cannot be explained by frequency considerations, because the reaction times for word identification did not correlate with the individual frequencies of case forms. For example, the genitive case is used almost as frequently in the language as the nominative; on the other hand, the instrumental case is ten times less frequent than the genitive, and yet they elicited the same reaction times. It was the morphological identification of the case form as either nominative or non-nominative that was critical to the reaction time, suggesting that the nominative form was in some way central in storage and access. The other case forms appeared to be clustered around the nominative case form like satellites, secondary to the nominative focal point but equal among themselves. These findings were interpreted as support for a whole-word access approach, but one in which the mental lexicon is organized to make use of the principle of organization of putting morphologically related words together as neighbors. The lexical entries are nonetheless accessed as whole words, though these whole words occupy adjacent spaces in the mental dictionary. The findings of previous experiments were thus interpreted as showing that entries for each form in the inflectional paradigm for nouns are represented completely and separately, and are not broken up into a single stem morpheme plus so many case affixes. Furthermore, such stems or base morphemes are not taken as the prime entry points for looking up noun entries in the Serbo-Croatian mental lexicon (see Lukatela, Gligorjevic, Kostic and Turvey (1980). In this satellite-entries explanation of the lexicon, the nominative form of the word serves as the hub of this satellite-like array of morphologically related words. The inflected words are strongly associated to the nominative form, but never as strongly to one another as they are to their hub nominative form. In keeping with this finding, the priming effects for the nominative to itself and the other inflected forms are strong, and vice-versa; these priming effects are in fact stronger than are the effects for the non-nominative case inflected forms to one another. Feldman and Fowler replicated the earlier pattern of results, supporting this satellite-entries account of lexical storage for inflected noun forms. They also found that nominative forms are more strongly linked to non-nominative case forms than the non-nominative case forms are to each other. Thus, regular forms do seem to refer back to a nuclear base form by which lexical forms are organized, and this base form is certainly the nominative case form. This was not exactly the case, however, for irregular nouns with alternating forms which change shape slightly by vowel deletion (nominative *petak* 'Friday' to dative *petku*) or consonantal shift (nominative *noga* 'leg' to dative *nozi*); nouns which have alternating phonological shapes may have a slightly different system of lexical organization. However, once the satellite entry of either a regular or irregular noun system has been accessed, then the entire noun system is activated. The nominative form stands in a nucleus-like relationship to non-nominative case forms regardless of whether the other case forms are identical in their phonological shapes or not. In sum, this data seems to point in the direction of all inflected cases of noun forms being represented fully in the mental lexicon; but they are grouped together, with morphological relatedness a basic principle of organization in the mental lexicon.

Spoken-Word Recognition

Some of the imbalance of experimental attention on morphological aspects of reading and written-word recognition has been redressed by increasing attention to spoken-word recognition (see Frauenhelder and Tyler 1987). One of the major problems in processing spoken words is determining where words and phrases begin. You will recall from Chapter 3 that Cutler (1989) successfully distinguishes between lexical prosody over individual words and metrical prosody over longer utterances, observing that the latter provides a statistically successful way of establishing word boundaries in continuous speech. Open-class content words typically begin with a strong syllable, allowing listeners to use this information in initiating lexical access procedures. But this aspect of word recognition has domain ties with some of what we discussed in speech perception under Studdert-Kennedy's stages, as well as syllable timing and stress patterning (see Grosjean and Gee 1987, and Cutler 1989), and so we will not repeat that information here. The second issue has to do with contextual information and the role it plays in lexical processing, since it is obvious that contextual information at some point influences how words are identified. But the role of contextual information is far from resolved. The two possibilities are that context has its effect in word recognition immediately, or that context plays a part after a decision has been made about the word's likely identity. Since this debate is similar to the one involving the role of context in ambiguity resolution, we will defer discussion of this matter until the sections on ambiguity and context in the chapters on syntax and discourse.

Some of the findings in written-word recognition have already been tested in spoken-word recognition studies. For example, Katz, Boyce, Goldstein and Lukatela (1987) investigated spoken-word perception for inflected Serbo-Croatian lexical items, and replicated their findings for recognition times for nouns which were auditorily presented. As in the experiments with written words, subjects showed fast reaction times for Serbo-Croatian nouns in their nominative case forms, but slower and equal reaction times for noun forms with other case endings. This "satellite-entry" pattern is certainly not accounted for by the frequencies of individual case forms in Serbo-Croatian, but must reflect the storage and access strategy that subjects employed. These results suggest that similar lexical access procedures are employed in word recognition tasks in either printed or spoken modes.

Parsing Strategies in Word Recognition

As we have seen, the main question in lexical access and word recognition is how the mental lexicon is structured. But this question raises another question, which is worth reconsidering before we move on. Are parsing procedures employed in lexical access in order to achieve word recognition? Some explanations simply expect that morphological parsing takes place and that while roots and stems are listed in the mental lexicon, affixes are not. Other explanations reject the need for parsing in the process of lexical access, and instead suggest that each word, inflected or not, has a separate entry in the mental lexicon. As we have seen in the preceding discussion, there is considerable variety in this latter position, ranging from the postulation of totally unanalyzed entries in the lexicon to satellite clusters in the mental lexicon. And are these unanalyzed entries the case only for words which arise from derivational processes, as for example, *happily* and *happiness*? Or is this true also for words which arise from inflectional processes, as for example, *happier* and *happiest*? Inflectionally and derivationally created words may not be handled by the same representation and processing mechanisms; in fact, it may be that there are even divisions in the class of derivationally created words, corresponding to etymological transparency, frequency, and phonological or orthographic similarity. Further research is needed to assess the possible different types, and the parsing strategies which different types elicit.

In the meantime, linguists have questioned the notion of an exhaustive listing of all possible lexical entries in the mental lexicon. Hankamer (1989) convincingly takes on believers of the Full Listing Hypothesis by using the agglutinative complexity of Turkish as an example. Hankamer demonstrates how morphological parsing procedures must be party to word recognition in such languages, for otherwise such a language would require over 200 billion full entries in the mental lexicon. This figure stands in dramatic contrast to an inventory of 30, 000 noun and verb roots tied to regularized parsing procedures. There is another inference to be made here, the fact that psycholinguistic theory will be unwise to rely overly much on the limitations of English structure, thereby momentarily forgetting that human language is characterized by unbounded creativity and uses a variety of means to achieve this.

Evidence from Tip-of-the-Tongue Phenomena and Malapropisms

Evidence for both phonological and orthographic considerations in the organization of the mental lexicon has also been gleaned from tip-of-the-tongue studies as well as studies of spontaneous malapropisms. Here we again see that various aspects of the stem- or root-shape are instrumental in achieving the retrieval of the correct lexical item in such mental dictionary searches.

The Tip-of-the-Tongue Phenomenon

"Tip-of-the Tongue" studies are one of the best places to see the interaction of phonological and semantic similarities in storage and recall. The word is on the tip of the tongue, and we are sure that the word we are seeking is out there; we know it, but just can't quite dredge it up. What we do come up with in such instances are usually words that overlap phonetically as well as semantically. Trying to get the right word out is like trying to tug on one strand of a spider-web without setting the others into vibration; all kinds of other words fall out, betraying the various features of relatedness along these two dimensions.

The tip-of-the-tongue experiments induced this experience by reading definitions of rare words, like *apse/cloaca/ambergris*, to subjects, and asking them to think of the word. Brown and McNeill (1966) asked subjects who could not recall the word to report on the words that did come to mind. A definition like "a navigational instrument used in measuring angular distances, especially the altitude of the sun, moon, and stars at sea" might not elicit the correct answer of *sextant*. But it often elicited a reliable idea of what the outline of the written word was, in terms of the initial and final letters of that word, as well as the number of syllables and where the main stress was. For example, they were correct over half the time on the number of syllables and on the initial letters. Chance would have provided considerably lower figures for such accurate guesses. They even came up with look-alikes like *secant/sexton/sextet*, as if they had stored a mental representation of what the desired word looked like. Brown and McNeill assumed that the mental lexicon is organized in a way that employs several indices of information, semantic and phonological. The phono-

logical index relies more on certain kinds of information, like the initial
and final sounds and syllables of words, than it does on middle ones.
Given that their method of used written responses for subject reports,
it is evident that orthographic information, as well as spelling-
pronunciation rules, also plays a role in such retrieval mechanisms.

Kohn, Wingfield, Menn, Goodglass, Gleason and Hyde (1987) have
further investigated lexical retrieval under tip-of-the-tongue conditions,
but with spoken language. Once again, subjects were given difficult
word definitions, and asked to say aloud the words which did come to
mind. Thus, subjects were given short (2 words) as well as long (12
words) definitions like the following, and asked to come up with the
right word.

1.   'female hog'
2.   'transformation from one form to another, as from a caterpillar
        to a butterfly'
3.   The answers here are *sow* and *metamorphosis*.

Their results showed that responses which are phonologically similar are good predictors of whether the word was likely to be retrieved.
If the responses are phonologically close to the target word, chances are
it will surface; the closest phonological shape was that provided by
production of a correct root morpheme. Producing semantically related
responses, however, was no great predictor of success. This is not hard
to see, for what is at stake is the retrieval of the phonological form of
the word; the semantic area has already been provided by the definition. Word fragments were good predictors, but the strongest indicator
of eventual success was the production of a correct root morpheme.
For example, producing *derm-* puts you well on the way to *dermatolo-
gist*; but *commencement* does not get you too much further towards
valedictory, though it does put you into the right semantic ball park.
The progression to the correct lexical item, for those who achieved this,
did not represent a straight orderly path, with each step more closely
approximating the correct word.

Spontaneous Malapropisms

This search process is also the origin of some malapropisms, the ones
which are unconsciously uttered through incorrect selection and not
ignorance of the word. The term *malapropism* is associated with literary characters like Sheridan's Mrs. Malaprop (*derangement* for
arrangement) and Norman Jewison's Archie Bunker (*epitaph* for *epi-
thet* and *Salivation Army* for *Salvation Army*). As Fay and Cutler
(1977) have shown, inadvertent use of the wrong word is a common
type of speech error in real life, but for reasons other than the ignorance Mrs. Malaprop and Archie Bunker were supposed to portray.
Real-life malapropisms show three characteristics. The malapropism is
always a real word, the error is unrelated to the target word, and both
are phonologically close. For example, contrast the target and error
words below:

1.   Target: If these two vectors are equivalent, then. . . .
2.   Error: If these two vectors are equivocal, then. . . .

Furthermore, the malapropisms are almost always of the same grammatical category, have the same stress pattern, and very often even have the same number of syllables. Just like with the tip-of-the-tongue searches for the right word, we see that the mental lexicon is organized in such a way that the speech production device must look into this mental dictionary to find an entry which has the meaning and syntactic category tags that match the specifications needed in the structure of the utterance. More than that, it also has a fairly good approximation of its phonological shape in the sense of number of syllables, stress patterning, and even the particulars of its phonetic shape.

Summary

Morphology is the study of how words are built, and of of how morphemes are organized into morphological classes to show grammatical functions in a language. Psycholinguistic studies have examined how morphological structure and the processes of word formation are related to the way in which words are recognized in comprehending natural language.

Morphemes, the minimal grammatical units with meaning in a language, are divided into two groups on the basis of what they do in the language. These two groups are content words and function words, also known as lexical classes and grammatical classes because content words display lexical meanings while function words carry the grammatical framework of the language. Content words in English are nouns, verbs, adjectives, and adverbs; function words are the grammatical pieces like articles, conjunctions, prepositions, and pronouns. Function words are complemented in their job of carrying the grammatical framework by grammatical morphemes called **inflections**; for example, English uses endings like the plural on nouns and the past tense on verbs. Grammatical morphemes like function words and inflections signal structural relationships between words or phrases, expressing a small set of conceptual distinctions that are crucial to establishing how objects and relations are organized into situations. Although different languages may express such conceptual notions with different grammatical morphemes, such notions typically occur in the grammatical part of the language rather than in the content part. These grammatically expressed distinctions organize both our production and comprehension of discourse by offering a framework for the construction of mental models for the situations described in discourse.

Of particular interest to psycholinguists is the structure of the mental lexicon, the mental dictionaries we carry about in our heads and that we refer to in comprehending spoken discourse or written text. The process of word recognition is sensitive to phonological, orthographic and semantic characteristics that words share, as well as characteristics like word frequency and the effects of context.

Considerable work has been done on written-word recognition. The major thrust of the research has been to determine whether words are represented in the mental dictionary in their root or stem shapes, stored separately from inflectional and derivational affixes. **Derivational affixes** build or **derive** new words, while **inflectional affixes** mark or **inflect** existing words for the grammatical features a given language makes use of. A related question is whether there are morphological parsing procedures by which a word is broken into its component pieces of root or stem AND possible inflectional and derivational affixes. The alternative to this is that words are stored as whole words, so that each possible word is stored independently in the mental dictionary. The evidence on these issues of storage and access is mixed.

There has also been increasing attention to spoken-word recognition. One of the major directions in spoken-word recognition has been to examine the role of cues like syllable timing and stress patterning in establishing word boundaries in continuous speech. Listeners must employ such information to initiate lexical access procedures. A second direction has focussed on contextual information and the role it plays in lexical processing, since such information must influence how words are identified.

Evidence for the organization of the mental lexicon has also been gleaned from tip-of-the-tongue studies and studies of spontaneous malapropisms. This evidence also confirms that phonological and orthographic aspects of the stem- or root-shape are instrumental in effecting the retrieval of the correct lexical item in such mental dictionary searches.

The current psycholinguistic interest in linguistic matters of morphological structure and word formation processes is directed at understanding the ways in which we identify words in hearing discourse and in reading text. Many in fact see the mental lexicon as a pivotal point in the comprehension process (see Marslen-Wilson 1989a). It is here that the physical acoustic characteristics of the speech signal must be translated into the appropriate mental representation for the lexical form, and then these values inform the syntactic and semantic interpretation of the intended message.

Chapter 5

Syntax

Introductory Comments to the Study of Syntax

The scientific study of language is the commitment that linguistics has undertaken. At best, the task of the linguist is to write a grammar for human language, language with a capital L, that abstract cognitive capacity that characterizes all languages of all types of all times. At the very least, the task of the linguist is to write a grammar for some specific human language, like English or Japanese or Zulu. A grammar of a specific language is a set of conventions that the language displays about which combinations of words carry which structural meanings. Sentence patterns are not random, but are structured according to definite restrictions. Their raw materials are morphemes and words, and the patterns in which they occur are hierarchically ordered; syntax is not a matter of mere juxtaposition of words. For example, read the following sentences in which the nouns *king/boy/slave* occur, but note that the meaningful relationships which they enter into are defined by their relative ordering according to the syntax of English. Thus, in the first sentence we know that the king was the giver, the boy the recipient, and so on.

1. The king gave the boy the slave.
2. The boy gave the king the slave.
3. The king gave the slave the boy.

Some languages, like Latin, also employ inflectional devices to show syntactic relationships, and then order is somewhat freer. A sentence like *Servus amat puellam*, 'The servant loved the girl', can just as easily be rendered with the unordered embellishments so favored by Cicero and still be understood. The sentence *Puellam amat servus* still has its case relationships marked by the inflectional endings *-am* and *-us*; the sentence retains the same meaning despite the change in positions. And lastly, languages, like English and Latin both, employ function words like *in* to also show syntactic relationships, as in the prepositional phrase *in silvis*, 'in the forests'. This fact of order, coupled with the use of inflectional endings and function words, is what made the *Jabberwocky* sentence in the last chapter so easy to 'understand', despite its being 'empty' of meaning.

There has been much argumentation about what form the grammar should take, but the options basically come down to two types of statements about how the implicit rules of language shall be stated in the grammar. The rules can be a statement of process, a generativist commitment, or a statement of arrangement, a structuralist procedure no longer much in favor. The above dichotomy of course pays no attention to the great debates between prescriptive grammars of years past (and even present) and the descriptive grammars of the structural and early generativist periods.

Linguists now are highly psychologized, since most consider the purpose of a grammar to be a description of the knowledge speakers have of their language; some linguists even see their discipline as very much an experimental science, so that the best method of ascertaining such knowledge is through empirical means (Prideaux 1979, 1985; Prideaux, Derwing and Baker 1980). Such a purpose is of course quite different from that of a grammar just describing a language, for a description of one's knowledge is clearly a psychological aim. Chomsky has himself asserted (1968) that linguistics is a branch of cognitive psychology, for the obvious reason that characterizing the abstract knowledge that speaker-hearers have is really an exercise in cognition. Chomsky has, however, never worked on an explanatory performance model, and has concentrated on formulating a theoretical model of the abstract capacity of grammatical competence instead.

Structuralism

Structuralism was the prevailing philosophy of science that organized and motivated much of linguistic research from the 1930s until the generativist period in the 1960s. The term **structuralism** derives its name from the fact that speech has structure, with structure defined as a limited number of items and arrangements in a language. The task of structural linguistics was to discover, describe, and make significant generalizations about these facts in A specific language. By inference, then, the task of the linguist is to describe languages by producing grammars of those specific languages. Structuralism was definitely a behavioral science, with that special fascination for operational definitions. In fact, some considered it the envy of many other behavioral sciences, for facts about language were to be observed and reported without any other assumptions made about extraneous social or psychological factors playing a part. One gathered a speech sample, and a set of operational definitions and discovery procedures allowed the linguist to derive rules on the basis of the corpus' inherent distributional characteristics. Of course, descriptions of a language, be they structural or generative, may not necessarily coincide with the conscious knowledge speakers have of that language. For example, most of us are unaware of the fact that the English plural is shown by a suffix /-s/ in words ending in voiceless segments other than voiceless sibilants and affricates. Still, we all employ the rule correctly in turning out the correct plural for the familiar *cap/caps* and even the unfamiliar *gip/gips*.

Structural linguistics was very much influenced by Logical Positivism, which had rapidly become a popular approach to science (see Morris 1938). Logical Positivism was a philosophy of science which held that meaningful scientific statements should be verifiable or at least confirmable by observation or experiment; theories which did not meet these criteria were considered empty metaphysical posturing. Bloomfield's (1933) book was often cited as the starting point for structuralism in linguistics, and Bloomfield himself was obviously sympathetic to the empirical Behaviorism, though he claimed to be neutral to psychology of any persuasion and stated that linguistics should be too. In his earlier book (Bloomfield 1914), however, he had been fairly reflective of the prevailing Wundtian psychology of the time (Kess 1983). Although linguistics of the Bloomfieldian variety was sympathetic to Behaviorism, it was not concerned with stimulus (S) conditions under which a verbal response (R) is produced, nor with nature of S-R connections, nor with the establishment of S-R connections in individuals. In this sense, linguistics was purely descriptive rather than interpretive and dealt strictly with language data. The linguist's special concern thus was with the STRUCTURE of language, though STRUCTURE could be used in several ways:

1.   utterances can be said to have structure
2.   a language can be said to have structure or structural patterns
3.   language in general can be said to have certain structural characteristics or general properties

The central maxim in carrying out structural descriptions was that each language was an entity unto itself. Thus, the methodological approach had to be inductive, and accomplished through observation, not deductive speculation. A linguist then built a theory which accounted for all the phenomena observed, thereby making generalizations which would account for all the phenomena which might subsequently be observed. The emphasis was thus upon specifics, even in terms of what work there was on language universals; for example, Greenberg's report on universal features (1963/1966) deals with language universals to be gathered largely by the inductive method, and even the later (1978) four-volume *Universals of Human Language* presents an invaluable inventory of cross-linguistically structural properties of language.

The methodology was obviously based on observation and its end was a taxonomic listing of language features. The starting point for the linguist was a single speaker or several speakers from one speech community; the interview was called **field work** and depended upon material gathered from a native speaker called an **informant** (now replaced now by the more professional term **consultant**). The language was thus taken at some arbitrary point frozen in time, and from a study of the utterances of such a **corpus**, one would arrive at a formulation of the total grammatical structure of the language (with continuing recourse to native speakers to amplify the data). Thus, **discovery procedures** based its methods on the notion of stimulus equivalence-- were two things the same or different? In their time, discovery procedures were felt to be a logical calculus which involved discovery of basic units; the procedure in principle was supposed to allow the linguist to pursue such units without reference to external meanings of linguistic forms. Examples of such procedures can be seen in the search for **minimal pairs** on the level of phonemes or the use of **slot equivalences** in

syntax. There is the example of Fries' (1952) non-semantic classification of the English parts of speech by using substitution frames, even
going so far as to rename nouns, verbs, adjectives, and adverbs as
Classes 1, 2, 3, and 4. Fries simply used a substitution-in-frame technique to define parts of speech formally as one class of words that
would fit into a slot in a standardized sentence frame that he had constructed; for example, a Class 1 form (noun) would fit into a frame
like *The* _____ *was good.*

The unit employed by structuralists was typically of the **etic-emic**
variety, or at least this was true on the level of phonology and morphology. The etic-emic approach was an entirely language-specific
approach which paid attention to a conditioned indifference to some
features, a learned non-perception of some linguistic characteristics.
For example, on the phonemic level the linguist attempted to suppress
the representations of phonetic features of the acoustic stimulus which
did not serve as cues for differential responses on the part of native
speakers. The variant etic manifestations of such emic units thus
appear differently in different contexts, being subject to conditioning;
this kind of contextual determination was supposedly found at all levels in language. In phonemicizing a transcription, then, one retained a
representation only of those features which do serve as a cue. And
presumably, this approach was analogous to the units (and their
descriptions) on other levels; thus, the allomorph, morpheme, and
morphology paralleled the notions of allophone and phoneme on the
level of phonology. This **etic-emic** approach was even used successfully
in a number of other descriptive applications, like Birdwhistell's study
of kinesics (1970) and the study of kinship systems in anthropology.
Pike (1964, 1967) even attempted to construct a total theory of structure of human behavior on basis of etic-emic principles, with an elaboration of other related concepts like spot, class, and substitution
frames.

In fact, this approach (and its units) was only successfully applied
on the levels of phonology and morphology; it never found a match on
the syntactic level, despite attempts by Pike and the tagmemic syntac-
ticans to apply such notions to syntax with units like the tagmeme,
syntagmeme, and allotagma. Syntax did pose real problems for
mechanistic structuralists for whom the application of semantic information was theoretically disallowed. For example, the ambiguity of a
sentence like *They were entertaining girls* depends upon charting the
syntactico-semantic differences inherent in an adjectival modification of
a noun phrase (*entertaining girls*) as opposed to a periphrastic verb
phrase (*were entertaining*). Here even mechanistic descriptions must
resort to mentalistic information of what speaker knows of the sentence and its meaning to determine the analysis of the sentence as
either containing a verb or an adjective. The basic problem of course
was that structuralist syntax did not bother to recognize the fact of
underlying structures, thus ignoring formal descriptions of sentence
alternations like active/passive, indirect object movement, and two-part
verbs.

A form of syntactic analysis called **immediate constituent** analysis, or IC Analysis, did postulate a hierarchical analysis of the relationships of parts within sentences, and was somewhat more abstract than just reliance on surface structure. For example, the sentence *They were entertaining girls* is ambiguous and can have two possible readings. One reading has the adjectival *entertaining* modifying the noun ('the girls were entertaining'); another reading has *entertaining* as part of the verb phrase ('Someone was entertaining the girls').

1. [They [were [entertaining girls]]]
2. [They [[were entertaining] girls]

Such syntactic analysis is useful, but since it is limited to charting the structure of the sentence immediately at hand, it is unable to show the relationships between sentence alternations like active/passive, indirect object movement, and two-part verbs.

1. John loves Mary---->Mary was loved by John
2. John gave Mary the book---->John gave the book to Mary
3. John looked up Mary's address---->John looked Mary's address up

Nor is such a syntactic analysis able to express the underlying differences between sentences which are really quite different, despite their surface similarities. For example, the sentences in (1) are really quite different from (2) in their underlying logical relationships.

1. John is hard to please; John is easy to please;
2. John is eager to please; John is glad to please

Markov Process notions were also quite attractive to structuralists and psychologists for this reason, with their emphasis on statistical analysis based on a left-to-right chain model of probabilities. Each word was considered to occur as a probabilistic function of the word(s) to its left, rather like alphabet probabilities from word sample counts, where one surveys the likelihood of what could fill the slot after a given letter like Q__ or T__. But on the level of syntax, there was no accurate prediction of what would come after the first word of a sentence; for example, a noun will certainly come sooner or later after an initial *The* . . ., but may be preceded by many potential fillers. Statistical probabilities work best with bounded sets, and natural languages are not bounded sets.

There was some, but not much, discussion of how arbitrary such descriptions were. For example, although Householder (1961) had characterized structural descriptions as either *hocus-pocus* (arbitrary) or *god's truth* (non-arbitrary), there was typically no compelling drive to seeking explanatory power beyond the data. In sum, the period known as structuralism viewed linguistics as a descriptive science, charged with the description of language systems. This description was to portray the set of distinctions that differentiate messages, as exhaustively, economically, and elegantly as possible. Its method was to carry out a logical analysis of the functional identities in data gathered by a linguist in field work with a language. As to the order in which this was accomplished, the linguist started with the large number of sounds actually produced (phones), determined the minimum number of classes of sounds that make a contrastive difference in this language (phonemes), the rules of their combination into meaningful units (morphemes), and the rules of combination of these meaningful units into utterances (syntax). There was more than enough to do here without rousing the unruly giant of semantics. In general, structural linguists avoided the problems of semantics altogether, though one finds the occasional structural incursion into semantics; for example, Ullmann (1966) employs a unit called *sememe*, keeping a perfect terminological parallelism.

Transformational Generative Grammar

Introductory Remarks on the Generative Approach

The major interest in psycholinguistic research in the 1960s and 1970s was on syntactic organization. In linguistics, **transformational generative grammar** was posed as a solution to problems found in dealing with sentence relationships, ambiguity, and the general lack of semantic answers. Transformational, or generative, grammar had a profound effect on psycholinguistics by attacks upon various models like Skinnerian behaviorism in psychology, structuralism in linguistics, and the Markov Process and Information Theory in general. For example, Skinner's *Verbal Behavior* was published in 1957, but reviewed by Chomsky in 1959 with such devastating effect that notions like mand, tact, and operant conditioning in general have seen few proponents in psycholinguistic circles since then. It also had a profound effect because of its generous accounts of the syntax of English, and later, other languages. But its most profound effect may be in its inherent psychologizing of linguistics, by some linguists attempting to provide a basis of psychological validity to theory and all linguists seeking to provide explanatory power for the complex abstract knowledge that is linguistic competence.

Chomsky essentially broke the paradigm; where linguistics was previously an empirically-based taxonomic science, (a "verbal botany", its critics would claim), it turns to the opposing position of rationalism. In sum, Chomsky, early and late, has had much to say about the status of linguistics as a science, and turned linguistics from what he suggested was a pre-scientific stage of collection and classification of interesting facts to a focus on theory construction and validation (see Lees' 1957 review of Chomsky's early impact on linguistics and Newmeyer's 1980/1986 chronicle for a summation of the period's triumphs and tribulations). The claim was that the rigorous methods stressed previously were trivial, and perhaps even leading to false conclusions. The linguist conjectures about linguistic facts and tests them against available evidence, but this results in a procedure for evaluating rival hypotheses, not discovering the "right" one in terms of real explanations. The two opposing linguistic paradigms, generativism and structuralism, simply clashed on the three main points of subject matter, goals, and methods. For structuralism, the subject matter was a corpus, its goal was the classification of the elements in the corpus, and the method was a set of discovery procedures. Generative grammar, on the other hand, took its subject matter as competence (the speaker's knowledge), its goal as the specification of rules underlying construction of sentences, and the method rested on evaluation procedures for adequacy of the grammar. At the very least, one required observational adequacy, a weak generative capacity whereby grammar should be capable of generating all and only grammatical sentences. Next best was a descriptive adequacy, a strong generative capacity whereby a grammar must do this **and** assign a correct structural description to the sentences generated. Ultimately, of course, one strives for explanatory adequacy, tied to whether there is one best type of grammar which can be selected out of all possible grammars.

Chomsky deduced that children must have some kind of innate ability which enable them to choose from among different kinds of grammars. After all, children are exposed to primary language data which differs from child to child, yet children all choose the same type of grammar. Thus, if there is only one appropriate kind of grammatical analysis, then it must be universal to all languages, and this universal grammatical theory would give an account of the grammatical forms and relations common to all languages. This is what a theory of language should be all about, a theory of linguistic universals, and Chomsky's most recent ideas confirm that this type of grammar will also be the most economical grammatical analysis of language, since that which is universal may eventually be left out of specific descriptions. Chomsky's original work was within the familiar framework of formal linguistics, and to some degree it still is, with clean, concise descriptions of language. But Chomsky has himself never elaborated a working performance model, considering it sufficient, and even preferable, to formulate a theoretical model of the abstract capacity of grammatical competence, with sentences as primary units. Some, like Steinberg (1982), consider Chomskyan grammar to be psychologically invalid for its assignment of the primary role to syntax and a secondary role to semantics. This is incompatible with any reasonable model of speaker performance, for production begins with ideas in the mind of the speaker who encodes them as utterances; comprehension takes those utterances as input and decodes them into meaning. In neither activity is syntax first or primary. The counter-claim might be that syntactic structure is determined by innate properties of the human mind, not by needs of communication. Thus it is no surprise that Chomsky's contribution has been to syntax, and that performance has been purposely overlooked.

The later Chomsky makes some far-reaching claims about the implications of generative grammar for the study of language acquisition and for the study of cognitive processes (see the 1968 *Language and Mind* which reads differently than Chomsky 1957 or even Chomsky 1965). Thus it can be appreciated that Chomskyan grammar is a changing, expanding theory. Chomsky's (1968) rejoinder that linguists are really cognitive psychologists is well matched some twenty years later by the number of linguists writing in journals like *Cognition/ Cognitive Science/Cognitive Psychology/Journal of Memory and Language*, as well as by the submissions with cognitive or psycholinguistic overtones in mainstream linguistics journals. And this is also reflected by linguistics bearing the responsibility for providing a theory of grammatical knowledge in the common cognitive science task of understanding the mind. And, despite early disinterest in such matters, many contemporary linguists are not averse to emphasizing the psychological relevance of modern transformational grammar (see Berwick and Weinberg 1985). The important criterion is no longer the nonpsychological criterion of simplicity, derived from scientific canons of theory-building, but the very psychological criterion of learnability.

For Chomsky, language is defined by syntactical structure, not by the use of structure in communication. Thus, a generative grammar is not a speaker-hearer analogue; it is only a formal analogue of the regularities which native speakers of a language conform to when producing or comprehending sentences in the language. Furthermore, a grammar in the generative sense simply enumerates sentences at random, and does not select a sentence appropriate to a specific context. A grammar simply accounts for the syntactic nuts and bolts that go into making up a sentence, any sentence possible in the language, and does not even attempt to account for all the false starts, incomplete utterances, and other imperfections that characterize real speech. The grammar dealt with an idealized set of abilities of an ideal speaker-hearer in an abstract sense, and did not take on the added responsibility for how, why, or when sentences were uttered. Later advances in the areas known as discourse analysis and pragmatics did undertake this task, in response to what was perceived by many as the failure of formal linguistics to address the functions of language, as well as the effect such considerations might even have on the very sentence formats of language.

The theoretical concept of **grammaticality** set the limits for the data that a linguistic theory was supposed to define, namely, a set of grammatical sentences, possibly infinite in number, but specifiable from a finite, perhaps even small, set of building blocks called syntactic slots (for example, subject) and part of speech classes to fill those slots (for example, nouns and pronouns). But grammaticality in its way also has a psychological import, for there is an underlying psycholinguistic truth here that ungrammaticality will likely involve longer processing times, since they are once removed from the norm of sentence expectations. Grammaticality is of course a useful expectation and supports processing strategies which are disrupted when this expectation is not met.

Basic Assumptions of Generative Grammar

What do generative linguists do then? They still write grammars of natural languages. But what is a language, we might further ask, and where is our entry point for analysis? Language as an object of analysis is for the generativist a set of grammatical sentences, infinite in number and grammatical in nature. And the grammar is a set of observations which codify our knowledge of how sentences are constructed, with a generative grammar laying out this knowledge by a set of explicit symbols and directives that produce all and only the sentences of a language. And a transformational generative grammar was committed to achieving this in a way that revealed differences of underlying structure that other syntactic approaches had failed to account for. Strings are of two classes for the idealized speaker: sentences and non-sentences, or grammatical and ungrammatical. The grammar then consists of a formal set of statements which generates all the possible grammatical sentences in a given language. Generativists tried to account for a potentially infinite number of sentences, but the number of simple sentences is large enough. For example, the time it would take to say the possible sentences just 20 words in length is reputed to be many times the estimated age of the earth (Miller,1964a); yet you will find little difficulty in understanding a 20-word sentence *The little girl who was waiting on the corner waved merrily at me as I passed by on the bus*. And you have the same abilities with sentences 4 words long, 8 words long, 17 words long, or 38 words long!

Generative descriptions now also described embedding and conjoining, the recursion processes that can occur over and over again to expand simple sentences into longer and more complicated sentences. Theoretically at least, there was said to be no limit to length of sentence. For example, any NP will allow an expansion, as in the Mother Goose rhyme *This is the cow/with the crumpled horn/that tossed the dog/that worried the cat/that. . . .*

Chomsky's basic unit was the sentence, and this quickly found its way into psycholinguistics as a basic working unit there as well. Every language was said to exhibit a small number of basic atomic sentences; for example, English has transitive, intransitive, and copulative verb sentences, plus sentences with some form of *be* as the main verb in the predicate.

1.   The boy hit the ball; John kissed Mary.
2.   The boy slept; John died; The sun set.
3.   The scholar remained a teacher; The scholar remained silent; The scholar remained in the garden.
4.   The boy is a student; The boy is well-behaved; The boy is in the garden.

Most sentences in a language are either simple sentences of this very type or elaborations on such basic syntactic formats. In turn, compound and complex sentences are combinations of such basic sentences, formed by following the rules of Engish for conjoining or embedding sentences. For example, a sentence like *The little girl who was waiting on the corner waved merrily at me as I passed by on the bus* is formed from the following basic sentences.

1.   The girl is little.
2.   The girl waits.
3.   The girl waves at me.
4.   I pass by.

The grammar is really an explicit system of rules which generates the grammatical sequences of the language. Transformational Generative Grammar takes its name from the nature of the rules.

1.   grammar: set of rules regarding the knowledge that native speakers have.
2.   generative: the creative aspect of generating sentences, and the mathematical explicitness of the way the grammar is constructed.
3.   transformational: alternations of sentence types (in the Chomsky 1957 sense of transformation from kernel to derived sentences). At least this is what many took the meaning to be, a transformation of a kernel into its possible altered shapes in sentence sets. The technical meaning was refined to refer to those rules which relate or transform the deep structure of a sentence to its surface structure.

Explicitness may need an example, and so for example, consider the following sentences:

1.   The happy minstrel loved a beautiful princess
2.   The angry dog chased the little cat
3.   A proud horse bit the unfortunate knight
4.   A wicked magician frightened the silly mailman

Each of these sentences consists of a subject NP and a predicate VP, and our first rule might say just this, namely, that a Sentence (S) is rewritten as a Noun Phrase (NP) and a Verb Phrase (VP). Thus, the rule S--->NP + VP. The VP in these sentences consists of a Verb Transitive and a NP, and thus the second rule would mark this second lower-level relationship by a rule like VP--->Vt + NP. And the NP consists of a Determiner (Det) like *the/a* and a Noun (N), represented by a rule like NP--->Det + N. We could put all this information into rules which would account for each such relationship until every piece of syntax was detailed. But recall that there is more to language than these four sentences, and we would also have to ultimately account for tenses like past tense, optional adjectives, *a/an* selection, plurals, a nd so forth. But it is worth noting the precision of the rules, and the economy by which we have achieved generalizations that only wordy descriptions could parallel. Not only are many ambiguities on the surface level labelled (recall *They are entertaining girls*), but deep structure ambiguities like *Visiting relatives can be a nuisance* are simply derived from different underlying simple sentences.

Early 1957 Chomsky and "Syntactic Structures"

The first appearance of generative grammatical notions in Chomsky's (1957) *Syntactic Structures* proposed a modest grammatical apparatus with three main subsections. The three grammatical components were the phrase structure rules, the transformational rules, and a set of morphophonemic rules to account for irregularities in the lexical items which could fill sentence slots. The rules were entirely formal, and thus entirely explicit; such rules were quite distinct from traditional grammatical descriptions and earlier structural descriptions in this respect. And the visual device known as the **branching tree diagram** would lay out the nested relationships contained within a sentence by giving vertically the structure of a sentence in terms of its generative history. The phrase structure rules were not too unlike phrase structure rules of other periods, except for their symbolic representation.

Transformational rules are what make this description different. They simplified the system enormously, by operating on strings of symbols. Thus, one rule could be stated to derive all passives for all active transitive sentences, thus showing their sentential relatedness. The other option, of course, would have been to have a separate set of syntactic rules for active transitive sentence types and another for passive sentences, thereby failing to show their ultimately identical origins. One of the underlying assumptions here is that a sentence has a grammatical status only as it stands in relation to other sentences in the language. Such transformational rules could thus be stated for the optional sentential changes like passives, questions, negatives, passive negatives, and so on, as well as for the obligatory transformations that occurred when one sentence type was transformed into another. For example, form the corresponding questions and negatives from simple active sentences like *John slept/John saw the mayor/John remained an American citizen.* Note how the auxiliary verb *do* obligatorily appears, and how the tense is attached to it rather than the verb in the corresponding questions *Did John sleep?/Did John see the mayor?/Did John remain an American citizen?* and negatives *John did not sleep/John did not see the mayor/John did not remain an American citizen.* The optional transformations worked on a notion of the kernel sentence, the simple, active, affirmative, declarative sentences, as being the starting point for sentences changing into one another, as for example, active to passive. Very simply, an active declarative can change into a question (optional), but a *do* auxiliary must be inserted and the tense marked must be attached to the auxiliary and not the verb root itself (obligatory). Lastly, the section on morphophonemic rules simply provided a formal set of rules to account for irregularities. Thus, while past tense could usually be stated as being /t/, /d/, or /əd/, depending on the final sound of the verb, a verb like *see* would simply have to have its past tense overtly listed as *saw*.

Chomsky's 1965 Standard Theory from "Aspects"

In the elaboration of syntactic theory that appeared in 1965, the phrase structure rules in the base component broke sentences into phrase units like NP, VP, AdvP, PrepP which in turn were filled by word class units like N, V, Adj, Adv, D. The rules were still written so that input terms like S are broken down into their component parts, and the word **generate** still meant 'to define', not 'to produce'. The motivating notion of sentences as a set (as in set theory) continued, with linguistic research directed at how to define members of that set.

To this conceptual array were added several new notions. The notion of deep vs. surface structure distinctions are added to the grammar itself, while the conceptual opposition of competence vs. performance is added to general theory. The **competence/performance** distinction was required simply because some things never turn up in the data. Such distinctions also reflected the emphasis the model placed on generating sentences in a way that characterized the underlying linguistic abilities that speakers of a natural language have. For example, it is obvious that native speakers can construct and understand a potentially infinite array of sentences never heard or uttered before. They can also accept or reject utterances as grammatically well-formed according to the syntactic rules of the language and they can also provide two interpretations of strings that are ambiguous. And this is what competence entails, the array of abilities that all such native speakers of a language share, without exception. The inference was that a grammatical theory of a language was better directed at understanding and portraying competence abilities rather than the particular and idiosyncratic set of utterances that a speaker might have happened to utter in a specific instance of the performance of these competence abilities.

This distinction was complemented by the fact that some things are known by speakers, but do not show up in the surface structure itself. The gap between **deep structure** and **surface structure** arises because there are just too many things to say, and only limited means of saying them. Note, for example, that many ambiguities arise from overlap on the surface level, yet we can sort them out because of our underlying knowledge. The surface structure, then, came to be equated with the surface or linear arrangement of clauses, phrase, words, and sounds, while deep structure evoked the notion of the underlying meaning and arrangement of propositions.

Chomsky (1965) thus seemed to radically break from 1957, though Chomsky claimed that the same basic notions prevailed. And so they did methodologically, for there were still the three components (syntactic, semantic, and phonological). Deep structures were now generated by phrase structure rules in the base segment, being largely equivalent to the underlying strings of 1957. The 1957 optional/obligatory split was lost, as was the implication that there were two classes of sentences (kernel and derived). It was this latter feature of 1957 that had led to so many experiments but which were now left without a theoretical home. Transformations in 1965 now clearly mapped deep structures onto surface structures.

The syntax now contained two components, a **base component** concerned with generation of base strings and their association in the deep structure of a sentence and a **transformational component** concerned with transformations that had to be applied to a deep structure to obtain the terminal string and appropriate surface structure. Thus, instead of the confusion over kernel and derived sentences, the base component had to include a representation of basic sentential structure, relating syntactic slots like S, NP, and VP, to the form classes (parts of speech) that filled those slots to yield basic strings. The syntactic rules continued to be applied in a linear order in the generation of basic phrase structures of sentences. But markers for P, N, Q, and Emph were to appear in deep structure formulations, and these would then trigger the appropriate transformations later.

The 1965 **Standard Theory** also introduced the notion of recursion into the grammar to account for the fact that sentences can be conjoined with other sentences or embedded into other sentences. For example, consider the origins of the conjoined sentence in (1) or the complex sentence with an embedded clause in (2).

1.   John is going to the concert and Mary is too<-----*John is going to the concert* is conjoined with *Mary is going to the concert*.
2.   He paid the courier who delivered the package<-----*The courier delivered the package* is embedded into *He paid the courier*.

Complex sentences can thus be explained as reduced sentences embedded into a matrix sentence. A rule like N--->Det + N + (S) adds the potential of an embedded sentence (S) after any noun (N), and thus simply starts the grammar through the rules again. In this way, all kinds of sentences can be described by reference to a simple set of sentences which may be conjoined with one another or embedded into one another. As an example, consider the origins of sentences containing appositives, locatives, and adjectivals, as in (1), (2), and (3) below.

1.   His father, a Nebraska farmer, wears overalls<-----*His father is a Nebraska farmer* is embedded in the matrix sentence *His father wears overalls.*
2.   The frost on the pumpkin is lovely<-----*The frost is on the pumpkin* is embedded in the matrix sentence *The frost is lovely.*
3.   The innovative speaker is named Copeland<-----*The speaker is innovative* embedded in the matrix sentence *The speaker is named Copeland.*

Overall, there was a neat conceptual organization to the theoretical framework. Some refinements were even made in the manner of including the lexicon, as **subcategorizational features** and **selectional features** appeared. The refinements basically incorporated notions outlined in Katz and Fodor's (1963) semantic theory based on atoms of meaning called semantic markers or features. Strict subcategorizational features categorized word classes like noun and verb into subclasses according to the syntactic frame in which they appeared. Thus, a sentence like *The time elapsed the harvest* could not be generated, because the syntactic frame specified for the sub-class that the verb *elapse* belongs to does not allow a following object noun phrase. Selectional features further subclassified parts of speech like verbs by assigning the contextual features of the nouns they could co-occur with. As a sentence would be derived, **lexical insertion rules** would allow only items with contextual features that matched in the particular sentence frame being generated by the phrase structure rules. One of the benefits of such refinements is that one now had a hierarchy of grammaticality, which allowed one to specify why sentences like *The time elapsed the harvest* seemed more ungrammatical than a sentence like *The time smoked a cigar.* It is all a question of how high up in the grammar the rule being violated is. The first sentence with *elapsed the harvest* violates a subcategorizational rule of syntactic framing, while the sentence with *time smoked* violates a selectional rule whereby *smoke* requires a human animate noun as its grammatical subject. Similarly, note how one finds sentences (2) and (3) below ungrammatical compared to (1), but in different ways, according to a violation of selectional versus subcategorizational rules, respectively.

1.   He bottles beer.
2.   *He bottles sincerity.
3.   *He bottles of.

Extended Standard Theory or Interpretive Semantics

The theory changes again (Chomsky 1971; Jackendoff 1972, 1977), with a revision of the relationship of surface structure to semantic representation. According to Chomsky (1975b:22), **Extended Standard Theory** was a modification of the Standard Theory, so that semantic representation is determined by both deep and surface structure. Grammatical relations of deep structure and the properties of lexical items that determine semantic relations, as well as other properties like anaphoric substitution by pronouns and related lexical items, the scope of both negation and quantifiers, and generally, logical form, are now determined by rules operating on surface structure. Standard Theory, of course, held that the deep structure of a sentence fully determined its meaning, but it soon was all too obvious that some aspects of sentence interpretation relate directly to the surface structure. Jackendoff's work changed this by suggesting that the semantic contribution of deep structure was limited to deep structure grammatical relations.

Transformational rules now functioned to introduce new meaning; surface structure now served to give cues to the semantic component as well as continuing to serve as input to the phonological component. A principal reason the theory was changed was to accommodate differences in meaning like those exhibited by emphasis, a definite surface feature. If there was to be a continuing commitment to assigning different deep structures to sentences with different meanings, the mechanics of this commitment meant that one had to include markers (like emphasis) in the surface structure of sentences which could result in meaning different from the one ultimately represented in the deep structure. Such a format meant that surface structure was now also allowed as input to the semantic component. Because of this shift in the way the grammar was organized, with both deep and surface structures introducing informational features for the semantic component, the Extended Standard Theory version of Transformational Grammar also came to be known as **Interpretive Semantics**.

Traces

Trace theory abolished any connection between the deep structure and the semantic component, and it is now the surface structure alone that determines how the meaning of a sentence is to be interpreted (see Chomsky 1975a:86-155, or Chomsky 1975b:22, for how the notion of **trace** fits into transformational theory as developed up until then). However, this "enriched" surface structure is now quite complex and includes "traces" which are markers identifying transformational rules which have been applied to deep structure. The idea is that transformations that move expressions leave a trace in the place where the item moved from, or can be postulated to do so. For example, we might represent the real structure of a sentence like *Gary wondered who Bill saw* as *Gary wondered who/(trace) Bill saw (trace)*. This allows us to have all the necessary information in a single representation, for we now simultaneously represent the independent but related facts that *see* requires an object and that *wonder* requires a following relative clause which in this case is introduced by a *who*, which is in turn the object of the verb *see*.

Chomsky's analogy with conventional systems of logic now portrays the system of grammatical transformations as a mapping of a system of grammatical relations (as expressed by deep structure) onto a logical form (as determined by surface structure). And the notation for traces ensures that surface structure is sufficiently detailed so that all of the meaning of the original sentence can be derived. Deep structure is thus no longer required to serve as input to the semantic component, as it was in Interpretive Semantics theory. And thus the grammar no longer requires a so-called deep structure to serve as input to a semantic component. And by the time we reach the next theoretical period, **Government and Binding**, the expressive power of the transformational component in the grammar is virtually eliminated.

One can easily see how syntactic theory changed quickly, and often rather extensively. This one procedural fact may have led many psychologists and psycholinguists to pay more attention to their own syntactic intuitions when constructing experiments, since these seemed no less fickle than those of professional syntacticians. The period of linguistic theory being the exclusive touchstone for psycholinguistic experimental insight had certainly by now assimilated to more eclectic and broader concerns. The changes in basic philosophical outlook were invaluable and remained, but the actual mechanics of the grammars written were now taken as only suggestive programmatic devices.

Government and Binding

As Chomsky's focus in syntactic analyses has turned to learnability, so also has that of modern syntacticians. Chomsky's interests (Chomsky 1981, 1982; see also Sells 1985) have turned increasingly to the notion of universals, attempting to portray grammars of individual languages in terms of settings for a limited number of **parameters**. The rest is derived from an array of universal principles which guide development of all grammars. Though GB theory has incorporated trace theory, the object seems to have become the quest to outline maximally simple grammars, which will contain universal principles that do not have to be learned, supplemented by language-specific rules which do have to be learned in each particular setting. This quest pays attention to language variation, with examples drawn from across the range of languages to provide comparisons of the specific settings for such parameters, as opposed to those design features derived from the universal list of organizational principles. One result has been that we see considerable discussion in the literature of the theoretical questions which motivate the strictures on universal grammar, and considerably less attention given to meticulous re-examination of grammatical constructions in well-known languages like English.

As Lightfoot (1982) has described, a particular Chomskyan concern lately has been to have Piagetian and other developmental theorists pay attention to the deficiency of the linguistic stimulus that young children learning their first language are exposed to. The desire is to have Piagetians show how their claims regarding generalized learning strategies explain how the child is able to circumvent the obvious explanatory problems posed by the fact of such variety, compounded by the deficiency of stimulation in the language that children are exposed to. The inescapable fact is that all children in all cultural communities learn to speak their native language and become competent speakers of that language, barring physical or mental deficits. This theme is not new in Chomskyan theorizing about language, and was already a motivating force behind much research as early as the 1960s. But the emphasis on learnability is very much in the forefront of modern linguistic theorizing under this GB phase, with demands that we come to understand how it is that human language can be learned so easily by humans.

We are reminded of the incomplete, and incredibly different, samples of language that children are exposed to, yet they consistently manage to create the same grammatical models for their language. Essentially, they all come to possess the same grammatical abilities in the language, suggesting that the human faculty for language exhibits certain innate characteristics that prescribes the limits within which human languages will be organized. The corollary of this fact is that human languages do not differ without limit, but are instead rather severely constrained in their actual construction. This has resulted in the particular emphasis on syntactic universals, in an attempt to define what it is that can be construed as the universal substratum for the structure of human languages. Though the preoccupation with universals is nothing new in generative theorizing and actual research, the vigor with which delineation of universals vs. language-specific parameters is being pursued is worthy of note.

Other Grammatical Theories

It is a fact of modern linguistics that much theorizing has either been reflective of or in contrast to the Chomskyan paradigm of transformational generative grammar. However, it is also worth noting that other syntactic models have been proposed which have claimed a fair share of theoretical attention of late, and these should be mentioned. The role of linguistics is to provide a reasonable theory of grammar which includes all our abstract knowledge about language. So far the leading contender for this responsibility may have been transformational grammar, but there have been other promising grammatical theories within the generative theoretical tradition, each with their own insights. There have also been alternatives to generative theories, as for example, Functional Grammar, Dependency Theory, and Guillaume's Psychomechanics. But these have not prompted nearly as much psycholinguistic experimentation, and thus we shall not attempt to cover these interesting theories in the small space available to us.

Generative Semantics

As we have seen, the generativist elaboration of syntactic explanation moved from explaining syntactic formats for sentences, to explaining their alternational (transformational) possibilities, and finally, to the structure of their underlying relationships. It should not be surprising that some generative syntacticians decided that semantic considerations were vital to syntactic explanation. Chomskyan syntax essentially believed that basic syntactic structures could be specified independently of semantic considerations. Other generative grammarians came to insist that only semantic structure could be specified independently, and that selection of syntactic structures is governed by semantic determination. They objected to the primary role assigned to syntax, with only a secondary or dependent role assigned to semantics. Instead of syntactic form determining semantic representation, the roles should be reversed, with semantics primary and syntax secondary. Very simply, a grammar should start with a description of the meaning of sentence, and only then be allowed to generate the syntactic structures through the introduction of syntactic and lexical rules. In this view, syntax became a collection of rules for expressing meaning.

Such a proposal essentially dispenses with the need for two levels of syntax. There is obviously no longer a need for deep structure and base rules, since the grammar simply relates the semantic level of structure to the syntactic level of structure. Such a requirement could be met by a set of transformational rules and a lexicon, with the transformational rules regarded as constituting the syntactic component of their grammar.

As many have noted, the conflict was carried on in a conceptual system given intellectual life by Chomskyan theorizing. The differences between **interpretive semantics** and **generative semantics** were not names of two contrasting positions on a single issue, but rather two packages of positions on a large number of issues. With typical candor, McCawley (1982) points out that the purported semantics camps were not completely homogeneous in their views, nor were they particularly tenacious in exclusively maintaining such theoretical views. But the theoretical conflict was useful in helping to clarify the need for a realistic view of semantics, and its possible relationships to the even more elusive human capacity of cognition.

For the generative semanticists, the major issue was that ideas be represented rather than words and syntactic structures. Semantic structure is to be a universal one, applicable to all languages, wherein different languages simply express the same idea in different ways (see Lakoff 1971). Much in the format of such discussions was often analogous to formal logic, with generative semanticists using semantic concepts and terms like **proposition, predicate,** and **argument** instead of syntactic constituents as the primary elements in the description. A **proposition** is the thought or idea which underlies a given sentence, and consists of a predicate and one or more arguments. **Arguments** are typically noun-like entities, while **predicates** are verb- or adjectival-like properties or actions that presuppose such entities to form a complete thought or proposition. For example, the verb predicate *put* takes noun arguments of actor, object, and location in a sentence like *John put the money on the table.* It is interesting to note that such considerations like **proposition** have come to play an important role in determining the depth of processing required for individual sentences, as well as discourse, in later work. And processing demands which require comprehension and storage measures may be better served by measures which reflect semantic content instead of just syntactic format.

Case Grammar

Other grammars have also considered the logical relationships that arguments (nouns) can have with their predicates (verbs). The most influential has been **case grammar** (Fillmore 1968, 1977), with its emphasis on the underlying case roles that nouns may have with their verbs. Languages may differ in how they mark such logical relationships. For example, in (1) English marks *slave* as agent and *girl* as object (or **patient**) by their position in the sentence. But in (2) Latin marks these same case roles by the endings -*us* on *serv-us* 'slave' and -*am* on *puell-am* 'girl'. The case roles are universal, despite differences in how they may be marked in languages.

1. The slave loves the girl.
2. Servus amat puellam.

And sometimes such case roles may not be marked at all. For example, *boy* and *key* both fill the subject position in the following sentences.

1. The boy opened the door.
2. The key opened the door.

But *boy* is an agent and *key* is an instrument, even if they do appear in the same sentence position. Logical relationships between the verb and its arguments are unchanging, no matter how the syntax of a particular language allows it to be shown. And if we did look, we would find further support for our assignment of the case roles of *boy* as agent and *key* as instrument. Sentences like (1) also appear, but sentences like (2) never do.

1. The boy opened the door with the key.
2. *The key opened the door with the boy.

Although case grammar never developed into an exclusive school of linguistic thought, with a readily identified following, it was extremely influential and its ideas were often incorporated into other theories. Case grammar notions have also been particularly useful in studies of child syntax, where noting the differences between form and function is crucial to understanding language development.

Lexical Functional Grammar, Generalized Phrase Structure Grammar, and Relational Grammar

Because of its concerns with considerations of psychological reality, **Lexical Functional Grammar**, or LFG, should be mentioned first in a textbook in psycholinguistics. It actively seeks to establish a theoretical linguistic framework for how humans process language, and has even been co-opted as a working model in at least one influential discussion of language acquisition and language learnability (see Pinker 1984:14-28). Grammatical theory is linked to processing considerations, so that a competence grammar is directly incorporated into a language processing model. LFG grammars would store any grammatical information needed to relate or differentiate sentence types within lexical entries themselves, meaning that there is no longer a hierarchy of sentences in grammatical derivations. Some discussion of LFG principles was given in the chapter on the history of psycholinguistics, and you may wish to refer back to that section for a re-reading of what a grammar with psycholinguistic commitments is willing to undertake.

Generalized Phrase Structure Grammar (Gazdar, Klein, Pullum, and Sag 1985), or GPSG, as it is known, makes no psychological claims for its formulations. GPSG has claimed much attention among syntacticians lately, however, for its computational possibilities in general, as well as its careful attention to generating all and only the grammatical sentences in the segment of the grammar being analyzed. This aspect of GPSG is so reminiscent of the earlier preoccupations of Extended Standard Theory, that GB and GPSG have often been likened to two sides of the same theoretical coin.

Relational Grammar, or RG, has been in evidence for about a decade (Perlmutter 1980; Blake 1990), but in an era beset by an embarassment of riches in the area of syntactic theory, has not received the attention it may have deserved. It claims that Chomskyan theorizing is basically unable to specify the essential structure of sentences in wholly syntactic terms, and has concentrated on accounting for the various syntactic and semantic relations noun phrases may have with the sentential main verb.

Sentential Relationships and the Derivational Theory of Complexity

Many earlier studies made the working assumption that transformational grammar might be directly involved in language comprehension and production. Most of this work reflected the basic premises of generative theory, that the number of potential sentences is infinite, but that they can be generated by a finite set of rules, and that these rules might somehow play a role in both understanding and storage. The question that was asked was what is the relationship between linguist's formal description and the actual processes employed in production and comprehension by real language users. Despite Chomsky's (1965) assertion that generative grammar was not to be understood as a model of either language production or comprehension, but rather a model of abstract linguistic competence of native speakers, many linguists would have rejected the suggestion that the construction of a grammar is just an arbitrary exercise.

The pressing psycholinguistic task is to elucidate the kinds of rules a language user actually knows, how those rules are used, and what kinds of mental representations are involved in processing and production. Perhaps these were linguistic rules of the type postulated for grammatical descriptions, and so the **Derivational Theory of Complexity** (DTC) was pursued actively as a working experimental hypothesis. It supposed that the number and complexity of mental operations performed by the reader or hearer during processing was a function of the number and complexity of formal transformations represented in the grammatical derivation of that sentence. For example, take a sentence family like the following.

1.   Active Sentence: John loved Mary.
2.   Passive Sentence: Mary was loved by John.
3.   Question Sentence: Did John love Mary?
4.   Negative Sentence: John did not love Mary.
5.   Negative Passive Sentence: Mary was not loved by John.
6.   Negative Question Sentence: Didn't John love Mary?
7.   Negative Passive Question Sentence: Wasn't Mary loved by John?

The Derivational Theory of Complexity can be illustrated as follows. The Negative Passive Question Sentence *Wasn't Mary loved by John?* is three transformational steps away from the Active Sentence *John loved Mary.* In the grammatical description of this sentence, it has undergone the transformations for passsive, negative, and question. Does this mean that this sentence is three times more complex in processing terms too? Does this mean that in reading such a sentence you backtracked through these transformational steps in trying to understand the sentence?

The DTC was pursued as a working experimental hypothesis, and what we learned was the following. No, we do not backtrack through the transformational steps of passsive, negative, and question in trying to understand the Negative Passive Question Sentence *Wasn't Mary loved by John?*. Nor is such a sentence three times more complex in processing terms than its Active Sentence counterpart *John loved Mary.* But experimental results certainly confirm the notion that sentences which were related transformationally were perceived to be related, giving support to the notion of sentential relatedness and sentence families (see, for example, Clifton and Odom 1966).

There was also some support for the psychological reality of structural constituents as posited by structural descriptions. That is, when measured by various techniques like click migration (see Garrett, Bever and Fodor 1966; Fodor, Bever and Garrett 1974) and transitional error probabilities (see Johnson 1965, 1966), structural constituents seemed to play a role in perception. Both the major syntactic boundaries and the constitutents which were posited to fill sentence slots appeared to be supported by the processing data derived from human subjects in experimental tasks. In other words, most studies seemed to substantiate the fact of major syntactic units, and that such syntactic units did have their effect on how we process the stream of speech. It also seemed to be reflected in how we produce speech, with evidence provided by pausing and hesitations at both major syntactic boundaries as well as at critical semantic choice points requiring cognitive choices. Thus, things like subjects, predicates, noun phrases, prepositional phrases, and so on, did seem to exist in the minds of speaker-hearers, as well as in the grammatical descriptions of language. So did most of the posited breaks between surface structure arrangements which separate constituents at points like subject-predicate break, the verb-direct object break, the verb-prepositional phrase break, and so on.

But the idea that the number of transformations required to convert a sentence from deep structure to surface structure in a grammatical description would translate into a metric of psychological effort in processing was not very well supported. For example, some sentences which were supposed to be more difficult, according to the way the grammatical description was laid out, just weren't. For example, **truncated passives** like (3) were derived from full passives like (2) in the grammatical description; but performance tasks with truncates were better than with full passives, and even equalled performance with active sentences like (1) (Slobin 1963; but see Gough 1965, 1966). Both findings contradict predictions derived from grammatical theory.

1.   Active: The thief stole the treasure.
2.   Passive: The treasure was stolen by the thief.
3.   Truncated Passive: The treasure was stolen.

Not only are truncated passives typologically more common in the world's languages, but acquisition data from children showed that truncates were comprehended and used earlier than full passives. Grammatical complexity and processual complexity are not necesarrily the same, and the processing path taken to get from one sentence type to another did not always mirror the path devised by linguists in creating elegant syntactic descriptions.

And some sentential types (like the three types of embedding) which were unmarked as to processing difficulty in a grammatical description were definitely ranked in terms of which were able to be comprehended by real subjects in real-time tasks. As if this were not enough, we also came to realize that some transformations simply were best viewed as rule manipulations essential to the creation of elegant and exhaustive grammars, but not as input for psychological theories of sentence processing, storage, or recall. For example, the affix-hopping rule which covered the possible appearance of English modals, as well as the movement of auxiliaries (like *do/be+-ing/have+-en*) and tense markers in verbal predicates, was a descriptive tour-de-force, but did not lend itself to considerations of psychological reality. Nor did other rules like particle movement in two-part verbs in sentences like *John looked the word up* derived from *John looked up the word*.

Not only did we come to realize that grammatical descriptions had no a priori predictive value in respect to processing considerations, we also came to realize that subjects really relied on the meaning or "gist" of a sentence, or sequence of sentences, and that transformational steps were largely forgotten, in recalling language material (Sachs 1967; Fillenbaum 1966). One could always claim this as deep structure, if one wanted to protect the primacy of the syntactic component, but essentially it required that we pay attention to the fact that recall is largely focussed on the meaning involved, and not the syntax. One might also add that if this was true, then surely some processing tasks must focus, or attend heavily, to meaning considerations.

Thus, although the early experimental DTC investigations suggested a promising, and in the beginning, seemingly fruitful, psychological theory of language to pursue, in the end support for DTC eroded and the hypothesis was finally abandoned. And as we have seen earlier in this chapter, grammatical theory continued to be drastically altered in each of its stages, as it passed from one era of theoretical refinement to another. And in fact the stage from Chomsky 1957 to Chomsky 1965 was more than a minor refinement as far as DTC tenets were concerned. Many psycholinguists simply concluded that there was no absolute relationship between the transformational operations posited by the linguist's grammatical description and the processual operations undertaken by the speaker in producing language and the hearer in comprehending language. Not all hold this view, however, and views contrary to this popular opinion can still be found. Berwick and Weinberg (1985), for example, maintain that a parsing algorithm mirroring the rules and representations of transformational grammar could predict the DTC results correctly, and they find little surprising about such results.

It is, however, easily agreed that we learned many facts along the way as the DTC and its successors were tested. As mentioned, many of the structural units posited in such grammatical descriptions, or at least analogues to such units, play a role at some point in both production and description. As we learned that there was far more to language processing than just syntax, experiments focussed on these factors and acquired much valuable information. For a specific example, note that relative clauses which are marked as such are easier to process; for example, in sentences (1) and (3), it is not until *arrived* and *would* that the hearer is forced to reconsider the analysis (see also Hakes 1972), whereas the relativizing pronouns in sentences (2) and (4) set out the relative clause as such immediately.

1.   The guest expected to be late arrived
2.   The guest who was expected to be late arrived
3.   Jack anticipated the answer would be difficult to uncover
4.   Jack anticipated that the answer would be difficult to uncover

Some experiments (Fodor and Garrett 1967; Hakes and Cairns 1970) even found this facilitating effect for relative pronouns in the categorically difficult self-embedded sentence type. Single center-embeddings can be handled, but two or more center-embeddings are difficult, if not impossible. The first sentence is common enough, but the second sentence is simply stretching the likelihood limits on what is grammatically well-formed.

1.   The cat the dog chased ran

2.   *The cat the dog THE MOUSE SAW chased ran

Still, contrast now the difficulty encountered in dealing with sentence (1) below, as opposed to sentence (2). Both are multiply self-embedded (and thus unlikely or impossible), and thus categorically difficult, but notice how the one with the relativizers is somewhat easier.

1.   *The pen the author the editor liked used was new.
2.   *The pen which the author whom the editor liked used was new.

Speaking of embedding, we also learned that the types of embedding vary in degree of difficulty, with self- or center-embedding and left-embedding more difficult to process than right-embedding. These are also known as left-recursive, right-recursive, and self-recursive in the literature, for embedding allows sentential productivity by its recursive power. This fact more than any other provides for the notion of a potentially infinitely long sentence, as well as for a potentially infinite number of sentences. First, some examples of center-, left-, and finally, right-embedding.

1.   Center-embedding: *The rat that the cat that the dog that the cow tossed worried killed ate the malt.
2.   Left-embedding: John's father's garage's roof's color is red.
3.   Right-embedding: This is the cow with the crumpled horn that tossed the dog that worried the cat that killed the rat that ate the malt that lay in the house that Jack built.

Now compare the following sentences where the truth conditions are the same, but where the information is carried by different embedding formats. The sentences are ordered from most difficult to least difficult to deal with in processual terms.

1.   Center-embedding: That for John to win the race was easy is obvious
2.   Left-embedding: It is obvious that for John to win the race was easy
3.   Right-embedding: It is obvious that it was easy for John to win the race

Embedding is also the way in which nominalizations are created, that is, the way in which one makes a single sentence out of simple sentences. Nominals in sentences (2) to (6) find their origins in the first pair of simple sentences in (1) below.

1.   John departed. That disturbed Mary.
2.   For John to have departed disturbed Mary.
3.   John's departing disturbed Mary.
4.   John's departure disturbed Mary.
5.   John's having departed disturbed Mary.

6.   That John had departed disturbed Mary.

What is interesting to note is that nominalizations seem to pose processing demands greater than the individual sentences. This is not surprising, for the process of nominalization usually requires several grammatical steps as one embeds sentences to create a complex multi-clause sentence. This may be easier to see going in the opposite direction, in tracing the steps by which the sentence *The sheriff pursued the cattle-rustling cowboys* is derived. The embedded nominalization derives from an underlying sentence *The cowboys rustled cattle*, and when this sentence is to be embedded in another, one must carry out several grammatical maneuvers. The direct object *cattle* is moved to a first position, followed by the verb *rustle*, now affixed with an *-ing*; this sequence *cattle-rustling* now modifies the original subject *cowboys* of the underlying sentence. One now has a noun phrase *cattle-rustling cowboys*, the result of the nominalization process, ready for service in any larger sentence.

In sum, what we have learned is that some syntactic formats make for processing constraints in a way that the grammar cannot predict, and that these processing constraints have their effect on the stages of comprehension, storage, and recall.

Sentence Processing and Sentence Comprehension

Sentence comprehension requires us to extract the semantic and syntactic characteristics of the surface form of the sentence, and even its underlying structure. Next we have to construct the meaning intended by the speaker, and in so doing, we pay attention to the surface meaning of the sentence, but may modify this by our understanding of the surrounding context. And finally, we may be required to retain some or all of the syntactic format, and certainly its meaning. But, as mentioned, there are often features of syntax which get in the way of one or more of these tasks, and we shall try to give some examples of what contributes to processing ease or difficulty in the following sections.

Negatives and Negation

Negatives seem to pose their own particular comprehension problems, with negatives typically taking longer to evaluate than their affirmative counterparts. First of all, recall that negation on the surface syntactic level is achieved by inserting the negative marker *not* after the *do* auxiliary, unless that verb is a form of copular *be*. For example, contrast the following negatives with the affirmative sentences they are derived from.

1.   John is not a student.

2.   John did not sleep.
3.   John did not eat the pizza.
4.   John did not remain a teacher.

Negatives typically take longer to evaluate than their affirmative counterparts. For example, sentence (2) is more complex in processing terms than (1). Chances are you have already had experience with sentences like (3) which are difficult because of the way in which they pile up negatives.

1.   Affirmative: Toronto is above Texas.
2.   Negative: Toronto isn't above Texas.
3.   "It is not necessarily the case that students will not be exempted if they are unable to complete the requirements."

Let us now add the factor of truth value, that is, whether the sentence is true or not. Verification is faster for true affirmatives than for false affirmatives, but faster for false negatives than for true negatives (Clark and Chase 1972; see also Carpenter and Just 1975). Negation continues to affect the length of time it takes to process a sentence, and so does whether it is true or false. Thus, (1) is the easiest to verify and (4) the most difficult.

1.   True Affirmative   Toronto is above Texas.
2.   False Affirmative   Texas is above Toronto.
3.   False Negative   Toronto isn't above Texas.
4.   True Negative   Texas isn't above Toronto.

Just and Clark (1973) have suggested that when a sentence is negated, so are its implications, while its presuppositions remain intact. A presupposition, of course, is that underlying propositional value of the sentence that we simply take for granted, since it is embodied, and thus presupposed, within the very sentence itself. For example, read the following sentence, noting its presupposition and its implication.

1.   Sentence: John managed to find his hat.
2.   Presupposition: John tried to find his hat.
3.   Implication: John found his hat.

Now read the following negative sentence, and you will see how its presupposition remains unchanged and how it is the implication which is negated.

1.   Sentence: John didn't manage to find his hat.
2.   Presupposition: John tried to find his hat.
3.   Implication: John didn't find his hat.

The position of the negative in the sentence can also make a difference in terms of processing difficulty. Contrast, for example, the following three sentences, which have the same truth value, but which differ in their processual demands.

1.   Affirmative: It is true that Toronto is above Texas.
2.   Predicate Negative: It is true that Texas isn't above Toronto.
3.   Denial: It isn't true that Texas is above Toronto.

The position of the negative in a sequence of sentences also elicits differences when comprehending for decisions like reasoning tasks. In trying to reason with negatives, Evans' (1972) subjects were presented with variations of the following simple syllogism. First, read the following straightforward syllogism, noting the first premise and the conclusion.

1.   If the letter is A, then the number is 3.
2.   The number is not 3.
3.   Therefore, the letter is not A.

If, however, you negate the antecedent in the first premise, it becomes three times harder to come to the correct solution. The placement of the negative, and the fact of then denying the negative, seems to be what is causing the processual difficulties.

1.   If the letter is not A, then the number is 3.
2.   The number is not 3.
3.   The letter is A.

Another example is offered by Johnson-Laird and Tridgell's (1972) substitution of a disjunctive for a conditional sentence so that a valid inference can be made as one of its components is negated. For example, the following syllogism is straightforward enough as long as the negative appears in the second premise.

1.   Either John is intelligent or he is rich.
2.   John is not rich.
3.   Therefore, John is intelligent.

The conclusion is the same, namely, that *John is intelligent*, in the second syllogism, but it is much more difficult to arrive at when the negative appears in the disjunctive first premise with *or*. The point seems to be that it is not necessarily negation which makes for processing difficulty, it is also the placement of where the negation appears in the sentence construction, and which sentence formats (like the disjunctive) it must interact with.

1.   Either John is intelligent or he is not rich.
2.   John is rich.
3.   Therefore, John is intelligent.

Inherent Negatives . There is also evidence for the existence of inherent negatives, that is, negatives which have semantic features of negation inherent in their underlying meaning (more will also be said on this in the chapter on semantics). For example, in testing whether subjects are able to access and make use of the presuppositions and implications of a sentence independently of one another, Just and Clark (1973) employed premise-question pairs with positively marked lexical items like *remember/thoughtful* and negatively marked ones like *forget/thoughtless*. Recall that if you *remember* to do something, it is likely to have been done, but if you *forget* to do something, then it has obviously not been done. In looking at premise-question pairs like *If John remembered to let the dog out, then where is the dog?*, questions about the implications of inherently positive and negative sentences took about the same time to answer. But in looking at sentence verification, they found that positive sentences are easier to verify than sentences containing inherent negatives. As an example, contrast the following sentences, and you will see that (1) is easier to deal with.

1.   If John remembered to let the dog out, then the dog is supposed to be out.
2.   If John forgot to let the dog out, then the dog is supposed to be in.

Negatives and Plausible Denials . But there are instances in which negatives are no more difficult than affirmatives. Such instances can be seen in utterances which describe the opposite to one's expectations, a situation in which what was expected to happen does not. Wason (1961, 1965) originally called these the "contexts of plausible denial", demonstrating that such utterances appear to be both appropriate and easily processed in such contexts. Imagine, for example, that the regularly scheduled 8:42 train, which is never even late, let alone missing, has not appeared by 9:25. Your companion turns and observes that *The train is not coming.* In such instances of plausible denial, there is little difference in processing this negative, and indeed, this utterance seems more appropriate than most.

Passive Sentences

Passive sentences in English are those transformations of active transitive verb sentences in which the direct object becomes the subject of the passive sentence, and its subject the object of a *by*-prepositional phrase. For example,

1.   The dog bit the mailman.
2.   The mailman was bitten by the dog.

The active and passive variants seem to differ in their function, but exactly how has been difficult to pin down and the distribution of passives has often been explained in vague stylistic terms. They do appear to differ in terms of what they focus upon or emphasize, and not surprisingly, they also seem to differ in respect to their processing difficulty.

Passives are less common than actives, and various counts of passives have shown them to occur anywhere from .7 to 10% of the time (Goldman-Eisler and Cohen 1970) or from 23 to 28% of the time (Krauthamer 1981), depending upon which sample and whose estimates you use. Some passivized forms, like the passive negative, was practically a non-event in Goldman-Eisler and Cohen's sample which included everything from speeches in the British House of Commons to spontaneous discussions of schizophrenic patients. But this distribution does suggest that there may be principles governing the appearance of passives. For example, it may be that when the agent is the given information, the active sentence type is used, but if the patient or object is the given information, a passive may be the more likely (see Krauthamer 1981). This is even more likely when the active sentence agent is an animate agent, since the preferred order seems to be animate before inanimate nouns in such sentences. There may be other reasons to do with style and planning prerequisites as well. Goldman-Eisler and Cohen (1970) did note that in their seven different types of real language samples, as the degree of planning and intellectuality went down, so also did the proportion of passive sentences. They conclude that passives are very much the product of rationality and conscious intellectual planning stages in the generation of sentences.

In general, passives take longer to process or verify for truth value than their active counterparts (see Gough 1965, 1966; Slobin 1966; Olson and Filby 1972). And so the exhortation to avoid passives has found its way into a number of applied psycholinguistic applications like document design (see Felker 1980, Felker et al. 1981) and the formulation of jury charges (see Charrow 1982, Charrow and Charrow 1979, and Charrow and Erhardt 1986). But there are some interesting exceptions to this rule. For example, when subjects are told to attend to the object of an action, as opposed to the agent, it is coded as the important feature, and passives are just as easy to deal with as actives (Olson and Filby 1972). Tannenbaum and Williams (1968) found that although active sentences take less time to produce, when their experimental subjects' focus was directed to the object of the action, they took more time to generate an active sentence and less time to generate a passive sentence. However, when subjects are instructed to attend to agents of the activity instead, actives retain their primacy in processual ease. And indeed, the active sentence may exhibit this processing characteristic because of the perceptual salience of agents.

Semantic expectations also play a role in comprehending passives. Some passive sentences like (1) can only go one way (see Slobin 1966). Because you know the semantic relationship between *girl, to water,* and *flowers,* you know that a sentence like (2) is impossible. As a result, (1) is just as easy to deal with as (3), the active from which it originated. This is not true for all noun-verb semantic relationships, and sentences like those in (4) and (5) contain nouns that could go in either subject or object positions. Because there are no semantic clues, passive sentences like those in (4) and (5) do take longer to process than their active counterparts.

1.   The flowers were watered by the girl.

2.   *The girl was watered by the flowers.
3.   The girl watered the flowers.
4.   The boy was chased by the girl; The girl was chased by the boy.
5.   The horse was followed by the dog; The dog was followed by the horse.

Truncated passives seem to function differently than full passives. Slobin (1968) gave subjects, ranging in age from 5 to 20, short stories which contained either full passives or truncated passives. Subjects were supposed to retell the story as accurately as possible. Recall for the stories which contained the truncated passives was significantly better; 60% of the truncated passives were retained in retelling, but only 25% of the full passives were. Moreover, truncated passives were recalled as active sentences far less than were the full passives, and they were rarely recalled as full passives. Charrow and Charrow (1979) also found that jury charges employing truncated passives are better understood by their subjects than jury charges with full passives, though passives in general presented problems. It seems obvious that truncated passives and full passives elicit different processing behaviors, and thus may not share the same cognitive relationships that their grammatical treatment suggests.

Slobin (1966) also gave children sentences which differed in reversible vs. non-reversible verbs; compare *The dog ate the cookie* and *The dog followed the horse*. Again, the finding was that in reversible passives, the verification of a particular picture, when it was to be paired with a sentence, was harder than for sentences containing non-reversible verbs. In general, passives are also harder to comprehend for children, so that *The horse was followed by the dog* is often interpreted as *The horse followed the dog*. Children seem to employ a basic strategy in which the sequence of N V N in English is usually taken as signalling Actor-Action-Object, and young children have just not straightened out the fact that this otherwise successful strategy does not always apply, as for example, in the case of passives.

Herriot (1969) also found that pragmatic expectations influence response latencies to passive sentences when there are strong expectations that one of the two nouns in the sentence should be the subject and the other the logical object. For example, compare the following sentences where (1) violates this expectation, while (2) fulfills it.

1.   The doctor was treated by the patient.
2.   The patient was treated by the doctor.

Very simply, doctors typically treat patients, and not vice versa, and our expectations in this regard influence the way we perceive such sentences. The lack of such cues may cause greater processing time and hence longer response latencies in such measured tasks. When there are such strong expectations as to which of the two nouns in the sentence will be the logical subject, the voice cue of passivation may not even be attended to; but when there are no such expectations, the voice cue is obviously an even more critical feature. Such findings suggest that in comprehension we may scan for, and pay more attention to, more prominent cues, letting the other minor features come in later for consideration.

Questions and Answering Questions

Questions are easier to comprehend when their form matches the form of the original information. For example, read the following sentences and consider which of its following two questions is easier to comprehend.

1.   John sold the book to Mary.

     a.   Did John sell the book to Mary?
     b.   Did Mary buy the book from John?

2.   Mary bought the book from John.

     a.   Did John sell the book to Mary?
     b.   Did Mary buy the book from John?

You probably found that (1a) was an easier question for (1), and that (2b) was an easier question for (2).

This even seems to extend to the actual syntactic format for questions. For example, in one of their five experiments with passives Olson and Filby (1972) asked whether questions about agents would be answered more quickly from the active voice, while questions about objects, phrased in in the passive voice, would be answered more quickly from the passive voice. When subjects were presented with either an active or a passive sentence, and then asked either an active or passive question, the results indicated that it appears easier to answer questions that correspond to the same surface grammatical structure of the sentence that formed the basis for the question. Wright (1972) also found that errors are typically fewer if both question and answer exhibit the same voice.

Koivukari (1987) has inquired into whether such "error-free answers" really demonstrate knowledge and understanding. She suggests that the input and questions determine the level of processing at either a deep or surface level, and that such questions can be manipulated in educational settings to effect student comprehension of subject matter in greater depth. Students can answer many questions by simply applying their knowledge of linguistic structure in analyzing the question posed in respect to the input. For example, answering *What do all daxes have?* or *Where do we have daxes?* can be accomplished by a simple turn-around linguistic analysis of the input, as in *All daxes have wobs* and *We have daxes in our dorf.* Such verbatim questions are likely to elicit rote answers, and although this may indicate knowledge and understanding of a sort, non-verbatim questions, which are preceded by lexically or syntactically varied input, are more likely to elicit non-rote answers requiring deeper processing for understanding of the material. Koivukari also points out the psychological message of verbatim questions is unfortunately one of conformity, so that knowledge is equated with repeating exactly what the teacher or the textbook said.

Some interesting work has been done on how answers to questions may not always come out of experience and memory storage, but may be the result of the syntactic or semantic frame used in asking the question. This has been of particular importance in legal settings, where achieving the truth has been shown to be clouded by introducing given information in the question which is untrue or uncertain, but which may be taken in unquestioned because of its appearance in the given information slot instead of the new information slot. Then again, not all questions are simple, with correspondingly simple answers. Asking the question *How do you shoot the moon?*, in the card game of *Hearts* is easy, but this is a hard answer to formulate. And in the opposite direction, some questions are difficult to formulate in a way that makes sense, though they receive simple answers. The best example of this may be the questions we received in elementary school as arithmetic problems that were called "word problems".

Semantic Expectations Influence Sentence Processing

Semantic expectations influence comprehension of sentences as well. Fillenbaum (1971b, 1974a, 1974b) asked for paraphrases of unusual sentences like *John dressed and had a bath* and *John finished and wrote the article on the weekend*. The sequencing of events is unusual, and 60% of subjects provided paraphrases which changed the sequence in accord with normal expectations. Even when asked to compare their paraphrases to the original stimulus sentences, 53% still provided incorrect paraphrases. Forster and Ryder (1971) found that even when unusual sentences are perfectly understood, they are understood more slowly; *Mary chewed spears throughout the corrupt talk* was less readily understood than *John smoked cigars throughout the dreary play*. Very simply, sentences whose structures match with our semantic expectations are processed more easily. This was also the essence of the Slobin's and Herriot's findings regarding semantic expectations in non-reversible passive sentences, and can also be applied to other syntactic formats which complicate processing, as for example, embedded sentences.

And we might add that Kintsch and Keenan (1973) found that reading time increases as a function of the number of semantic propositions within a text, even when the number of words is held constant. The number of propositions may be larger than the number of sentences in a text, or even the number of words in a given sentence. Compare, for example, the following, where the second sentence has three associated propositions while the first sentence has only one.

1.   The settler built the cabin by hand.

2.   The crowded passengers squirmed uncomfortably.

Syntactic Ambiguity

The study of ambiguous sentences has been a central area of study
in both linguistics and psycholinguistics. In linguistics, ambiguous sentences demanded independent syntactic analysis for sentences which
allowed more than one interpretation or "reading". Sentences can be
ambiguous on at least three levels: on the lexical level of word meaning (**lexical ambiguity**); on the surface level of syntactic relationships
with ambiguity in the surface structure (**surface structure ambiguity**);
and on the deep structure level of logical relationships between underlying syntactic constituents (**deep or underlying structure ambiguity**).
Examples of each may be seen in the following trio of sentences.

1.   Lexical ambiguity: *The visitors enjoyed the port.*
2.   Surface structure ambiguity: *Old men and women are advised
        to apply for their benefits.*
3.   Deep structure ambiguity: *Cheating students will not be toler-
        ated.*

In psycholinguistics it was felt that understanding sentences with
multiple meanings would shed light on how simple, "normal" single-
meaning sentences were comprehended. Many earlier psycholinguistic
studies investigated whether, and less often, how, ambiguity affects
sentence processing (see Kess and Hoppe 1981a, for an account of this
paradigm of research activity). Some results suggest that context
determines which reading of an ambiguous sentences is to be accessed,
while others claim that the more common reading is accessed first, and
is discarded only after it has been determined that it is inappropriate
in the context. The third view is that all readings are accessed at first,
and then the correct reading is decided upon, at which point the others
are discarded. This last view, while seeming to be counter-intuitive,
has considerable experimental evidence to support it. These have been
variously labelled as: the prior choice hypothesis, the ordered search
hypothesis, and the all-readings hypothesis (Hirst 1987); the single-
reading, the ordered search, and the multiple-reading hypotheses (Kess
and Hoppe 1981a); and the single-reading, the context-dependent, and
the ordered-access models. The bulk of earlier psycholinguistic literature favors the interpretation that the human parser considers all
readings for ambiguous syntax. Apparently, at some unconscious level
of performance, all possible readings of an ambiguous sentence are processed, and one is finally selected at some point in the overall comprehension process. Ambiguous sentences are different from unambiguous
sentences in this crucial feature.
      There has been no complete resolution of the way in which multiple
readings for ambiguous utterances are reviewed and selected from in
actual sentence processing. The real challenge is to find out what
makes this pervasive ambiguity relatively unobtrusive, and what fea-

tures in natural language processing we make use of in comprehending the meaning of utterances.

Single Reading or Multiple Readings? . A few early experimental studies argued for a single reading procedure, or at least an ordered approach to a single reading based on the probability of the most likely single reading (Foss, Bever and Silver 1968; Carey, Mehler and Bever 1970a, 1970b; Hogaboam and Perfetti 1975; Bock 1978). But generally the experimental results have pointed in the other direction. Experimental results have tended to suggest that the processing of ambiguous sentences does differ from unambiguous sentences, and that multiple readings are in fact unconsciously considered in the process of deciding upon a single interpretation. In general, experimental findings for ambiguous sentences in isolation suggested that multiple readings are in fact computed, and the processing effects of such a requirement leaves traces when measured by various experimental tasks that presume that the processing system has limited capacities (Cairns 1973; Cairns and Kamerman 1975; Foss 1970; Foss and Jenkins 1973; Garrett 1970; MacKay 1966; MacKay and Bever 1967; Olson and MacKay 1974). Bever, Garrett and Hurtig (1973) did provide some explanation in suggesting that both meanings are processed during an ambiguous clause, but that once the clause is completed, it is recoded with only one meaning retained.

There was even evidence that multiple readings are activated for ambiguous sentences despite the presence of context (Foss and Jenkins 1973; Conrad, 1974; Holmes, Arwas and Garrett 1977; Lackner and Garrett 1972; Tanenhaus, Leiman and Seidenberg 1979). And such experiments continued to demonstrate that both readings are available or that some processing difference is to be found which distinguishes ambiguous sentences from unambiguous sentences. One widely cited example of such studies was a dichotic listening experiment (Lackner and Garrett 1972). Subjects were presented with an ambiguous sentence in one ear and a disambiguating context sentence in the other ear, and were required to attend to the ear in which the ambiguous sentences were presented. They were then to immediately paraphrase the ambiguous structure which had been presented in the attended ear. Although the disambiguating material in the unattended ear was below active comprehension recognition, the biasing contextual information it provided significantly influenced the interpretation of the ambiguous sentences being consciously attended to.

Lackner and Garrett's experiment demonstrated that analysis of the linguistic material presented to the unattended ear did take place. The input was linked to the multiple readings for the ambiguity which were being scanned, for how else could the correct meaning have been chosen. This is of course the only reasonable explanation of how the ambiguous sentences were able to be biased in the way in which they were. Both of the readings of the ambiguous sentence must have been considered during the actual processing procedure for the biasing to have effectively taken place. How else was it possible to bias the subjects in either direction, in favor of the preferred or the less likely interpretations of the ambiguous sentence? For example, imagine that sentence (1) below was the ambiguous sentence given in the attended ear. In the unattended ear, the disambiguating sentence (2) is given.

1.   The spy put out the torch as our signal to attack.
2.   The spy extinguished the torch in the window.

Despite the fact that subjects could not provide any information about the unattended channel, they significantly paraphrased the attended channel, with its ambiguous sentence, in line with the disambiguating context. If, on the other hand, sentence (1) was now presented with a different sentence, like (2) now below, the paraphrase was now in line with the new (2).

1.   The spy put out the torch as our signal to attack.
2.   The spy showed the torch in the window.

Thus, their findings seemed to conclude that all the readings of an ambiguous sentence are considered, since the biasing sentence was provided simultaneously with the ambiguous sentence. The processing of both readings had to take place in the light of the contextual information which was being presented to the unattended ear and analyzed.

Foss and Jenkins (1973) showed a processing effect for lexical ambiguity when the ambiguous word was preceded by a biasing context within the same sentence. Such results also seemed to suggest that even prior context has its effect **after** lexical retrieval, meaning that even in the presence of context, all meanings of an ambiguous word are considered before the processual decision as to correct reading is rendered. Although Foss and Jenkins had expected that a biasing context would prioritize the readings of an ambiguous item, reaction times to their phoneme monitoring task were longer in both neutral and biased contexts when the target phoneme in the monitoring task was preceded by an ambiguous word than when it was preceded by an unambiguous word.

Other experiments which employed varying types of context, as well as different experimental tasks, also seemed to show differences for ambiguous structures. Holmes, Arwas and Garrett (1977) showed effects for ambiguous lexical items with a biasing context in an experiment using the RSVP technique. Conrad (1974) found effects for ambiguous words in a color-naming Stroop task with a biasing context. Several experiments used semantic priming as a measure of access. Swinney (1979) used sentences with a semantically biased context, like *John saw several spiders, roaches, and other* **bugs**. Subjects had to respond to target words, related to either the biased meaning ('insect') or unbiased meaning ('spy') of *bug*. Tanenhaus, Leiman and Seidenberg (1979) investigated noun-verb categorical ambiguities in biasing syntactic contexts; for example, **rose** has the two potential meanings of 'stood up' and 'flower', but is biased in *They all rose*. Both experiments report a two-stage process in which all readings of ambiguous words are initially accessed and then the false interpretations rapidly eliminated. And some studies even indicated that all meanings of a lexically ambiguous word are called up in a biased context (Onifer and Swinney 1981; Seidenberg, Tanenhaus, Leiman and Bienkowski 1982), or when that ambiguity is preceded by a prior disambiguating syntactic context (Tanenhaus and Donnenworth-Nolan 1984). The multiple access route seemed to be a fairly reliable finding for lexical items within the framework of a single sentence, and according to these studies, syntactic context does not guide the initial access.

Parsing Strategies. Some theoretical studies in linguistics have suggested that syntactic ambiguities might have preferred readings, and postulate first-order parsing strategies. The fundamental claim of such explanatory devices is that the parsing procedure accepts a complete but minimally complex analysis in the absence of other information. Thus, it is suggested that, in analyzing an incoming sentence, phrases are attached so as to create a logical analysis as far to the right as possible or are attached so as to minimize the complexity of the analysis (see Pereira 1985 or Kurtzman 1985). For example, compare sentences (1) and (2).

1.   Rose read the note, the memo, and the letter to Mary.
2.   Rose read the letter to Mary.

The principle of Local Attachment accounts for the common interpretation which attaches the phrase *to Mary* into the local noun phrase *the letter to Mary* in sentence (1). Incoming words or phrases are typically incorporated into structures which also contain the other nearby words. In contrast, the preferred interpretation for (2) is to incorporate *to Mary* into the verb phrase, as in *to read (something) to Mary*.

Another principle, Minimal Attachment, suggests that we take the incoming words or phrases to build an analysis with the smallest number of syntactic nodes. For example, take sentences like (1) and (2) below.

1.   *They told the girl that the boy liked the story.*

        a.   [[They told the girl] [that the boy liked the story]].
        b.   [They told the girl [that the boy liked] the story].
2.   *Tom said Sue left yesterday.*

        a.   [[Tom said] [Sue left yesterday]].
        b.   [Tom said [Sue left] yesterday].

Both (1a) and (1b) are plausible analyses for (1), but (1a) has fewer possible nodes than (1b), and is thus the typical parse for an ambiguous sentence like (1). In (2), is *yesterday* a sentential adverbial modifying the sentence as a whole, or does it just modify the clause *Sue left* as an adverb of time? Again, the principle of minimal attachment takes the first available analysis which will construct a syntactic analysis with the fewest permitted syntactic nodes, and therefore (2a) and not (2b) is the likely first parse (see Frazier and Rayner 1982).

   Garden path sentences may be the best examples of how we build
the most likely syntactic tree until contrary information tells us otherwise. Obviously, the interpretation that is ultimately the most successful in specifying the appropriate reading is the correct one (Crain and
Steedman's (1985) principle of referential success), but garden path
sentences suggest that there is an active strategy at any given point in
the parsing of sentences. For example, read sentence (1) below to a
friend who has not heard it before (taken from Lashley 1951). You
will note that he or she will interpret it as (1a), until realizing that the
word could not possibly be *writing*, but has to be *righting*, as in (1b).

1.   Rapid /raytɪŋ/ with his uninjured hand saved from loss the con-
        tents of the capsized canoe.

        a.   Rapid writing with his uninjured hand saved from loss
              the contents of the capsized canoe.
        b.   Rapid righting with his uninjured hand saved from loss
              the contents of the capsized canoe.

   Such principles, however, do not always predict parsing behavior
on slightly different ambiguous sentences of the same type. For example, you may initially parse (1) as (1a) instead of (1b). But you will be
less likely to initiate such an incorrect parse for potentially ambiguous
sentences like (2) and (3) than you will for (1) (see Kurtzman 1985).

1.   The horse raced past the barn fell.

        a.   [[The horse raced past the barn] [fell]].
        b.   [The horse [raced past the barn] fell].
2.   A horse raced past the barn fell.
3.   Horses raced past the barn fell.

   Recent studies have claimed that we employ parsing strategies
even when pragmatic considerations would be expected to override the
initial syntactic preference for minimal attachment (Rayner, Carlson
and Frazier 1983). Ferreira and Clifton (1986) have shown results
that suggest that syntactic processing is independent and that the initial syntactic analysis given to sentences is not influenced by the
semantic information already processed. They used eye movements as
a measurement, and examined whether semantic content or pragmatic
context would influence the initial syntactic analysis of the sentence.
They found that some syntactic parsing preferences do indeed appear
to operate independently of such semantic or contextual factors, and
that Minimal Attachment influences sentence parsing in context as
well in isolation. Ferreira and Clifton conclude that there are first-
order independent syntactic parsing strategies even in coherent discourse. This does not mean that semantic or pragmatic information
does not play a role, but rather that the input it provides is employed
at a later stage. Garden path strings like the following thus undergo a
preferential parsing strategy which constructs a structural description

using the fewest syntactic nodes allowed by the grammatical rules for forming sentences in the language. For example, read the following strings.

1.   The editor played the tape
2.   Sam loaded the boxes on the cart

The expectation, according to Ferreira and Clifton, is that the preferred analysis of the first phrase will be to mark it as an active sentence. Similarly, even the more subtle ambiguity in the second fragment will be analyzed so that the prepositional phrase *on the cart* will be attached to the whole verb phrase *loaded the boxes*, instead of having it modify just the noun phrase *the boxes*. In accord with this general principle, they found that when sentences containing these fragments are embedded into longer sentences, and in turn embedded in coherent discourse, they still show this parsing preference at first. For example, now read the following sentences, and note how your perception of the sentences changes as you are forced to reanalyze it.

1.   The editor played the tape agreed the story was big.
2.   Sam loaded the boxes on the cart onto the van.

Frazier and Rayner (1987), however, found that subjects delayed the assignment of an analysis for lexically ambiguous sentences which involved syntactic category assignments, until they received disambiguating information. They examined the principle of Minimal Attachment in sentences with categorially ambiguous lexical items by also using eye movements as a measure of on-line parsing. For example, a string like *The warehouse fires. . . .* could be interpreted as Noun + Verb **or** Adjectival + Noun, as in (1) and (2) below.

1.   The warehouse fires numerous employees each year.
2.   The warehouse fires harm some employees each year.

Such ambiguities of syntactic category can be modified by prior context; for example, the appearance of *this* and *these* might be expected to set the syntactic processor for the noun+verb combination or the adjectival+verb combination, as in (1) and (2) below.

1.   This warehouse fires numerous employees each year.
2.   These warehouse fires harm some employees each year.

However, their results still seem to favor a delay strategy, in which readers delay syntactic category assignments when there is a syntactic category ambiguity. Moreover, reading times on ambiguous words seem to be shorter in sentences with following disambiguation than in sentences with preceding disambiguation, suggesting that readers delay syntactic category judgments under such conditions of ambiguity and that readers do make immediate judgments on syntactic parsing assignments when this type of ambiguity is not present. This finding slightly modifies Frazier and Rayner's (1982) previous findings that the human parser adopts the first logical syntactic analysis available, only revising this first analysis if it turns out to be ungrammatical. It also shades Rayner, Carlson and Frazier's (1983) findings that pragmatics did not override the initial syntactic preference for Minimal Attachment as a parsing principle. One explanation is that there are complementary, but unique strategies for different kinds of ambiguities; for example, lexical ambiguities like *pipe*, categorial ambiguities like *The warehouse fires. . . .*, and syntactic ambiguities like *The spy saw the cop with binoculars. . . .* may not all elicit the same processing procedures. Clearly, the role of grammatical theory within models of natural language processing is being tempered by the emphasis on discovering independent strategies that explain how we deal with ambiguous structures (Pritchett 1988).

Modularity vs. Interactionism . Ambiguity and the question of syntactic parsing strategies is one of the best places to view the debate between **Modularity** and **Interactionism**. You may recall that the modularity position claims independent input systems, with these modules transmitting their processing decisions on input to a central processing system which correlates the information (see J. A. Fodor 1983). Processing at any given level is assumed to be essentially free of influence from processing decisions about the input on any other level. For example, a modular view would claim that the initial syntactic analysis of ambiguous sentences is made **without** taking into account semantic or pragmatic information. In sharp contrast, the interactionist position maintains that processing at any given level takes into any and all information from other processing levels. Comprehension would involve integrating information derived from **bottom-up** analysis of the actual data as well as **top-down** information derived from the higher levels. Thus, an interactionist view would hold that syntactic decisions about ambiguous sentences are definitely made in the light of semantic or pragmatic information.

The evidence which bears on this does not unequivocally point to an easy resolution and is the source of considerable experimentation. Some sense of the debate can be seen in a recent volume (Marslen-Wilson 1989) which in part examines the role of lexical representations in syntactic parsing and semantic interpretation. The modular representatives argue against any initial lexical influence in syntactic processing. Frazier (1989) claims that only item-independent information of the syntactic type guides the initial analysis of input; item-specific information of the lexical type did not alter the initially preferred parsing strategies exhibited by her subjects. In contrast, the interactionists assign a central role to lexical representations in integrating linguistic and nonlinguistic knowledge in sentence processing. Tyler (1989) thus presents evidence that the syntactic implications of verbs are immediately constrained by the semantic context in which they occur, and Tanenhaus and Carlson (1989) show that the argument structure of verbs is utilized during sentence comprehension. The stakes in this unresolved debate are high, nothing less than understanding of the architecture of the human language processor.

Memory and Sentence Recall

Short-term and Long-term Memory

It may be worth first noting the distinction between tasks that demand different things of the memory. In short-term memory we store the exact wording for brief periods of time. It has a limited capacity and information is either quickly moved into long-term memory in distilled form or it is simply discarded. Our long-term memory has two distinct components: an episodic memory in which we recall particular episodes or events which we have experienced, and a semantic memory, which deals with what we know about the real world, and stores that information in a way that is compatible with information from other inputs. This cognitive code is the subject of much debate, as we wrestle with the question of what the "structure of mental representations" must be.

Memory for Form vs. Memory for Gist

We usually store only the meaning of a sentence, and not the actual format, unless we are instructed to retain the surface form. By and large, what we tend to remember is the gist of what we have read or heard, rather than the actual format of the sentences we have been exposed to. This was learned fairly early on in the experimentation with syntactic structures, for subjects were poor at recalling specific sentences from instances they were exposed to, but had little trouble in providing meaningful, and relatively accurate, paraphrases for what they had been given (Fillenbaum 1966; Sachs 1967).

Some modification of these findings may be required by findings on memory for conversations, as opposed to transformationally altered sentences given without context. Hjelmquist (1984) has pointed out that there is a substantial memory for certain surface structure aspects of discourse. His work with memory for dialogues four days after the conversations demonstrates that there is a significant recognition memory for the actual surface forms of the utterances which appeared in that conversation. The dialogues were spontaneous and natural, and subjects were unaware they would later be asked to differentiate between utterances that were exactly as appeared in the conversation, paraphrases of those utterances, and new utterances that had not appeared at all. Not surprisingly, and in keeping with the preceding observation about the reliability of gist conservation, memory for content was very accurate; subjects also easily rejected utterances that had not appeared in the original conversations. But they showed a considerable memory for surface structure characteristics of utterances that had been embedded in those natural dialogues. Keenan, MacWhinney and Mayhew (1977) similarly found that in recalling natural conversations from group discussions at lunchtime exchanges, subjects were very good at recalling statements that were high in interactional value (recalling both their form and their meaning), but were poorer at recalling form and meaning when the interactional value of the statement was low. They explain this finding of memory for what was actually said by noting that this memory is connected to interactional aspects of the actual conversation. Such **interactional** utterances are those which not only convey an important role in establishing the memory value of of statements in natural conversations, but also convey the attitude of the speaker to the listener. The argument is that the pragmatic value of such utterances lies in the way they transmit the speaker's intentions, beliefs, and attitudes toward the listener, but much of this is embedded in discourse contexts, and thus the topic will be taken up again in the section of the book which deals with discourse.

Imagery . Other considerations like **imagery** may also enter into our accurate recollection of the actual sentence format, in addition to its content (Begg and Paivio 1968; Jorgenson and Kintsch 1973). Free and cued recall of concrete words is typically superior to that for abstract words. And when lexical items with a high-imagery value were used in several experiments, the sentences were not recalled as well in terms of their original syntactic formats as in terms of their meaning. Even in production, subjects who had to provide sentences for abstract words like *dominance* vs. concrete words like *car* took longer to produce the first word of abstract sentences, suggesting that it may take longer to create sentence frames for low-imagery items (Taylor 1969). It is as if the imagery value of such "picturing" lexical items pushes listeners to "view" such sentences in terms of their meaning components more readily. On the other hand, sentences with vocabulary items exhibiting a low-imagery value exhibit a better retention rate for the actual syntactic formats. It also seems that high-imagery sentences are evaluated more rapidly for their truth values than sentences with low-imagery values. It is as if samples of language which are not easily imaged in terms of other sensory and storage media require us to rely more on the syntactic frames the information comes in. This is true both for how we comprehend the information, and how we then store it. Basically, it comes down to language being easily defined or matched by other storage modalities, or language which must rely on itself to be stored. As an extreme example, imagine storing away the following two sentences, and then trying to recall them; incidentally, both sentences have the same number of words, though they may not seem to.

1.   Labrador Retrievers are among the smartest of the species we know commonly as dogs.
2.   Infinitival forms are among the vaguest of the categories we know as predicates.

There is some question of the general functional role of imagery in human cognition and memory, as for example, whether images can be assumed to be the way that even concrete verbal information is stored in long-term memory; very simply, the form of human conceptual memory is yet to empirically established (see Marschark, Richman, Yuille and Hunt 1987). But there does seem to be considerable support for the imagery system as specialized to immediately deal with information about nonverbal objects as well as relatively concrete verbal information (see Paivio 1986). Some modification of this finding seems called for by the finding that there is equivalent recall for concrete and abstract sentences when presented in paragraph order, suggesting a discourse effect. However, concrete sentences continue to show a recall advantage when presented in random order, in keeping with an explanation based on discourse schemas having an effect (see Marschark 1985). Still, the notion of imagery offers a powerful explanation for learning, comprehension, and memory strategies in dealing with list learning or sentences in isolation, but does not always successfully generalize to more complex linguistic stimuli like discourse prose (see Marschark, Richman, Yuille and Hunt 1987).

Temporal vs. Syntactic Sequencing . Early experiments (Clark and Clark 1968) had noted that the sequencing of temporal events in syntax has an effect on recall from memory. Typically, recall is poorer when the sentence order does not match up with the temporal order of the events in the sentence. Using arbitrarily related events (dress up/ brush teeth; rake lawn/wash car) in separate clauses linked by conjunctions like *before/after*, they found that verbatim recall was poorer; so also was recalling the correct ordering of the events and even the sense of the sentence. Obviously, one has to attend to the stated order of events, if they are not already causally related, as in *He turned on the ignition before his car started*. This, however, is not always the case, as when the sequence of events is arbitrarily related, as in the following.

1.   He washed the car before he raked the lawn.
2.   He raked the lawn before he washed the car.

You can complicate this fact by having the syntactic order of mention different than the temporal order in which they actually occurred; for example, when sentence (1) is given as *Before he raked the lawn, he washed the car*.

Clause order is also important in recall; sentences containing a causal subordinate clause are harder to memorize if the subordinate clause precedes the main clause, than if the subordinate clause follows the main clause (Clark and Clark 1968), as in the following semantically identical sentences.

1.   Because the food was gone, the dog bit the cat.
2.   The dog bit the cat because the food was gone.

Propositional Content . Kintsch and Keenan (1973) had already found that reading time increases as a function of the number of propositions within a text, and Kintsch and Glass (1974) found that recall is better for single proposition sentences than for multiple proposition sentences in texts, even when the number of words is constant. Subjects recalled surface form more correctly (91%) for unipropositional sentences, as opposed to 74% for multi-propositional sentences.

Inference

We recall more than we actually hear, because we make inferences or deductions from sentences that we hear. Often the inferences we make are not based directly on the linguistic material itself, but on the extrapolations we make on the basis of that material. We integrate various pieces of meaning, some directly from the sentences we have actually encountered and some constructed as inferences from those sentences. For example, in hearing that *I lost my key and couldn't get into my apartment last night*, you might logically infer that the door was locked, even though that is said nowhere in the sentence.

Sometimes we may even make inferences which may not be true on the basis of what we have actually encountered. For example, Loftus and Palmer (1974) have demonstrated that witnesses can be misled easily by inserting verbal material in the syntactic slots for given information. Their subjects made incorrect inferences about a scenario they had in fact witnessed. Memory is a constructive, dynamic process, and what happens is that the subjects incorporated their new inferences into their reproduction of the situation, based on what they had derived from the questions asked of them. For example, in hearing *smashed*, instead of the less evocative words *hit/collided/bumped/ contacted*, subjects were more likely to give higher estimates of speed for automobile accidents they had witnessed on film. The two sentences have different values in terms of what they evoke immediately, as well as in longer-term memory, for the subjects who had received the first question were more likely to report having seen broken glass when re-tested a week after the films.

1.   About how fast were the cars going when they smashed into each other?
2.   About how fast were the cars going when they hit each other?

We tend to fill in blanks in comprehension, in order to integrate meanings into coherent and complete pictures of the meaning. This may in fact be the intended meaning, or it may even be the meaning that we thought was intended, or that we used to make sense of the incoming information. This integration may again lead us to forget the actual syntactic format, and pay attention to only the semantic gist. In testing subjects for recognition of sentences, Bransford and Franks (1971) found that subjects were prone to admit having seen sentences which they had not. The crucial point was that the sentences they were most willing to accept, as having been present in the sets they had been exposed to, were more complex than the originals. Such complex sentences actually incorporated many of the ideas of the simpler sentences of the original list, and Bransford and Franks' three experiments in memory for semantic ideas demonstrate the integration process for construction of holistic ideas from single sentences. For example, although sentence (1) below would not have been in the original list, this complex sentence would be readily accepted as having been seen. One can easily see how it might have been constructed from originals, like those exemplified in sentences (2) through (6).

1. The ants in the kitchen ate the sweet jelly which was on the table.
2. The ants were in the kitchen.
3. The ants in the kitchen ate the sweet jelly.
4. The jelly was sweet.
5. The sweet jelly was on the table.
6. The ants ate the sweet jelly which was on the table.

Two points can be made here. On the basis of Bransford and Franks' work, we learn that inference is an integrational process, and the confidence levels that their subjects exhibited toward the more comprehensive, holistic sentence seems to point to this fact. Their subjects exhibited the highest confidence ratings in claiming to have seen the more complex sentences; and the confidence ratings went down as the comprehensive quality of the sentences did. Very simply, the more informational propositions tucked into a sentence, the more likely that subjects were to say that they had seen it. The second point to be made here is that one is actively constructing a chunk of memory, and makes inferences as to how everything fits together in some unified sense. In this case, one is actively inferring what took place in some sense of the essence of the scenario. The explanation offered at the time was that a theory of sentence storage and recall could not be based on an interpretive model, whereby sentences are viewed as objects to be remembered (Bransford, Barclay and Franks 1972). Instead, a better explanation seemed to rest in a constructive approach whereby semantic representations of the situations described by the sentence's information are constructed. One thus constructs such a mental model in memory, and sentence memory is also geared toward the semantic representations contained in the information conveyed by the sentence, as well as to the actual sentence itself. The original sentences themselves are only an information-carrying means to that end, and once the scope of the scenario has been extracted, the original sentences do not carry the same weight they did as input. The experimental subjects here acquired complete ideas from exposure to partial ideas, namely, the multi-propositioned complex sentence from the single sentences. In constructing the total semantic model of the situation in their minds, they came to think that they might have heard the sentence expressing the complete idea when in fact they had not. Since their subjects were so confident that they had heard the three- and four-proposition sentences, they must have been actively constructing, and then storing, the holistic semantic model that they had prepared from the individual sentences which had been non-consecutively presented. Thorndyke (1976) seems to have found much the same in discourse comprehension, noting that what seems to be stored in memory is a structure which encodes the total situation described by a series of related propositions and their logical inferences.

An extension of this notion of inference, coupled with general world knowledge, is seen in the Bransford, Barclay and Franks (1972) experiment which presented subjects with sentences containing spatial relations. For example, they would be presented with sentences like the following.

1. Three turtles rested beside a floating log, and a fish swam beneath them.
2. Three turtles rested on a floating log, and a fish swam beneath them.

They were then tested on whether they had seen sentences like the following, sentences which they had in fact not been given.

1. Three turtles rested beside a floating log, and a fish swam beneath it.
2. Three turtles rested on a floating log, and a fish swam beneath it.

The test sentences differ in one crucial feature in respect to the spatial relationships beween turtles, fish, and log. If the original stimulus sentence had the turtles **on** the log, then it was inferred that the fish must have swum not only under the turtles, but the log they were on as well. A common sense piece of knowledge, of course, but one which depends upon making inferences from the information presented in the stimulus sentence, and then putting this information to work in conjunction with one's generalized world knowledge of how spatial relations work between objects. Thus, it is not surprising that the sentence with *it* for the *the log* was accepted if the turtles had been presented as having been on the log, but not beside it. The sentence itself does not contain this piece of information, and it is only explained through the inference-making process so actively engaged in by the listener. The listener obviously goes beyond the mere syntactic format of the sentence itself, and even goes beyond the actual information presented in the sentence, to infer appropriate relationships and construct a plausible scenario. The listener has actually gone beyond the surface syntax and even the propositional textbase here, and has constructed a model of the situation that is described by the text; it is this model that is stored and that is consulted (see Perrig and Kintsch 1985). More will be said on this notion of mental model in the section on discourse.

Johnson, Bransford and Solomon (1973) further continued this notion of comprehension involving the making of inferences and devised a similar experiment to determine whether subjects were likely to think that they had heard information based on such inferences. Two types of inferences were tested: the first involved the implication that an instrument like a gun was used, as in sentence (1) below; the second was an implication that a particular action had a consequence like the window breaking, as in sentence (2) below.

1.   The man was shot.
2.   The boy hit the baseball and watched as it flew into the picture
     window in the house.

The sentences were presented, embedded within stories; the controls
did not imply instrument or consequence. Subjects were tested for recognition of sentences which had appeared, sentences which had not,
and sentences which were inferentially true. And indeed, subjects did
respond to the inferentially true sentences more often than the controls, claiming that they had seen them in the previous text exercise.

The nature of instrumental inference was also investigated by
McKoon and Ratcliff (1981), who attempted to determine whether
instrumental inferences are necessarily made, given that such inferences are rarely needed to produce a connected text representation. For
example, does the appropriate scenario, and mention of a hammer, set
the inferential stage for an instrumental relationship between the hammer as instrument and the activity of pounding. If you read the following paragraph, you may test this for yourself.

> Bobby got a saw, hammer, screwdriver, and square from his toolbox.
> He had already selected an oak tree as the site for the birdhouse. He
> had drawn a detailed blueprint and measured carefully. He marked
> the boards and cut them out. Then Bobby stuck the boards together
> with glue.

McKoon and Ratcliff's subjects took longer to respond to whether they
had seen the test word *hammer* in this paragraph, than they did to
respond yes or no when the paragraph was altered by replacing the
final sentence with the following.

> Then Bobby pounded the boards together with nails.

The conclusion they drew was that the appropriate action does
appear to activate the inference of a specific instrument. They then
tested this conclusion with a test word, like *mallet*, which was semantically in the same field, but not highly associated inferentially. They
found that the response times for such test words were not significantly
different for the two versions of the paragraph. And extending the
investigation to long-term memory in yet another pair of experiments,
they found similar results for inferential connections between instruments and actions.

Sentence Production

Much of what we will want to say about sentence production will have domain ties with what we would like to say about discourse. What we typically achieve with language is to communicate with our fellows transmitting both the informational content of our ideas and our intentions. We not only communicate facts, feelings, and figures, that is, informational and ideational content, but we typically wish our co-locutors to do something with those ideas, namely, to follow, or at least to be aware of our intentions. This dichotomy between **information** and **intention** is further taken up in the next section on discourse, since the realization of actual sentences is very much tied to considerations larger than the boundaries posed by the single sentence in isolation. Obviously, speakers are very much aware of the preceding and ongoing structure of the discourse, and the way that each new sentence contribution can be expected to fit in with what the conversational partner already knows from the exchange and what he or she is likely to understand as the dialogue unfolds. In this respect, discourse also has structure, and it is this structure that we are about to survey next, as we inquire how information and intentions are conveyed in monologic text and dialogic discourse.

Summary

Syntax is the study of sentence-building, and a grammar of a specific language is a set of rules about how words are combined to carry structural meanings. But linguists also consider a grammar to be a description of the complex abstract knowledge speakers-hearers have of their language, clearly a psychological aim.

Structuralism, the dominant paradigm from the 1930s until the generativist period in the 1960s, characterized syntax as a limited number of items and arrangements in a given language. Semantic information was theoretically disallowed, and structuralist syntax did not recognize underlying structures in sentence alternations like active/passive. Transformational generative grammar attempted to explain sentential relationships, paraphrase and ambiguity, and the role of semantics in the grammar, and had a profound effect on psycholinguistics in the 1960s and 1970s. It also held that children have an innate ability to learn language, and that this is what a theory of language should be about, a universal theory which gives an account of the grammatical forms and relations common to all languages.

The basic unit of analysis was the sentence, and this found its way into experimentation as psycholinguists probed distinctions like deep/surface structure and competence/performance. Such distinctions reflected the emphasis placed on generating sentences in a way that characterized the underlying linguistic abilities that native users of a natural language have. Syntactic theory has changed quickly, and often rather extensively. For example, generative theory expanded to introduce recursion into the grammar and was later revised to include an enriched surface structure with traces which identify transformational rules that have been applied to deep structure. Though Government and Binding theory has incorporated traces, its goal is to outline maximally simple grammars, with universal principles that do not have to be learned, but are supplemented by language-specific parameters which must be learned and set in each particular language.

Much of modern linguistic theorizing has either complemented or contrasted with generative grammar. But such syntactic models, like Generative Semantics, Case Grammar, Lexical Functional Grammar, Generalized Phrase Structure Grammar, and Relational Grammar, have claimed our attention too and provide their own unique insights.

The Derivational Theory of Complexity examined whether the number and complexity of mental operations performed by a reader or hearer during processing was related to the number and complexity of formal transformations given in the grammatical derivation of that sentence. There was support for the psychological reality of major syntactic boundaries and their structural constituents, but little support for the role of transformations as such. We did learn, however, that some syntactic formats make for processing constraints that the grammar cannot predict, and that these constraints have their effect on the stages of comprehension, storage, and recall. For example, negatives and passives generally take longer to process or verify for truth value, questions are easier to answer when their form matches the form of the original information, and semantic expectations influence comprehension. Recent work on ambiguous sentences focusses on whether the human parser considers all readings for ambiguous syntax or employs first-order parsing strategies, and reflects the fact that grammatical theory now also emphasizes processing strategies in models of natural language. Ambiguity is also an excellent test case for probing the explanatory power of the respective claims of Modularity and Interactionism. Modularity claims independent input systems, whereas Interactionism integrates information derived from **bottom-up** analysis of the actual data as well as **top-down** information derived from the higher levels.

Storage and recall of sentences are sensitive to several factors, such as imagery, interactional value vs. gist, and propositional content. We recall more than we actually hear, because we not only make inferences from the sentences that we hear but we actively construct chunks of memory. We integrate all this information into a mental model of the situation, and it is this model that is stored and later consulted for recall.

Chapter 6

Discourse

Discourse and Discourse Analysis

Sentence structure and sentence comprehension are no longer alone at center-stage in linguistic and psycholinguistic studies. Nor do we see the same preoccupation with the sentence as the primary naturally occurring unit of language. The concern with syntax has been complemented by concerns with the larger structures of discourse, and the last decade has seen a boom of intellectual activity in trying to chart the systematic aspects of discourse[3] (for example, see the multi-volume *Handbook of Discourse Analysis*, edited by Van Dijk 1985). For discourse, like sentences, can also been seen to exhibit structure. Utterances in discourse carry meaning of a more intricate type than just morphemes and words, and in a very real sense are the typical means by which we transmit both ideas and intentions in communicative exchanges.

While there is little question that discourse analysis is a field that is to be reckoned with, the crisp formalism which came to characterize syntactic studies has yet to be realized in some areas of discourse studies (see Frawley 1987; Kess 1986). Part of this may be due to the convenient boundaries afforded by the nature of the sentence as a unit of study, in contrast to the enormity of what a sensitive analysis of discourse will require us to cover. However, when one looks at discourse syntax, discourse semantics, or narrative grammars, that desired crispness is evident; but since most work on discourse is not on syntax, a singularly formalistic paradigm has not yet emerged. In fairness, however, it is also true that much work in other areas of language, for example, semantics, is no less intuitive and not always formal (van Dijk, personal communication). Part of this failure in self-realization is also due to a lack of a standard unit (for example, we had phonemes and distinctive features in two approaches to phonology and basic sentence types in early formal syntax) and an agreed-upon methodology to deal with the data of discourse (again, see Frawley 1987, and Kess 1986).

---

[3] One methodological point worth making is that the study of discourse at times refers to the terms **text** and **discourse** as dealing with the separate phenomena of written chunks of language and spoken chunks of language, respectively. Elsewhere it employs the terms almost interchangeably, as if they could refer to the same fact of larger sequences of language (see Stubbs 1983). In this chapter, and throughout the book, we will try to use the terms **text** and **discourse** to refer to written and spoken pieces of language, though at times the distinction between them may be blurry. Terms like **verbal discourse/reading/conversation**, and so forth, still refer to their more traditional values in discourse about discourse.

Nonetheless, it is obvious that discourse is an critical area on which to concentrate more of our psycholinguistic resources, for the problems there are both meaningful and rewarding if resolved. It also seems obvious that some unanswered questions of sentence grammars, like the problems of anaphora and topic reference, may be resolved by recourse to discourse features. Other sentential phenomena like passivization in languages as different as English and Tagalog may also find some more satisfying explanation for their distribution in the architectural features of discourse design; for example, explanations for what conditions the appearance of the nearly half-dozen passive sentence types in Philippine languages like Tagalog (Kess 1979) and the dichotomy between active and passive sentences in English may profit from attention to the ways in which thematic structures are maintained and developed in discourse. It is, however, unlikely that discourse grammars will entirely take the place of sentence grammars, and as Morgan (1982) correctly notes, such a move would require us to re-invent syntax anyway.

Speech Act Theory and Discourse

Because the function of language is communication, we are typically more interested in and aware of what speakers really mean in using a given sentence than we are interested in the surface structure of the sentence. Speakers usually have intentions; that is, they intend to have some effect on their listeners by acting in a linguistic way. That is, language is action, and individual utterances are actions. Austin (1962) has reminded us that we act through language, doing things through words, getting others to do things for us through our words. Some activities in fact are only carried out as language acts; apologizing, for example, is not something you can do any other way--you must produce a particular utterance, "perform a language activity", to apologize.

Language is used just as much to perform functions as it is to carry meaning. We should be aware of these two facets of language as having equal claim on our attention, that is, the facets of **informational content** and **intentional activity**. Kasher (1985) has called these **communication** and **action**, Steinberg (1982) has termed them **proposition** and **purpose**, but we may employ the more transparent labels of **information** and **intention** for our discussions here. Language has a dual function, realized in language as communicating information and language as communicating intentions. The notion of information is the belief that language is a vehicle of communication, intended for transferring the informational or referential content of ideas from one person to another. Obviously, psycholinguistic inquiry must include a method of representing the transferrable information independent of language itself, not unlike the need to know the nature of water to talk intelligently about the nature and design of water pipes (Kasher 1985). Noting the problems with truth conditions, Kasher has suggested that there are serious obstacles to pursuing an information-oriented theory of language, stating that the discovery of flimsy conceptual bases should send us in search of the alternative foundations to be found in the selection of intention as a primary working assumption in discourse analysis. The implication is that natural language involves a human action, done on purpose, employing words and sentences in some appropriate contextual setting, and a framework for describing such speech acts will have to be stated in terms of ends, means, roles, and products. However, it is going to be much more difficult to put forward generalizations about speech acts, or discourse in general, than it is to make generalizations about syntax, which is much more amenable to explanation in terms of rule designations. The most promising area for generalizations in this area may be the discourse counterpart of "universal grammar" on the syntactic level, and efforts are being made in this direction (Kasher 1985).

When we speak, we not only transfer information in a technical sense, but we also convey our intentions by performing activities like suggesting, promising, inviting, requesting, or even prohibiting our co-locutors from doing something. Thus, language activity is not just transferring information like *Snow is white*, but it is also an activity by which we do things with words, things like demanding, demurring, or displaying our erudition about commodities like snow. Once listeners have figured out the informational content of what we are saying, they then must decide what to do with it, and this they do by assessing what the real force of the speech act is. The general outline of discourse is thus directional, in that speakers intend both to have listeners recognize their intentions and to have them do something about those intentions. For example, conversational exchanges often have embedded with their development a programmatic build-up to some main goal-oriented theme; think, for example, how your last conversation went when you wanted someone to lend you something.

If the speech act is the unit of analysis for intention, we may call the informational content of the ideas its propositional content, using Kintsch's (1974) system of text analysis. This system employs the **proposition** as the basic unit of analysis, with predicators and arguments as units of those propositions. As outlined in the preceding chapter on syntax, predicators express relations, states, and activities, while arguments provide referential information. These notions are very compatible with computational versions of memory structure and hierarchical concept organization in artificial intelligence. For example, Schank (1980) speaks of a system of conceptual representation independent of language, whereby verbs are classified according to a set of primitive acts, which in turn requires a definition of noun-like objects that fulfill roles like agent, object, recipient, instrument, and so forth. In both producing and comprehending natural language, we are guided by the expectations that a given action primitive has in memory storage, and case grammar was at least one theory of syntax that had similar commitments to the notion of underlying semantic primitives. Thus, for example, an action like *put* requires both an agent and object, and even an obligatory locative; an action like *send* requires only an obligatory agent and object, with the locative and beneficiary as optional. The important point here is that in Kintsch's model of meaning in memory, as well as in discourse comprehension, it is the elemental set of meaningful propositions that we extract and store, not an elemental set of sentences. We do of course process sentence structure as well, and even remember stylistically or emotionally striking uses of surface structure verbatim, but it is the underlying informational content that we are really after, in the sense of the basic propositions.

Conversational partners in dialogues, as well as passive listeners to monologic discourse, are also very aware of the thematic structure of the discourse, so that after they manage to identify the incoming speech act and its content, they must then ascertain if there is anything in the working memory to which they can attach the old and new information coming in. Most utterances in discourse play on this theme of old and new, or **given information** vs. **new information** (Haviland and Clark 1974). The new information is that which the utterance brings to the exchange as being new and of value in expanding the discourse, while the old or given information is that which the hearer can already be expected to know. As the thematic structure develops, it relies on the fact that the given information is shared in common by both speaker and hearer. The new information is usually marked by some syntactic marker like the article *a* or an intonational feature like the heaviest stress in the sentence. Contrast, for example, the following English sentences with *the* and *a*.

1.   I walked in with a map.
2.   I walked in with the map.

When what I walked in with is characterized as *a map*, it is immediately perceived as new information, for this is not a map you have presumably seen before. If, however, it is reported as *the map*, then I as speaker and you as listener presumably already know something about this map, for it is not just any old map, but rather it is **the map**.

There are other devices too, as for example, the way that we keep track of what is already mentioned in coversations by the shift from proper names to pronouns, as in *she* from *Mrs. Vidmar*. In English, subjects not marked by *a* are usually the given information and the predicate the new information; the subject and predicate are often like topic (given) and comment (new). Fowler and Housum (1987) report that speakers shorten "old" words in monologs, while "new" words appearing for the first time are not attenuated. One result of this acoustic marking was that old words were also less intelligible than new words when presented in isolation. Listeners were thus able to identify words as old or new in the discourse, and used that information to integrate related material. If old words are repeats of earlier presented information, and no less identifiable in context, then this reduced acoustic signal may not only be more economical, but flags the fact that the word relates to something that was said earlier.

In investigating psychological subjects and predicates, Hornby (1972) found evidence for the notion that given information is what the sentence is about. He showed pairs of pictures to subjects, and then read them sentences about the pictures which were in fact wrong in one important feature. When he asked subjects to select pictures to match the mistaken sentence read to them, the errors revealed a pattern whereby subjects usually picked the picture showing the given information. Hornby's explanation is that subjects treat pictures like the themes in sentences, portraying the given information, and they do not expect to be misled by sentences which do not adhere to this principle. Hornby also tested for verification strategies in the relationships of the pictures to the erroneous sentences, by showing pictures which were true or false in respect to the sentence. The general results demonstrated that when the picture contradicts the new information, fewer errors occurred. But when the picture contradicted the given information, the error rate increased dramatically. Readers and hearers don't expect to have the given information contradicted or misrepresented, and the language does not support a strategy in which the slot fillers for the given information is out of line with the demands for informational cohesion as the discourse develops.

Other languages have their own devices which either signal given vs. new status, or focus on a specific piece of information, or both. For example, in Japanese one of the uses of the *wa* vs. *ga* particles is for given vs. new information.

1. Kotaka-sensei wa, ikanakatta desu ka? 'Didn't Professor Kotaka GO?'
2. Kotaka-sensei ga ikanakatta desu ka? 'Didn't PROFESSOR KOTAKA go?'

The Philippine language Tagalog has *ang* for given, but an *ang* + *ay* inversion will signal new information. Compare the following Tagalog sentences which convey the same content, but differ in terms of how they view that information in terms of focus and newness.

1. Matalino si Cory Aquino. 'Cory Aquino is intelligent.'
2. Si Cory Aquino ay ang matalino. 'The intelligent one is Cory Aquino.'

Information vs. Intention in Production and Perception

Earlier we observed that sentence comprehension requires us to extract the semantic and syntactic characteristics of the sentence, then to determine the meaning intended by the speaker, and finally, to retain these features in whole or in part in the permanent memory storage. In simplest terms, when we hear an utterance we try to determine what its content is and then decide what to do with it. In so doing, we must first of all process the utterance by identifying the speech act and determining its content both in speech act terms and in information transfer terms. Then we must check memory to see if there is anything there that matches that information in the utterance. And lastly, we must deal with both the new information and the speech act intention which tells us to do something with the utterance in a specific way. For example, *Do you think you could shut that door after you?* is an utterance which is really a command, and as such, requires its hearers to fulfill the command rather than answer a question about information regarding doors and one's purported ability to close them.

Thus, the objective of the production process is to turn out a set of speech forms for the thought that speaker wishes to convey. The objective of the comprehension process is to retrieve the speaker's intentions in constructing the production sequence by identifying the speech act. Both sides must take into consideration the fact that the process consists of a duality of function for language users, fulfilling both the needs for communicating intention as well as information.

The Force of Speech Acts

Intention is the speaker's underlying purpose when he or she produces an utterance. This is the basis of the development of **Speech Act Theory** in philosophy of language circles, with its notions of **speech acts** and **illocutionary acts** originating with Austin (1962) and elaborated by Searle (1969, 1976, 1977). The fundamental principle is that every sentence is designed to serve some function like to inform, to warn, to question, to demand, or to apologize. Every time we speak we expect to accomplish something by the act of speaking, hence the term "speech act". Each speech act has its **illocutionary force**, its real function or intended meaning in terms of the intention it was supposed to fulfill. Austin also spoke of **locutionary act**, the act of just saying something, but the actual utterance is merely the starting point for the really interesting analysis of what it means (illocutionary force) and what the speaker had hoped it might accomplish in terms of listener response (**perlocutionary force**). Perlocutionary force concerns the goal of the speech act and whether or not it has achieved its purpose. Purpose, or goal in the perlocutionary sense, has been the weak link in Speech Act Theory, however, and the least elaborated area for obvious reasons of lack of rigor in ascertaining the effectiveness of the range of speech acts. For example, in saying *He'll be leaving soon* to please the addressee, or in saying *Did you really think you did so badly?* as consolation or commiseration (instead of as a straight question) to soothe feelings over a poor exam performance, we uttered an assertion and a question, respectively; but our goal in a perlocutionary sense was really some specific effect on the listener! But it is difficult to deduce the actual perlocutionary effects of individual speech acts. The classification of speech acts is essentially a taxonomic question, whereas assessing their effects is a behavioral question, and philosophers of language are traditionally better at the first than the second. This particular difficulty, however, certainly does not stop advertising and public relations enterprises from continuing to use persuasive language to achieve some desired perlocutionary effect for their claims on the listening population at large (see Schmidt and Kess 1986). Very simply, they cannot persuade us by simply saying *I persuade you*, and so instead they employ all manner of more indirect language to achieve the same effect.

A Taxonomy of Direct Speech Acts

Many utterances are **direct speech acts**, utterances which have the same illocutionary force as the literal reading of the sentence. That is, a question really is a question, as in *Can you speak Japanese?* (contrast the 'non-question' *Can you pass me the salt?*). If illocutionary force is the purpose an utterance can be expected to convey to the listener, then the number of speech acts must be limited in both scope and variety, for there are only so many basic things speakers can do with a language. The range of uses of human language as an activity is neither infinite nor indeterminate; if this is so, we should be able to analyze and list the types of activity that we employ language for-- hence a taxonomy of speech acts (Searle 1977). But trying to characterize speech acts and then classify them reliably on the basis of easily recognized features is not always straightforward, even if the classes are limited. For example, Austin's original (1962) work only listed five types of speech acts which were as follows:

1.   **Verdictives** like *acquit/calculate/describe* which present evidence, reasons, or are evaluative of truth.
2.   **Exercitives** like *order/direct/nominate/appoint* which decide or advocate particular actions.
3.   **Commissives** like *promise/pledge/vow/swear* which commit the speaker to a particular action.
4.   **Expositives** like *affirm/deny/emphasize/illustrate* which elaborate on the speaker's views.
5.   **Behabitives** like *applaud/deplore/felicitate/congratulate* which provide reactions to the behavior of others.

However, the problem with speech acts is well illustrated by Austin's choices, which are the result of no particularly consistent or exact principles of classification. This has led some like Searle (1977) to reformulate the taxonomy of speech acts and others like Wunderlich (1980) to criticize the methodologies used in Speech Act Theory. Searle's (1977) classification also has five classes of speech acts, but they differ from Austin's considerably, in that the reformulation of the taxonomy of speech acts is based on twelve classificational principles which are subject to verification to reach agreement. Searle's five classes of speech acts, together with examples of their illocutionary force, are as follows:

1.   **Representatives** like *suggest/state/insist/swear/hint* which commit the speaker to the truth of some expressed proposition. Assertions like *John is a student* are typical of the representative class, and one can easily expand on the quality of the assertion by adding the appropriate representative-type compatible verb, as for example, adding *I suggest that/I state that/I insist that/I swear that/I hint that. . . .* to an assertion.

2.   **Directives** like *order/command/dare/desire* which attempt to have the listener do something. Questions, commands, and requests are all common types of directives.

3.   **Commissives** like *promise/vow/guarantee/pledge/threaten* commit the speaker to some future action.

4.   **Expressives** like *thank/apologize/deplore/congratulate* express the speaker's affective, psychological state on some matter.

5.   **Declarations** like *excommunicate/appoint/declare/christen*, as well as some uses of *suggest/state/insist* in formalized settings, bring into reality some new state of affairs noted in the propositional content of the declarative. For example, *I hereby appoint you Executor of this Will.* As can easily be seen in choosing examples, many of these declaratives seem to take place within specialized systems like legal, cultural, or religious activities. Examples like marriage vows, business contracts, and oaths of citizenship or allegiance pay great of attention to the actual wording, and the ramifications of such wording, if actually uttered.

Each category of speech acts conveys something from the speaker, but it may also require something on the part of the hearer. Austin (1962) may have said it best in describing such activities on the part of language users as "how to do things with words". The three most common speech acts in everyday discourse are **assertions, questions**, and **commands**. These three speech acts are so common in most languages that they are typically shortened in normal conversational practice. For example, sentences (1-3) are followed by the form in which they typically appear, that is, in their shortened version. We may also take the assertion as the syntactic starting point, the unmarked form, because the question and command must be marked by changes like interrogative words, deletion, or emphatic intonation.

1.   *I assert/declare to you that it is raining out*, typically shortened to *It is raining out.*

2.   *I ask you to tell me where the Safeway is*, typically shortened to *Tell me where the Safeway is.* And recall that the array of question types in a language is usually an extremely rich one; for example, in English, we have at least the following:

     a.   **echo questions** like *John is in the library?*, expressed by intonation contours.

     b.   **wh-questions** like *Where is John?*, signalled by a question word of the wh- type.

    c.   **yes/no questions** like *Are you going to the library?*.
    d.   **tag questions** like *You are going to the library, aren't you?*.
3.   *I command/order you to stand still*, typically shortened to *Stand still!*

Performatives . Some speech acts even have words telling you what speech act it is, as for example, **performative verbs** like *sentence, pronounce, bet, promise, appoint, nominate, bequeath.* Such verbs have a special place in the sentence, having the same frame in all instances, and they often have a special place in the society or culture that makes use of such performatives. These performatives are the clearest examples of things we do with words (to again use Austin's terms), of actions that can only be performed through language. You cannot bet or promise or announce anything without performing this activity through language, and it is in fact the saying that makes it so, and in the case of some performative verbs, makes it legally binding. In fact, there are often legal penalties if such utterances are not taken with the seriousness of purpose for which they were intended; for example, *I swear to tell the truth, the whole truth. . . .*

In English, the sentence pattern is *I...performative verb...you...sentence complement*, as in sentences like *I christen thee Joseph Anthony* or *I sentence you to twenty years hard labor.* One way of ascertaining whether the verb is a performative is to see whether the only way that an act can be performed is by saying the utterance itself. Another less satisfying method, suggested by Austin himself, is to test whether the word *hereby* can be inserted before the verb, as in *I sentence you/I hereby sentence you.*

Indirect Speech Acts

We have seen how direct speech acts are utterances in which a speaker utters a sentence and means exactly and literally what the surface form of the sentence suggests he or she is saying. For example, *Can you speak English?* is a question and is intended to be answered with a yes/no answer. It is not to be answered with a display of one's ability in the English language, as might be the response if the question were instead an **indirect speech act**, like *Can you say the word 'supercalifragilisticexpialidocious' for me?*. It is for this reason that although the utterance *Can you reach the salt* may look like a question, the appropriate response to this interrogatory doppelganger is not a yes/no answer, but to pass the salt over. **Indirect Speech Acts** are those expressed by sentences which have a literal reading other than the illocutionary force of the sentence, that is, utterances in which one illocutionary act is performed indirectly by way of producing another (Searle 1975). As in our examples above, some requests are performed by uttering what seems to be a question. An assertion like *Oh, I see your glass is empty* can really be a question like *Shall I give you a refill?*. Or an assertion like *Gee, I'm on a diet* is really a polite negation to the offer *Have a piece of cheesecake.*

We do not always say what we wish to say in the most direct fashion. For example, in the company of unfamiliars we might say something like *Would you mind terribly if I asked you to open the window?*, instead of *Hey, open that window!*. Both are directive requests, or commands, and both have the intention of seeing that window opened, but the first is literally a question while the second is literally a command. Yet both are commands in their underlying intent, in their true illocutionary force, but the first achieves this by being indirect in its appearance--hence the term "indirect speech act".

This fact of speech conveying a message other than its direct content is not unfamiliar to us. Think of the many situations of **phatic communication** in which empty utterances serve simply to establish communication channels. Recall the last time you made a trite observation like *Looks like it's raining out again* to someone standing next to you at a bus stop, or perhaps less wisely, ventured *Got a flat tire, eh?* to some flustered motorist at the side of the road. Such conversational gambits are informationally empty and pragmatically pointless in that they assert what is already known, and are simply indirect ways of opening a possible conversation channel.

The way in which indirect speech acts are organized can be different in other languages, as anyone who has learned another language will testify. And genetic relationships are no guarantee that the organizational values of indirect speech acts will be the same in related languages. For example, although English and Norwegian are both members of the Germanic language family, our indirect commands may be interpreted as weak desiderative forms while their imperatives may be considered too direct by our reckoning. Similarly, Serbo-Croatian and Czech are both Slavic languages, but Serbo-Croatian is more like English in its deployment of indirectness.

Different words or constructions may be substituted because of politeness and formality conventions; for example, there are all sorts of variations on commands to close the door, ranging from impolite to polite. Sentences (1-3) below probably verge on the impolite, while (4-7) seem to move up the politeness gradient.

1. Open the door!
2. I want you to open the door!
3. Do open that door!
4. Would you mind opening the door?
5. Could you open the door?
6. Won't you open the door?
7. Can you open the door?"

The actual ranking of these is somewhat subjective, but we are certainly aware of social values in terms of who gets what and what is actually being conveyed in the social interaction. Kemper and Thissen (1981) have given us evidence that the level of politeness has a memory effect when that politeness level violates conversational conventions. Introducing the factor of social status level into the equation, they found that subjects could accurately recall polite requests which came from high-status speakers, but not when they came from low-status speakers. The implication is that it is appropriate and in keeping with the social role of high-status speakers to issue more direct requests, while it would be impolite for low-status speakers to do so. Thus, that which is expected (namely, indirectness and politeness) from lower status speakers is not unusual, and is not particularly prone to being registered in the startling verbatim quality that directness and impoliteness might be from the same low-status speaker. Conversely, as expected, the subjects did not accurately remember impolite requests from high-status speakers, but they certainly did from low-status speakers.

Responding to Indirect Speech Acts . Deciding how to respond to indirect speech acts is the other side of the conversation. After all, in hearing an utterance we must first decide whether it is to be taken directly or indirectly, and having done that, we must then decide what its indirect meaning is in order to plan our verbal response (see H. Clark 1979). For example, take the utterance *Is Julia at home?*. One can take such an utterance at literal face value, that is, as a question; or one can take it as an indirect request, with responses of either a one-part or two-part nature. Depending upon which of these is meant, we try to decide among the following responses.

1.   Response to a literal question: *Yes, she is/No, she isn't.*
2.   One-part response to indirect request: *I'll get her/Just a minute/Hold on a second.*
3.   Two-part response to indirect request: *Yes, she is--I'll go get her.*

Clark observes that the one-part answers respond to the single possible meaning alone, while the two-part responses answer the literal question with the first part and the possible indirect request with the second part. It is worth recalling that a verbal response is quite necessary; you cannot get away by giving no response at all, for questions and requests literally demand responses. But there does seem to be some explanation for how indirect speech acts are actually understood, and how we decide upon what our actual verbal responses will be. The responses given above are answer to the question, information about the response to the command, answer to the question followed by information about the response to the command, respectively (H. Clark 1979:439). The way of interpreting the indirect speech act, and then producing the correct response, is related to the seriousness of the literal meaning and the uncertainty of its meaning. For example, *How are you?* is hardly likely to be taken seriously as a real question, and thus the standard pro forma response to its typical usage as a greeting is what is likely to be elicited. Uncertainty of meaning is another matter. In an experiment involving a telephone survey, merchants reponding to questions over the telephone split on their responses to being asked *Do you accept credit cards?*. They essentially had to guess at whether the caller meant the question literally, or wanted more information (like a

list of credit cards accepted), and thus their responses reflect their com-
putation of probabilities of which was intended. Essentially, the merchants in Clark's sample, like the rest of us, rely on several informational sources in assessing what is likely to be meant, in order to plan
one's responses.

Among these may be counted the conventionality of both form and
means, special markers (like *please* signalling a command), the transparency of the indirect meaning as opposed to the implausibility of the
literal meaning, and lastly, the speaker's imputed plans and goals.
Gibbs (1981) has given us an idea of how conventional some forms are,
by further investigating Clark's (1979) conventions of means and form
as they interact with context in interpreting the nature of indirect
requests. By the convention of means we refer to the way in which an
indirect request can be performed. English speakers typically question
whether another has the ability to do the activity that is being requested. For example, we might typically ask for a window to be closed by
querying whether the other person is capable of doing it, with such
phrases as *Can you close that window?* or the more oblique *Do you
think you could close that window?*. The convention of form, on the
other hand, refers to how commonly a given form is used to convey an
indirect request. For example, of the following two sentences, the first
is the more likely to be issued as an indirect request though the second
may also see some occasional use.

1.   Can you open the window?
2.   Is it possible for you to open the window?

Gibbs predicted that the more conventional a request was, the easier it should be to find an appropriate interpretation, and his subjects
did indeed take less time to comprehend and judge paraphrases for conventional indirect requests in conversational contexts. Unconventional
indirect requests took longer to comprehend and make paraphrase
judgments for. Gibbs also had his subjects generate their own indirect
requests for a number of common everyday scenarios from everyday
life. He found that there are a limited number of conventions by which
indirect requests can be realized, and that subjects are very sensitive to
what is conventionally appropriate in given contexts.

Indirect Speech Acts in Isolation and in Discourse Context. There is
some interesting experimental evidence that demonstrates how ultimately what we are interested in is the underlying speech act intention
of the utterance. Clark and Lucy (1974) found in general that indirect
meanings take longer to process than direct meanings, exactly what we
might expect from a simple computational model point of view. That
is, we analyze the incoming sentences for their structure and for what
that structure might usually convey in a direct speech act interpretation (that is, x usually means y). But if this does not fit for some reason, we then compute the other possible indirect interpretations (x usually does mean y, but in this particular circumstance and for this
particular reason, x really means q).

But they also found that the underlying meaning of the utterance has an effect on processing. Similar to what we have seen with negatives in studies of negation in sentence comprehension, negative speech act requests take longer when they are indirect speech acts. And more importantly, Clark and Lucy report that this also happens when the real meaning of the indirect speech act is negative in nature. For example, if you consider the utterance, *Can you open the door?*, you will note that it is really positive, and means *Do go open the door!*. On the other hand, *Must you open the door?* is really negative, and means *Don't go open the door!*. Yet both sentences look superficially positive. In a test in which subjects were to judge whether or not a picture satisfied a request, subjects took .3 seconds longer to judge the underlyingly negative sentences with *must* than they did the underlyingly positive sentences with *can*.

But this is even more dramatically demonstrated when the superficial positive format of the sentence contradicts the real underlying negative meaning. The finding here was that the real underlying meaning of the sentence is what we ultimately process for. It is this underlying illocutionary force, in terms of the real discourse intention of the speaker, that hearers actively process the input for; its complexity may be what ultimately is responsible for levels of processing complexity. Despite their surface markings, the indirect speech act *Why not open the door?* is really positive, meaning *Open the door!*; but *Why open the door?* is really negative, meaning *Don't open the door!*. Despite the surface structure appearance of a negative, the first sentence was processed more quickly (.3 seconds) than the second underlyingly negative one.

We are typically required to evaluate incoming pieces of the discourse on several levels. At the very least we have to analyze the actual syntactic format of the sentence to make sure that the underlying illocutionary meaning of that piece of syntax is the same as the literal reading of the sentence. But it is the intended meaning we are after, and indirect meanings are common, so it is not unusual to proceed from the first to the second level of discourse analysis. There is some evidence from Gibbs (1979) on contextual information in this interpretation process. In using contexts for some sentences, Gibbs investigated the question of how quickly such indirect meanings are computed when in contextual surroundings. Clark and Lucy had of course found that in general indirect requests took longer to process than when the sentences were direct requests with a literal reading of request. However, since these findings were derived from experimental tasks with sentences in isolation, the embedding of such sentences in context might provide a different set of results. And they did, for in context subjects did as well or better with extracting the intended meaning of indirect request. Preceding context provided sufficient information to either give, or allow to be inferred, a thematic structure which allowed subjects to proceed directly to the intended meaning of the utterance, even if it was cast in an indirect form of speech. It makes sense, on the basis of such results, to assume that we do not always need to process the literal reading of an utterance before arriving at the intended reading. In the context of story settings, the indirect request *Must you open the window?* takes no longer to comprehend than its direct request analogue *Do not open the window!*.

It is worth noting, however, that Gibbs did replicate the Clark and Lucy findings for sentences in isolation, for it did take subjects longer to understand indirect requests than it did literal requests, when these utterances stood in isolation. But with sufficient story context, indirect meanings were no problem at all, and do not support the hypothesis that we first compute the literal meaning of an utterance before we derive its intended meaning from an indirect form. This, by the way, is also what Glucksberg, Gildea, and Bookin (1982) found for metaphor, namely, that they are understood without having to first go through the literal interpretation of the metaphor. Such evidence suggests that discourse factors effect an immediate semantic interpretation for literal, indirect, and metaphoric sentences.

Conventions, Conversational Postulates, and Conversational Implicatures

Utterances in conversations abide by a set of shared conventions that we are all aware of and adhere to as speakers and hearers. Such conventions may be implicit rules, but they are nonetheless rules we expect to be followed. We assume that the discourse rules are being followed, but always check to see if other channels like context, nonverbal behavior, and so forth match this expectation. Much of the impetus for looking at discourse as employing a set of conversational postulates, with corresponding conversational implicatures, comes from Grice's (1975) lectures on logic in conversation. Conversational exchanges are not normally just a succession of unconnected remarks, but are best viewed in the abstract, as cooperative efforts in the ideal sense. Ideally, conversational partners expect one another to be truthful, informative, relevant, and clear.

This means that each participant recognizes in their discourse contributions a common purpose or set of purposes, or at the very least, a mutually accepted direction in the way the conversation is laid out both in its structure and in its underlying intention. One must remember that we are speaking of the ideal, the abstract goal of any and all conversations. This means that we are speaking of the first level of priorities. It is of course true that some conversations may not actually work this way, not corresponding to the ideally projected format and goals of cooperative conversations. For example, you can lie and deceive your conversational partner in some actual conversation, but note that the only reason you can lie and deceive people is because in some ideal sense they expect you **not** to do so. That is neither the reason people converse nor how!

At each stage of the conversational development, some conversational moves are acceptable, while others are quite unacceptable or unsuitable in either their format or their intent. Grice has put such idealized notions together in a package he termed the **Cooperative Principle**, which goes as follows:

Make your conversational contribution such as is required, at the
stage at which it occurs, by the accepted purpose or direction of the
talk exchange in which you are engaged.

Essentially, what the cooperative principle says is that parties
assume that each person in the conversation means what he or she is
saying and is speaking with a purpose. One can extract from the cooperative principle four maxims:

1.   Maxim of Quality
2.   Maxim of Quantity
3.   Maxim of Relation
4.   Maxim of Manner

The **maxim of quality** essentially demands that we are truthful,
and that our contribution is one of sufficient quality to merit being
included in the conversation. The contribution should be true, and
ideally we do not say that which is false or which we believe to be
false. Similarly, we do not venture forth with that which we lack adequate evidence for. Examples of flouting the maxim of quality can be
seen in irony, metaphor, meiosis, and hyperbole. In irony, the listener
knows, or comes to realize, that what the speaker is saying is not really the case, and thus the other meaning emerges, as it did in Mark
Anthony's eulogy over Julius Caesar and *honorable men*. Metaphor
characteristically involves categorical falsity, so that there is a contra-
dictory quality to what the speaker is saying; since the statement cannot possibly have such a meaning, it must have another, as in *You are
the light of my life*. Metaphor, incidentally, is an intellectual path
through which we humans explore new paths or analogize in order to
better understand unfamiliar concepts; metaphoric extensions take
advantage of the plasticity of the human mind, and much learning
takes place through metaphor. Meiosis essentially means "too little"
and hyperbole "too much"; by such under- and overstatement the
speaker usually achieves another meaning, as in *He was a "little" out
of it that night!* and *They gave "mile-high" ice cream cones to the kids
at the birthday party*.

The **maxim of quantity** expects that we be succinct, but complete,
providing as much information as needed, but not more than is
required for the purposes of the exchange. Making the contribution
more informative than is required is a waste of time, if perceived as
unnecessarily and overly informative; more often it is just confusing in
that it is liable to raise other issues because the hearer will be misled
into thinking that there is some particular point to the information
excess. Some, of course, use language purposely this way, as a smokes-
creen, throwing out all sorts of verbiage just to cloud the original point.
The reason it can be effective is because of our expectations according
to the maxim of quantity.

One can err in the other direction, perhaps purposely, in giving too
little information. Thus, a recommendation for a lecturing position in
linguistics may not be well served by a letter of recommendation which
says:

> Mr. Blatnik is a fluent speaker of both English and Slovene, and
> he reads German very well.

As a letter of recommendation, this is far too short and uninformative, and from the perspective of the **maxim of relation**, says little indeed about his abilities in the matter of linguistic analysis. The implication, of course, is that although the letter says only good things, one cannot say enough on the true point at hand to write what is a really "good" letter of recommendation. Hence this must be taken as a poor letter of reference!

Into such violations of the maxim of quantity may also be put those tautologies like *Boys will be boys!/All's fair in love and war!/That's the way the cookie crumbles!*, all of which are totally uninformative. Because of their empty value as conversational contributions, they are rightly interpreted as pre-closings or signals that a new topic is in order. The maxim of relevance demands that we be relevant, and make our contribution bear directly on the issue at hand in the conversational exchange. That is why a letter of reference like the following would be even more devastating than the above example.

> Mr. Blatnik can type 63 words a minute in English, Slovene and
> German.

Lastly, the **maxim of manner** relates to how the information must be expressed, requiring that it be presented clearly and concisely. One is expected to be brief and orderly, avoiding purposeful ambiguity and obscurity of expression. For example, purposeful, deliberate ambiguity is one way of flouting the maxim of manner. In uttering lure remarks like *I think his paintings lack a little daring* or *His exams may be a little too hard*, the speaker intends the listener to see the possibility of two subtlely related meanings. We then ask what would make the speaker go out of his or her way to make this conversational contribution. The answer is that the utterances can be taken as either a statement of opinion, or more likely, as lure remarks intended to encourage conspiratorial criticism.

Others have added to Grice's conversational postulates by suggesting that rules like *Be polite!* and *Be idiomatic!* also guide our conversational contributions. For example, Leech's (1977) **tact maxim** suggests that the more tactful a directive is, the more indirect and circumlocutionary it will be, while Lakoff's (1973) **rules of politeness** suggest that we typically avoid imposing, give options, and in general, attempt to make the listener feel good. We also speak idiomatically, or colloquially, unless we wish to convey another meaning by not doing so (see Searle 1975). In saying *Knowest thou him who calleth himself John Paul Smith?* or *Is it the case that you at present have the ability to reach over and convey the salt cellar to your table partner?*, we usually confer a meaning over and above the words by not being colloquial. Whether or not these can also claim the status of conversational maxims is open to question, but they are part of our constellation of conversational strategies. The activity known as conversation is to be viewed as a rational and purposeful type of behavior. We observe conversational maxims with the ideal understanding that, all other things being equal, the purpose of conversation is to achieve a maximally effective exchange of information.

However, all other things are not usually equal, and the abstraction and the reality are not always the same. A conversational partner may decide not to fulfill a maxim, and in so doing, expects that the real meaning will be quickly grasped by the hearer because the maxim has so obviously been flouted or ignored. The real meaning is then obtained by implication, but it must be able to be worked out by the listener. One might take our example of the letter of reference and go through the likely sequence by which the appropriate conversational implicatures have been made (paraphrasing Grice 1975:50). Recall that we have received a letter of recommendation which says that *Mr. Blatnik is a fluent speaker of both English and Slovene, and he reads German very well.* Now we know that although the originator of the letter has said this complimentary thing about Blatnik, we also realize that this is far too short a letter of reference, and a bit off the mark about abilities as an analyst of language, a teacher of the discipline, his possible contributions to the smooth running of a department, and his personability as a colleague. Now there is no reason to suppose that he has failed to realize the obvious violation of the maxims, and that he would not be doing this unless he thought something more or something other about Blatnik's suitability. Certainly, the originator knows all this, and furthermore, knows that I know that he knows; he expects that I can see the supposition that he also expects that something other than his "complimentary" sentence is required. Yet he has done nothing to stop me from thinking that something is awry here, and in so doing, he has in fact implied that something else is the real message. Very simply, it may very well be true, and indeed to his credit, that Blatnik can speak English and Slovene fluently, and even read German very well, but as far as hiring him, the **conversational implicature** is clear--forget it!

Criticisms and Modifications of the Gricean Principle . The Gricean insights regarding the nature of conversation and implicature are obviously only a starting point for us to think about discourse in a functional way. Some have specifically addressed shortcomings in Grice's account of how conversational implicatures are actually made by listeners. For example, linguists like Wilson and Sperber (1986) have focussed on **relevance** in an attempt to formalize exactly how it is that implicatures are constructed. They offer a formal account of the implicational process by relying on a deductive logical model to achieve this, but place emphasis only on relevance in contextual assumptions and the probabilities that can be attached to the possible inferences drawn from them. Because the problems in establishing mutual knowledge are enormous, they try to avoid appealing to such assumptions by instead assuming that speakers try to be as relevant as possible in a given situation. Speakers rely on the listener's search for relevance, knowing that it is the task of the listener to recover new information that is relevant and that can be integrated with old information. This new information may strengthen a tentative assumption the listener has, or it may combine with existing assumptions to produce new ones; or it may weaken, contradict, or even destroy that assumption. To paraphrase, it is not enough to recover information that you did not have before; you must be able to relate this new information to what you already know or believe to be true. You must establish that it is relevant!

The Wilson and Sperber approach is clearly a linguistic approach in that it extends Chomskyan principles to a clearly pragmatic arena, but with an important difference. Propositions are treated as psychological representations, and not just logical objects (see Blakemore 1988). They would maintain that psychologically real deductive processes do indeed play a key role in the recovery of implicatures, and that such a theory of relevance makes specific claims about the constructive role of implicatures in comprehension. Relevance thus becomes a matter of degree, reflecting the fact that the more cognitive effect a utterance has, the more relevant it is.

Computational scientists like Wilks (1986) and psychologists like Gibbs (1987) also offer a different view of Grice's much-quoted insight about understanding being a matter of inference from not only what is said, but from what is assumed. Neither Wilks nor Gibbs believe that an objectively correct set of propositions can be assumed to exist independently (and with any value) of the speaker's and listener's belief sets. Mutual knowledge, according to Gibbs, is not only a result of comprehension, but is in fact a prerequisite for it. And speakers and listeners must coordinate what they mutually know in order to truly comprehend utterances. Wilks would even extend this to their beliefs about one another's belief sets. For example, doctors and patients talking to one another typically have different ideas about where the stomach actually is. The doctor accommodates the belief that the patient is likely to have about where the stomach is, a folk anatomical belief which does not entirely coincide with medical belief. The point is that in order to carry on efficient discourse with the patient, the physician must both recognize and accommodate to the erroneous belief held by the patient as they discuss the location of feelings of discomfort in the patient's "stomach".

Gibbs (1987) has demonstrated that we do indeed employ mutual knowledge in formulating our questions in conversations. This means that speakers and hearers must assume a common mental model for the knowledge and beliefs shared in the conversation; such a mental model explains how speakers frame their questions in the light of the mutual knowledge that exists between speaker and listener, and then how listeners answer them. Gibbs had subjects read short scenarios with two or more characters, and had subjects choose from among three alternative questions the one that best fit the context. For example, read the following short description of events, and then pick the question which is best suited to the scenario given.

Bob and Ann are eagerly waiting for a weekend visit from their
friend, Ken, who is supposed to arrive in time for dinner on Friday
evening at a local restaurant. On Friday morning, however, Ken
phones Ann at work and tells her he will not be arriving in town until
Saturday morning due to engine problems with his car. Ann phones
Bob at work and leaves a message with a co-worker, Sally, for Bob
concerning Ken's delay. Later on Ann runs into Sally who says that
she gave Bob the message. That evening when Ann and Bob meet at
home Ann says to him. . .

1.   Do you still want to go out to dinner with me tonight?
2.   Did you find out that Ken won't arrive until tomorrow?
3.   Shall we go out even though Ken won't arrive until tomorrow?

In this case, Ann and Bob both know that Ken is not arriving in
town for dinner tonight, and both also know that the other knows. The
correct choice in this case is sentence (1), and this is the alternative
that subjects picked significantly more often than the others. The scenarios were manipulated to depict different degrees of mutual knowledge between the two main characters, and the other two questions
were significantly chosen in accord with such manipulations of mutual
knowledge in the scenarios.
    Others like Wierzbicka (1986) have argued that the potential ambi-
guity of an utterance as one or another speech act is not problematic.
We assign the illocutionary meaning of incoming speech easily and
accurately, and on the basis of unmistakable linguistic clues, not
according to vague conventions of usage or conversational implicatures.
Even without resorting to intonation as an explanatory feature, there
are many language-specific linguistic indicators of well-defined illocutionary force. For example, there are English function words like *still/
therefore/although* with the illocutionary force of *I insist that/I conclude
that/I concede that* (Austin 1962; see Wierzbicka 1986:97). Although
it may be true that many such illocutionary forces cannot be stated by
single speech act verbs (for example, as assertions can be by *assert*),
the illocutionary force can be fully and unambiguously stated by means
of feature-like meaning components. And "it is surely part of the work
of the linguist who wants to describe English to say what this meaning
is (1986:74)," by posing for each construction a minimal set of components which will jointly account for all the aspects of its use. For
example, declarative sentences with tag questions of the opposite polar-
ity, like sentence (1), exhibit the illocutionary force that follows in
numbers (2) through (5).

1.   Maria is Italian, isn't she?
2.   I think that X
3.   I don't want to say that I know that this is right
4.   I want you to say that it is right or that it isn't right
5.   I assume you will say that it is right

On the other hand, for matching polarities on the tag questions, the tag is typically an echo of the earlier speaker's utterance, as in the utterance *Sally is pregnant, is she!*.

However, such matching tag questions can also be used to solicit confirmation of one's interpretation, as in (1) below. The corresponding meaning components of the illocutionary force can be stated in the following sequence numbered (2) to (5).

1.   You're going to pieces, are you!
2.   I think that X, because of what you say
3.   I am not sure if this is right
4.   I assume it is right
5.   I want you to say that it is right or that it isn't

Textual and Conversational Cohesion

Discourse is coherent if its parts relate to one another. This cohesion has been formally explained by describing the coherence relations between propositions; one or more macro-themes set the entire discourse episode, and sub-themes bridge the gaps between sections in the discourse. The semantic structure of texts can thus be described at two levels, a local micro-level and a more global macro-level (Kintsch and van Dijk 1978). In van Dijk's (1977a) terms, these larger macro-themes are usually called **macrostructures**, the overall main theme of the discourse and its sub-themes, while the **microstructures** are the actual propositions expressed by the sentences of the text, and their relations. Any proposition derived from more than one proposition is a macroproposition. A macrostructure characterizes the overall meaning of the discourse as a whole, while a microstructure refers to the structure of individual propositions and their relationships to other microstructures within the discourse. Both contribute to the realization of the overall thematic structure. In processing a piece of discourse, comprehension requires that we reduce all the propositions to their basic informational content, and then sort them into the higher-level sets of macropropositions in order to ascertain how they relate to the higher-level organizational units. This assignment to more abstract, higher-level topics allows us to organize the mass of micro-details into memory.

The basic assumption here is that discourse has a structure to it, and that this discourse structure is not necessarily shown by the words or sentences in it. In fact, much discourse rarely has identifying signals of this type. We know that some text formats, like books, have structure, in which the various pieces are organized into a hierarchical progression by a set of conventions which delineate one part from another. For example, the typical indexical subdivision for a book like this one usually goes as follows:

1.   chapter

2.   section
3.   subsection
4.   paragraph
5.   sentence

We might well ask whether discourse formats like conversation also have a structure similar to this one, and whether there are behavioral conventions for both the content of the conversational contributions and when to make them by claiming, utilizing, and then relinquishing conversational turns.

Conversational Cohesion

If discourse is any unit of language beyond the sentence, then **conversation** is any discourse which is produced by more than one person. And while discourse broadly includes both dialogues and monologues, either written or spoken, conversation more narrowly refers to just spoken dialogues (see Schiffrin 1988). Speakers and hearers engaged in talking to one another are in fact fact **constructing** the conversation; they create joint meanings and coordinate conversationally relevant acts.

Conversation is thus sensitive to considerations of cohesion, and when a given contribution is not in step with the ongoing conversation, that turn has a disruptive effect on the conversation. Since conversations are linear, cohesion is shown in the sequential cohesion of a contribution dependent upon the preceding contributions. Such cohesive turns are taken for granted, in much the same way that a series of moves constitute a properly executed game. Only when one is out of order and inappropriate do we notice that the property of cohesion is marred. Language is no different in this respect, and can also be considered a game, a set of exchanges with definable and regular properties; a non-cohesive conversation takes place when these rules for ongoing contributions have been in some way violated.

An excellent example of this is offered by Vuchinich (1977), who demonstrates that if a norm necessary for conversational stability is violated, this infraction results in the breakdown of the interaction or its being marked as very special indeed. While waiting for a purported sociology experiment, a subject and a confederate were told to "get acquainted" before the experiment was to begin. However, the confederate had been trained to give non-cohesive turns in a normal intonation, and with a normal set of body postures, as if everything was in order. The subject responses exhibited a systematic regularity in the way in which they exhibited their extreme sensitivity to non-cohesive turns. Such responses included the following conversational features in the turns taken by subjects after an incoherent turn by the experimental confederate.

1.   Remedy sequence which tries to repair possible misunderstandings and offenses during the conversational flow; for example, saying *Huh?/ What?/What do you mean?*.

2.   Latency in which the gaps of silence as noticeable events indicate the listener's preoccupation with "trying to figure out" the previous speaker's turn.
3.   Topic Reference Effects which indicate the listener's attempt to deal with the speaker's odd contribution as a new topic by one of four mechanisms.

    a.   Focus: the previous topic is dropped and the non-cohesive turn is focussed upon as the new topic.
    b.   Die: the previous topic is dropped and some new topic, unrelated to both the previous topic and the non-cohesive turn, is adopted.
    c.   Ride: the old topic is continued on and the new non-cohesive turn is simply ignored.
    d.   Contribute: the non-cohesive turn is incorporated into the previous topic somehow, being made out to be an actual contribution to it.

4.   Immediate Internal Reaction in which the listener actively thinks to himself or herself that "something is very wrong here!". Needless to say, such conversations, if peppered with bizarre conversational non-sequiturs, are ones we try to exit from as quickly as we can.

Denials . A discourse view of sentence production places many previous facts of sentence comprehension into better perspective. As an example, recall that affirmative sentences are generally easier to process that negative sentences, but that one of the uses of the negative was to connected to discourse cohesion. Wason (1965) explained that one of the uses of the negative is in the context of plausible denial, that is, denying or negating something that is likely in the situation, but which does not materialize as such. In such instances when we use a negative to describe an exception to one's expectations, the negative is processed with the same ease (or even more quickly) than an affirmative sentence is. For example, sentences like *It is not raining*, when it usually is, and *The train is not on time*, when it usually is, can be processed as quickly as affirmatives, given these contextual surroundings. And this is of course a matter of discourse cohesion affected by pragmatic constraints.

Even regular negatives, outside the special circumstances of the context of plausible denial, often have some relationship to the expectations of the developing discourse. In general, negatives seem to cancel the assertion a sentence makes, specifically by negating the new information and leaving the given information intact in the overall assertion. However, there is some evidence (Givon 1978) that negatives do more than just cancel the given information. Givon's work suggests that negative sentences elicit different assumptions from the listener, and commensurate with Wason's work, function to correct false beliefs. For example, contrast the different responses to the following pair of sentences, positive and negative.

1.   We saw a movie last night.   Response: Oh! That's nice!

2.   We didn't see a movie last night.   Response: Oh! Were you
      supposed to?

Conversational Turn-Taking

The facts of conversational turn-taking parallel the way in which cohesion is achieved by conversational partners. The notion of turn-taking is common in other ordered systems like games and traffic, even language activities like debates and ceremonies, and looking at conversations as a rule-ordered language game has allowed us to grasp much about how the flow of conversational discourse is actually organized. In real conversations, in which speakers turn out hundreds of syllables per minute, there have to be rules that govern such a fluid activity in daily exchanges. In contrast to when we have to stand and give a monologue, most of us encounter little difficulty in exhibiting a high degree of fluency when engaged in natural conversational exchanges where all the turn-taking clues are present and the content is established by the ongoing thematic development. Indeed, we often seem to be more conscious of matters of conversational strategy and interpersonal turn-taking conduct than we are about matters of syntactic construction and even vocabulary choices. The reason that we achieve such fluency is because many exchanges, and the rough outline of many longer exchanges in a conversational sense, are ritualized speech events, in which the alternative forms of expression are highly restricted. For example, there are many exchanges which are simple two-part ritual exchanges, **adjacency pairs** or utterance pairs in which an utterance by one speaker requires a particular type of response by the listener (see Goffman 1976; Sacks, Schegloff and Jefferson 1974; Schegloff 1968). Among these may be included paired sequences like the following.

1.   complaint followed by apology
2.   summons followed by answer
3.   invitation followed by acceptance
4.   compliment followed by acknowledgement
5.   greeting followed by a different, but complementary greeting

The ritual element of such pairs can be seen in the social expectation which compels us to answer a summons like *Could you tell me the time?*. Most of us reply, and readily, even with the strangest of strangers. In fact, contrary to what transformational grammar has claimed about most sentences being novel in some way, it would appear that many sentences are really recurrent patterns of discourse structure. There are indeed truly novel sentences, but thousands of such clauses are probably memorized and stored in long-term memory, to be retrieved as wholes and used at appropriate moments. And, of course, some patterns see particularly heavy use in generating both the novel and not so novel sentences.

An excellent example of this can be seen in Manes and Wolfson's (1981) report on the amazingly limited range of compliment formulas in English. Quite the opposite of being highly original and innovative, it would appear that compliments are instead severely constrained in both their structure and lexical content. When one thinks of what is at stake here, this is not particularly surprising; for in giving a compliment one wants to ensure that it is received as just that, without possible mistaken interpretations. And sometimes the compliment is so ritualized that there is a typical single phrase, which does service for practically all such encounters, as with the Japanese *Gochisoo-sama desita*, literally 'It was a feast', but more like 'It was a wonderful meal'. Such a discourse fixture serves us well in many instances, even when the 'feast' was just a cup of coffee; the point is that it ensures we have made the appropriate contribution at that point in the discourse.

Many longer exchanges in a conversational sense operate according to some rough, but generally accepted outline. The rigorous notions of structure are not left at the level of simple pairs of utterances like adjacency pairs. Indeed, many conversations operate on the basis of a general formula that looks something like the following:

1.   Give greetings
2.   Transact the business at hand
3.   Issue a farewell

But it is rare that in conversations we come right to the point of the business at hand, saying what we mean and meaning what we say. Anyone who has indulged in even the most casual of conversations knows that this is just simply not so. There are entry and exit rules here as well, and what we say and when follows patterned guidelines as well. Say, for example, that we wanted to borrow something from neighbor X. Chances are that as we phone the neighbor, we first exchange the usual greetings and pleasantries, slowly getting to the heart of our conversational intent. Finally we get to the point, saying something like, *Oh, by the way, do you still have that new lawnmower you showed me last time I was over? Do you think I could borrow it on Saturday?*. Mission accomplished, we continue to exchange a few conversational pleasantries, provide ourselves with an exit by saying, *Well, I'll let you get back to your television program*, or whatever other activity our telephone partner was involved in when we first called. Such information, obtained early in the discourse, is recycled as we make our way out of the discourse, purporting to be attentive to the listener's needs.

The general sequence in our example above was greetings, followed by business, and then capped off by farewell. But even within the final phase of the conversational progression, we might look at the structure of conversational closings, for conversations do not end abruptly. Rather they come to a close by **pre-closings**, in which the partipants signal that it is time to end (Schegloff and Sacks 1973). The current turn-taker may utter something like *well/OK/yeah/soooo* with a drawn-out intonation, or perhaps even an empty observation like *It'll work out for the best, things always do.* This essentially passes the turn back to the listener after an empty turn. The new turn-taker now has the opportunity of initiating a new topic, and thus a new set of turns, or the new speaker can take the hint and close out too. In fact, as we opened the conversation, either in person or over the phone, we probably already gathered thematic material for our closing by asking questions like *What're you doing?/What're you reading?/What're you working on?/What're you watching (on TV)?.* Then, when it is time to close, we can always refer to the other party's interests in seemingly altruistic gestures (see Lakoff 1973), and close out by saying *Well, I'll let you get back to your books now* or *You're probably missing the best part of your program.*

The non-verbal cues for turn-taking have been nicely captured by Duncan (1969, 1972) and Duncan and Fiske (1985). There are behavioral clues of a non-verbal, vocal type, as well as kinesic and postural clues, that signal what the speaker-state is. For example, when there is a shift from being an auditor (hearer) to speaker, the new speaker marks this shift by at least one of two cues, either shifting the head direction away from one pointing directly at the conversational partner, initiating gesticulation (tensing the musculature of the body, finger-pointing, thrusting the head forwards, and so on), or both. Similarly, there are cues for yielding a turn, which can be recognized in unfilled pauses, termination of gesticulation motions, relaxation of body posture, change in intonation contour (with a terminal juncture other than a sustaining terminal juncture; see Kess 1976c:137), decrease in amplitude or loudness, or the use of empty stereotyped expressions. Any, or all of these, in conjunction with the completion of a grammatical sentence, can elicit a move to take the conversational turn by the auditor.

And even the hearer must signal a less than passive participation by what Duncan has termed the auditor back-channel signals. These do not constitute a speaking turn as such, nor are they a claim of turn, but they are issued at regular intervals to signal that we are there and actively listening. For example, as auditors we typically give out back-channel signals like head-nods, brief requests for clarification (*You mean x?*), brief re-statements of the speaker's own wording (*I bought a station wagon* mirrored by the auditor saying *a station wagon, eh?*), and sentence completions which anticipate the obvious phrasal completion by the speaker. Very commonly, one singly or doubly inserts fillers like *mm-hhmmm/uh-huh/yeah/right/yes/I see/that's true.* Such fillers are found across many languages, and this author can recall having overhead a lengthy Japanese conversation on a subway, in which one conversational partner did nothing but provide the appropriate back-channel signals to keep the conversation very much alive. Perhaps the important thing to be learned from back-channel signals is that conversational discourse is actively produced by the cooperation of both parties, and we are reminded of this at every turn, in the abstract ideal underlying the cooperative principle, the notions of conversational cohesion, and even the verbal signals given off to indicate that we are attentive and eager to participate when our turn comes again.

Similarly, Keller (1981) has written of discourse **gambits** that speakers may use to introduce what they are about to say. Such gambits also play a role in acting as conversational signals which introduce level shifts in the conversation or prepare listeners for directional changes in the logical development of the argument. As Keller points out, in looking at discourse from a psycholinguistic point of view, such gambits are verbal signals which can be used on several levels of conversational strategy. They can be semantic introducers, framing the topic about to be introduced into the conversation; for example, personal opinion introduced by *The way I look at it. . . .*, or a piece of unpleasant realism with *Whether we like it or not. . . ..* A gambit may also signal the speaker's state of consciousness, as in saying *I'd like to hear all about it*, to denote readiness to receive information. In signalling social contexts, such gambits can be used to either pass or gain turns, as for example, in using *Well, what you do think of it?* to pass off an unwanted turn. And lastly, some gambits can fulfill the metadiscourse role of monitoring whether the conversation is really going where it was intended to go, as for example, in asking *What I've been telling you all night is. . . ..* Indeed, such gambits are common in conversational discourse, as well as in some written texts, with metalinguistic markers commenting on the progress of the discourse or text. Discourse allows such metacommentary in a way that sentential organization does not.

Attention and Selective Listening

Discourse and other conversations swirl about us, so that much daily activity involves selective listening. We pay attention to certain messages, tuning out environmental noises and other messages, perhaps even tuning out the conversation we are in. The intelligibility of messages goes down if two messages arrive simultaneously, instead of one right after the other. But comprehension of either of two simultaneous messages can be achieved if the listener is instructed to ignore one. But two messages together cannot both be easily understood, even though the information is there for the ear to hear (Broadbent 1962). The human central processing unit seems to have a limited capacity, so that preferential treatment is usually given to one message, the attended one, over the other message, the unattended one. This "selection" of an attended message means that there is selective attention paid to simultaneous discourse inputs.

Cherry (1953; 1957/1966) reports that subjects are in fact very good at shadowing messages, ignoring speech presented to the opposite ear, or even to the same ear in the same voice and loudness (though this is more difficult). Subjects did not notice when the input channels were switched to opposite ears, nor when the language switched from English to German. They did notice, however, when the message changed from speech to a pure tone, when it reversed from forward to backwards, or when the sex of the speaker changed. They often noticed when their own name turned up, or when the message was identical, though it could not be delayed any more than five seconds.

Their memory for the contents of the unattended message was poor, even when they were forewarned that they would be later asked for words which occurred as often as thirty-five times.

We can process unattended messages in the discourse around us when the content is very limited in the possible alternatives that are drawn from, as when you overhear a competing conversation at a cocktail party. But when the messages come from a large range of possibilities, we only let one message through and filter the other one out (Broadbent 1962). In general, if an individual listens to two messages at once, only one is understood, for the brain has an attention mechanism for selecting the desired information.

But we also have evidence that subjects are processing the unattended message at some level below threshhold. For example, if both channels consist of cliches, subjects will unwittingly switch the channel between cliches. Or, if the messages are very close semantically, the more errors in reporting the attended message, suggesting a semantic spill-over. Generally, the more differences spatially, acoustically, and semantically, the fewer errors made in attending to the correct message. There are obvious implications here for attention and information transferral tasks. The efficiency of information control systems can be improved by attention to these facts in settings which require selective attention. One major cause of failure in these systems is that listeners have too much information from different sources to handle simultaneously. One should avoid giving too much information to be handled simultaneously, or risk reaction to what is effectively an unimportant signal. Such considerations are important in situations like air traffic control, or even for the efficient moving of passengers in transportation centers like air terminals. One cannot simply expect that hearers will ignore one message and attend to another, but one can enhance this likelihood by having the messages differ in their physical characteristics, as for example, male vs. female voice, spatial separation of the two voices by selective mounting of speakers, or by having the loudspeaker remove the lower tones from one voice (see Broadbent 1962).

Memory for Form vs. Memory for Gist

We have said that we usually store only the meaning of a sentence, and not its actual format, unless we have been instructed to retain the surface form. There are discourse considerations which may enter into our accurate recollection of the actual sentence format, in addition to its content. The surface manifestation of an utterance can be quite accurately remembered if it has sociolinguistic connotations (recall Kemper and Thissen 1981). But it can also be remembered quite accurately if it has pragmatic implications, for we are also sensitive to utterances as carriers of information about social relationships, beliefs, and personal characteristics, especially when they are contrary to expected norms or perhaps even our own expectations of what the norm is. For example, contrast the following questions, considering your reaction to the impression that they might make on you if they appeared in an exchange. How likely would you be to store these away for future reference?

1.   Do you always walk to school?
2.   Do you always talk so much?

I actually used the second sentence once in friendly teasing, but only its objectionable values were registered, and to this day that acquaintance still remembers the remark, and probably no amount of reassurance can make up for the unfortunate inference taken from the surface form. This is what Keenan, MacWhinney and Mayhew (1977) found when their subjects could recall segments from natural conversations from lunchtime exchanges 30 hours earlier. Statements that were high in interactional value were recalled in both their form and their meaning, but this was not so when the interactional value of the statement was low. They suggest that **interactional** utterances are those which also convey the attitude, beliefs, and intentions of the speaker to the listener, perhaps even over and above information. The argument is that the pragmatic value of the stylistic formulation of such utterances has an important role in establishing the memory value of of statements in natural conversations. Consider, for example, the following utterances, the first with low interactional content and the second with high interactional content.

1.   I think there are two fundamental tasks in this study.
2.   I think you've made a fundamental error in this study.

Discourse Structures

Much attention has been directed to the area of text and discourse comprehension lately. Recall that we have learned that sentences are obviously structured both at their surface and their underlying levels. In extracting meaning dependent upon the actual meaningful components and their logical relationships, we have also noted that the propositions inherent in a sentence are often a better metric of sentential and discourse complexity than simple word-count or even number of syntactic relationships. Some psychologists have examined sentences to determine the actual number of propositions in that sentence, in order to measure its complexity. Recall Kintsch and Keenan's (1973) finding that reading time increases as a function of number of propositions within a text; although later modified, it seems generally true that a sentence with a larger number of propositions will take longer to read and comprehend than a sentence equal in length but with fewer propositions. Subsequent modifications recognize that reading times for sentences are facilitated when related knowledge-based materials precede them, so that the integration of entire sentences with prior text is enhanced by the activation of knowledge structures which imply causal connections (Sharkey and Sharkey 1987). But the notion of proposition as a basic unit complementary to the sentence unit is a useful starting point. Propositions in longer pieces of discourse may be ranked in terms of how directive they are in setting out an order or organizational schemata for those propositions which follow. And we rely on these thematic structures and schemata in our understanding of stories, scripts, and scenes, for they provide the unifying topic which provides a frame of reference through which the meaning of each sentence can be measured against the meaning of the discourse as a whole (see Kintsch 1977; van Dijk 1977a, 1977b, 1979; Kintsch and van Dijk 1978). Such commonly understood structures guide us in the comprehension of stories, texts, and even conversations, as well as in their production, as we strive to turn out a piece of discourse that meets the expectations the rest of the linguistic community has about a particular piece of language activity. In fact, the conceptual representation of the knowledge underlying the ability to deal effectively with a text requires more than just a script. Scripts are in their way generated by plans, which in their turn are generated by goals, and ultimately fall under the rubric of themes (see Schank 1980). Even scripts are to be viewed as dynamic structures, which are not stored in memory directly as unchanging and unchangeable wholes, but which are to be constructed afresh from the general procedural rules in memory organization.

Such an approach claims that a discourse is coherent when its individual sentences and constitutent propositions are connected by being organized at some macrostructural level. The primacy of the sentence as the crucial processing unit in psycholinguistic terms seems to have given way to a more realistic view of natural language processing, which concentrates on larger pieces of discourse and the knowledge base that they must rely on. This is probably due in part to what we have learned from the newer computational paradigm and its demands for processing by artificially intelligent devices. In an early article on understanding natural language from a computer's point of view, Winograd (1972) had to remind us linguists that humans make full use of their knowledge and intelligence to understand sentences. But a computer cannot be expected to deal reasonably with language unless it understands the subject that is being dealt with. This does not entail a full replication of what humans know, but it does require the formal specification of those pieces of knowledge that are so automatically accessed about a given situation before we can expect computers to handle "natural" language as "naturally" as we do.

A crucial issue in artificial intelligence is specifying computer programs that outline the essential knowledge that is to be included in memory. And part of this task is then specifying how this knowledge is to be organized. Some of the terms for the way such knowledge structures could be organized are quite well-known as plans, frames, scenarios, schemata, or scripts, and these structures have been elaborated to deal with very minimal, but surprisingly rich, knowledge-based activities like eating in a restaurant (for a well-known and effective example of **script**, see Schank and Abelson 1977, or the similar "memory organization packet" in Schank 1982). Such scripts are proposed as knowledge-based frameworks for information about prototypical events, like eating in a restaurant, and one runs through the general script of what one does and what one expects to happen when one eats in a restaurant in order to either predict or understand behaviors there. Thus, one expects such scripts to contain a sufficient level of generality that they can inform about eating in restaurants, be they French, Italian, Japanese, or whatever, for they all conform to the same general knowledge framework. Artificial intelligence concerns in computer science has required its practitioners to postulate a variety of complex memory structures like scripts, plans, and goals to properly understand how knowledge is stored and inferences made (see Schank and Burstein 1985). It is simply not sufficient to understand only the verbal script, and such concerns have had to branch out further and further to include a perspective on the entire scenario, and to even assess the plans and goals of the participants. Grosz and Sidner (1986) give equal billing to matters of linguistic structure, the participants' intentions, and their focus of attention in a computational processing model to determine the coherence of discourse. Thus, the entire discourse will exhibit a discourse purpose, and discourse segments in the linguistic structure will be driven by specific discourse segment purposes. They suggest that a specification of the intentional structure of a discourse is as important to computational understanding of discourse as the actual linguistic structures themselves.

Man and machine may be different in matters of knowledge, but such applications demonstrate well the uses of computer models in testing our ideas on which features of naive language analysis must provide a framework for extracting and storing knowledge from textual input. The benefits derived from such artificial intelligence exercises is that it provides linguists, psychologists, and psycholinguists with an example of a pragmatic research program with computational goals which either succeed or fail. Our theoretical models will also develop and grow as we learn from the successes and failures of the computational paradigm. As a simple example, there is a compelling analogy between our observation that sensory input is only the start of our processing for real meaning, and the artificial intelligence experience that has been forced to provide an enormous knowledge background for even such simple scenarios like eating in a restaurant or taking a bus.

A central issue in such artificial intelligence tasks remains how to provide reliable formalisms for drawing inferences from spoken discourse or written text, and that issue does have a compelling similarity with the same central issue in discourse processing. The point made by Schank and Burstein is that computational understanding is essentially a memory-based process, and others (Reiser and Black 1982) echo exactly such views for human information processing models. This is another example of how computational concerns with modelling memory for language understanding may provide us with metaphors for modelling human language processing.

Reiser and Black argue persuasively that memory representations for discourse should be functional rather than descriptive. In other words, rather than models of comprehension putting so much emphasis on the structure of the text, they should instead concentrate on explaining how knowledge structures are used to make the inferences that connect the concepts in a text. Such models of comprehension should also show how such knowledge structures are used to guide the retrieval of information from mental representations. There is a theoretical and pragmatic parsimony here in that the knowledge structures used to understand discourse will also be expected to function as storage and retrieval structures. Such a view is more akin to the active, dynamic aspect of language processing that will be necessary to understand the role of inference in comprehension of discourse. As Reiser and Black point out, much work in cognitive science had tended to portray discourse representations as static descriptive structures, instead of as functional structures which actively participate in language processing. Adopting a functional model of discourse comprehension has had its benefits for cognitive scientists working with mechanical information processing systems, and a similar working hypothesis has its obvious benefits when transferred to problems of understanding the human information processing system.

Thus, a piece of naturally-occurring language in the form of a written text or spoken discourse cannot be viewed as merely an unrelated list of propositions, but a set of propositional units which are cross-referenced to one another and catalogued under one or several macro-propositions. If such propositions are not directly expressed or inferred in a given piece of text or discourse, they will be actively constructed by the listener, either on the basis of general world knowledge or in accord with typical knowledge of the restrictions surrounding a specific script or scenario (see Mandler 1984 for an excellent review). Such organizational macrostructures are what provide semantic coherence to a text or discourse, thus making for a meaningful whole. If this were not so, a given discourse sequence would be just a list of unrelated propositions, each of which has to be evaluated for its possible meanings and corresponding interpretations. But as suggested in the section on **Syntax**, we process the incoming discourse for the gist of the text, and it is the construction of this meaningful gist that consumes our attention. There is always an overriding schema which controls this comprehension stage, and we extract one from the discourse which is readily available. One example of how discourse headings influence our perceptions of the discourse comes from Bransford and Johnson (1973). Subjects were read a short passage in which the following sentence appeared.

The landing was gentle and luckily the atmosphere was such that no special suits had to be worn.

However, two groups of subjects differed in the title of the discourse they were given, being provided with either (1) or (2) below.

1. Watching a Peace March from the Fortieth Floor.
2. A Space Trip to an Inhabited Planet.

Not surprisingly, the group with title (1) had a poor success rate in recalling the sentence in question, since there was no appropriate thematic motif to relate it to.

In cases where the discourse does not offer a readily available schema, we construct one in order to have the input make sense to us. For example, Bransford and Johnson (1973) constructed a prose passage by stringing sentences together to produce a textual whole that was essentially nonsense. They then provided some subjects with a pragmatic setting for the piece of pseudo-discourse by giving them a picture; the other subjects did not have the picture to be able to construct a context for the discourse. The important finding is that those subjects who did have a picture from which to construct a context for the bizarre passage fared much better in recall (twice as successful), and even rated the comprehensibility of the passage as reasonable. Without the pragmatic setting available, the other subjects rightly rated the passage as just a sequence of well-formed individual sentences, but without integration into a whole; to them the passage was essentially meaningless.

Thematic macro-structures in effect define what is most important about a given discourse sequence. According to van Dijk (1979), they are defined in such a way that propositions which are not relevant are either deleted or taken under the heading of a more general organizational proposition. Such discourse structuring has led many psycholinguists to posit explanations for how stories, narratives, and general discourse is structured. Many of these take the form of outlining a framework for discourse instances in much the same way that a structural framework for sentences was set out in transformational descriptions for individual well-formed sentences. That is, a piece of discourse like a story is either well-formed or it is not; and if it is well-formed, one can point to the constituents of such a well-formed story and the order in which the constituent pieces appear. For example, the simplest of stories usually consists of a main character and a problem, efforts at solving the problem, and then some resolution of the problem. Thorndyke's (1977) "Grammar Rules for Simple Stories" is essentially a **story grammar**, a generative grammar of plot structures for simple narrative stories of the single-goal single-protagonist type. Thus, just as a well-formed sentence in English could be expected to consist of a Noun Phrase and a Verb Phrase, and in exactly that order, so also we expect a simple story to consist of a Setting, a Theme, a Plot, and a Resolution, and in exactly that order. This is at the highest level of structure for both the sentence and the story, respectively. We further expect that a Verb Phrase in a sentence might contain a Transitive Verb and a Direct Object Noun Phrase; a well-formed story will have its Setting further developed into its Characters and the Location and Time of the story. The point is that we typically generate stories and other such examples of discourse by such rule-ordered formats, and we typically rely on such specific knowledge both when producing and comprehending discourse events like stories.

Thorndyke (1977) tested for exactly this in looking at comprehension and memory for narrative discourse. He found that the probability of recall for individual facts from the story were related to the structural centrality of those facts to the organizational framework of the story. Facts which were found at a higher level of organization in the framework of the story were remembered better than facts which operated at a lower level of organization in the abstract story schema. Subjects also seemed to make good use of structural characteristics of the story grammar type in organizing their summarization of stories, even over content as a mnemonic device. There is considerable evidence that the higher the level of the proposition in the organizational structure of the discourse, the more likely it is to be remembered. In reviewing the evidence for narrative texts and expository texts, Yekovich and Thorndyke (1981) note that this particular "levels effect" is very robust and reliable across studies.

More recently, Gee and Grosjean (1984) have provided more empirical evidence for story grammars of narrative structure. They found that spontaneous pause durations at sentence breaks could be correlated with the importance of those breaking points in the theoretical plot development of the story. Thus, pausing above the level of the sentence unit seems to reflect a higher-order level of structure, and that structure seems to be associated with the structure of the discourse as a whole, in this case, that of a story or narrative.

There is also evidence (Mandler and Goodman 1982) that we read and comprehend stories faster when the constituent sentences in the story match the order expected by the story schema. Using traditional stories, in which one expects that the story progresses forward by citing events in the order in which they actually happen, it was found that even minimal movements which reversed the temporal order of story constituents slowed reading times down. The explanation seems to rest in the violation of expectations of how the story schema will be realized, rather than to a lack of comprehension of the individual sentences themselves. Mandler (1986) has offered a further wrinkle on this finding by pointing out that temporal order plays a part only when the events are arbitrarily related. When the events in the narrative are causally related, a mismatch between actual temporal order and their order of mention in the narrative did not really affect comprehension. In the case of arbitrarily related events, such a mismatch does affect comprehension.

Van den Broek (1988) also found causal as well as hierarchical factors in determining the role a statement plays in a narrative. Judging the importance of a goal statement has to do with the number of other statements it can be seen to be related to. The more causal connections a statement has, whether to individual statements or to episodes, the more important a statement is judged to be. Thus, in addition to hierarchical ordering and statement category as predictors of the importance of a statement in a story, causal relations play an equal, if not more important role. In general, statements which are high in the hierarchical ordering scheme, statements with categorially important content like topics, goals, and outcomes, and lastly, statements that have a large number of connections with other statements in the narratives are all recalled and summarized more frequently and more accurately.

Along these same lines, procedural directions are read faster when the general organizational information for a task is found at the beginning rather than at the end of the directions. Directions for performing a task usually consist of the component parts, namely, which specific steps you must follow to perform the task, and the organizational information, the task designation and rationale for doing it. Dixon (1987) reports that information order has an effect on the reading time. For example, a sequence like *You can make a wagon by drawing a long rectangle with two circles underneath* takes 7.3 seconds to read, but the reverse order of component steps first, as in *By drawing a long rectangle with two circles underneath you can make a wagon*, takes 9.0 secs. to read. If mental plans can be said to have a hierarchical structure, with general plans at the top stages of the mental model and the specific steps for their realization at a lower stage, then we might have predicted the need for additional processing time whenever this order is violated. Even in simple part-whole tasks like these, the mental representation is constructed from the top down, with the higher-level information required before the lower-level components. Dixon notes that these results may generalize to other tasks and materials of a more complex nature. The implication is that there is an effective ordering sequence to the way that written instructions are processed, with organizational information to be placed ahead of component steps.

Mental Models

Such work is congruent with the notion of mental models in processing text and discourse. Such mental models represent what a piece of discourse, like a narrative or a set of directions, is all about, rather than simply representing the discourse itself by way of a description. Thus, the highest level concerns what the discourse deals with, and once established, this in turn controls interpretation of the component parts of the discourse, guides inference making, and even predicts judgments of coherence. As Glenberg, Meyer and Lindem (1987) have summarized in an experiment with foregrounding, the postulation of mental models provides explanations for comprehension results which demand inclusion of a representation of what the text describes, not just a description of the text itself. Indeed, the notion of mental models is very attractive in the sense that it also allows for the integration of information from different input modalities, as for example, visual and verbal input while attending a play.

We have moved from focussing on one level to the next in psycholinguistic studies (Perrig and Kintsch 1985). From syntactic and semantic processing of sentences in the 1960s, attention moved to discourse processing and the comprehension of the propositional framework of the talk or text in the 1970s. From there we also considered models of the situations described by the text, as Bransford and colleagues so nicely showed in the 1970s. In the 1980s this notion of model and the role it plays in comprehension and inference has been considerably elaborated. Two influential texts appeared in the same year, calling attention to a level of representation best described as a

mental model (Johnson-Laird 1983) and to the strategies employed in discourse comprehension and corresponding **situation models** (van Dijk and Kintsch 1983). In such a view, words and sentences act as cues in the construction of familiar mental models. The resultant mental model may be closer to the structure of the events described in the discourse than it is to the propositional format, because it reflects the non-linguistic contextual inferences that the discourse triggers.

Discourse comprehension is a strategic activity, and such mental models are constantly being altered and upgraded, in line with the listener's current state of knowledge, past and present, and with what the discourse now conveys. New information can be added, old information changed or deleted; the mental model is there as a ready reference, to be manipulated or reorganized as it is brought to bear in a given discourse situation. And it provides answers for how reasoning is carried out, over and above syntactic rules of inference which are at times simply inadequate. For example, reasoning about the relationship of being seated to the right or left of someone must involve a mental model of the details of size and shape of the table to be able to infer that some persons are seated to our left (and not to our right!) at a round table. Given general purpose rules of reasoning, John may be seated to the right of James who is seated to the right of Peter who is seated to my right, but John is envisioned as being to **my left** at a four-person round table. This is true even if I was not told this explicitly in the sentences presented to me. Such a conclusion is both valid and supportable if one accepts the notion that we formulate mental models of situations and events, and that reasoning processes are mental operations applied to such models.

Culture-specific Discourse Structures

An interesting twist on the notion of well-formedness for stories, narratives, folklore, and literature in general is that the structural expectations may be posed by cultural norms. This is what Bartlett's classic (1932) study of memory came up against in having English speakers try to recall folk literature examplars from the Northwest Coast. What constitutes an acceptably formatted piece of folk literature in Kwakiutl, an Amerindian language of northern Vancouver Island in British Columbia, is completely strange to English raconteurs, and not surprisingly, English-speaking subjects tended to reproduce such stories on a more familiar model of story-telling. Not only were some of the details different, but so also was the general structure of the way the story was rendered, in an unconscious attempt to bring the story in line with more recognizable forms of story-telling. Bartlett's explanation was that recall is not a reproduction of the important ideas to found in that narrative, but rather that recall is an inferential reconstruction. That reconstruction is based on inferences which not only reflect the expected schema for how such tales should be organized, but also the expected values of the individual event within that story, as well as the appropriate bridging inferences between those events to make it all meaningful in its development.

Inference

We already have seen that we know or recall more than we actually hear, and that we are constantly making **inferences** or deductions from sentences that we hear. This is all the more true in the realization of discourse. Speakers rarely lay out everything to the last detail, for they know that we will grasp not only what is being said, but far beyond that to the tiny details that "everyone takes for granted". What "everyone takes for granted" is the background knowledge that we share, and the inferences that we typically make from a piece of discourse input often consist of these or rely on these details. As a result, much is usually left out, and we fill it in by inference as the discourse proceeds. Take, for example, the following piece of discourse (from Johnson-Laird 1986:43).

> When I returned to my house last night, I discovered that I had lost
> my keys. There was no one there and the door was locked. I broke
> the glass and turned the lock from the inside. Someone heard the
> noise and came running.

Much of what follows is not explicitly stated in the discourse, yet most of us would have inferred all of the following to be true or likely to be true (from Johnson-Laird 1986:43). The inferences help to tie the discourse together, for they act as bridges from one sentence to the next, helping to make sense out of what appear to be separate sentences by tying them together into an integrated whole picture of what happened at each turn of events.

1. The keys the speaker lost included the key to the door of his house.
2. There was no one in his house.
3. The door that was locked was the door to his house.
4. He broke a pane of glass in the door to his house.
5. He reached in through the resulting hole and unlocked the door.
6. Someone (not in the house) heard the noise of the breaking glass and came running to investigate its cause.

The fact is that we make many inferences as to what the discourse structure is, and how the macro- and micro-propositions are realized, as well as what their relationships to one another are as the discourse unfolds. An **inference** is thus a piece of information or meaning in the underlying discourse that we draw out of it. It may not be overtly expressed by the speaker, but it is nonetheless there and is crucial to understanding either the discourse itself or the reason for the discourse. And it must be drawn by the listener.

For example, consider these three answers to the question *Would you like to join us Saturday night for supper?*:

1. I have to visit my great-aunt at the hospital that evening. She's very lonely, and no one seems to find time for her on the weekends.

2.   I'm not really into visiting anybody these days . . . too many
        things on my mind!
3.   Sorry, I have to paint my canoe.

The first is a reasonable refusal, and allows both the asker and the
invitee to feel good about their continuing relationship. But the second
allows the asker to make some judgments, given the context of his or
her friendship with the invitee up to that point, as to whether one
should leave this "friend" alone for a while. The third flatly solicits the
inference that a friendly relationship is just not desired.

We integrate various pieces of meaning, some directly from the
sentences we have actually encountered and some constructed as inferences from those sentences. But knowledge is not just derived from
input in a linguistic or other sense. We actively analyze and evaluate
that input to infer what that piece of knowledge is or could be, fitting
it to what we already know of the world and how it can be expected to
operate. The acquisition of knowledge in a linguistic sense, or through
any other sensory modality, is not a passive process. We are actively
matching and re-arranging our stock of evaluative judgments and reaction strategies on the basis of what we are exposed to each passing
day. But the input is only the first step in this sequence, it is what we
infer from this input and then how we store it and what we do with it
that constitutes the full range of the dynamic capacity we loosely refer
to as "general knowledge of the world". As one can see, inference both
relies on our ability to refer to this storehouse from previous experience, as well as the capacity to alter it.

We seem to fill in blanks in comprehension, in order to integrate
meanings into coherent and complete pictures of the meaning intended.
This coherent picture may even rely on what we thought was intended
or what we used to make sense of the incoming information. As noted
in the section on syntax, we saw that what seems to be stored in memory is a structure which encodes the total situation described by a
series of related propositions and their logical inferences. Thus, a
major function of the inferential process in comprehending discourse is
to construct an integrating context through which to interpret incoming information, and it is this active process by the hearer which
strives to establish coherence and maintain continuity as the discourse
proceeds.

Sometimes the inferential process is aided by script-based knowledge which makes certain informational features of the situation
directly accessible. Walker and Yekovich (1987) found this to be true
for antecedents during the resolution of anaphora. Anaphora occurs
when we refer back to persons, things, or concepts in the preceding
text; for example, a very common type of anaphora is pronoun use, as
when we refer to Walker and Yekovich the second time as *they*. They
have demonstrated that central concepts are automatic in script-based
discourse models in memory, and that antecedents which are central to
typical scripts are available regardless of how a given text is organized.
But peripheral concepts in such texts do depend upon features of their
presentation in the text for their recall prominence, because they are

peripheral in pre-formed scripts on the topic. The stylistic manner in which referential ties are made between antecedent and anaphor can be explicit by the direct reference of a repeated noun phrase or implicit by the inferred reference of an understood noun phrase. Or the referential tie may not be made at all between the anaphor and its possible antecedent, in which case the reader must make a series of situational inferences from general knowledge to construct the possible relationship. Examples of each are as follows:

1. Explicit referential tie: Allison fed the dog chow to Duffy. The dog chow tasted good.
2. Implied referential tie: Allison fed Duffy. The dog chow tasted good. (Requiring the inference that Allison fed Duffy something, and that something was dog chow.)
3. No referential tie: Duffy barked at the cabinet. The dog chow tasted good. (Requiring the inferences: Duffy is a dog. The cabinet contains dog chow. Someone fed that dog chow to·Duffy.)

For peripheral concepts, it does make a difference whether the referential tie is direct or not; for those concepts which are inherently central because of their pre-set role in scripts, comprehension time is unaffected by whether the referential tie is explicit, implied, or completely absent. According to Walker and Yekovich, scripts are organized in such a way that certain concepts are more central. For example, the well-known script for eating in a restaurant revolves around concepts like *table* and *meal*, but only peripherally involves *hostess/salt and pepper/cocktails/napkins*. One expects that such central concepts will automatically be part of the mental model of discourse when that discourse has domain ties to a given script, and that these central concepts will be available as antecedents no matter what the exact features of the text that is read. Thus, the time required to comprehend a sentence like *The table was near the window* should be the same regardless of which of the three antecedent-setting formats it follows.

1. Explicit referential tie: The hostess seated Jack and Chris at the table. The table was near the window.
2. Implied referential tie: The hostess seated Jack and Chris. The table was near the window.
3. No referential tie: Jack and Chris walked into the dining room. The table was near the window.

The organization of well-known scripts thus counts as a systematic and far-reaching set of prior knowledge, which has its effect by automatically adding central concepts to the working discourse model for any text that activates that scripted knowledge set. Comprehension of anaphoric sentences referring to central concepts reflect this organizational set; anaphoric sentences referring to peripheral concepts do not, instead reflecting the stylistic manner in which referential ties were made in the language of the text itself. However, this difference in comprehension set does not obtain when the concepts appear outside of a scripted context, and central concepts no longer have a prior knowledge set to be facilitated by. In this case, Walker and Yekovich note that inferences regarding anaphoric sentences which are out of a scripted context depend upon the features of the text itself.

Ambiguity Resolution and the Influence of Discourse Context

Sentences normally follow one upon the other in a discourse flow which has a structure and pattern of its own. A shift in emphasis from the attention paid to the isolated sentence to instead questioning the role of larger discourse patterns may shed light on how ambiguity is resolved. It seems logical to look at the processing of larger chunks of normal discourse to provide some idea of the role that context plays in the processing of ambiguities.

Knowledge as Context . But before we look at discourse patterns, we should first recall that context also has a broader meaning. When we encounter a sentence, we typically bring all our past knowledge and experience to bear in dealing with that sentence. General knowledge of the world interacts with our knowledge of the grammar of the language, and is usually reflected in our probability rankings for the various meanings that words and syntactic structures can have in that particular language. This is what accounts for the inherent bias that certain lexically ambiguous words have (see Simpson 1981), and also for the bias exhibited by structures which admit more than one reading (see Kess and Hoppe 1983b). Ambiguous structures exhibit degrees of sensibleness which provide their own bias. For example, in looking at the following three ambiguous sentences, you will note that (1) is most likely to have the car associated with the boy, while (2) is most likely to have the bone associated with the dog. Sentence (3) can go either way in terms of likelihood. But if you look more closely, you will note that the possibilities are many, and that the sentences admit more than one interpretation. After all, dogs in cartoons drive cars, dogs in families with children often run off with a toy car in their mouths, pioneer boys on the prairies could easily find a shin bone to use as a weapon to chase a dog off with, and so on. Nevertheless, even with this information in mind, you will probably still see the most sensible interpretations as the following: (1) a boy in a car chasing after a dog; (2) a boy chasing a dog who has a bone clenched between its teeth; and lastly (3), **either** a boy with a stick doing the chasing or a dog with a stick in its mouth refusing to come back.

1.   The boy chased the dog with a car.
2.   The boy chased the dog with a bone.
3.   The boy chased the dog with a stick.

While there are obviously biases in the preferred reading for an ambiguity, we are still interested in whether both readings are unconsciously processed anyway. If this is so, generalized world knowledge would only enhance the attractiveness of the preferred reading, but would not exclude the other less likely reading. Some interesting evidence comes from an experiment with newspaper headlines, a written genre which is syntactically minimal, and thus often syntactically ambiguous (Perfetti et al. 1987) Space constraints cause headlines to be syntactically compressed, omitting definite and indefinite articles, auxiliaries and even copulas. A verbless headline violates the computational centrality of the verb, and readers may incorrectly analyze the internal sentence relationships. For example, consider the following such headlines.

1.   **Deer Kill 130,000**
2.   **Purdue Game It for Winless Pitt**
3.   **Rumours about NBA Growing Ugly**

You would expect the parsing of Headline (1) to rely on the fact that every reader knows that deer are harmless and that they are the hunted ones. But even real-world knowledge apparently does not bypass syntactic processes, for the experimental results showed that parsing procedures for ambiguous headlines are the same as for other instances of syntactic ambiguity. At some unconscious level of analysis, subjects did consider both potential readings before settling on the correct one. The headline **Deer Kill 130,000** has no verb, and one possible analysis might have *deer* as the subject of *kill*; a second reading is in fact the correct analysis, with the words linked in the compound noun *deer kill*. Apparently, even though we are primed to expect more ambiguity in newspaper headlines as a discourse genre, and despite our knowing the real-world facts about deer and hunters, ambiguous headlines require more processing than unambiguous ones.

Discourse as Context . Now let us examine the possible influence of contextual cohesion in extended discourse on the resolution of ambiguities. Some previous findings in psycholinguistic investigations of ambiguous sentences in isolation do not always replicate when such sentences occur in discourse settings with pragmatically available motifs. A discourse view of context would expect that an organizational, and perhaps even processual, effect is set before the ambiguous item. And indeed, some previous studies making limited use of context in this sense have shown a bias in the selection of the appropriate reading (Swinney and Hakes 1976; Schvaneveldt, Meyer and Becker 1976; Tyler and Marslen-Wilson 1977; Kess and Hoppe 1981b, 1983b, 1985). Swinney and Hakes (1976), for example, employed a phoneme monitoring task to demonstrate that prior context, in the same sentence as well as in the preceding sentence, serves to restrict access to the possible readings of ambiguous lexical items. In a phoneme monitoring task, subjects are supposed to listen for a given sound, and told to press a button as soon as they have heard it. As a way of testing for processual effects present because of ambiguity, the hypothesis is that there will be less cognitive room for the attention required to monitor for a given phoneme because of the extra attention required to deal with the two meanings of the ambiguity. Subjects' reaction times after ambiguous words were longer than to unambiguous controls in the neutral condition where there was no conditioning factor of context which sensitized the subjects to one reading. But the reaction times between ambiguous words and unambiguous controls were not significant when there was a biasing context in either the same sentence or the preceding sentence conditions. Reaction times after ambiguous lexical items in biasing contexts were faster than those which occurred without a biased context. Such results are supportive of a selective access explanation of ambiguity resolution in the context of discourse.

But most such experiments are not particularly supportive of a single reading model, or even a strong selective access approach. For example, Cairns and Hsu (1980) also employed a phoneme monitoring task, and eliminated monitoring effects for lexical ambiguity in the presence of a prior biasing context. But they conclude that their data are insufficient to choose between the prior- and post-retrieval hypotheses, suggesting that the effect of context is simply to speed the final decision process in the retrieval of and selection between multiple meanings. Cairns and Hsu are representative of a number of similar experiments, in that they favor a post-retrieval role for prior context.

There have been methodological criticisms of the phoneme monitoring paradigm (Mehler, Segui and Carey 1978; Newman and Dell 1978), severely weakening its usefulness in demonstrating differences for ambiguous items. In response to such criticisms, Swinney (1979) used a more refined experimental task with the Swinney and Hakes (1976) materials. His experimental task attempted to avoid the shortcomings of the phoneme monitoring task by replacing it with an auditory presentation of an ambiguous sentence coupled with a visual lexical decision task. These results suggested that lexical access is at first autonomous of the effects of semantic context. The entire inventory of information stored for a lexical item is made available during the comprehension process, and a post-access decision process selects a single meaning from the inventory. This decision process is obviously very fast, and appears to be completed by the time at least three syllables of additional information have passed. It is presumably here that preceding semantic and pragmatic information are brought to bear.

Some experiments have pursued the effects of various types of contextual conditions. An experiment by Schvaneveldt, Meyer and Becker (1976) on lexical ambiguity, semantic context, and word recognition found results which favored a selective-access interpretation, since semantic context influenced the recognition of ambiguous lexical items in their study. Investigating the on-line effects of semantic context on syntactic processing, Tyler and Marslen-Wilson (1977) suggest that syntactic decisions can be influenced by prior semantic context well before a clause boundary is reached. Although they do not demonstrate that only the syntactic structure compatible with the prior context is computed, they do suggest that the interpretation which is consistent with the context is preferred.

Several experiments (Hoppe and Kess 1986; Kess and Hoppe 1989) have specifically attempted to extend the notion of context in normal discourse by offering linguistic constraints in the form of thematic contextual conditions. They call attention to a difference between **theme** and **context**; although a general context may suggest one reading, it does not necessarily exclude the other reading. A better candidate for contextual effects is the superordinate thematic framework which guides the entire discourse (see Kess 1982), for it may serve to narrow or block the range of interpretations before the actual ambiguous items occur. Although some experiments like Foss and Jenkins (1973) did use prior linguistic context, that biasing context was a single word within the same sentence. For example, an ambiguous and neutral sentence was said to be one like *The merchant put his straw beside the machine*. Sentences which were also ambiguous but which could be considered "biased" because of the preceding word were sentences like *The farmer put his straw beside the machine* and *The child put his straw beside the machine*. But it is a question of bias, and one can move the biasing quality of such sentences up a notch by sharpening the contextual contributions. Note, for example, how one can increase the bias by more relevant context, as in *The cattle farmer left the straw beside the machine* and *The soda jerk left the straw beside the machine*.

An earlier study by Perfetti and Goodman (1970) had already suggested that decoding is determined by sentence context, and that single words in lists have little or no effect. When one looks at the sentences used in the Perfetti and Goodman study, one notices that the context provided by the sentential surroundings seems to have a thematic context, for it provides a macro-structure around which the sentence can be organized, providing a reference point for meaningful interpretation. Consider sentences like the following, each of which contains a lexically ambiguous word like *country*.

1. Many families rent a house in the country for the summer months.
2. The developing country is ready to take any steps necessary to ensure its independence.

The word *country* is potentially ambiguous, but it is disambiguated by the inference of a theme from the entire sentence, taking one beyond the local context. This disambiguation does not arise from the immediately surrounding contexts of *the developing country* or *house in the country*.

When subjects are required to judge the relative likelihood for the two interpretations of ambiguous sentences, Oden (1978) reports that they employ a scale of continuous semantic constraints. Contexts were manipulated within the sentence in one experiment, and in the preceding sentence in another experiment. Oden's results show that judged likelihood of the interpretation chosen is a direct function of the relative sensibleness of the particular reading of the ambiguity, and that semantic constraints in effect determine this degree of sensibleness.

His subjects judged which interpretation of an ambiguous sentence would be more likely as the meaning of the sentence, and how likely that interpretation was in comparison to its alternative. As exemplified in the *straw* sentences above, it is possible to highlight any particular reading of an ambiguous sentence by manipulating the sensibleness of the alternative interpretations. Oden's conclusion is that the degree of sensibleness might be used to eliminate interpretations completely, so that it would not be necessary to process more than one reading. An alternative conclusion is that such information might eliminate all but the most sensible interpretation, but only after enough processing has been performed. Such considerations are now seen as central to successful outcomes in artificial intelligence, for any viable system of semantic interpretation which allows computational understanding of natural language must replicate common-sense knowledge in both language comprehension and problem solving (see Hirst 1987).

Simpson (1981) has also demonstrated that dominance and context make independent contributions to the processing of lexically ambiguous items. His experimental materials used sentences which ended in ambiguous words, biased to either the dominant or subordinate meaning of the ambiguous item. When a sentence was biased strongly toward either meaning, dominant or subordinate, it was that meaning which was retrieved. If the sentence was weakly biased toward the subordinate meaning, then both meanings were accessed. And when the sentence was simply ambiguous, without biasing, it was the dominant meaning that was retrieved. In another experiment, subjects retrieved the dominant meanings for ambiguous words when lexical decisions had to be made to possibly related words. These results underscore the importance of not only context and dominance, but the order of their interaction, and clearly establishes that interpretations for ambiguous lexical items exhibit ordering priorities in the semantic memory. This order determines which meaning of an ambiguous word will be retrieved when that ambiguous word is encountered in a neutral context or in the total absence of context. However, when the context is highly suggestive of just the one meaning, regardless of whether it is the dominant or subordinate interpretation, it is the meaning consistent with the context which is highlighted. Lack of context is the exception rather than the rule in normal language processing, and this frequency bias may be a default procedure which is overridden by context (Simpson 1981:134).

Similar results were obtained by two experiments (Hoppe and Kess 1986; Kess and Hoppe 1989) which established biasing contexts based on thematic relevance. The prediction was that listeners would be guided by the organizational frame of reference provided by preceding discourse context to choose one reading for an ambiguous sentence. A thematic, organizational context of this type would, in theory at least, force listeners to evaluate the ambiguities in only the one direction.

One experiment (Hoppe and Kess 1986) used a dichotic listening task modelled on the influential Lackner and Garrett (1972) experiment (explained in the chapter on **Syntax**). It was hypothesized that the effect of a thematically restrictive context would be powerful enough to override the presentation of an interpretation presented to the unattended ear. Since Lackner and Garrett's previous results clearly establish the contribution of such simultaneously presented disambiguating cues, one might expect that the disambiguating effects of such cues would continue in the presence of such context. Thus, subjects were dichotically presented with ambiguous sentences to an attended ear and disambiguating cue sentences presented to the other, unattended ear. But each of the sentences was preceded by a thematic paragraph biased for one meaning of the ambiguous sentence. One-half of the contexts biased a meaning consistent with that of the disambiguating sentence, while the remaining half biased the meaning of the ambiguous sentence in a way which was inconsistent with the meaning of the disambiguating sentence. For example, paragraphs (1) and (2) each provide a thematic context for the final sentence which is ambiguous.

1.   Night after night, the city had been torn apart by drunken brawls. Drunken driving was such a problem that any driving was dangerous. The churches banded together to oppose the free beer being given away at all the local pubs. A committee of concerned citizens demanded a meeting with the mayor. Their appeal was favourably received. The police chief was called to city hall. *The mayor ordered the police to stop drinking.*

2.   The city council was adamant. The police force must do everything it can to win back the respect of the people. They had bought new, faster cars, dressed the men in impressive new uniforms. They even increased the policemen's salaries. But still the citizens jeered at them and refused to obey. Perhaps the police force would have a better image if they behaved better. *The mayor ordered the police to stop drinking.*

Subjects almost exclusively reported readings of the ambiguous sentences that were consistent with the biasing context, even when that meaning was inconsistent with the meaning of a disambiguating sentence presented to the unattended ear. And this effect operated across all types of ambiguity (lexical, surface, and underlying). Clearly, such a thematic context strongly influences the perceived meaning of the ambiguous sentence, even overriding the influence of a disambiguating sentence presented to the unattended ear.

A second experiment (Kess and Hoppe 1989) used the same materials to modify the classic phoneme monitoring task used by Foss (1970), and later extended by Foss and Jenkins (1973). Recall that subjects in such experiments are required to monitor sentences for a given phoneme after the presentation of lexically ambiguous words, with reaction times to target phonemes typically longer when preceded by ambiguous words than by unambiguous words. Most experiments used a phoneme monitoring technique with lexical ambiguities, but Kess and Hoppe used the technique with both syntactic and lexical ambiguities, after a thematic context as well as after no context.

Foss and Jenkins (1973) had shown an effect for lexical ambiguity when the ambiguous word was preceded by a biasing context within the same sentence, suggesting that even in the presence of context, all interpretations of an ambiguous item are considered before the processual decision as to correct reading is rendered. But the Kess and Hoppe results showed no significant differences between the reaction times to the monitored phonemes in ambiguous and unambiguous sentences in the context conditions. Generally, the reaction times to the phonemes in ambiguous sentences were longer than in unambiguous sentences, but these differences were not significant when the sentences were preceded by the thematic contexts. In general, when ambiguous sentences were preceded by a thematic context, it did not take significantly longer to react to a critical phoneme that was to be monitored than when the sentences were unambiguous. Ambiguous sentences in isolation show processual differences when compared with unambiguous structures, and this is also true for ambiguities in context which is minimal or non-directive. However, when embedded in larger, more normal discourse contexts of a thematically relevant kind, ambiguous sentences act very much like the other utterances one encounters in reading or hearing a language.

No matter which way the ambiguity debate between single-reading or multiple-reading procedures is resolved, however, it seems clear that listeners and readers only carry forward one reading for an ambiguous structure (see Perfetti et al. 1987). What a theory of ambiguity resolution will ultimately have to achieve is to explain how the successful identification of the correct reading is achieved. Obviously, the mechanism which is the most successful in specifying the appropriate reading is the correct one (Crain and Steedman's (1985) principle of referential success). The real question is how information about meaning, context, bias, and pragmatic use cooperates with the parsing strategies we employ in a syntactic analysis of the sentence. The real task in ambiguity research must be to find what these mechanisms are and the degree to which they influence, narrow, or erase the range of alternatives potentially available to the listener or reader.

Reasoning from Discourse

Some important work is being done on the natural language question of discourse episodes which elicit specific types of reasoning. Two important themes have focussed upon the forms of mental representation which are employed in the reasoning process as derived from discourse input, and the role of the strategies of inference and coherence in dealing with natural language. Inference and coherence has been partially dealt with in previous sections, but the questions of mental logic, reasoning, and utilization of inductive vs. deductive strategies are worth contrasting for the role they play in inference and verbal reasoning. Johnson-Laird (1986) has claimed that valid inferences are arrived at by following general semantic procedures, instead of by applying the invariable deductive rules of a mental logic. He simply discards the notion of a mental logic as sufficient or even necessary as the basis of human reasoning, noting that valid deductions can be made without recourse to formal rules of inference. This suggests that a theory of reasoning should instead be based upon a knowledge of truth conditions. Given semantic information, he suggests that spontaneous inferences arise which reflect information not explicitly stated in the premises but which maintain their semantic content. Very simply, logic does not make a good theory of deductive competence, for there can be reasoning without logic. The experimental evidence from psycholinguistics points to a theory of rational competence based on truth conditions. Certainly theories of performance based on the doctrine of mental logic could be easily abandoned, and as Johnson-Laird puts it, "indeed, once the search for a logic of the mind is abandoned, it is possible to make better sense of the psychology of reasoning (p. 14)."

If there are formal rules of inference in the mind in the sense of a mental logic, then such rules should apply to sentences whatever the semantic content of the problems. However, humans appear to be very much influenced by the semantic content of the premises. In addition, such a form of logic has so far not been able to predict the specific valid conclusions which people draw spontaneously. It is obvious that an adequate theory of competence, let alone an adequate theory of performance, will have to account for the inferences that people actually do make, leading to the conclusions that they then arrive at.

Syllogisms present tidy mini-reasoning situations in which to test inference and the notion of mental models (Johnson-Laird 1980), though they are not necessarily the only paradigm for how reasoning occurs. Still, as a test case, they are ideal, for syllogisms offer two premises and a conclusion which can be logically derived. They are couched in straight syntactic formats, and formally invite inferencing to obtain the logical conclusion. But as Johnson-Laird (1980, 1986) notes, they may actually invite incorrect solutions; and for a satisfying explanation of reasoning from discourse, we should have answers as to why and when incorrect conclusions are arrived at. But one cannot always rely on the current formal models of logic to be even adequate to the task of explaining all correct solutions from language-based reasoning. For example, Johnson-Laird (1986:33) notes that neither theories of rational competence based on logical techniques for the syllogism nor those based on predicate calculus can accommodate the simple inferences made from the following premises.

1.   More than half the teachers are men.
2.   More than half the teachers sing in the choir.

Such a pair of premises give the valid conclusion that *There is a man who sings in the choir.* Though even children can draw such a conclusion, this deduction cannot be captured in predicate calculus because there is no way to express the quantification over individuals given in the utterances. Theoretical linguistics has of course shown much interest of late in formal logic as the way of explicating the semantics of natural language, but Moore (1986) reminds us that form cannot be separated from content in the inductive reasoning sequences used in natural language. Meaning contained in the premises, and the body of knowledge related to the relevant "facts", have as much to do with reasoning from language as does the sentence form. Unfortunately, there are no reliable standard techniques for doing exercises in inductive logic, and given that such inductions on our part typically rely on a sliding scale of knowledge and experience, it is not surprising. Yet it would appear that probabilistic logic will tell us much about how human reasoning works, and that a model of inductive inference is one which may be more appropriate for linguists and psycholinguists seeking to understand real-time natural language. Very simply, inferences derived from natural language are very often of the "probably true" instead of the "necessarily true" type. For example, compare the following examples of deductive and inductive inference, each which derives a conclusion from its preceding two premises.

Deductive Inference:

1.   If Max is hungry, he is ratty.
2.   Max is hungry.
3.   Max is ratty.

Inductive Inference:

1.   When Max is hungry, he is usually ratty.
2.   Max is hungry.
3.   Max is ratty.

The difference between the two conclusions is that the first is necessarily valid, for all such logically based exercises produce conclusions that are either true or not true. However, the conclusion arrived at in the second syllogism is not necessarily valid, though it seems a likely enough conclusion to come to, and more importantly, is one that we might likely come to. Natural language may more often pose discourse problems of such a probabilistic kind to us than do exercises in formal logic, and a theory of reasoning from natural discourse should serve to account for this fact (Moore 1986). For this reason, Lakoff (1987) observes that formal syntax and semantics in the tradition of mathematical logic are also artificial constructions invented for mathematical purposes, and that they are not exclusively about natural language syntax and human reason.

Even if all discourse only dealt with valid conclusions, we still have no principled way of predicting which conclusions subjects will always give and in which rankings. Citing from his extensive experimental experience on reasoning with quantifiers, Johnson-Laird (1986) notes that the formal and semantic approaches to quantificational reasoning diverge. In experiments where subjects are asked to state in their own words what conclusion followed from syllogistic premises with quantifiers, the findings show that some syllogisms usually show a logically correct response, while other syllogisms rarely do. For example, read the following syllogism and try to make the correct conclusion.

1.   Some of the scientists are parents.
2.   All the parents are drivers.

Chances are that you drew the first conclusion below, though you might have instead chosen the second conclusion below. In fact, both conclusions are equally valid, but subjects typically (90%) choose the first conclusion, though a smaller number (5%) draw the second conclusion.

1.   Some of the scientists are drivers.
2.   Some of the drivers are scientists.

Now try the following syllogism, carefully reading it first and then posing the correct conclusion.

1.   All of the beekeepers are artists.
2.   None of the chemists are beekeepers.

Now, given this syllogism, you, like many of the subjects in Johnson-Laird's experiments, probably came up with something other than the logically correct response, which is that *Some of the artists are not chemists.* The following list gives an idea of the array of the actual conclusions (and their percentages) that subjects came up with; recall that only the last one is the correct one! Such results are certainly a reminder that most of us are neither well-trained nor particularly motivated to use formal reasoning procedures based on logic of formal language, without the benefit of some real context. At the very least, if human subjects behave differently than the calculus predicts, it may not be that humans are behaving illogically, but rather that the calculus is simply inappropriate for such applications (see Broadbent 1984).

1.   None of the chemists are artists.   (60% of the subjects)
2.   None of the artists are chemists.   (10% of the subjects)
3.   No valid conclusion   (20% of the subjects)
4.   Some of the chemists are not artists.   (10% of the subjects)
5.   Some of the artists are not chemists.   (0% of the subjects)

It is obvious from results like these that any theory of deductive performance must be based on what we actually do when confronted with problems of verbal reasoning, and not on what we might expect the rigors of scholastic logic to predict as logical conclusions. Certainly, the very range of difficulty of syllogisms in the variety of actual responses they elicit as conclusions must be accounted for if we are to understand what verbal reasoning actually is, and not what we think it should be. A better candidate for a method of inference is one based on

semantic procedures, for experimental results from work with syllogistic reasoning seem to better support a semantic theory (Johnson-Laird
1986).

Reasoning across Languages

Reasoning from discourse procedures may be manifested in different ways across languages. Citing data from Luria's work with Uzbek
peasants, Cole and Scribner's work with Liberian villagers, Tversky
and Kahneman's work on probabilistic reasoning with North American
university students, Moore (1986) has called attention to features of
discourse reasoning that can hardly be ignored from a performance
point of view. The course of reasoning examines the content and plau-
sibility of the information rendered and this is further matched against
personal experience and judgment. For example, according to Luria's
interpretation, his unschooled peasant subjects in Uzbekistan simply
refused to accept some of the premises given to them or simply
replaced aspects of the expected inferential process by their own, one
often based on experience, rumour, or culturally approved ways of presenting such new inferential knowledge. Even in syllogisms with
semantic content familiar to them, they were reluctant to offer conclusions of the syllogistic type until prodded to do so. For example, when
given the following premises and prompted with a transparent question, they typically declared they had never been to England, and thus
couldn't really be expected to know.

1.   Cotton grows well where it is hot and dry.
2.   England is cold and damp.
3.   Question: Can cotton grow there?

This reluctance to respond deductively was even more pronounced
in syllogisms containing information that was not commensurate with
real experience. For example,

1.   In the Far North, where there is snow, all bears are white.
2.   Novaya Zemlya is in the Far North.
3.   Question: What colour are the bears there?

The metacognitive point that Luria strove to make (Luria
1976:107-110, cited in Moore 1986) is that deductive reasoning processes may reflect matters of personal knowledge and experience.
Some interpretations of discourse problems may respond to the semantic content of the words and sentences, and not their particular
arrangements, as in syllogistic presentations. The Vygotskyan point
that Luria also strives to make on the basis of this data has to be modified by a re-interpretation of his data. The Vygotskyan expectation is
that various features of mental competence depend upon other social,
cultural, and experiential factors like literacy and schooling; for example, Luria's literate Uzbeks had no difficulty performing well on the
deductive syllogisms. Indeed, there is a heated contemporary debate

over the effects of orality vs. literacy, in both an individual and a cultural developmental sense (see Ong 1982, and Olson, Torrance and Hildyard 1985) which addresses largely these same questions. However, as Moore (1986) nicely reminds us in his reinterpretation of the data, it is not that illiterate Uzbeki peasants cannot perform deductively on familiar, or even unfamiliar, syllogisms. Rather they may choose to provide answers which are deductions from different premises, instead of according to our expectations. Indeed, some of their answers even seem to reflect what our sense of formal logic might require deductively, but their actual answers honor what they are allowed to deduce and answer publicly. For example, consider the following answer.

1.   What colour are the bears in Novaya Zemlya?
2.   We always speak only of what we see; we don't talk about what we haven't seen.

And in the larger view, it may even be that some prelogical forms of encoding are extrinsic to logic and language, and causally antedate linguistic or reasoning competence. On the basis of evidence from experiments with adults, children, and even non-human primates, McGonigle and Chalmers (1986) suggest that ordering devices used by sophisticated adult subjects in the solution of linear transitive inference problems are not the result of logical procedures but derive from prelogical forms of encoding.

Document Design and Discourse Design

Lastly, it seems appropriate to end a chapter on discourse by calling attention to the interesting work that has been going on in the areas of **document design** and **discourse design**. Here indeed is an area which eagerly awaits practical applications of what we have learned in the field of sentence and discourse processing. Much analytical work has obviously been carried out on the nature of written text and spoken discourse, and some of these findings are now also beginning to find their way into practical design applications for both documents and discourse. Legal and medical discourse (see Kess 1985 and West 1984, respectively, for examples) have been extremely fertile areas because of the structured nature of the discourse, as well as the critical import of how effective conversational partners must converge to achieve a mutual goal of understanding complex facts (see Kess 1989). In the area of document design, government documents promulgating laws and regulations or solicitation of information through questionnaires, insurance policies (Shuy and Larkin 1978), paper inserts that come with medical prescriptions, and a whole range of textual discourse have profited from making such document prose clear and easier to read and understand. But the principles of clarity are a derivative of our understanding of ordinary discourse and the way that we typically take meaning from chunks of language. The corollary of this fact is that simplicity does not equal clarity, but that clarity is better achieved by ensuring that a textual document or conversational exchange is organized in a way that lays out the alternatives in a way that matches what we have discussed here of how humans actually process discourse for information.

Summary

Discourse utterances typically have a dual function, communicating informational content as well as communicating intentions. When we speak, we not only transfer information in a propositional sense, but we also convey our intentions by performing activities like suggesting, promising, and requesting. The speech act is a useful unit of analysis for describing the intention of an utterance, as is the proposition for showing its informational content. This informational content is either given information or new information in respect to the thematic structure of the discourse. Old information is that which the hearer can already be expected to know. New information moves the discourse forward by adding novel and relevant information, and it is often overtly marked by some linguistic feature.

Many utterances are direct speech acts, meaning that they have the same illocutionary force as the literal reading of the sentence. Illocutionary force refers to the intention or function a speech act is supposed to fulfill; that is, utterances serve some function, such as to inform, to warn, to question, to demand, or to apologize. Illocutionary force can form the basis of a taxonomy of speech acts, which includes representatives (assertions), directives (questions, commands, and requests) commissives (promises and threats), expressives (thanks and apologies), and declarations (appointing). The most common speech acts in everyday discourse are assertions, questions,· and commands, and as such, they are typically shortened in normal conversational practice.

Indirect speech acts have a literal reading other than the illocutionary force of the sentence, and this relationship exhibits varying degrees of conventionality. The convention of means reflects the way in which an indirect request is carried out; for example, in English we typically question whether the listener has the ability to do the activity that is being requested (*Can you close that window?*). The convention of form reflects how commonly a given form is used to convey an indirect request; for example, *Can you close that window?* is more common than *Is it possible for you to close that window?*. The more conventional an indirect speech act is, the easier it is to comprehend in conversational contexts.

Utterances in discourse abide by a set of shared conventions that we are all aware of and adhere to as speakers and hearers. Such rules may be implicit, but they are nonetheless conversational postulates that we expect to be followed, for we refer to them in making conversational implicatures of what was really meant. Conversational exchanges are thus not normally just a succession of unconnected remarks, but are best viewed in the abstract, as cooperative efforts in the ideal sense. Ideally, conversational partners expect one another to be truthful, informative, relevant, and clear.

Discourse exhibits structure in both its written and spoken forms, and is coherent if its parts relate to one another. This cohesion has been formally explained by describing coherence relations between propositions; one or more macro-themes set the entire discourse episode, and sub-themes bridge the gaps between sections in the discourse.

Conversation is a specific form of discourse, realized by more than one person in spoken dialogues. Speakers and hearers are in fact constructing the conversation, for they create joint meanings and coordinate conversationally relevant acts. Conversation is also sensitive to cohesion, and when a given contribution is not in step with the ongoing conversation, that turn has a disruptive effect on the conversation. Conversational turn-taking parallels the way in which cohesion is achieved by conversational partners.

Discourse considerations affect the accurate recollection of the actual sentence format, in addition to its content. For example, the surface form of an utterance can be quite accurately remembered if it has sociolinguistic connotations, pragmatic implications, or carries information about the social relationships, beliefs, and personal characteristics of the listener.

A discourse view of ambiguity suggests that context has an organizational effect on ambiguity resolution. Listeners and readers carry forward only one reading for an ambiguous item, so that a theory of ambiguity resolution must explain how the successful identification of the correct reading is achieved. How does information about meaning, context, bias, and pragmatic use cooperate with parsing strategies to influence, narrow, or erase the range of alternatives potentially available to the listener or reader who encounters ambiguity?

We rely on thematic structures and schemata in our under tanding of stories, scripts, and scenes, for they provide the topical frame of reference against which the meaning of each sentence is measured. But these should be viewed as dynamic structures, reflecting plans and goals; they are not stored in memory as unchanging wholes, but are constructed afresh from procedural rules in memory organization. Reading times for sentences in discourse are facilitated when related knowledge-based materials precede them, and thus activate knowledge structures which imply causal connections.

Story grammars provide a generative grammar of plot structures for simple narrative stories, and reflect the fact that we read and comprehend stories faster when the constituent sentences in the story match the order expected by the story schema. The higher the proposition in the organizational structure of the discourse, the more likely it is to be remembered. Causal relations play an equally important role; the more causal connections a proposition has, whether to individual statements or to episodes, the more important it is judged to be. In general, statements which are high in the hierarchical ordering scheme, statements with categorially important content like topics, goals, and outcomes, and lastly, statements that have a large number of connections with other statements in the narrative, are all recalled and summarized more frequently and more accurately.

We represent mentally what a piece of discourse is about, rather than simply representing the discourse itself by way of a description. Words and sentences act as cues in the construction of such mental models, and so also does information from other input modalities. The resultant mental model may be closer to the structure of the events described in the discourse than it is to the propositional format, because it reflects the non-linguistic contextual inferences that the discourse triggers. Listeners are constantly making inferences or deductions from sentences that they hear, and these inferences help to tie the discourse together. They act as bridges from one sentence to the next, creating an integrated picture of what happened at each turn of events. Reasoning processes are mental operations applied to such mental models of situations and events.

Inductive and deductive strategies can be contrasted for the role they play in inference and verbal reasoning. Valid inferences are arrived at by following general semantic procedures, and can be made without recourse to formal rules of a mental logic. This suggests that a theory of reasoning should instead be based upon a knowledge of truth conditions, for spontaneous inferences arise which reflect information not explicitly stated in the premises but which maintain their semantic content. Moreover, inferences derived from natural language are very often of the *probably true* instead of the *necessarily true* type. Many of these psycholinguistic findings in how humans actually process discourse for information are useful in the refinement of document design and discourse design in technical areas like legal and medical discourse.

Chapter 7

Semantics

The Nature of Meaning and The Nature of Semantic Inquiry

An adequate theory of language must have an adequate theory of semantic structure. And it has to be a real theory of semantic structure, too, not just one that happens to fit into some current theory of language. It has to be able to specify certain universal relationships and how we interpret and employ these. A major psycholinguistic issue in semantics continues to be the nature of semantic representations in the mind, and our goal is to understand how semantic information is stored and organized in the semantic memory, as well as how that information is retrieved when needed.

Philosophical Background to the Study of Meaning

The study of the meaning of linguistic forms is as old as philosophical inquiry itself. There have been two traditional views about the role of language in mediating the external world for us, and how this mediating role comes about. Plato claimed there was a natural and necessary link between words and objects, but Aristotle thought the link to be put there by humans. We can understand the world in a way that is separate from language, and Aristotle was correct in assuming that things are named with arbitrarily selected words. This position was the basis of medieval Scholastic thought, as well as of modern Linguistics.

Modern philosophers have also split into two camps, asking different questions with different answers (see Katz 1966). We have had 'non-linguistic philosophers', like the logical positivists of the Vienna Circle, whose work was largely with artificial languages and concerned with naturalness conditions in unnatural languages. Such logical empiricists were concerned with a formalized theory of linguistic structure in general, especially with theories of reference and meaning. Under 'meaning' they pondered significance, intension, synonymity, and analyticity, and under 'reference' they examined naming, truth and extension; their approach to such matters, however, was quite distinct from the concerns of linguists. There were also 'linguistic philosophers' like Wittgenstein, whose work emphasized acceptable usage in natural languages. They were instead concerned with naturalness conditions in natural language; instead of explicit axioms and rules, they employed introspection and intuition in examining what would be reasonable to say in a given instance of ordinary language. Such 'ordinary language' philosophers would demand that linguistic descriptions be concerned with and governed by the facts of natural languages. Rather than asking the enormous question of *What is meaning?*, such philosophers of language posed simpler, more tractable questions which are part of the larger question; the questions and their answers, however, are essentially language-based. For example, what is the difference between sentences like *Colorless green ideas slept furiously* and *Colorful calico kittens played happily?* We may define it as the difference between language-based definitions of meaningfulness and meaninglessness. This was later reflected in the attempt to define semantics in a way that was compatible with syntax, by determining that meaningfulness had much to do with how nouns, verbs, and adjectives collocated with one another in sentence patterns. The compatibility which allowed words to go together had to do with their semantic features, and this gave us a formal explanation for not only collocation, but also certain aspects of synonymy, ambiguity, redundancy, and paraphrase.

At the very least, a theory of meaning has to account for the basic imperfection in the relation between form and meaning. Every language has synonyms, instances where two or more expressions have the same meaning (for example, *thin/skinny*). Every language also has homonyms, where a single expression has two or more meanings (for example, *saw*). And every language has polysemy, instances in which word has more than one meaning, although they are often related through a more central meaning (for example, the word *mouth* for animals and rivers).

Units of Semantic Analysis

Three linguistic units have claimed our attention as carriers of meaning: the morpheme, the word, and the feature. As we have seen, linguists have considered the smallest meaningful element in the utterances of a language to be the morpheme, not the word; later, the range of inquiry focussed upon yet another, even smaller unit, the feature. Words have an intuitive appeal as units for native speakers; for example, Aristotle defined words as the smallest significant units of speech, and Sapir's Amerindian consultants were acutely aware of the word as a conceptual unit, just as we usually are. But it is one thing to identify words intuitively and another to state the criteria by which one identifies them; the word as a basic unit has thus never figured as prominently in linguistics as it has in psychological investigations. Although there are units of meaning smaller than the word, semantic inquiry has often focussed upon the word, and as we shall see, also upon the morpheme and the semantic feature.

Models of Semantic Analysis: Lexical Semantics

Referential Theory of Meaning

This ancient view of lexical semantics claims that the meaning of a word is some object, event, or state of affairs in the real world specified or referred to by that word. But such a referential theory of meaning permits two linguistic expressions to refer to the same object, though the two forms do not mean the same thing. Compare the meanings of 'personal name/political office' for *John/the president*, which accounts for why *John is the president* is meaningful in a way that *John is John* is not. Then, too, words like *unicorn, infinity, truth* can be meaningful without having any real-world referent at all.

Ogden and Richards (1923) attempted to remind us of the mediational status of the sense of a word, as standing between the actual word as a symbol or name and the referent or thing it stands for. The basic elements in meaning are therefore three, and not just two.

1. **Symbol** or **name**=the phonetic shape of the word
2. **Thought** or **reference** or **sense**=the information which the name conveys to the speaker
3. **Referent** or **thing**=the non-linguistic feature or event we are talking about

American structuralism in linguistics and behaviorism in psychology were mechanistic, anti-mentalistic, and thus tried to avoid dealing with the psychological factors inherent in the correlated mental processes. Both posited a direct relationship between symbol and referent, suggesting that the meaning of a linguistic form is essentially the situation in which speakers utter a particular linguistic form and the response which it calls forth in the hearer.

Denotation vs. Connotation

A **denotative** theory of word meaning notes that a word refers to an abstract class of objects, namely, to our mental concepts. The word *dog* refers not to a particular object but to our mental category of dogs. But there is more to word meanings than just reference. Language users have attitudes, feelings, and opinions about words and their referents that is very much a part of the meaning of a given concept. This is the **connotation** of a word, and several extremely clever measuring devices have been developed to measure this aspect of meaning.

Semantic Differential

Osgood and his colleagues found that there was a way to measure the connotative aspects of meaning with some precision, for humans universally use the same qualifying attributes in assigning connotative values to words. These attributes were based on three variables of evaluation (good-bad), potency (strong-weak), and activity (active-passive). In the application of this technique, termed the **semantic differential**, subjects locate a given stimulus word on a 7-point scale anchored at either end by a pair of bipolar terms like 'strong/weak' or 'good/bad' (Osgood, Suci and Tannenbaum 1957; see also Snider and Osgood 1968). Thus, *tornado* has been evaluated by American English speakers as 'strong, active, and bad', *lazy* as 'weak, passive, and bad', and *baby* as 'weak, active, and good' (Jenkins, Russell and Suci 1958).

The semantic differential also allowed for cross-cultural semantic analysis in the area of affective, connotative aspects of language. Since the basic criteria of evaluation, potency, and activity are assumed to underlie connotative meaning in all semantic systems, one can use the criteria as a metric for comparing the connotative meaning of words in different languages and cultures (Osgood 1964; Snider and Osgood 1968). Moreover, one can also use the same criteria to trace the changing connotative meaning of a concept in the same society; for example, in Jenkins et al. (1958), *divorce* was 'weak, active, and bad', but thirty years of change in societal attitudes may have altered this evaluation, and the semantic differential allows us to measure this over time.

The semantic differential is a neo-behaviorist attempt to provide an account of meaning in a behaviorist framework, which demands that meaning is ultimately a response derived from observable behavior. Behaviorist accounts of meaning were typically too simplistic, and the semantic differential attempted to remedy this by accounting for at least the connotative aspect of meaning. Meaning is now related to a mediating response, the internal response to some expression. This response is considered to have been originally made to the referent of the word, and is now conditioned to the word as an internal mediating response. Thus was neo-behaviorism able to maintain both its commitment to stimulus-response explanations and yet tackle the problem of meaning.

Word Associations

An association theory looks for latent relationships, the covert links that words have with other words, images, and thoughts. Experiments with **word associations** attempt to transform associative relationships from latent relationships into relationships which are sequential and tangible. The system is like a spiderweb, with words in the mental network related to other words via associative links of varying strengths.

In a free association test, the subject is given a word and asked to respond with the first word that comes to mind. There is a surprising consistency across subjects for many words like *boy, black*, but not for some others like *aardvark, sepia*. Associationist experiments try to determine the frequencies of associations to gain knowledge of the psychological space in which a word is located.

Word association responses can be classified in respect to type.

1. Members of the same part of speech class (paradigmatic) or not (syntagmatic)

    a. paradigmatic responses: (often synonyms like *thin/ skinny* or antonyms like *black/white*
    b. syntagmatic responses: *dig/hole*
2. Members of the same taxonomy

    a. subordinate: *dog/retriever*
    b. superordinate: *dog/animal*; superordinate responses are more common than subordinate
3. Rhyming or clang responses: *yellow/mellow*

Word association responses are sensitive to the context in which the task is posed. If subjects must respond quickly, clang responses like *sister-blister/yellow-fellow* are common. If subjects have more time, responses which are similar in semantic features are given, as in *man-woman/sister-brother*. And if subjects are under no time constraint to respond, then more idiosyncratic responses like *man-door/ sister-summer* emerge.

Some have taken the associated meaning of a word to be the sum of all the associations offered by subjects. For example, one can ask subjects to cite as many words as they can think of as associations for the stimulus word, or to take the most common associations and have subjects then associate with those words. Thus, for a word like *butterfly*, Deese (1965) found not only a frequency matrix for associations, but also how they clustered into feature groupings like *animate (bees, fly, bug, wing)* and *inanimate (sky, yellow, spring)*. The associative meaning of a word, then, is the sum total of all the things that a person thinks of upon hearing a word (Deese 1962). Interestingly, incorrect words produced by aphasic patients are often related in meaning to the intended word, so that their erroneous naming responses resemble the word associations of normal speakers (Caramazza and Berndt 1978).

Associations have been ordered in systematic ways, in an attempt to mirror the organizational process which occurs during the act of word associating. For example, Hormann (1971/1979) once summarized the categorial associations for *needle* as follows.

1. definitions, including synonyms and supra-ordination (for example, 'instrument, tool, article, sewing')
2. completion and predication (for example, 'sharp, steel, pointed, eye, work')
3. coordinates and contrasts (for example, 'thread, cloth, pin')

4.   valuations and personal associations (for example, 'prick, hurt, blood, useful')

Semantic Fields

Some semanticists have assumed that related words participate in
a **semantic field** whose properties and dimensions are defined by members of the set themselves. That is, the meaning of a lexical item is a
function of the meaning relations that hold between words in the same
domain (Fillenbaum and Rapoport 1971). It is reminiscent of Gestalt
psychology in that a group of words together form a semantic field,
much like the stones of a mosaic made up a patterned field with visual
integrity. Although field theory lends itself readily to feature analysis,
the specific features are derivative from the set of items under investigation, and usually distinguish finer differences than feature theory.
And field theory does not require binary features like feature theory,
because it examines differences among members of a class, while feature theory invokes general features to distinguish among the classes
themselves.

The methodology used is similar to that used to explore semantic
differential and word association studies. One studies how semantic
information is organized, stored, and retrieved, by simply asking subjects how they perceive the relationships between various lexical items
and their categories. For example, Fillenbaum and Rapoport studied
the mental organization speakers have for related words in fields like
color, kinship terms, pronouns, names of emotions, prepositions, conjunctions, verbs of possession, verbs of judging, and evaluational 'good-
bad' terms. Such lexical fields are highly organized, tightly knit groupings of lexical items; each word within a field like kinship terms
derives its meaning from the system as a whole and its contrastive
position vis-a-vis the other words. College students made judgments of
relative similarity among members of a given set by constructing a
graph with linkages among words determined by perceived closeness of
meaning. Their results with color terms are quite informative; color
can be technically described by the physical properties of hue, brightness, and saturation, but for their subjects, however, hue was most
important dimension, with little awareness of brightness or saturation.

Miller (1967) also employed a sorting experiment by subjects that
provided a cluster analysis set of results. Subjects were given a stack
of file cards, each with a word printed on it. When asked to sort the
cards into piles according to how similar the words were to one
another, subjects showed results that provided clusters of words that
they perceived to group together. For example, most put *plant* and
tree together, and almost as many added the word *root* to that grouping. One clustering was broken into three general sets: *yield, exhaust*;
battle, kill, deal, play, labour; *joke, question, vow, counsel, help*. Sub-
sets show how some vocabulary items have been characterized as closer
to one another in the semantic field; for example, in set three, *joke,
question, vow* constitute an even closer subset, as distinct from *counsel,*

help. The basic problem with this approach, however, is that the set is chosen by the experimenter, and the classification is imposed upon the set by subjects who assess and relate a set of terms. The relative salience of some features is always a function of the particular set being analyzed.

Feature Theory

The meanings of words are assumed to be broken down into separate components or features, so that the basic meaning of any lexical item can be specified by an independent set of **semantic features** (Katz and Fodor 1963; Katz and Postal 1964; Chomsky 1965). The more features shared by a set of words, the more closely related they are semantically. The notion of features already had appeared in phonology and in the componential analysis of bounded structures like kinship systems in anthropology.

In phonology, the notion of distinctive features described sound units as actually composed of simultaneously occurring features. The features were drawn from a universal set of distinctive features, and the features intersected to allow cross-classification in defining classes. Any sound could thus be matched with any other sound which exhibited similar properties, simply by specifying a rule involving that specific feature or subset of features. For example, Chomsky and Halle's *Sound Pattern of English* (1968) has a rule which deals only with those sounds in English which have the feature of +coronal; this involves only those sounds (dental, alveolar, and palato-alveolar) which involve the tongue tip and blade (the crown, or "corona"), thus excluding those sounds which are -coronal (labial and velar) sounds. This grouping can obviously be neatly and accurately specified with just one feature.

The importation of distinctive feature methodology into anthropology led to componential analysis for such lexical classes as kinship terms (Lounsbury 1956). For example, a whole kinship system like the English set of *father, mother, uncle, aunt, son, daughter, nephew, niece* can be described by only three features of generation, sex, and lineality. A kin term like *father* is thus taken to be a bundle of simultaneously occurring features like male, non-collateral, and first ascending generation.

In the acquisition of a semantic system by children, it was assumed that the meaning of lexical items would be acquired a feature at a time, with the perceptually most salient or most important features acquired first. Where a feature cut across a number of words, for example, animate, it was also assumed that the feature would be learned once and apply right across these various categories. It was also hoped that the semantic features chosen would be based on universal semantic features, and thus representative of the attributes of the conceptual system that structures the human mind. For example, Langendoen's (1969:37) suggestion is representative: "semantic features do not represent properties of the universe but innate properties

of the human mind itself and of the human perceptual apparatus."
Feature theory largely grew out of generative grammatical concerns to
have a semantic theory that would somehow build upon, or at least
complement, the syntactic theory. The primary consideration in
semantics focussed on what must go into a dictionary or lexicon entry
in the grammar, and how selectional restrictions are to be formulated.
Thus, sentences which are anomalous, ambiguous, or paraphrases at
the semantic level had a formal treatment and a corresponding explanation within the grammatical formulations themselves, for semantics
was now a formal part of the grammar. For example, Katz and
Fodor's (1963) example sentence *The bill is large* has at least three
readings, corresponding to 'dollar bill', 'restaurant bill', and 'toucan's
bill'. The use of semantic features in describing the unique identity of
such semantic entries like *bill* was intended to mirror the speaker's
ability in determining the number of readings a sentence has by
exploiting semantic relations in the sentence to eliminate potential
ambiguities. Speakers were thus characterized as having some internalized lexicon which is employed in the production of sentences. This
internalized lexicon is not the kind one might find in a dictionary
entry, where all the meanings are organized loosely according to defini-
tional sentences. For example, *bachelor* might be there defined as 'a
man who has never married' or 'one who possesses the first university
degree'. Instead, what was considered crucial in a feature theory
approach were the criterial features by which words are similar and
different. In this view, the first definition of *bachelor* contains the features *human* and *male*, while the second contains only *human*. Only
males can be unmarried bachelors, while males or females can matricu-
late and become university graduates possessing the degree.

Nouns were characterized by a primary set of features like **Common, Count, Animate, Human, Abstract** (Chomsky 1965). The **Count**
feature refers to the grammatical property of pluralization; for example, nouns which are +count (*dog-dogs*) can take plural inflections,
but those which are -count (*dirt-*dirts*) cannot. **Common** refers to the
individuality of the noun, and is like the difference between proper and
common nouns, except that it also has overtones of collocation with
determiners; for example, since there is only one *Egypt*, we rarely say
*the Egypt, *an Egypt*. The other features seem straightforward
enough without further explanation. Thus, any given noun could be
defined in terms of its semantic features, like the following (see Chomsky 1965).

1.   boy = +common, +count, +animate, +human
2.   dog = +common, +count, +animate, -human
3.   book = +common, +count, -animate
4.   sincerity = +common, -count, -animate, +abstract
5.   dirt = +common, -count, -animate, -abstract
6.   John = -common, -count, +animate, +human
7.   Fido = -common, -count, +animate, -human
8.   Egypt = -common, -count, -animate,

One thus has a set of grouping characteristics which can be applied to other nouns; for example, *woman* obviously has the same general characteristics as *boy*, *table* the same as *book*, *confetti* as *dirt*, and so forth. One also has cross-classificational possibilities immediately available, so that we can now call up all those nouns with the feature of +animate, or those with the feature of -count, varying the size of the set we wish to address, without naming individual nouns. The idea in such feature classification of words is that grammatical markers like **noun** and semantic markers like **animate** mark that which is regular and systematic in the language. But the idiosyncratic features of word meanings would still have to be marked in an individual fashion, since they vary from word to word.

There was now provision for a set of rules which would combine lexical items in ways that correspond to the sequences that comprise the grammatical sequences of the language. In a generative syntax, the motivation for such feature designations was simply to be able to avoid ungrammatical sentences like *The boy persuaded the tomato* or *Sincerity plays golf*. The motivation was also to explain why sentences like *The boy persuaded the teacher* or *The girl plays golf* were grammatically well-formed. With the introduction of features as the essential defining characteristic of nouns, one now had a way of describing in formal terms the way in which nouns and verbs co-occur with one another, for verbs are now defined in respect to the nouns they will co-occur with in sentence patterns. For example, *persuade* is a verb which can only co-occur with animate human nouns as direct object; *play* is a verb which requires an animate human noun as subject, particularly when the direct object is a sport like golf. In this way, we can characterize the second pair of sentences as grammatical and semantically well-formed, while the first pair is not.

Once the notion of features is accepted, one finds further uses for it in delimiting meaning. An excellent example is McCawley's (1970) example of semantic components in complex verbs like *kill*. *Kill* has the underlying features of 'cause', 'become', 'not alive'. In a sentence like *John almost killed Harry*, there are three possible readings for the sentence because the adverb *almost* can modify any of the three features. One meaning has John mad enough to go and shoot Harry, but cooling down and seeing reason; this would be the adverb modifying the feature of **cause**. Another meaning would be John actually taking a shot, but missing; this would be the adverb modifying the feature of **become**. And the third possible meaning is John taking a shot, wounding Harry seriously, but not enough to do him in; this would be the adverb modifying the feature of **not alive**.

Similarly, the verb *lend* may be decomposed into the features of temporary possession and the fact of transfer. In a sentence like *John lent Harry his bicycle until tomorrow*, the phrase *until tomorrow* modifies the feature of temporary possession, not the fact of transfer. Indeed, when one looks closely at certain word pairs, they only differ by one such feature. For example, pairs like *present-absent* differ in a single feature of negativity; some pairs like *kill-die*, *feed-eat*, *teach-learn* differ in the feature of causality; and some pairs like *die-death*, *melt-liquid* differ in the feature of realization. But such facts are better dealt with in a theory of semantics than in a theory of syntax, and we can conclude this discussion of semantic features by agreeing with McCawley (1973) that what is needed is a set of explanatory semantic principles rather than a souped-up syntax. Not surprisingly, the notion of feature finds better use in the prototypicality and network models, and the notion of subcategorization (see the section on subcategorizational rules in the chapter on **Syntax**) finds a logical home in the postulation of verb-type assignments in compositional semantics.

Prototype Theory

Typicality is also an important factor in the organization of concepts in the semantic memory. Some defining properties are more salient than others; for example, some birds are typically conceived of as more bird-like than others (see Rosch 1973, 1975, 1978). Semantic categories are best explained by a graded type of membership rather than absolute inclusion of membership. Rosch has explained natural classes as clustering around a **prototypical** member, a categorial example which has the best cluster of attributes that characterize the class. Some members of a class are more central to the class, in that they share more of the relevant attributes; other members are more peripheral, because they have only one or several of the attributes. For example, robins seem more birdlike than chickens or penguins, though both belong to the category of bird; wooden chairs with straight backs, well-defined seats and four legs seem more chair-like than a polyester bean-bag chair flopped on the floor; plums and cherries seem more like fruit than coconuts and olives. Rosch has noted that this is true for taxonomies as different as that of trees, birds, fish, fruit, musical instruments, tools, clothing, furniture, and vehicles (Rosch 1978).

Rosch and Mervis (1975) had subjects evaluate furniture, vehicles, fruit, weapons, vegetables, and clothing to determine the ranking of members according to their typicality and representational value in respect to the category. Not only was this an easy task, but the results were very consistent from subject to subject. The most prototypical members of a category are those with most attributes in common with other members and the least in common with members of other categories. Thus, a robin is more prototypically a bird because it shares more defining characteristics (sings, perches in trees, has feathers, flies, is medium-sized) with other members than a penguin or chicken does. Folk taxonomies are usually based on gross morphological characteristics and behavior, and it is for such reasons that the whale is viewed as more similar to the shark than other mammals. Instead of expecting an absolute set of necessary features that define the concept, prototype theory suggests that we instead pay attention to the description of a given instance of that concept. Semantic categories have an internal structure that is not captured by absolutes or hierarchies; very simply, some instances are more typical of a category than others, just as robins are "birdier" than chickens. Natural classes have some members closer to the central cluster of attributes for a class, and others as more marginal. Yet the class exists with a membership of both. Prototype theory answers the problem of fuzziness within the membership of a category, and the fact that some items seem to be better carriers of family resemblance than others. Semantic categories are mentally structured in terms of shared attributes, with some members of the category judged as being closer to the prototypical member and therefore better representatives of the category than others.

Apparently, listeners have the prototype in mind as the reference point when they process or produce sentences. One of Rosch's experiments had subjects compose sentences with category names, as for example, *I heard a bird singing outside my window.* The category name was then replaced with a specific name like *robin* or *ostrich*, and other subjects were asked to rate the sensibility of such sentences. Not surprisingly, the more typical a category member was, the more easily it could replace the category name.

Other findings indicate that the more typical a category member is, the more quickly sentences containing that word are judged as true. For example, both of the following sentences are true, but sentence (1) is judged more quickly as true or false.

1. A robin is a bird.
2. A chicken is a bird.

Subjects overwhelmingly agree about how good an example is of a given category, even when the atypical members are frequent and familiar words. Prototype theory thus reflects the fact that the boundaries for concepts are usually fuzzy and less than clear-cut, allowing for the plasticity in categories that allows us to expand them or divert them by metaphoric extension. But this does not mean that 'fuzzy set' theory, as developed to answer the shortcomings of standard set theory for imprecise concepts, can be applied to how exemplars represent categories within a taxonomy. This particular mathematical model cannot correctly portray the situation for exemplars of natural categories at different levels within the taxonomy (Roth and Mervis 1983; Mervis and Roth 1981). The attributes or properties of a category are directly related to typicality, in the sense that the greater the overlap, the greater the typicality. In fact, the properties of natural categories tend to occur together in clusters; thus, animals with wings and beaks usually also fly and have feathers instead of fur (see Malt and Smith 1984).

Such cognitive activity is reflected in the basic principles that underlie the formation of basic categories. Rosch (1978) notes that the principle of cognitive economy allows as many properties as possible to be predictable from knowing any one property; this reduces the infinite differences among stimuli to manageable proportions. The second principle has to do with perceived world structure, in that the material objects in the world are perceived to possess a high correlational structure, as for example, wings with feathers more often than with fur. These two basic principles of categorization underlie how categories are abstracted and how the internal structure of categories are formed.

The degree of representativeness for an item depends upon how many attributes it shares with other members of the same category, and how few attributes it shares with members of other categories. For example, whales are mammals, but because they swim, are found in the sea, and have sleek skin, they seem to be less like dogs and horses and more like sharks and other large fish; a similar argument could be made for penguins as less representative of birds, which normally do fly and don't swim. Thus, the more attributes an item has in common with one category, and the fewer it shares with other categories, the more representative it will be of its own category (Rosch 1978). Prototypes are simply members of a category which best reflect the redundancy structure of the relationships among the attributes that are taken to characterize the category.

Malt and Smith (1984) have demonstrated that there are systematic property relationships across members of natural categories, and that such clustering relationships can affect typicality. Their findings also seem to support a set of intermediate groupings, in much the same way that intermediate groupings operate in folk taxonomies, indicating the presence of perceptual or functional groupings that are recognized even though there may not be single-word names for them. For example, it is true that a *robin* is a *bird*, but it is also true that we recognize an intermediate grouping in which robins can be said to belong to a category of small, chirping, worm- or seed-eating birds which fly up into trees.

Categorial Networks

The basic issue in semantic storage and memory is how the meanings of words are stored in memory, how they are related, and how this affects the processing of sentences which contain those words. The **categorial network** approach assumes that each category name is a part of a taxonomy, and that each word thus belongs to a network of words. The meaning of a word is given by its relationships to all other words in the network. Collins and Quillian (1969) set into motion a paradigm of research devoted to understanding how words relate to one another in a network of relationships and how different features of these relationships, as defined by the network, might account for reaction time differences. Their technique employs a simple verification task which requires subjects to make true-false decisions about assertions like *An ostrich is a canary*.

Quillian's work had originally been an attempt to provide a computer simulation of how semantic memory is searched in the process of comprehension. The semantic memory is portrayed as a network, with each concept in that network represented as a node, with links to other such concepts at nodes more or less distant. The full meaning of a given concept is thus the whole subset of the network as reached by pathways from the node in question. Words are thus interconnected by a number of relationships, and the most easily represented of these is their hierarchical relationship in the network. Some words can be specified as subordinate to others, as *retriever* is to *dog*, or superordinate to others, as *animal* is to *dog*. Words are said to be hierarchically arranged, and this hierarchical organization is reflected in how words are accessed in the semantic memory. The size of the category and its inclusiveness in the hierarchy was a major feature of such hierarchical network models in attempting to model semantic memory.

Collins and Quillian (1969) demonstrated that subjects are better able to verify sentences which require classification when the category is small than when it is large. The processing implication of this approach is that the longer one has to search through this network, the longer it will take. Thus, sentences (1) and (3) are easier to judge as true or false, because the number of steps are fewer. A hierarchical path to *retriever* or *canary* starts at *animal*, moving through the intermediate nodes of *dog* and *bird* before getting to the actual words.

1.   A retriever is a dog. (1 step)
2.   A retriever is an animal. (2 steps).
3.   A canary is a bird. (1 step)
4.   A canary is an animal. (2 steps).

Some have argued that semantic relatedness is more important than inclusion and category size, and that a feature-based model is a better explanatory device. Several experiments (Smith, Shoben and Rips 1974) have instead suggested that such response times reflect the fact that *canary* and *bird* are more closely related in meaning than are *canary* and *animal*. And, in fact, Rips, Shoben and Smith (1973) did show that some smaller categories exhibit lower response times for their verification, though McCloskey (1980) has suggested that such results may be due to differential familiarity with the stimulus words. That is, the word *mammal* is not as familiar as *animal*, and this accounts for why sentence (1) takes longer than sentence (2) to process.

1.   A bear is a mammal.
2.   A bear is an animal.

Smith et al. (1974) claim that a feature-based model is a better explanatory device, and that the amount of priming activation is really reflective of the degree of feature overlap between the words or concepts in question. One can also define words in the network by specifying their properties, as for example, dogs have four legs, tails, and pointed teeth. Thus, the more features that are activated in both the initial word and its related word, the more readily processed will both be when they are processed together. The semantic features or properties of such words may be unordered. So for example, the feature of *yellow* might be stored directly with *canary*, but the property of *having wings* would stored at a higher level in the hierarchy, at the level of *bird* (see Perfetti 1972). This would explain why it takes longer to judge whether sentence (2) is true or false.

1.   A canary is yellow. (1 step)

2.   A canary has wings. (2 steps).

There has been some evidence in support of this approach, but there has also been much against it. It would seem that mental categories are not the same as the scientific ones developed in the natural sciences or even the deductive ones developed by language philosophers. For example, the hierarchical path to *horse* would take one from *animal* through *ungulates* (hooved animals), but this is obviously not a much-used category in the English folk taxonomy. If you ever consciously had to learn that the whale is a mammal, like the bear, and not a fish, like the basking shark, you will easily understand that folk science is not the same as academic science. Not only do folk taxonomies have a higher profile in our common semantic usage, but even the scientific ones break down at times, as does the common phylogenetic scale when faced with egg-laying mammals like the platypus and the echidna.

Spreading Activation Models

The most satisfying network model has been the **spreading activation** model of the lexicon (Collins and Loftus 1975), an improvement on Quillian's notions which incorporates the results of a number of experimental findings on semantic memory. The basic assumption is still that the semantic memory is organized around the basic feature of semantic similarity, but the network of relationships between words is no longer hierarchical. Words are connected to other words by more than strict subordination or superordination ties, but also by how typical they are for that particular class (a retriever is more typical of dogs than a Borzoi), and how typically a feature is associated with the particular word in question (for example, *dogs have fleas* vs. *dogs have ribcages*). In a spreading activation model of the lexicon, the activation of a single word then spreads over its network of associated words, being strongest with the most closely associated words and weakest as the strength of the relationship decreases with semantic distance. When any one concept is being processed, its activation spreads out along the pathways of the network; its effect decreases in time, much as the ripples on a pond weaken as they distance from the original starting point. Thus, if *vehicle* is primed, so also will be *fire engine/ truck/bus*, and they in turn will prime one another as well. Thus, one can expect that sentences like *Retrievers are dogs* or *Dogs chase cats* will be easier to verify as true or false than sentences like *Retrievers are omnivores* or *Dogs chase philosophers*.

The Collins and Loftus model thus explains how semantic priming operates, by spreading activation of nearby related concepts in the semantic memory. The highly replicated finding that related words are more easily processed when presented after a related word, than after an unrelated word, is a result of the rich connections between concepts in the semantic network. It is also responsive to the experimental results reported for multiple access in lexical ambiguity. However, this attractive explanation may be task-specific, since Lupker (1984) has found that the priming effects may be different from lexical decision to lexical naming tasks, and that the amount of priming provided by a related stimulus pair may depend on the task.

Lexical Ambiguity and the Notion of Spreading Activation . Although we have considered the psycholinguistic study of ambiguity in the chapters on **Syntax** and **Discourse**, it worth recalling that ambiguity can and does occur at the semantic level of word meaning (**lexical ambiguity**). Sentences like *The visitors enjoyed the port* and *The young man picked up the pipe* are ambiguous because a particular word has more than one meaning. The fact is that many sentences are ambiguous or vague because lexical items are ambiguous or vague, exhibiting a semantic range larger than a single and unique referent. For example, even the preceding sentence is an ambiguous example, if you read as far as the word *because*. That is, as you were reading along the printed line, two readings were possible up to that point. There is a second possible reading for *many sentences*, as used in the judicial sense, with courtroom judges handing down ambiguous or vague sentences at the conclusion of criminal proceedings. Try reading it again: *The fact is that many sentences are ambiguous or vague because . . .*.

The important processing question for lexical ambiguity is the same as it is for syntactic ambiguity, and can be re-stated as follows. Does the reader call up and maintain all possible readings for an ambiguous word until the correct interpretation is decided upon? Do listeners do the same in processing spoken language? Or do they employ some short-cut which avoids the need for this? If they do use such short-cuts, do these occur before the lexical search begins? Or does the short-cut occur early in the search for word meaning?

Not surprisingly, lexical ambiguity has generated more research in the past decade than syntactic ambiguity because it is special case of what is involved in word recognition. Like syntactic ambiguity, the possible answers to the problem of lexical ambiguity are of three types. One claims that context determines that one and only one meaning of an ambiguous word is to be accessed; another claims that the more common meaning of an ambiguous word is accessed first, and is discarded only after it has been determined that its meaning is inappropriate in the context. The third answer is that all meanings of an ambiguous lexical item are accessed at first, and then the correct meaning is decided upon, at which point the others are discarded. Hirst (1987) has labelled these the prior choice hypothesis, the ordered search hypothesis, and the all-readings hypothesis, respectively; they have also been termed the single-reading, ordered search, and multiple-reading hypotheses (Kess and Hoppe 1981), as well as the context-dependent model, the ordered-access model, and the exhaustive access model (Simpson 1984).

A quick summary of the research on ambiguous lexical items seems to indicate that the third answer is correct and also provides strong support for the notion of spreading activation. All meanings of an ambiguous lexical item are accessed at first, and then the correct meaning is decided upon, at which point the others are discarded. To be more specific, all meanings of an ambiguous lexical item are accessed during the first 200 milliseconds of the search, after which time the appropriate meaning has been chosen, and the other meanings are then discarded (Hirst 1987:93). A crucial consideration is how far along the lexical decision path one taps the processing that the listener/reader is going through. For example, if you check immediately after the presentation of an ambiguous word, all its meanings are apparently being accessed (below the level of awareness, of course!). But if you check after 1.5 seconds, a decision has already been reached and the subjects will only be sensitive to the contextually correct meaning (see Foss 1988). As an example, recall how we determined that **semantic priming** activated faster recall for the word *nurse* after the word *doctor*, but that this did not happen for the word *horse* after the word *doctor*. This was because the words *nurse* and *doctor* are semantically related. The same thing happens with an ambiguous word like *mint*, but it happens with **both** meanings. For example, the ambiguous word *mint* has two associated meanings, one being *candy* and the other *coin*. If you present the word *mint* to subjects, they are semantically primed for **both** meanings and will respond to either meaning, *candy* or *coin*, within the first 200 milliseconds after presentation. But if you check at 1.5 seconds after the word has been presented, only the contextually appropriate meaning is responded to.

Models of Semantic Interpretation: Compositional Semantics

Semantics is not just about the meaning of words. The semantic interpretation of an utterance in natural language is derived as much from the ways in which its words are combined as it is from the meaning of the individual words. What we have done up till now is lay out different approaches to the analysis of word meanings. But a complete picture of how we understand natural language requires a set of principles for how lexical interpretations are combined to yield full semantic interpretations for utterances which are syntactically more complex than a single word (see Ladusaw 1988). But before we look at compositional semantics, however, we should recall several earlier theoretical developments that prepared the way for the current focus on semantic interpretation.

Earlier Semantics-based Grammars

We saw how semantic theories within a generative grammatical framework tried to fulfill the requirement of adding a semantic component to a grammatical framework which also had components that would describe phonology and syntax. Structural grammar had attempted to locate the processes of formation in the area of surface structure and failed; generative grammar tried initially to locate the processes of formation in an imaginary deep structure, avoiding an outright commitment to semantics. Since the grammar required a theoretical continuity and presentational symmetry, later theories of semantics (Interpretive Semantics by Katz, Extended Standard Theory by Chomsky and Jackendoff, and even Generative Semantics by Lakoff) were constrained in the form they could take. As grammars took a more semantic approach to formulating descriptions of what languages do, this suggested to many a directionality which starts with a semantic structure for principles of well-formedness, and then ends with the actual phonetic realization. For those that specified semantics as the essential component of the grammar, there was little reason for specifying anything like deep structure, if it is not itself the underlying semantic structure. For such theorists, there was no longer a real boundary between syntax and semantics, only a methodological one. Indeed, this tension between the domains of syntax and semantics continues to be the source of theoretical debate in linguistics (see Ladusaw 1988 and Enc 1988), and the mapping between the two domains is of central concern to psycholinguists interested in natural language processing.

Earlier Case Grammars

More and more emphasis came to be placed on the underlying functional values of elements in the grammar (see J. D. Fodor 1977). Several grammars called attention to the fact of functional or **case roles** for noun phrases, and the fact that formal generative treatments had not addressed this important fact (Fillmore 1968, 1977; Chafe 1970).

Fillmore observed that in sentences like the following it is always the boy, as agent, who sets the action into motion; it is always the key, as instrument, by which the action is accomplished; and it is always the door, as object, that moves as a result of the action. We can thus speak of the three nouns *boy, door, key* as being in the agentive case, the objective case, and the instrumental case. Even though the surface syntax may shuffle their positions about, their case function roles remain identical.

1. The door opened.
2. The boy opened the door.
3. The key opened the door.
4. The door was opened with a key by the boy.

Such underlying functional differences also explain other semantic niceties, like the differences between verbs like *build* and *destroy*. The first results in something which had not previously existed, while the second requires an already existent product to act upon. This same type of ambiguity is seen elsewhere, as in sentences like *John paints nudes*, which can have either of the meanings exemplified by sentence (1) and (2), respectively.

1.   *Modigliani and Rubens painted nudes, creating canvases that were masterpieces.*
2.   *Psychedelic painters in the sixties painted the nude bodies of young women, but this is an art fashion which is no longer with us in the nineties.*

Although Fillmore's notions never formed a school of linguistic thought with an easily identified following, they have been extremely influential. Psycholinguists often refer to the functional notions embodied in case roles, and developmental psycholinguists have found such functional notions more useful in discussing early language development than purely syntactic notions. Moreover, Fillmore's ideas fit right in with the intellectual flow that culminates in the current focus on compositional semantics.

Chafe similarly suggested that there are simply things and actions, and that the intersection of these provides defining qualities. The possible co-occurrence of these depend upon their real-world relationships, and how we see them; conceptually, the universe is broken into nouns (things and abstractions) and verbs (states, conditions, qualities, and events). For Chafe too, the verb is central, because in every language there is a verb present semantically in all sentences, except for marginal utterances. The nature of the verb determines what the rest of the sentence will look like, and how it is interpreted. For example, in a sentence like *The chair laughed*, we interpret the use of the verb as odd, not the noun. This is not really very far from the compositional view that one can generalize about the relationship between syntactic categories and semantic objects, by saying that verbs provide the predicates for individuals while their associated noun phrases provide their arguments.

The Compositionality Principle

The meaning of a sentence is determined only in part by the meanings of its words. The full semantic interpretation of a sentence is also a function of how those individual lexical items have been combined, that is, a function of the syntactic relations holding between the parts. To refresh your memory, sentences like (1) and (2) below receive different semantic interpretations for this reason. Certain syntactic differences lead to differences in the assignment of semantic roles, and thus to differences in truth conditions. But not all syntactic differences have the same effect. For example, consider sentences (3) and (4); despite the syntactic arrangements for passivization and topicalization, you will note that they exhibit the same semantic roles as (1) and thus have the same truth conditions. And if you substitute other human nouns for *John* and *Mary*, or another transitive verb for *love*, the assignment of semantic roles will remain constant (see Enc 1988).

1.   Mary loves John.
2.   John loves Mary.

3.   John is loved by Mary.
4.   John, Mary loves.

This is known as **Frege's Principle** (Frege 1952/1960), or the **Principle of Compositionality**, namely, that "the meaning of the whole is a function of the meaning of the parts and their mode of combination" (Dowty, Wall and Peters 1981:8). Obviously, syntax is an important aspect of compositionality, but understanding the nature of compositionality is nothing less than being able to assign semantic interpretations to the output of syntax in a systematic way (see Enc 1988).

We require a grammatically neutral way of stating the logical arguments of a predicate. The notion of compositionality thus also implies that the lexical representations we postulate should make provision for the way that lexical items are combined. For example, our lexical representations for verbs must reflect the fact that verbs take one or more arguments. Sentences like (1) through (4) each contain a verb type that differs in the number and kind of arguments it takes.

1.   *The baby slept.* Verbs like *sleep* denote functions that take only one argument.
2.   *The baby saw the rattle.* Verbs like *see* denote functions that take two arguments.
3.   *The baby put the rattle under the blanket.* Verbs like *put* denote functions that take three arguments, one of which must be a location.
4.   *The baby hoped that her mother would come back into the room.* Verbs like *hope* denote functions that take two arguments, one of which is a sentential complement which is itself a proposition.

This information is commonly presented as a set of **semantic roles**, or **thematic roles**, like **agent, goal, patient, source, experiencer**, and **location**. The terms for such semantic roles are reminiscent of earlier work in case grammars, and serve as a syntax-neutral way for specifying arguments for those predicates that enter into the semantic interpretation of an utterance. Such notions have been supported by experimental results as well. For example, Tanenhaus and Carlson (1989) have demonstrated that the argument structure of verbs is utilized during language comprehension, and even suggest that the directive role of such thematic information weighs in on the modularity side of the modularity-vs.-interactionism debate about the immediacy of lexical effects in sentence comprehension.

Mental Models Again!

We have seen that comprehension of discourse requires construction of a mental model of the situation described by the discourse. The individual words contribute to this, as listener constructs a mental model by using inferences made on the basis of context about the specific referents that the words point to. A semantic theory which is psychologically adequate will have to take into account the implications of a theory of mental models which also includes the real-world functional or categorial relationships between words. More than a decade ago, Miller and Johnson-Laird (1976) argued for a conceptualization of meaning in which mental representations are different from the actual features of lexical items and their syntactic arrangements in the surface forms of language. They demonstrated that propositional language offered a better explanation than actual language devices, and for some like Oden (1987), the sooner we return to a conceptual framework based on a propositional model, the sooner we will be able to have a realistic account of concept, knowledge, and thought.

Johnson-Laird (1980, 1981, 1987) has more recently suggested that none of the major theories of semantics in psycholinguistics (the decompositional or feature theory of meaning, the semantic network theory of meaning, and the meaning postulates theory of meaning) can address the way that semantic constraints figure in information processing. The task facing a well-reasoned theory of semantics is to provide a framework of conceptual representation, common to all forms of cognition (see Jackendoff 1983). A theory of semantic interpretation for linguistic forms is unquestionably linked to conceptual structures which represent knowledge gained from other sensory modalities and are cognitively integrated in the mind.

Johnson-Laird (1981) suggests that a mental model of procedural semantics is a better explanation than the previous three models, because such a theory assumes that the mental representation of a sentence will take the form of a mental model which pictures the situation described by a sentence. This answers the necessity of specifying the semantic relations between words in a way that reflects how they relate to the world. Johnson-Laird (1983) has further suggested that we construct mental models in our heads to represent the outside world and that we perform operations on those models. As Broadbent (1984) has pointed out, such a system can put together a model of the world from individual inputs, to then call up properties of the model that were not present in the original inputs. We can have inference without logic, for we are no longer dependent on the actual syntactic format for the knowledge base that humans employ in understanding the meaning of an utterance or in reasoning with it. This internal representation of the outside world also means that the type of linguistic analysis that is most appropriate is one that analyzes sentences into semantic representations rather than just syntactic relations.

What goes on in the mind, in respect to semantic representations, is simply not satisfactorily explained by formal rules that relate semantic representations to one another; rules must provide some idea of how they are related to the outside world. In this use of mental models, Johnson-Laird (1987) points out that the specifications of truth conditions will be the necessary factors required for procedures that initially construct, and then modify or manipulate mental models. The logical properties of words can arise from either the representation of a set of explicit verbal relations or from the consequences of the representations of their truth conditions. Thus, you may either hear that *Elephants are animals*, or you will know what configuration of attributes must be present for something to be an elephant, and knowing what is required for something to be an animal, you will arrive at the same conclusion.

Metaphor

Metaphors and figurative language are pervasive in everyday life, as many as 4 per speaking minute (Pollio, Barlow, Fine and Pollio 1977) and perhaps 21 million over an average lifetime (Hoffman and Honeck 1980). Lakoff and Johnson (1980) suggest that conceptually we live by metaphors, that much of rational thought involves the use of metaphoric models. Metaphors rely on perceived similarity of some aspect of meaning to transfer a familiar concept to an unfamiliar one. Such transfers are dependent upon the inherent 'fuzziness' of category boundaries, allowing us to extend a category label or a **word** in its meaning range. An excellent example is the use of familiar terms for unfamiliar scientific concepts. Consider, for example, how much easier it is to gather some sense of what *black hole, solar storm, radiation belt, DNA chain* mean, as opposed to new concepts like *quasar* or *quark*. Indeed, this fact is congruent with what we learned from Rosch's work in establishing a theory of prototypes. Categories are not simply defined as a unique set of objects all equally sharing a set of common properties; we learned instead that some objects display those properties to a greater or lesser degree, and that the properties of a given object may overlap with other categories to a greater or lesser degree.

Metaphors have been of considerable interest to psycholinguists of late, because novel metaphors are not just decorative language; we use them to experience one kind of thing in terms of another and create new conceptual realities. The fascination with metaphor is far from frivolous, for categorization is the primary cognitive means by which we make sense of experience, and metaphor is central to this process. Conceptual categories, in this view, are radically different from what an objectivist view of the categorization process would claim, namely, that categories exist in the world independent of humans and that they are defined only by the characteristics of their members. But symbols used in thought do not get their meaning by simply corresponding with things in the world. Lakoff (1987) claims that thought is in fact *embodied*, arises out of bodily experience, and is directly grounded in perception, body movement, and physical and social experience. Thought is also *imaginative*, in that concepts which are not grounded in experience employ metaphor and mental imagery, and go far beyond the literal mirroring of external reality. It is this imaginative capacity that allows for abstract thought and takes the mind beyond what is seen or felt. Thought is more than just a mechanical manipulation of abstract symbols, and cognitive models that attempt to describe conceptual structure must recognize such properties. Very simply, rational thought goes far beyond the literal or mechanical (Lakoff 1987), and metaphor is often the vehicle that carries us there.

Psycholinguistic theories of metaphor comprehension suggest that we may accomplish this in one of three possible ways: attribute matching, analogical reasoning, or transferring perceptual characteristics into novel applications (Pitts, Smith and Pollio 1982). Attribute matching suggests that when we understand a metaphor like *The man is a wolf*, we assess the attributes of *wolf* and of *man*. Irrelevant ones like the number of legs are ignored; we pay attention to those attributes that could be shared and that might be salient, like ferocity, predation, and so forth. These attributes are then transferred for the metaphor to be understood. Analogical reasoning relies on our recognition of the parallel in metaphors like *Abraham Lincoln is a lion among presidents*. A perceptual, or *Gestalt*, approach explains that we perceive the potential relationships between the two topics (*Lincoln* and the *lion*) and establish these perceptual characteristics as mutually shared.

Historically, the quality of a good metaphor in English literature has been related to how similar the things are that are compared, as for example, *A butterfly is a winged rainbow* or *A pond is nature's mirror*. I would argue that the really striking metaphors are the ones that have a small point of contact, largely differing along the rest of the semantic continuum; for example, consider *The portfolio has become the stockbroker's conscience in the 1980s*. Ortony and his colleagues (1979, 1985) have also demonstrated that the more metaphorical the comparison, the less symmetrical it is likely to be; the putatively shared attributes are highly salient for one concept, but of low salience for the other.

Certainly, different points of contact are favored in culturally-defined historical periods. Smith, Pollio and Pitts (1981) examined trends in figurative metaphors produced by American authors from 1675 to 1975. Not surprisingly, different issues served as focal points for metaphoric extension in each of six 50-year periods in that 300 years, depending upon what were significant issues and events in American history.

Semantic Considerations in Sentence Processing and Production

Memory and Information Processing

It may be worth again noting the role of memory in information processing, particularly in respect to how semantic representations are stored, as opposed to syntactic or discourse structures. There is considerable evidence for a dichotomous memory, with short-term and long-term storage capabilities (Loftus and Loftus 1976). In **short-term memory** we store the exact wording for brief periods of time. But this is a limited capacity, and typically holds seven chunks of information like numbers, words, or even wholistic units like prose or poetic passages (see Miller 1956). If the information is not further processed, it is either quickly moved into long-term memory in distilled form or it is simply forgotten after about fifteen seconds. Our **long-term memory** for meaningful memory is mainly semantic and has two distinct components: an episodic memory in which we recall particular episodes or events which we have experienced, and a semantic memory, which interacts with our knowledge of the real world, storing that information in a way that is compatible with information from other inputs. This cognitive code is the subject of much debate, as we wrestle with the question of what the "structure of mental representations" must be. But we typically remember the gist of information, not the details, and this also applies to remembering the semantic values of language input, and usually not their syntactic or discourse format--unless, of course, there have been significant or unusual features! The sense of the word is acquired through definitions or, as may be more often the case, from encountering instances of the word in actual use. Although use may give us an incomplete 'meaning', it usually gives us enough to grasp the state of affairs described by the context provided by the sentence. For example, the sentence *The explorers survived on pemmican and truffles* is easily comprehended, though few can give a definition of either *pemmican* or *truffles*. Johnson-Laird (1987) has described how subjects know that *pemmican* is consumable, while *verdigris* is not, underscoring that people often are aware of what is important. As another example, people are also more likely to know whether a substance is solid or liquid than whether it is natural or man-made. Such gaps in lexical knowledge remind us that the way in which concepts are acquired will be reflected in the form and content of their lexical entries.

Typically, memory is a constructive process, and we reconstruct a mental model of the relevant facts, features, individuals, and relational premises for the consistent details of a situation (see Johnson-Laird 1980), usually within the guidelines of well-established scripts that we call upon for a framework. Recognition memory is better than recall memory because one does not have to conduct an active memory search. And intentionally stored information is better recalled than incidentally stored information because we consciously establish cues to guide ourselves in recall; intentional and incidental information, however, appears to be equally well-recognized.

Much research in how semantic considerations affect sentence processing has to do with how reaction times in sentence verification tasks are affected. Sentence verification tasks simply ask whether the information provided in the sentence is true or false, and how long it takes to make this judgment when word characteristics like category size, membership, or relationships are manipulated. The notion of typicality, for example, has shown that more typical, core members of a category will be learned more easily and more quickly, that they will be given more commonly as examples of the category in free listing tasks, and that they are more easily judged as being members of a given category.

Imagery also has an effect in processing the semantic content of sentences. Paivio's **dual coding hypothesis** (1971, 1986) suggests both a pictorial coding scheme and a linguistic one. The more imageable an item is, the better it is recalled in memory or the better or faster that sentences containing such a lexical item is processed. The more concrete an item is, the more likely it is to be stored in a nonverbal semantic form; abstract items are more likely to be stored in verbal forms. Though there has been some question about the exact contribution of imagery to mental representations, it is generally found that concrete sentences are superior to abstract sentences in both comprehension tasks and in memory tasks. For example, Moeser (1974) found that subjects were almost always better at identifying meaning changes in concrete sentences; subjects were better at recalling concrete sentences, suggesting that imageability of a sentence does affect how easy it is to store or retrieve that sentence. But they were also faster at both encoding and decoding concrete sentences; in fact, they were also better when instructed to encode for wording, suggesting that concrete sentences may have easy access to both verbal and semantic information. Most evidence points to the fact that semantic information is more rapidly accessed for concrete stimuli (see Belmore, Yates, Bellack, Jones and Rosenquist 1982). Abstract stimuli are evaluated more slowly in semantic classification tasks with pictures and words, as well as in tasks regarding the grammaticality of sentences where subjects have to decide whether a sentence is meaningful or anomalous. Although the evidence is not unanimous, in that some results show no differences or superiority for low-imagery sentences in sentence comprehension tasks, the majority of the reported results indicate faster response times for high-imagery sentences.

Belmore et al. (1982) have even reported that this distinction extends to the processing of implicit meaning. Subjects certainly comprehend the explicit meaning of concrete sentences more quickly than abstract ones, but this also extends to the role of such imagery in processing for implicit meaning. An experimental task which required subjects to paraphrase sentences confirmed the well-established observations about explicit meaning, and a task which required inference from either concrete or abstract sentences demonstrated the role of imagery even in processing for implicit meaning. Thus, a paraphrase for the concrete sentence (1) would be verified faster than a paraphrase for sentence (2); and the inference made in sentence (4) from the concrete sentence (3) was faster than an inference that might be made from an abstract sentence.

1. Concrete: The drain of the bathtub was clogged up with hair.
2. Abstract: The energy of the people was used up by war.
3. Stimulus: The karate expert hit the thick board.
4. Inference: The karate expert broke the thick board.

Marked vs. Unmarked

One of the most influential semantic concepts in sentence processing studies has been the concept of the unmarked form as a semantic primitive. The **unmarked** item is the usual or normal case, while the **marked** one is considered special or unusual. It is easy to see markedness when it is shown by extra added morphemes, as in the second member of the following pairs *dog/dogs, happy/unhappy, sleep/will sleep*. But in semantics one finds markedness expressed by more covert features, like contextual neutralization; one of the members of the pair has a wider neutral use in more contexts than the other. For example, the unmarked member of the pair names the dimension specified by the pair, as in depth (*deep/shallow*), length (*long/short*), height (*tall/short*), and so forth. A question about the dimension named makes no assumptions about how deep the river was, when we use the normal unmarked label for that dimension. But it does make certain assumptions when we use the marked member of the word pair. When words like *bad, young, uninteresting* appear in sentence frames like *How _____ is the teacher?*, instead of the normal *good, old, interesting*, they usually carry some special, and thus **marked**, sense (Perfetti 1972). Contrast, for example, sentences like *How short was teacher?* and *How tall was the teacher?*. One also normally encounters sentences like *The Koksilah River was two feet deep*, not *The Koksilah River was two feet shallow*, even though two feet is not very deep. Unmarked forms are more general than marked forms, and do not carry the same marked or distinctive values that sentences with the marked form of the word pair do. Contrast sentences like *John is thirty years young, The board was six feet short*, and *The boulevard is 23 feet narrow*, with their normal unmarked counterparts. Lastly, marked forms more often elicit unmarked responses in word association tasks than the opposite way; thus, one gets *young-old* more often than *old-young* (Perfetti 1972).

From a processing and recall point of view, the implication is that the unmarked form in word pairs is the easier or simpler of the two to deal with in syntactic and semantic terms. In memory tasks, semantic features may be lost for the marked form, such that the unmarked item is the one that is remembered or better recalled. In recall tasks, it appears that if there is no motivation from context to focus on a marked tense or aspect, sentences are stored and recalled in their unmarked forms. This is also true for the unmarked member of adjective pairs (Clark and Clark 1968; H. Clark 1969). Clark and Card

(1969) found that subjects tend to recall unmarked comparative forms better than marked ones in stimulus sentences like *X is deeper/ shallower than Y.* And errors tended to change marked comparative adjectives to their unmarked counterparts. Marked adjectives make more processing demands and thus take longer than their unmarked counterparts. For example, a sentence with *better*, the comparative form of the unmarked adjective *good*, is easier to process than a sentence with *worse (bad)*, as in the following.

1.   Peter is worse than John.
2.   Peter is better than John.

This is further reflected in deductive reasoning problems (H. Clark 1969). Problems are solved faster if the sentence contains an unmarked adjective like *good-better-best*, than if it contains a marked adjective like *bad-worse-worst*.

1.   If John is better than Bill, who is best?
2.   If John is worse than Bill, who is worst?

Lastly, we might treat certain words like *absent* as carrying the semantic feature of negativity. The word *absent* has the same negative meaning as *not present*, and may be considered an implicit or **inherent negative**. Recall that negative sentences like *John isn't present* take longer to judge than corresponding affirmatives like *John is present*. Subjects use similar processing rules for verifying sentences containing implicit negatives (H. Clark 1974). When the sentence contains the *present/absent* opposition, instead of the *present/not present* opposition, we find the same distinction in processing true and false assertions. That is, *not present* takes longer to judge than *present*, but so also does *absent*. Inherent negatives seem to take less time to deal with than explicit negatives, but they do take longer to process than positives.

Summary

An adequate theory of language contains an account of both lexical semantics and compositional semantics; that is, it should explain the semantic structure of lexical items, as well as being able to assign semantic intepretations to the output of syntax in a systematic way. The major psycholinguistic concern with respect to semantics is the nature of semantic representations in the mind, and how semantic information is stored, organized, and retrieved from memory.
Three linguistic units, the morpheme, the word, and the feature, have claimed our attention as carriers of meaning, with the word being the most commonly explored. The referential theory of meaning claims that the meaning of a word is some object, event, or state of affairs in the real world referred to by that word. A denotative theory of word

meaning claims rather that a word refers to an abstract class of objects, namely, to our mental concepts. This is complemented by the connotative meaning of the word, namely, the attitudes, feelings, and opinions about words that language users have. A technique called the semantic differential measured the connotative aspects of meaning by using the three qualifying variables of evaluation (good-bad), potency (strong-weak), and activity (active-passive).

A theory of word associations attempts to make the latent relationships that words have with other words, images, and thoughts into relationships which are sequential and tangible. Some have even taken the associated meaning of a word to be the sum total of all the associations offered by subjects. Other semanticists have instead claimed that related words participate in a semantic field whose properties and dimensions are defined by members of the set themselves. The meaning of a lexical item is thus a function of the meaning relations that hold between words in the same domain. Still other semanticists assume that the meanings of words can be broken down into separate components or features, so that the basic meaning of any lexical item can be specified by an independent set of semantic features. Feature theory largely grew out of generative grammatical concerns to have a semantic theory that would complement syntactic theory by specifying how selectional restrictions within sentences interacted.

Typicality is also an important factor in the organization of semantic structure, because some defining properties are more salient than others. Prototype theory suggests that semantic categories are best explained by a graded type of membership rather than by absolute membership. Some members of a class are more central to the class, in that they share more of its relevant attributes; other members are more peripheral, because they have only one or several of the attributes. Certain basic principles thus underlie the formation of categories; for example, the principle of cognitive economy allows as many properties as possible to be predictable from knowing any one property, thus reducing the infinite differences among stimuli to manageable proportions.

A categorial network approach to meaning assumes that each category name is part of a taxonomy, with the semantic memory portrayed as a network. Each concept in that network is represented as a node, with links to other such concepts at nodes which vary in distance. The full meaning of a given concept is thus the whole subset of the network, as reached by hierarchical pathways from the node in question. However, mental categories are not the same as the hierarchical categories one sees in science or philosophy, and the experimental support for this model is limited.

The spreading activation model of the lexicon has been an extremely well-received explanation for the properties of lexical semantics. It too is a network model, but assumes that the semantic memory is organized around features of similarity, and that the network of relationships between words is not hierarchical. Words are connected to other words by shared features of typicality or by how typically a feature is associated with the particular word in question, rather than by strict subordination or superordination. The activation of a single word then spreads over its network of associated words, being strongest with the most closely associated words and weakest as the strength of word relationships decreases with semantic distance. This semantic model not only explains how semantic priming operates, but is also responsive to the experimental results reported for multiple access in lexical ambiguity.

But semantics is not just about the meaning of words. The full semantic interpretation of a sentence is also a function of how its individual lexical items have been combined. This is known as Frege's Principle, or the Principle of Compositionality. A theory of compositional semantics also implies that lexical representations should specify the way that lexical items are combined, but in a grammatically neutral way. Thus, lexical representations for predicates will specify that a verb takes one or more arguments, commonly presented as a set of semantic or thematic roles like agent, goal, patient, source, experiencer, and location. Some experimental results have shown that the argument structure of verbs is utilized during language comprehension.

The comprehension of discourse results in the construction of a mental model of the situation described by the discourse, which includes the relevant facts and relational premises consistent with the typical details of such a situation. Our mental models also include the functional or categorial relationships between words, and we both infer from properties of the model that were not present in the original input and perform operations on those models. This suggests that an adequate theory of semantics cannot just relate semantic representations to one another; it must provide some idea of how they are related to our knowledge of the real world and specify truth conditions.

Metaphors and figurative language are so pervasive in everyday life that some suggest we live by metaphors conceptually. Metaphors have been of considerable interest to psycholinguists of late, because rational thought goes far beyond the literal or mechanical and often involves the use of metaphoric models. Psycholinguistic theories of metaphor comprehension suggest that this modelling may be based on attribute matching, analogical reasoning, or transferring perceptual characteristics into novel applications.

Experimental results show that semantic considerations affect sentence processing and sentence recall. For example, tasks like sentence verification and deductive reasoning demonstrate that prototypicality, imagery, marked vs. unmarked, and positive vs. negative vs. inherent negative features all have an effect on the ease with which sentences are processed, as well as the way in which they are remembered.

Chapter 8

Language and Thought

Introductory Comments on Language and Thought

The questions at issue are whether language is necessary for thought, whether the nature of language determines the nature of thought, or whether there is simply a partial dependence between the two, with some aspects of language structure influencing or determining some aspects of thought. It might also be that language is simply the tool by which we express what we think, the typical vehicle of communication that humans make use of in dealing with one another. For the sake of discussion, let us accept thought as a theoretical primitive, the exact dimensions of which await the results of future inquiry in the field of cognitive science. But thought is not a kind of speech behavior, in the way that behaviorists wished to reduce cognition to the observable and measurable, rejecting mental processes entirely. The fact that measurable activation of the musculature was found, when subjects were told to think of moving their arms, fit in with their attempt to reduce thought to simply physical phenomena. Some behaviorists went as far as self-administering the muscle-paralytic curare in an attempt to see whether thought processes would be as paralyzed as the laryngeal muscles. But we know that children and the deaf comprehend and think, and so can those with various handicaps that preclude speech production.

Nor is language fundamental to thought, though many have suggested that it is. Cognition in its general sense is largely independent from the peculiarities of any language, and can develop to a certain extent in the absence of the knowledge of language (Lenneberg 1967). Furth (1966) found no difference in intelligence between normal and deaf persons (though construction of intelligence tests which do not have a verbal component is not a simple task). This is not to deny that certain types of linguistic knowledge, like vocabulary words (and the discriminations illustrated by those word forms), does not aid certain types of cognition, like memory tasks.

As an inventory of a given culture, language will typically represent what a given society concerns itself with. The relationship between language and thought is not the same as the relationship between language and culture. The catalogue of culture known as language will list what is available in the culture, including its social beliefs and corresponding values. But language can also transmit new ideas which bring about changes in those beliefs and values, and so cannot be the exclusive basis of thought. But this has been a central question in much research in linguistics, anthropology, and psychology since the turn of the century, and we should survey what we have learned. We will examine the relationship between language and thought by first looking carefully at the **Linguistic Relativity Hypothe-**

sis. We do this for two reasons: first, because this has been the most provocative statement of the problem; and secondly, because this aspect of language life has captured the popular imagination more than any other in a century of linguistic scholarship.

Linguistic Relativity Hypothesis

How does the structure of one's language affect one's thought processes? Does the structure of the language one speaks affect one's perceptions of the world in a way that would be different if one happened to speak another language instead? There have been various versions of this question, the most recent and influential having been the **Linguistic Relativity Hypothesis**, also known as the **Sapir-Whorf Hypothesis**. The boldest presentation of this notion was made by Benjamin Lee Whorf (1956), who saw thinking as largely a matter of language and inescapably bound up with systems of linguistic expression. For Whorf, all higher levels of thinking are dependent upon language, and the structure of the language one habitually uses influences the way in which one understands his or her environment; the picture of the universe differs from language to language. This was a departure from a tradition as old as Greek philosophy, which commonly believed that there was a universal, uncontaminated essence of reason, shared by all thinking humans, and that this unity of thought process was expressed in any and every language. The implication is that such unity allows for translation into any other language without loss of meaning.

Linguistic relativity was not entirely novel to Sapir and Whorf, but was an idea that resurfaced in America in this century. What may have been novel was that it became widely known and accepted in many circles. Indeed, the notion resurfaced in a congenial intellectual climate, given Einsteinian notions of relativity in the physical sciences, and Whorf himself may have been influenced by this movement (see Heynick 1983). An influential version of linguistic relativity had already been proposed by the German philosopher Herder and the ethnographer Humboldt in the 18th and 19th Centuries, respectively. Wilhelm von Humboldt, in keeping with the Romantic inclinations of his period, thought that language embodied the spirit and national character of a people, a philosophy which coincided with the rise of European nationalism and which is still a major component in most ethnic movements. The Sapir-Whorf Hypothesis is exactly in this intellectual tradition, claiming that one's language is the principal determinant of thought processes.

The radicalism of linguistic relativity was a reaction against the patronizing attitude toward "primitive" languages in the last century. The European languages were felt to be inherently superior to the languages of the rest of the world, undeveloped and uncivilized as most of it seemed to be to Europeans. Their own languages were held to be better suited to the demands of the modern world they felt they had created. Such notions had an unmistakable Darwinian ring, and it was this intellectual atmosphere that Boas, Sapir, and later his student Whorf, attempted to put right. Research in unwritten non-European languages began to demonstrate the logic and systematicity of all languages. Nor were languages given to the evolutionary stages that 19th Century anthropology used to picture the development of human cultures. The anthropologist Boas showed for the first time since the ancient Indian grammarian Panini that a language could be analyzed in its own terms, without imposing the classical Greco-Latin grammatical tradition upon it. But Sapir possibly did more than anyone else to call attention to the linguistic underpinnings to thinking and make it of scientific concern (he did later shift the emphasis of his views, but not their basic outlook (Hymes 1964)). And Whorf seemed to suggest that such an approach might even have hidden benefits of its own. An Amerindian language like Hopi, for example, might have an entirely novel form of logic, and might even have a correspondingly innovative picture of the universe, one only discovered by the occasional genius in our own language and culture. Linguistic relativity was simply the farthest swing of the reactionary pendulum in the attempt to prove that every language and culture was unique as well as logical. As Kay and Kempton (1984) have observed, this doctrine of radical relativity may have led to certain intellectual excesses, but it was very much a needed corrective posture to counter ethnocentric evolutionism. And its intellectual excesses were trivial in social terms, for radical relativity can really only be accused of concentrating on particulars in language and culture, instead of looking for universals in linguistic and anthropological theory.

It was Whorf who captured the popular imagination with his vivid examples, and it was he that made the boldest, and, possibly, best publicized claims of this tradition. He seemed to say that the language of a cultural community not only embodies its world-view, but that it also perpetuates that world-view. The languages of the world are pictured as so many molds of varying shape into which infant minds are poured; the mold determines the cognitive shape of the infant's adult mind as it grows up in a particular linguistic and cultural community (Whorf 1956; Brown and Lenneberg 1954). Whorf was eminently quotable and dramatized the inquiry with questions which essentially asked whether there are obvious ties between behavioral patterns and language patterns.

Whorf's actual field work was with Hopi, an Amerindian language of the Uto-Aztecan family from the American Southwest. He also researched Mayan writing systems, and did semantic analyses on language data collected by other linguists. His examples are often from Hopi and Shawnee, an Algonquian language originally spoken in what is now Ohio. Whorf observed that Hopi had no reference to time, and contemplated whether different, equally valid, descripions of time and space were possible. He was particularly interested in what different languages did to what he called "the flowing face of nature" (1956:241), implying that our macrophysical analysis of the cosmos pretty well follows our segmentation by language categories. Do time, space, and matter appear the same to all humans, or are they filtered through the structure of one's language? Does European physics explain the universe by objects and process-like activities because the Indo-European languages see things in the grammatical categories of nouns and verbs. Whorf came to believe that observers are not led to the same picture of the physical universe by the same evidence, unless their linguistic backgrounds were the same. Sapir and Whorf's examples from Amerindian languages suggested that even basic concepts like nouns and verbs were not universal; Nootka might not have a noun-verb dichotomy, or might use verbs where English is fond of using adjectives.

But there may be an element of paying too much attention to the exotic in Whorf's examples, as well as looking for deep-seated meanings for phrasings which no longer have such meanings. For example, phrases like *Good-bye* and *It is raining* neither signify the pervasiveness of our beliefs in the deity ('God be with you!') nor our belief in the animistic universe implied by 'it'. One can entertain extreme or conservative versions of the Linguistic Relativity Hypothesis. An extreme version would see a language system as completely organizing human cognition, while a conservative version would simply suggest that linguistic structure predisposes individuals to pay attention to some things more than others, or to perceive things in one mode rather than in another (see Carroll 1963). Linguistic influence on cognition really is limited to the fact that language is the primary, but by no means the only, tool by which humans represent, store, and communicate information. Brown and Lenneberg's (1954) concept of **cognitive deck** and Herskovits' (1950) ethnographic concept of **cultural focus** wisely contrasted habitual behavior from potential behavior; what humans in a given setting typically do is different from what they can do. Even so, there are probably more similarities than differences in the way that human languages code concepts, simply because human societies exist within a physical and social environment that itself exhibits many uniformities.

Language is, of course, an index of culture, if we take culture as whatever it is that one has to know or believe to act in a manner acceptable to the members of that society. Culture is neither rational nor irrational; it simply exists as a potential guide for the behavior of humans. The culture shapes the way that life is structured and organized, the way things fit into one's life. The language, as a metalinguistic catalogue of a particular culture, will typically list those cultural concerns, communicating much, but not all, of a culture. For example, the fact that Japanese has different words for 'older brother' and 'younger brother' is an indication that there must be some difference in the way the kinship system is organized; compare English, which only has one word for both, *brother*. Benedict (1946) once presented an overview of Japanese culture by describing the full meanings of a few key words; for example, a full description of *ani* 'elder brother' involves a complete description of Japanese law and family life.

Matching Linguistic Structures with Cognitive Structures

Cultural considerations aside, we should now examine the claim that a language constitutes a logic or general frame of reference, which molds the thought of its habitual users like a mathematical system. The relationship between the mechanisms of language and the perception and organization of experience is really an empirical question. But Whorf never really collected or reported any non-linguistic data to do with the cognitive behaviors possibly related to linguistic behaviors. He did speculate about the possible physics, metaphysics, or general cognitive structures of a group, but his data are always linguistic (see R. Brown 1976). The existence of non-linguistic cognitive differences which match linguistic differences is really a psychological question which can be answered by experimentation. But first let us separate out several aspects of language structure which are distinct from thought and which might be compared to it (see Henle 1958).

1. vocabulary
2. grammatical categories and mode of inflection
3. manner of sentence formation
4. part of speech designations

Vocabulary . As a fire insurance investigator, Whorf had observed the suggestive power of words. Gasoline drums which were called 'empty' elicited an undue carelessness by employees who seemed to forget that 'empty' did not make residual vapors any less flammable. Words certainly do mean different things in different languages, even though they seem to be direct translational equivalents. For example, Haida *xa* and Japanese *inu* may be glossed 'dog', but they stand for a range of man's best friend that is not the same in referential extent as English *dog*. *Rice* is important in the lives of Filipinos, and so Tagalog has *palay* in the field, *bigas* in the bag, and *kanin* on the dish. The vocabulary of a language reflects the physical and social environment of a people, constituting an inventory of the various ideas, interests, objects, and experiences that take up the attention of a cultural community. But we cannot simply assume that the world appears different to a person using one vocabulary than it does to a person using another vocabulary. The use of one vocabulary may call attention to different aspects of the environment, suggesting that some distinctions which are left unnoticed are habitually made. Simply because Navaho, Yakuts, and Japanese have a single term for the color continuum we label blue and green does not mean they are incapable of making color distinctions that are familiar to us. They do not suffer from a particular kind of color blindness any more than we do because we lack words for the two sorts of black found in darkness of night and objects like coal, or the two types of blue found in the lighter Russian *sinii* and the darker *goloboi*. In fact, more differentiated societies will often develop both specific and generic terms for a given area of experience, corresponding to the needs of individuals; for example, Eskimos have an elaborate vocabulary for snow, but so do some English-speaking skiers.

And it is always possible to name a new category that falls into one's realm of experience, even though we may not have had a word for it previously.

But it is true that having words for something may suggest expectations for how things should be represented or stored. A classical experiment by Carmichael, Hogan and Walter (1932) presented individuals with drawings which could be linked with either of two possible linguistic labels, as for example, paired labels like 'bottle or stirrup', 'crescent moon or letter C', 'beehive or hat', 'eyeglasses or dumbbell', 'ship's wheel or gun', and 'gun or broom'. The figures were ambiguous in that either label could apply. They were typically recalled in a form that suggested a reproduction of the figure in a way that matched the original stimulus word used to name the ambiguous figure at first exposure. For example, if the ambiguous figure was called *eyeglasses*, it was likely to be reproduced with a figure that looked like a pair of eyeglasses; on the other hand, if the same ambiguous figure had been called *dumbbell*, it was likely to be reproduced with a figure that looked like a dumbbell. Nor are such effects limited to naming practice for nouns, as we have seen with Loftus and Palmer's (1974) work with courtroom uses of descriptive verbs like *smashed*. Such results show the power of linguistic input in deciding upon the semantic representation of the information received.

Lenneberg and Roberts (1956) found interesting differences for color terms in English and Zuni, an Amerindian language of New Mexico. Colors that were highly codable in English were not always highly codable in Zuni, and Zuni speakers had more difficulty recognizing and remembering colors that were poorly coded in Zuni, but that were well coded in English. The opposite was also true for ranges that were better coded in Zuni than they were in English. For example, orange and yellow are covered by a single term in Zuni, while they are obviously represented by two terms in English. The monolingual Zuni frequently confused the orange and yellow colors in the stimulus set, while the English speakers never made this mistake; bilingual Zuni fell somewhere in between in their recognition performance. Very simply, Zuni speakers were better at remembering and recognizing colors that were easily and unambiguously named in the Zuni language; colors which were easily named in English did not fare as well.

Brown and Lenneberg (1954) demonstrated that the increased frequency of a perceptual categorization will mean a generally greater availability of that category. They visualized the more nameable categories as nearer the top of the **cognitive deck** of perceptions that we play with every day. Zipf's Law (1949) had already demonstrated that there is a tendency for the length of a word to be negatively correlated with its frequency of usage. The more frequent a word, the shorter it will be either phonologically or orthographically; words which are less frequent are typically longer. Building on this finding, Brown and Lenneberg speculated that the length of a verbal response provides an index of the frequency with which the relevant perceptual judgments of difference and equivalence are made. For example, although types of snow are nameable in both Eskimo and English, in English each type of snow requires an entire phrase, whereas in Eskimo the snow is named with a single word. From this fact, they concluded that the Eskimo must distinguish types of snow more often than the average English speaker does. Thus, they essentially suggest that codability is an indicator of the frequency of usage which in its turn is an indicator of the frequency of judgments made in respect to that category. The basic assumption is that a given set of cognitive categories is more available to the speakers of a language that lexically codes these categories than to the speakers of a language in which the categories are not represented in the lexicon.

One assumes that all subjects with normal vision can make approximately the same set of discriminations. Whorf's claim that cognitive differences correlate with lexical differences can be examined in the relationship between the variable of codability and subjects' performance with color recognition. Five judges were asked to pick the best 8 colors (for red, orange, yellow, green, blue, purple, pink, and brown) out of 240 colors from the Munsell Chart. Other subjects were then shown the color chips tachistoscopically and asked to name them. The result was that some colors can be named with a single word like *red*, while others are named with a phrase like *reddish-orange*. The differences in length are found to be correlated with the latency of naming response AND the reliability of response from subject to subject. If a given color was named by a single word which was used commonly by subjects, then that particular instance of a color seemed to be easy to identify from memory too. The length of a verbal expression (its codability) did seem to reflect its frequency in speech, and in turn the frequency with which relevant judgments concerning this category are made. Thus, a perceptual category that is frequently used is more available than one that is less frequently used, so that shorter monolexemic items are nearer the top of the **cognitive deck**, and more likely to be used in ordinary perception. At the time, this set of results was taken as support for linguistic relativity in its weaker form, though not its strong form.

Grammatical Categories and Mode of Inflection . Do the grammatical rules of inflectional categories force us to use a set of alternatives that other languages might not? For example, does the fact that English has the compulsory category of plural for most nouns force us to think in terms of singularity or plurality? Of course, one can always paraphrase a plural like *homeowners* with *anyone who owns a home*. Although English has a past tense which occurs with most verbs, our verbs do not require a time observation for every utterance we produce. Amerindian languages like Hopi and Wintu have affixes which designate hearsay from first-hand information, but this does not mean that speakers are always aware of the evidence for every statement they make. What can be expressed in one language can be expressed in another language, though it is often true that what is expressed easily and quickly in one language by a single word can only be expressed by a lengthy phraseology in another language.

Carroll and Casagrande (1958) tested whether grammatical categories like these have any effect on perception. Their subjects were reservation Navaho children between the ages of three to ten who were either English-dominant or Navaho-dominant. Athapaskan languages like Navaho, Chipewyan, and Hupa have elaborate classificatory schemes with nouns falling into the following groups: living beings; round objects; long rigid objects; broad flexible objects like fabric; long flexible objects like rope; empty containers; containers with contents; bundles or packages; liquid; loose items like grain, sand or hay; dense, viscous substances like mud or dough; and aggregates or sets. Navaho has eleven such sets, with correspondingly special forms for the verbs of handling like 'to pick up', 'to drop', and 'to hold in the hand'. The results of a sorting task did indicate that Navaho-dominant children tended to group objects according to shape classes, while English-dominant children tended to group more according to color. But these results were later confounded by the results with white middle-class school children of similar ages in Boston, who also did much better on shape sorting than on color sorting.

Maclay (1958) also found no particular support for the Whorfian hypothesis in a sorting task with Navaho and English subjects. Maclay had even included a third group of non-Athapaskan-speaking controls, native Indians from Pueblo groups like Zuni, as a safeguard against Anglo or Indian preferences in such tasks. His sorting task employed three categories based on physical characteristics: long/slender-rigid (for example, cigarette); rope-like/slender-flexible (for example, rope); and fabric-like/flat-flexible (for example, blanket). The three groups failed to show the expected differences in either sorting or latency effects. Maclay noted it is almost impossible to conceive of objects that can be linguistically classified in only one way, for every language has a variety of alternative ways of classifyng stimuli. It cannot be reliably predicted that a known linguistic category (like verbs of handling in Navaho) will correlate with a non-linguistic behavior (like sorting).

Manner of Sentence Formation . Is there some connection between sentence patterns in a language and the way in which perceptions are ordered? But there are only so many possible orderings in syntactic patterns, so the range is not unlimited. For example, there are only six possible orderings for noun subject (S), verb (V), and noun object (O) in declarative transitive sentences in the world's languages. Of the six logically possible arrangements, only SVO, SOV, and VSO occur commonly (Greenberg 1963/1966, 1975; see also Comrie 1981). English, Swahili, and Indonesian are SVO; Japanese and Turkish are SOV; Tagalog and other Philippine languages, as well as Welsh, are VSO. The VOS sequence is rare; Malagasy, a far-flung Austronesian language found off the east coast of Africa, is an example. The Object-initial orders are limited to indigenous languages of South America; OVS appears almost exclusively in the Carib family and OSV in several small language families in the Brazilian Amazonian basin (Derbyshire and Pullum 1981). The tendency is for subject nouns to precede object nouns, with verb placement more of a variable (Greenberg 1963/1966, 1975). There is no strong empirical evidence for sentence type correlating with perceptions. Sentence type may be driven by considerations of style or discourse cohesion. The English active and passive sentence types seem to reflect this fact. So do choices between the four or more voices found in Philippine languages. For example, choosing among the following Tagalog sentence types is a matter of establishing or maintaining discourse focus on the agent, the goal, the location, or the beneficiary.

1.   Bumili SIYA nang bigas sa palengke. 'HE bought the rice in
      the market.'
2.   Binili niya ANG BIGAS sa palengke. 'He bought THE RICE
      in the market.'
3.   Binilhan niya nang bigas ANG PALENGKE. 'He bought the
      rice in THE MARKET.'
4.   Ibinili niya ANG NANAY nang bigas sa palengke. 'He bought
      the rice FOR HIS MOTHER in the market.'

Part of Speech Designations . Those who believe in linguistic determinism feel that the semantic character of the part of speech classes fixes the basic conception of reality. For example, this implies that Nootka, with a grammatical overview which does not sort words into nouns and verbs at the first level of analysis, might look at objects and actions differently than English. But the mere fact that a language sorts words into different part of speech classes does not require that speakers of that language₄will find themselves driven by the semantic correlates of those classes.[4] Recalling our own experiences, which of us was intellectually limited by the elementary school definition which insisted that nouns were the names of persons, place, or things? Even then, some of us put up our hands to ask where *sincerity* fit!

Whorf was fond of quoting the Hopi conception of time, arguing that Hopi metaphysics is radically different from what he called Standard Average European. It seemed that Hopi suggests nothing about the shape of time, except the 'getting-later' quality of it. In English, time is conceived of as a stable physical object; events are spoken of as if they were stable objects, and the fluidity of the passing experience seems to be ignored. Thus, we are conceptually able, Whorf would claim, to 'save time', to isolate segments of it, to treat time like any other object with shape, size, and definable qualities. However, in arguing for this conceptualization of time in Hopi, critics have pointed out that Whorf's description of this aspect of Hopi metaphysics has been presented quite adequately in English, a Standard Average European language, and that the notion is not entirely unlike the French

---

[4]   In fact, contemporary scholars of the Wakashan and Salish language families now consider that a noun-verb distinction does indeed exist in languages like Nootka and Spokane, although there is a transition between the two grammatical classes (B. F. Carlson, personal communication).

philosopher Henri Bergson's philosophy of the lifestream. Others have
not only criticized Whorf's grammatical generalizations about Hopi as
faulty, but have even dismissed his claims about the representation of
time in European languages (see Hill 1988 for a summary of such criticisms).

The Language of Experience . Lenneberg and Roberts (1956) once produced an invaluable procedural handbook for reviewing the language-
and-thought hypothesis. They required universality, variation, and
simplicity in the choice of language data for experiments in linguistic
relativity. The features in question must exist in every culture (universality), and must vary at the same time they are commensurable
(variation). It would also be enormously helpful if they required few
parameters of measurement (simplicity). The one area of language
which seemed to fit these requirements best are vocabulary words that
constitute 'the language of experience', lexical items which refer to the
most elementary forms of experience, like sensations of temperature
and light. Until we have ordered and conclusive experiments in such
realms of experience, we must simply consider notions of linguistic relativity as tenable only in their weaker version, and as applicable only
to codability and frequency of perceptions for that area of language
structure called vocabulary.

Language and National Character . One area that definitely does not
qualify is the popular correlation of national character with linguistic
features. English thrift is supposed to match its predilection for monosyllables, German militarism with its harsh consonants, and French art
and culture with its melodious contours. Even the late President De
Gaulle observed that the wonderful thing about the French language is
how it expresses thoughts in their natural order. But obviously all
such judgments are subjective. After all, what are 'harsh consonants'
and 'melodic contours'? By this reckoning, we should expect Nootka to
be more militaristic than German, and Vietnamese to have an even
more well-recognized tradition of art and culture than French. Such
arguments are circuitous and unfruitful, for what constitutes thrift,
militarism, art and culture is subjective. This is a case of making
inferences from a piece of ill-defined linguistic data to an equally ill-
defined nonlinguistic factor (see Lenneberg and Roberts 1956).

    Such observations about language and national character are
embarrassed by the imperfect correspondence between language and
culture areas. One would suppose that such characteristics, if the
notion were true, would be exhibited by all members of a linguistic
family or subfamily. Language and culture areas, that is, language
and national characteristics, should coincide. But Finns and Hungari-
ans in Europe are pretty much like their Indo-European neighbors, and
the culture of the Navaho is more like that of their unrelated Uto-
Aztecan neighbors, the Hopi, than it is like that of the Navaho's Athapaskan cousins, the Apache.

    Similar, but less far-reaching, claims continue to abound in the
popular literature, and occasionally even in the scholarly literature.
For example, Kearney (1984) has recently claimed that the obligatory

appearance of personal pronouns coincides with the rise of individualism in Europe society. It might seem possible if you limit yourself to
contrasting data like Latin *sum* 'I am' with its modern (presumably
individualistic) counterparts in English, French, and German, namely,
I am, Je suis, and *Ich bin*. But as Hill (1984) points out, Italian *sono*
and Spanish *soy* exhibit optional pronouns, but were certainly not
excluded from the rise of capitalism and its emphasis on individual
attainment. And **pro-drop** (pronoun-dropping) is one of those variable
parameters that Chomsky (1981) considers to be immune from extralinguistic factors; its random distribution in related languages like
those above certainly seems to support this interpretation of such
phrase structure features. Lastly, the widespread use of English as a
first or second language around the globe seems to have neither precip-
itated a new wave of individualism in the world-view held by its speakers nor even a greater respect for individual human rights.

Linguistic Universals

Inherent in any discussion of relativity is the notion of linguistic
universals. Indeed, Linguistic Relativity arose in the period known as
American Structuralism, which held the compatible belief that language could differ in unlimited and entirely unpredictable ways. Looking at only the surface structure of languages makes it appear that
languages are very different indeed, and it is not suprising that few
language universals appear in a period when no one is looking for
them. We now know that languages are relatively constrained in their
design, though languages can differ quite a bit in their surface characteristics.
Universals can of course be imputed to be present in languages by
theoretical fiat; that is, a language can *a priori* be said to have transformations in syntax or semantic features in its lexical organization.
Because one has defined 'language' by particular features, the array of
languages will naturally have such features. But to be fair, most, if
not all, universals are a matter of definition and extrapolation from
some definition. Although the assignment of universals is in a sense a
reflection of some definition, one can take an inductive approach, saying that language universals must truly be found to be shared by all
languages. There should be no exceptions, and the presentation of a
universal is in effect a generalization about language (see Hockett
1963/1966). But unrestricted universals, which apply to all languages
in an unconditional fashion, seem to often be self-evident, because they
do reflect the design architecture of human language. For example,
the fact that all languages have vowels, that human language makes
use of the oral-aural tract, or that every human language has proper
names does not seem particularly startling. They seem self-evident
because they constitute the essence of language anyhow.
Greenberg (1963/1966, 1968) has also called our attention to near-
universals, those specific exceptions to the general rule. Quileute and
a few other Amerindian languages in the Pacific Northwest fail the

general rule of having nasal consonants; Nootka does not seem to have
separate noun and verb stem classes, since all inflectable stems have
the same range of inflectional possibilities (but whole inflected words
have a noun or verb designation). Such statements allow frequency
distributions, in that statistical universals allow us to group and classify languages according to more or less common typological features.
   There are also implicational universals of the type that if x is
present, so also must be y. For example, Slavic languages like Slovene
and Lusatian have a dual number, which automatically implies that
there is not only a singular number, but also a plural number. The
implication is one way, however, for languages with a plural number
(like English) do not necessarily have a dual number.
   Interest in the features of universal grammar has also had an
influence in shifting the attention in cognitive anthropology from the
specific to the particular. As more ethnographies have been examined,
we find that there are some very compelling parallels among languages
in respect to how certain knowledge domains are organized and how
they develop historically. Parallelling the pursuit of formal and subs-
tantive universals in the structure of language has been the search for
universals in culture and cognition. As a result, we have been reward-
ed with a better understanding of perceptual categories and folk taxonomies, and the universal features which underlie them.

Perceptual Categories and Folk Taxonomies

   Are there universals which derive from the human capacity to
organize and categorize perceptual information? Are these reflected in
lexical universals? Recent research has revealed that there are universals in the way semantic structures are organized in classificatory
frameworks. Lexical categories in the domains of color (Berlin and
Kay 1969), botany (C. Brown 1977), and zoology (C. Brown 1979)
seem to be encoded in a historical sequence of development with implicational consequences. If a language has a word for *yellow* it will
always have a word for *red*; the presence of the one term implies the
occurrence of the other. The presence of a category for *grass* or the
herbaceous *grerb* implies that the folk botanical category of *tree* has
already been encoded in the language. The presence of the categories
of *wug* 'bug' or *mammal* implies the presence of *fish/bird/snake* in the
zoological domain (see Witkowski and Brown 1978). And languages
will encode certain categories first, *black/white* in the color domain, *tree*
in the botanical domain, and *fish/bird/snake* in the zoological domain.

Naming Objects

Naming requires that we identify the object to be named and select the appropriate word for it. But there are also usually competing names for a given object. What we often do is choose among possible names by selecting a name at the optimal level of utility, naming objects by not being too general (for example, *animal*) nor too specific (*Labrador Retriever*). This might be a **basic-level term** like *dog*. In acquisition, mothers often take the child's presumed point of view, naming things at what would seem to be the child's presumed **level of usual utility** (R. Brown 1976). Thus, for very young children a metallic object might be called *money*, because it is not to be thrown away, not to be put in the mouth, to be valued when Uncle Tony gives a sample at birthday time, and so forth. As the child matures a bit, the larger scope of cultural values in naming comes into greater play, and that same metallic object is now named at the level of usual utility as culturally defined (see R. Brown 1958b). It is now a *dime*, worth two nickels or ten pennies, enough to buy a jawbreaker, but not a popsicle, and so forth. This is how the folk science of a people, with its own special taxonomies, is passed on to the next generation of users.

Ethnoscience and the Lexicon

It is a truism in anthropology that many of the important cognitive categories in a culture will be represented in the way the lexicon is structured. A particularly compelling example of this is seen in ethnoscience areas of knowledge like the folk taxonomies of ethnobotany and ethnozoology. Ethnoscience in cognitive anthropology attempts to describe folk classifications that a given culture makes use of, the system of culture-specific meanings by which a people organizes the external world around them. Often these appear as folk taxonomies which differ from, though they may parallel, scientific domains. For example, Haida folk botany does not exhibit our scientific classifications for ferns, dividing them into those which are useful, edible, or medicinal, and those which are not; this is as important a codification as ours, and probably more useful, given the goals of Haida knowledge. Still, many categories seem to overlap, and Berlin (1978) notes that 60% of his field data for folk plant and animal kingdoms correspond to scientifically named species. Some folk taxonomies, like the North American preoccupation with cars, exhibit frames of reference which may not even have a scientific counterpart.

Ethnobiological classifications are an excellent example of relationships between language, culture, and the cognitive abilities underlying classificatory systems in semantic structures. As civilized or primitive as we are, every society must interact in some way with the living world around us. The biological diversity of plant and animal kingdoms is particularly rich, and in some preliterate societies, knowledge of the biological world constitutes a large and important chunk of knowledge. This body of knowledge rests upon human recognition of visible similarities and differences inferred from features of morphology and behavior, not simply from utility. Berlin's (1978) field work with the Tzeltal Maya of Mexico and the Aguaruna Jivaro of Peru revealed that fully a third of plant names lack any cultural utility.

Humans in all cultures classify things like plants and animals into categories, and these categories differ in their levels of class inclusion. English, for example, has a category of living things called *plants*, which can be further subdivided into classes like *bushes/trees/grasses/vines*. In the *tree* category are included *firs/oaks/maples/sycamores*; in turn, *firs* in British Columbia can be *Douglas fir/Grand fir*. These common-knowledge classifications of biological phenomena in the botanical world are called the folk taxonomy of **ethnobotany** used by English speakers. A **folk taxonomy** organizes the physical world around us and allows us to understand it; the biological world is organized into a small number of easily recognized plants and animals which are embodied in a taxonomic hierarchy that all members of a given language and cultural grouping make use of. For example, think of the concept *evergreen*, a folk botany concept which you never encountered in biology class. Yet you can probably go right out and identify one without a textbook.

All cultures seem to divide the plant and animal kingdoms into categories, each of which is given a name. The domains are large, and the average plant and animal vocabulary of a preliterate society can easily consist of 1000 to 1200 basic-level names. There can be as many as six levels of classification in such natural systems of classification, although systems with three or four levels are common too. The most inclusive domain is the kingdom ("unique beginner"), and as the most inclusive folk level in the hierarchy, includes every other class in the semantic domain in question. It is often named with a phrase instead of a single word, as for example, Tzeltal "those things that don't move, don't walk, possess roots, and are planted in the earth". The other classes are ranked beneath it as follows (see Berlin 1978).

1.   kingdom assignment of domain as 'plant' or 'animal'
2.   life forms like 'tree' or 'fish'
3.   (intermediate designations like 'evergreen' or 'freshwater fish')
4.   generic names like 'pine' or 'bass'
5.   specific names like 'white pine' or 'black bass'
6.   varietal names like 'Western white pine' or 'large-mouthed (black) bass'

Folk taxonomies may lack categories at the rank of unique beginner and life-form levels, but classes are always found at the generic and specific ranks. A general principle of nomenclature assignment labels life forms and generics as primary lexemes, and both levels are typically named with a single word. The generic rank is the level in which the members are defined in reference to an ideal prototype, endowed with an array of criterial attributes in the sense that Rosch has defined semantic categories. Generic classes are always more numerous than specifics; specifics are often longer than a single word, and marked in respect to the generic category that they fall under. Thus, the generic might be *oak*, and the specific member might be *white oak/pin oak/post oak* (Brown and Witkowski 1980).

The generic rank is the core of folk biological taxomonies, for at this rank both plants and animals appear perceptually most distinct to human classifiers. They are easily perceived as morphologically and behaviorally most distinct, and seem to "cry out to be named" with a distinctive name. As a result, there are usually a large number of such highly salient categories at the basic generic level. It is this category which is felt to be primary and the most useful, and constitutes the first names that children are given to learn and are expected to use.

Berlin suggests that we organize folk classificatory systems around the generic level of categories and that this level is basic to the process of classification. It may also reflect the way that our basic perceptual and cognitive apparatus deals with the external world, for the generic level develops before other ethnobotanical classificatory levels. Perhaps the human perceptual apparatus is geared to deal with certain attributes in nature which cluster together to form categories. The generic category has the tightest and best distinguishability criteria; its members are all very similar to each other, and very different from other categories.

Some levels above the generic rank may not be named; for example, the entire kingdom may not have a linguistic designation which is easily recognized as a linguistic title, though it is a cognitive category which is pervasive in its influence. There may also be a covert category of an intermediate rank above the generic level; it includes an arbitrary subset of generic ranks in a loose perceptual array, based on gross morphological or behavioral characteristics. *Evergreen* is an example of a covert intermediate category in English. At levels below the generic rank, the specific and varietal levels seem to be distinctive in respect to cultural utility. Perhaps it is here we can speak of linguistic relativity, for these relate to the needs and uses of the particular cultural community, or even a sub-group within the community. For example, there are often sub-group differences in expertise, and the expert makes distinctions that novices don't. Thus, there is a basic category *tree* for the city dweller in Vancouver, but *Douglas fir* and *Grand fir* are the basic categories for a logger in British Columbia. We can always learn what we need to or want to, and the structure for carrying out this basic process is to move up or down a level for the basic categories of usage.

Recent research has confirmed that lexical items for such domains are added to languages in a fixed order. C. Brown (1984) has described lexical encoding sequences for life-form categories in folk biology. A universal zoological sequence seems to be that the categories *fish/bird/snake* are encoded in languages before *wug* 'bug' and *mammal*. Similarly, a universal botanical sequence for languages always has *tree* as the first category, followed by *grerb* 'small herbaceous plant' or *grass*. Once *grerb* or *grass* is encoded in the language as a category, the other appears, and will then be followed by *bush* or *vine*. Such folk biological classes are built upon natural discontinuities in nature which allow clustering features of objects around a focal point of attributes based upon obvious physical characteristics of gross morphology. Very simply, the categories of *tree* vs. *grerb* match the features of large size and woodiness vs. small size and herbaceousness, respectively.

The basic zoological classes of life-forms are based on the form of the whole animal, on their gross morphology. C. Brown (1979, 1982) suggests the following five zoological life-forms as the most pervasive.

1.   fish: creature possessing fins, possibly gills, and a streamlined body; may even include mammals like dolphins and whales.

2.   bird: creature possessing wings, usually feathers and a bill or beak; may include flying mammals like bats.

3.   snake: featherless, furless, elongated creature usually lacking appendages; may even include reptiles and elongated reptile-like insects.

4.   wug: small creatures like bugs, insects, spiders; may even include snails, lizards, frogs.

5.   mammal: large creature; may even include large animals like iguanas, crocodiles, tortoises, and even large frogs.

Folk zoological life-form terms are added in the following sequence (C. Brown 1982).

1.   bird, fish, or snake, added in any order, but all three appear before wug or mammal.

2.   wug or mammal, added in any order, but after bird, fish, or snake have been encoded as life-form categories.

C. Brown (1977) has also shown that folk botanical life-form terms are also added in a specific order.

1.   tree

2.   grass or *grerb* 'small herbaceous plant': If grerb is encoded as a category before grass, it will include grasses until the life-form category of *grass* appears, at which point it will contain only small herbaceous plants; if grass is encoded first, grerb will contain only small herbaceous plants when it appears.

3.   vine or bush, in any order, once both grass and grerb have appeared as categories.

4.   the final complete inventory a language might have would be tree, grass, grerb, vine, and bush.

There are some obvious correlations between the possible diversity of botanical species and life-form terms. Languages of groups living in desert and arctic areas have fewer botanical life-form classes, while those living in areas which favor botanical diversity, like temperate woodlands or tropical rain forests, have more (C. Brown 1977). The size of folk botanical and zoological vocabularies for life-form terms are also correlated with societal scale (C. Brown 1984). Small-scale societies, with less political integration, social stratification, and technological complexity, seem to have more biological life-form categories, while the large-scale societies usually have fewer. Individuals in small-scale societies are more reliant on the natural world, and can commonly identify 500 to 1000 separate plant species, while their modern urban counterparts might only be able to name 50 to 100 (Witkowski and Brown 1978). The more general life-form terminology is typically more useful to large-scale societies, since these groups are increasingly separated from dependence on the natural environment. Detailed knowledge of plants and animals is no longer required, and the specific and generic names both are replaced by more general terms of the life-form variety.

C. Brown (1986) has also claimed that there are differences among small-scale societies. Hunting and gathering peoples have sizable inventories of labelled plant and animal classes, but small-scale farming peoples have even larger ones, with five times the number of plant classes and twice the number of animal classes. The transition from foraging to agriculture may lead to an increased interest in plants and animals, with these domains playing an enhanced role in the lives of such societies.

Developments in the classifications in ethnobiology and color seems to have run in opposite directions. Societies with few basic color terms are typically at relatively primitive levels of economic and technological development. The basic color lexicon seems to increase and become more specific with greater societal complexity (Witkowski and Brown 1978).

Basic Color Terms in the Lexicon

Berlin and Kay (1969) discovered that color naming is far from arbitrary, and that there is cross-cultural regularity in color naming. There are basic color terms, which have the least complexity and yet still cover the color spectrum. They have also shown that the nomenclature for color categories expands in a regular and predictable evolutionary sequence in languages.

They investigated genetically diverse languages like Arabic, Hungarian, and Thai, using four criteria to identify basic color terms. The terms had to be:

1. monolexemic, that is, they must consist of one lexeme.
2. they must not be contained in another, as *scarlet* is in *red*.
3. they must not be restricted to a small number of objects, like the term *blonde*.
4. they must be common and known; for example, *yellow* vs. *saffron*.

Not all languages had the same number of color terms, and ranged from a maximum of 11 (like English) to a minimum of 2 (like Dani in New Guinea). But Berlin and Kay discovered that all languages take terms from the following basic list of 11 color names. Thus, if one knows the number of color terms in a language to be five, we can predict that that they will be black, white, red, yellow, and green. Such semantic development cannot be random, for there were 2, 048 possibilities, but Berlin and Kay discovered that only 22 combinations, or less than 1%, did in fact occur. There are also historical implications for semantic development, for the following ordered sequence is also the way that languages expand the color lexicon.

1.   black and white
2.   red
3.   yellow and green
4.   blue
5.   brown
6.   purple, pink, orange, gray

Only minor changes (Kay 1975) have been made to the original order of encoding for color they described. The main change has had to do with the finding that basic color terms may encode categories with multiple foci rather than always a single focus. Thus, one change has been the addition of a stage labelled as *grue*, representing the combination of green and blue hues, a term that covers the blue and green regions of the color space. This color category focusses on neither blue nor green, and precedes the appearance of blue and green as separate basic color terms, but only after the yellow focus has been named as a basic level color term. The color gray also seems to be something of a 'wild card' color in that it can appear at any point after the first basic colors, probably because black, white and gray also exhibit a dimension of brightness, as distinct from hue.

Kay and McDaniel (1978) explain constraints in color classification across languages as a consequence of the neurophysiology of color vision in humans. They argue that the physically continuous color spectrum is divided into categories which are neurophysiologically determined. The encoding of color is strongly constrained by the fact that humans are programmed for the natural categories of hue found in the basic colors of red, yellow, green, and blue, with red being especially salient. Black and white are also salient because of the brightness dimension. Kay and McDaniel thus find no differences in color perception for speakers of different languages; their conclusions from a large cross-cultural survey was that perception determines language, rather than language determining perception.

Kay and McDaniel also suggest that color categories are best understood as 'fuzzy sets', with members varying in degree of membership. But there has been some objection to the application of fuzzy set formulations of logical containment to the relationship between the membership functions of a super-category and its subcategories. Mervis and Roth (1981) report two experiments which applied Kay and McDaniel's criteria, but failed to distinguish basic from non-basic color categories. They suggest that every category contains at least one member which is a better example of its own category than any other category, and that this is true for categories in general.

Focal Colors . A number of studies have shown a sensitivity to focal colors as the most salient colors, regardless of cultural naming differences. Rosch (1973) reports that three-year-old children pick focal colors, when asked to choose among color chips, and four-year-olds do better at matching focal chips than they do at matching non-focal chips. Adults seem to match focal chips better, faster, and with shorter names; they also remember focal chips better in tasks like delayed matching. They also learn focal colors better when they are introduced to new color terms. For example, the Dani, a Stone Age agricultural group in Indonesian New Guinea have only two basic color terms, *mili* for dark and cold hues, and *mola* for bright and warm colors. This of course does not mean that Dani cannot name other colors, it just means that they need to devise elaborate phrases when they wish to be more specific, as we do with phrases like *robin's egg blue*. But when taught arbitrary names for colors, the Dani who were taught names for focal colors learned faster than the Dani control group which was taught names for non-focal colors. The Dani also did better with focal colors in a recall experiment. Dani and English subjects seem not to have been too different in their recognition abilities, though the Dani were generally less successful than the English subjects (Rosch Heider 1972; Rosch 1973).

Indeed, this is a case where differences in the naming structures in the lexicon were not paralleled by differences in cognitive structures as evidenced in behavioral tasks. Rosch's work shows that codability is not so different across languages, and that the perceptual salience of focal colors is a better determiner of how well a color is picked out, described, or remembered, than are the features of the language in question. Focal colors exhibit the best codability scores, regardless of language, for focal colors are a human perceptual universal. R. Brown (1976) concludes that a given color lexicon, like the English one, is not just another arbitrary break-up of the color spectrum, but is determined partly by the universal set of focal colors. There is not an infinite array of possible color lexicons, but a fairly constrained set, the design of which reflects universals in color perception. There are 11 focal areas which are the best instances of color categories named in any particular language, and the number of basic color terms will reflect this fact, with languages varying from 2 to 11 as a result.

Conclusions on the Linguistic Relativity Hypothesis

It may be useful to end this section by now offering some conclusions about the extent of relativity in the relationship between language and thought. Whorf's impact was great in promoting the examination of ties between language, culture, and thought processes like perception and recall. Some, like Lakoff (1987), go so far as to consider him to be the most controversially stimulating linguist of this century. His intellectual legacy, at least insofar as it prompted careful investigation by others, can be summarized in three striking hypotheses (R. Brown 1976; Kay and Kempton 1984).

1.   Structural differences between language systems will be paralleled by nonlinguistic cognitive differences for native speakers of the two languages.
2.   The structure of one's native language will influence or determine one's world-view.
3.   the semantic systems of different languages will vary unpredictably and without limit.

Kay and Kempton (1984) note that empirical research inspired by the Sapir-Whorf Hypothesis falls largely into two independent traditions, with psychologists evaluating hypothesis (1) and linguists and anthropologists evaluating hypothesis (3). The bulk of research in both traditions has concerned color. Much of the work before 1969 tended to provide weak support for (3), while recent work has shown this hypothesis (3) to be clearly wrong. Indeed, color is an excellent example to show how we have moved from the extreme relativity of Whorfianism to a univeralistic view based on nativistic views of language, perception, and behavior. Instead of a deterministic role for language, we are now inclined to believe in perceptual universality, with language simply reflecting that universality. Hypothesis (3) is obviously unsupportable; (2) is and always has been vague and not given to experimental validation; and (1) has some merit only in a much weakened sense.

An example of this weakened sense can be seen in Kay and Kempton's (1984) experiment with English and Tarahumara, a language of Mexico. Tarahumara does not have a lexical boundary for the *blue-green* categories, as English does. A first experiment found Whorfian effects in English judgments of colors in the blue-green range, but not for Tarahumara. Though there are some differences in nonlinguistic cognition, as expressed by a task which involves subjective judgments of similarity of color chips matched by a difference in linguistic structure, the differences are not deterministic in the sense that Whorf is often taken to have proposed. And when correcting for the influence from a naming strategy based on lexical category boundaries, the effects disappear. There appears to be some influence of linguistic categorization on non-linguistic processes, since some judgments may be made on other than a purely perceptual basis. These results seem to be best explained by a naming strategy, in which a language-user confronted with a difficult task of classificatory judgment may use lexical classifications of objects to be judged. And they will do this as if the lexical classification were correlated with the required dimension of the judgment even when it is not, as long as the structure of the task does not block this possibilibity.

In general, the experimental findings do not support determinism, but they do show results in which some strategies (like the naming strategy) borrow a ready-made lexical classification from language to handle a difficult and unfamiliar task. This is not the Sapir-Whorf Hypothesis as we have usually understood it, but the nonlinguistic effects are there. We can conclude with Kay and Kempton that linguistic differences may induce nonlinguistic cognitive differences in a weakly related way, but never to the degree that universal cognitive processes fail to appear in other appropriate contextual conditions. Finally, we should say that Whorf's notions on relativity are far from discredited; although they are considerably modified, they still serve to remind us of the cognitive areas where the force of linguistic habit exerts its influence on how we tend to view things. And perhaps more importantly, Whorf's ideas successfully challenged the smug ethnocentricity of European and North American mainstream culture, calling attention to the insightful elegance of other linguistic frames of cultural reference.

Piaget and Vygotsky

Piaget

Piaget's insights have told us much about the developmental sequence of stages in cognitive development (Piaget and Inhelder 1958, 1969), most specifically in the acquisition of concepts fundamental to knowledge. He has approached the acquisition of knowledge as a process of transformation and growth. The child's cognitive abilities are typically inferred from the behavior of one or several children dealing with some spontaneous or elicited task. His **genetic epistemology** tracks the development of knowledge as universal structures of rational thought in the individual. These develop in progressive stages, with each stage evidencing an increased logical capability in the child.

Language is secondary to his interest in the development of thought in children. Language is neither causal nor even particularly instrumental in this development. The child's language merely follows his or her development of cognitive structures, and is only important in the child's later development, as it reflects intellectual growth as a result of verbally interacting with others. Language appears as the medium in two different functions for the child, in moving from egocentric to socialized speech. Utterances in the egocentric stage have little communicative intent, because the child speaks solely for its own purposes. Eventually, the child begins to be more social in orientation, perceiving language as needed to satisfy the communicative needs of others. It is at this time the child becomes conscious of the point of view of others.

Piaget rejects pre-programming in the Chomskyan or any sense, and considers all cognitive acquisition, including language, to be the outcome of a gradual process of construction. The child gradually is more and more able to make sense of the world, and is constantly constructing new levels of cognitive organization as he or she matures (see Rieber and Voyat 1981). Cognitive structures, in the Piagetian sense of a coherent system of mental operations, allow one to arrive at concepts, to solve problems, and to make conclusions, and without necessarily being aware of those operations in order to do them. Such cognitive structures must be taken to explain language structures, as well as their acquisition, since cognition is logically prior to language in the human species (see Sinclair 1975). Logical organization is obviously not derived from language, and intellectual development is obviously possible without language. Acquiring language is just another expression of the general human cognitive capacity for organizing experience, albeit a special one.

Piaget argues that intelligence is derived from experience after birth; his is an operational theory of intellectual development, in which many of the child's concepts are developed without being taught, but independently by doing and manipulating. The stages develop with a finality that allows previously elusive concepts to become crystal-clear with the snappiness of the 'aha' experience we have witnessed in the conservation of matter experiments with water in variously sized glasses. The corollary of this fact is that when adults try to impose concepts on the child prematurely, the child may seem to learn, and even respond verbally, but true understanding must await the actual cognitive stage which allows its true assimilation.

Piaget's opinion (1979) of the Chomskyan school of linguistics is that it is rather impoverished, and that in positing a fixed innate mechanism, it evades explanations by throwing language into biology. Piaget would rather place language among the self-regulatory mechanisms where all the cognitive processes belong. Piaget does, however, give some credit to Chomskyan linguistics for having made us see that intelligence is not subordinated to language. He sees the existence of the discipline of psycholinguistics as a pledge of collaboration which is full of promise (Piaget 1979), and that any realistic and successful future theory of psycholinguistics will have to be interdisciplinary (Rieber and Voyat 1981) and amenable to answers which can be tested experimentally (Piaget 1979).

Vygotsky

Vygotsky (1962) also sees the study of cognitive development as central to understanding thinking processes, and as taking place in stages. Language and cognitive development begin as separate and independent processes, at least until about the age of two, at which time this prelinguistic thought mode interacts with the emerging facility of language and is gradually transformed by it. Language and thought are not identical, but do share a very close relationship. Once the child establishes the connection between experience and language, developments in the one will enable or influence developments in the other. Language also serves to mediate the external world for the child.

Vygotsky knew of Piaget's concept of egocentric speech, but differed in his interpretation of it. Piaget described egocentric speech as appearing around 3 and disappearing by 7, preceding social speech, and having no particularly useful function. Vygotsky instead saw this speech form as a necessary transition from external to inner speech, and suggested that egocentric speech has social origins, and develops into the inner speech which generates the functions of controlling and regulating human activities (Wertsch 1986).

Vygotsky's work spanned the decade between 1924 to 1934, just after the Russian Revolution. His particularly Soviet view of issues in terms of society and social controls is thus not surprising. Though his book on *Thought and Language* appeared in 1934, it was not translated into English until 1962. It was the product of an intellectual climate within a revolution against a particular past, and with a planned future. His psychology was formulated along Marxist lines, inspired by social applications designed to help with the massive practical problems facing the new socialist state.

He was particularly concerned with the field of education, and both Vygotsky and his followers are best known for their studies of child development and education (see Wertsch 1986). His approach has often been labelled as 'interactionist' because higher level thought processes are derived from social interaction, and is directly reflective of the socio-cultural setting that it takes place in. Vygotsky conceived of the development of higher level thought processes as inherently social. The child's development is always embedded in a social environment in which interaction with the more expert adult aids the child's mastery of increasingly complex cognitive structures. This is particularly true for how the child interacts with adults in specific problem-solving situations.

This is reflected in Vygotsky's interest in the way that language reflects and even transmits social, cultural, and historical experiences, and how this fact might channel higher levels of thought. The child's developmental stages of thought reflect mastery of the mediating tools of thought that humankind has developed in the course of his social history. This accounts for his preoccupation with issues of literacy and schooling and the educational process, and their implications in a new society. The most important tool for Vygotsky was language, since it allows the child to be exposed to and master increasingly higher thought processes. He even wrote that concepts are impossible without words and that thinking in concepts does not exist beyond verbal thinking, meaning that the child's acquisition of scientific frameworks and taxonomies is enabled by the child's acquisition of semantic concepts in word meanings and making the generalizations that underlie those categorical meanings (see Lucy and Wertsch 1987). And considering what we have seen in this chapter, such notions are entirely compatible with what we know of how language may be related to thought processes.

Modularity in Cognition

Finally, we should again raise the issue of **modularity** in cognition, since this question is at the very heart of current psycholinguistics. J. A. Fodor (1983) has proposed that the mind is modular, with different kinds of information processed by separate and distinct modules; their output is then submitted to a central processing component for final processing decisions about what has been comprehended. There are well-recognized modular systems like visual and auditory perception. Vision is fast and automatic, as well as being immune to contextual information in the first stages. For example, knowing the truth about an optical illusion does not change your visual perception of the illusion; you will still see lines without diacritics at the ends as longer than lines with them (see Carston 1988).

Does the language processing system exhibit the same modular properties that vision does? We know that linguistic theories have their grammars divide the information they present into separate components or modules, and that such theories differ as to the number of such modules and where the boundaries between them should be drawn (J. D. Fodor 1988). But the way in which a given grammar is organized is often just a convenient organizational framework. How shall we view the organization of the mind? The question in cognition, then, is whether there are such modules in the mind. Can we simply assume that all the higher mental functions operate according to the same set of cognitive principles? Or is it possible that cognitive domains as different as vision and hearing, perhaps even language and mathematics, each follow a separate set of principles?

Chomsky (1975a) was an early advocate of the second view, suggesting that the explanation needed to account for behavior in one domain may be different from that needed in other domains. He in fact proposed that cognitive capacities like vision, hearing, language, and even deductive reasoning and mathematics can be construed as distinct faculties in the mind. J. A. Fodor (1983) has less drastically suggested that the mind is like a computational system, with separate input systems (modules) for vision, hearing, and language, and a central processing system. The language processing system, then, can be compared to other complex systems in which the various input systems feed information to the next higher level of the central processor which in its turn organizes the information. A feature of such a modular view of language processing is that the separate input systems operate quite independently of one another at initial stages, and are correlated by the central processing unit at some higher level, a level which may in fact override input decisions made by the lower-level modules. There is a certain elegance to such a proposal, as well as a certain efficiency to such a working model. Central processors which deal with a restricted range of informational input, already vetted by the modular input systems, operate more quickly and more efficiently than a system which has to consider all the various types of information simultaneously. J. A. Fodor simply assumes that there must be some ordering to how the information is dealt with efficiently, and the notion of modularity is one way of explaining how this could happen.

This may be the best example of how the pervasive computational paradigm that we mentioned in the first two chapters has offered a stimulating metaphor for understanding the human mind. The mind-machine analogy between language processing by humans and language processing by computers is the basis of the metaphor. Just as a computer system for modelling a language capacity might have a sentence parser, a semantic component, a semantic analysis and lexical insertion, a speech output system, and a general problem solving system, we might think of human language itself having such separate modular components, acting separately at first and then being correlated at higher levels. J. A. Fodor (1983) has essentially posited the operation of the same kind of modular, domain-specific system for language that we have for vision and hearing. The language processing system is in turn composed of a set of processing modules, which function autonomously, and do not have access to the internal operations of the other subsystems as they are in operation. But they do interact upon output, at which point the end product decisions in processing are made available to the next module.

Some support is derived from studies of lexical and syntactic aspects of language comprehension in aphasic patients, which seem to point to the functional independence of the various components in language processing. For example, studies of sentence comprehension by aphasics suggests that syntactic mechanisms are independent of lexically based heuristic strategies for assigning meaning (Caramazza and Berndt 1978). Linebarger (1989) presents evidence from agrammatic patients who can analyze some aspects of syntactic structures which they cannot interpret, thus suggesting that form and content are computed by distinct processing mechanisms.

Modular theories of the language processing system face strong opposition from interactive theories of language processing, however, for interactionism also presents evidence in its favor (the debate is nicely captured in Carlson and Tanenhaus 1989 and Marslen-Wilson 1989a). Is processing modular or is information shared throughout the system at any given time and on any given piece of input data? It will be interesting to see which position the evidence will support or delete in the next decade, modularity or interaction in cognitive processes.

Summary

What is the relationship between language and thought? Is language necessary for thought? Does language in some way determine the nature of thought? These have been central questions for linguistics, anthropology, and psychology in this century. The most provocative statement of the relationship between language and thought has been the Linguistic Relativity Hypothesis, also known as the Sapir-Whorf Hypothesis. Thought was pictured as inescapably bound up with systems of linguistic expression, so that all higher levels of thinking are dependent upon language. The structure of the language one habitually uses was held to influence the way in which one understands the world, so much so that the picture of the world would differ from language to language.

Language and thought are distinct from, but do reflect culture. Language serves as a representative catalogue of a particular culture, communicating many, but not necessarily all, of a society's concerns. The existence of non-linguistic cognitive differences which match linguistic differences, however, is really a psychological question which can be answered by experimentation. Several aspects of language structure, namely, vocabulary, grammatical categories and mode of inflection, manner of sentence formation, and part of speech designations, have been examined for such effects. The general result is that only vocabulary and lexical structure have a modest effect in perception and classification, offering support for linguistic relativity in only its weaker form and only for this one aspect of language structure. In general, the experimental findings do not support determinism, although they do show results in which naming strategies may co-opt the ready-made lexical classification of a language to handle a novel task. Instead of a deterministic role for language, we are now inclined to believe in perceptual universality, with language simply reflecting that universality.

Looking for language universals, we should remember that languages are relatively constrained in their basic design, although they do differ quite considerably in their surface characteristics. Unrestricted language universals, which apply to all languages in an unconditional fashion, are often self-evident, because they reflect this architecture. For example, universals like the fact that languages have vowels, use the oral-aural tract, and have proper names seem to reflect the essential design of language. But there are also useful observations we can make about near-universals, those specific exceptions to the general rule; for example, a few Amerindian languages in the Pacific Northwest fail the general rule of having nasal consonants. Such statements allow frequency distributions, in that statistical universals allow us to classify languages according to typological features. There are also implicational universals of the type that if x is present, so also must be y; for example, two Slavic languages exhibit a dual number, which automatically implies that they also have both a singular and a plural number.

Certain universals derive from the human capacity to organize perceptual information. As a result, there are lexical universals in the way that semantic structures are organized as classificatory frameworks. Lexical categories in ethnoscience domains of knowledge like color, botany, and zoology are added to a language in a fixed order, suggesting a lexical encoding sequence with implicational consequences.

There are usually competing names for a given object, but we often choose among possible names by selecting a name at the optimal level of utility. Instead of being too general (for example, *animal*) or too specific (*Labrador Retriever*), we often name things by a basic-level term like *dog*. Parents and caretakers typically take the child's presumed point of view, also naming things at the level of usual utility.

In this way, the folk science of a people, with its own special taxonomies, is passed on to the next generation of language users. A folk taxonomy organizes the physical world around us and allows us to understand it; for example, the biological world is organized into a small number of easily recognized plants and animals which are embodied in a taxonomic hierarchy that all members of a given cultural group make use of. All cultures divide the plant and animal kingdoms into categories, each of which is given a name. The domains are large, and the average plant and animal vocabulary of a preliterate society can easily consist of 1000 to 1200 basic-level names. There are anywhere from three to six levels of classification in such natural systems of classification, but folk classificatory systems are organized around the generic or basic-level categories because they have the tightest and best distinguishability criteria.

Color naming is also far from arbitrary, for basic color terms have the least complexity and yet still cover the color spectrum. The perceptual salience of focal colors is a better determiner of how well a color is picked out, described, or remembered, than are the features of the language in question. The constraints in color classification across languages arise from the neurophysiology of color vision in humans; for example, humans are programmed for the natural categories of hue found in the basic colors of red, yellow, green, and blue, as well as for the brightness dimension of black and white. But even color categories contain at least one member which is a better example of its own category than any other category.

Piaget has approached the acquisition of knowledge as a process of transformation and growth, with language neither causal nor even particularly instrumental in this development. The child's language merely follows his or her development of cognitive structures, and is only important in the child's later development, as it reflects intellectual growth derived from verbal interaction with others. Vygotsky also sees the study of cognitive development as central to understanding thought processes, and as taking place in stages. Language and cognitive development begin as separate and independent processes, at least until about the age of two, at which time thought interacts with the emerging facility of language and is gradually transformed by it. Language serves to mediate the external world for the child, but once the child establishes the connection between experience and language, developments in the one will enable or influence developments in the other.

The issue of modularity in cognitive processes is at the very heart of current psycholinguistics. Some have proposed that the mind is modular, with different kinds of information processed by separate and distinct systems; their output is then submitted to a central processing component for final processing decisions about what has been comprehended. There are well-recognized modular systems like vision and hearing, and some have posited the operation of the same kind of modular, domain-specific processing system for language. The language system is in turn composed of a set of processing modules, which function autonomously, and theoretically do not have access to the internal operations of the other subsystems as they are in operation. Each interacts upon output, at which point its processing decisions are made available to the next module. Some support is found in studies of lexical and syntactic aspects of language comprehension in normal subjects and aphasic patients, suggesting the functional independence of these components in language processing. But there is also evidence to support an interactionist position, claiming instead that information is shared throughout the system. It will be interesting to see which position the growing body of evidence will finally support, modularity or interaction in cognitive processes.

Chapter 9

Biological Prerequisites

Introductory Comments to the Biology of Language

We know that there is no natural language among the world's languages that is more logical or natural than any other. There is no past or contemporary language by which the others are to be measured as being more or less developed. We also know that no current language is the predecessor of our contemporary array of modern languages, at least not in the sense that one of them has an antiquity that the others do not possess. There is no present living or even recent ancestor for the world's array of languages. Each modern language is simply descended from an earlier form of that language, and is thus simply a continuation in the way that modern French, Italian, Spanish, Romanian, and Portuguese are just Latin spoken some 2000 years later. In fact, this is true of earlier forms of language as well, so that Latin itself is just a continuation of an earlier Proto-Italic language which survived better than its less aggressive sister languages Oscan, Umbrian, and Faliscan. Every known language is relatively recent, whether it be Latin, Greek, Sanskrit, or Hebrew, and none of these has any claim to priority or superiority when measured against the world's array or languages, past or present.

The search for origins and directionality was a common fallacy in the Middle Ages, and one even finds it occasionally in the 20th Century. Just as Goropius Becanus patriotically derived all languages from Dutch in the 16th Century, Stalin's approved linguist, N. I. Marr, observed that highly inflected languages (like Russian) represented an advanced stage on some possible evolutionary scale of language development. But no 'primitive' language will provide us with insights into what our primitive ancestral languages were like, because there are no primitive languages. Whether they were a hoax or not, when the Stone Age Tasaday recently walked out of the Mindanao forests, they turned out to speak another form of Manobo structurally similar to other languages of the southern Philippines.

Nor is there much point in studying the stages of child language to show us the stages of language development in history, because we have no evidence that ontogeny recapitulates phylogeny. We have come to re-think and re-assess our view that language is purely cultural as a purely learned behavior. Rather, the current thinking is that language is a species-specific behavior, part of our genetic endowment as human beings, and is acquired in a way that presupposes innateness considerations. Very simply, we think that babies are born with an instinct for language--not for any particular language, but for human language in general. Humans enter the world with certain genetic propensities, like bipedality, for walking on two feet is simply a feature of being human as we know it. Language is like this, and we have found that there are even physiological correlates that support its presence in the human species. There is the much-celebrated hemispheric specialization in the human brain. The organs of speech are shaped as much for speech as for mastication and digestion, and the small mouth opening makes for a better resonating cavity. The tongue is extremely agile, and the human ear has a sensitivity to the point where we can detect a sound which moves the eardrum one-tenth the diameter of a hydrogen molecule.

Rationalism vs. Empiricism

Is what humans know and do the product of experience, or is it there to begin with? This is an old debate between two positions contrasted as **empiricism** (experiential) and **rationalism** (innate). Empiricism holds that no linguistic structures are innate, and that language is learned entirely through experience. Modern behaviorists like Skinner (1957) explain that humans learn languages through general learning principles, which are assumed to be the same for many species of organisms. This means that very little psychological structure is innately specified and that children have no special ability for language, other than that derived from general learning principles.

Rationalism, or **nativism** in Chomsky's terms, claims that the structure of language is specified biologically as part of the genetic endowment of humans. The function of experience is not to teach, but to trigger the capacity for language. It is self-evident that animals can only learn that which their anatomy, central nervous systems, and general level of cognitive abilities will allow them to master. Language is within this range for humans, and rationalists believe in a specific capacity for language. According to Steinberg (1982), both empiricism and rationalism are really forms of mentalism, in that all mentalists agree on the existence of mind and that humans have knowledge and ideas in the mind. But they do not agree on how those ideas got there; the empiricist position is that ideas are derived entirely through experience while the rationalist position is that some ideas are already in the mind at birth. Rationalists may disagree about which processes activate innate ideas and as to what kinds of ideas are innate in the mind. How such ideas became innate in humans remains a problem for rationalists, though for some like the 17th Century philosopher Rene Descartes, the answer was simple--God placed such ideas in human minds. Modern rationalists claim that such knowledge is specified by biology and our genetic endowment, an equally satisfying and equally vague answer.

Human Origins and Language Origins

Humans have existed for several million years. The australopithe-cine hominids became distinct from other primates at least 4.5 to 5 million years ago in East Africa, and probably had some primary mod-elling system for conceptualization in the brain. Our ancestor, or a near relative, Australopithecus, of 4 million years ago, boasted a crani-al capacity of 400 cubic centimeters (cc), while Homo habilis of 2 mil-lion years ago had a brain of 500 to 750 cc. Homo erectus, of .4 to 1.2 million years ago, had a brain of 900 to 1300 cc, no doubt useful in controlling fire and organizing the large-scale elephant hunts which we credit them with by at least .5 million years ago.

The early forms of Homo sapiens, with a brain of some 1400 cc, appeared about 300, 000 years ago. Neanderthal, or Homo sapiens neanderthalensis, of 100,000 years ago, had a brain of 1500 cc, and was a tool user. There were several strains of Homo sapiens, so that Homo sapiens sapiens co-existed with Homo sapiens neanderthalensis over 100,000 years ago. Cro-Magnon, perhaps the best known of the Homo sapiens sapiens strain, appeared about 40,000 years ago and had a brain averaging 1500 cc. Cro-Magnon had a lunar calendar, pro-duced cave paintings, and were likely right-hand preferent and cere-brally lateralized, since they have left us with traced outlines of their left hands. The evolutionary history of basic neurological asymmetry appears to be even more ancient, and some research indicates that nonhuman primates, although they may have lacked language, were characterized by lateralized brains. Handedness and language may represent elaborations based on this asymmetrical configuration (Falk 1987). For example, Homo habilis of 2 million years ago has left arti-facts which display a level of technological complexity.

It is commonly asserted that there is a left-right brain asymmetry, but many no longer assume that the functional and anatomical asym-metry found in the brain is uniquely human (Kimura 1985). Brain asymmetry does not reflect a specialization of function related specifi-cally to human language; various types of brain asymmetry are present in a variety of mammals, and it also controls singing in certain birds. It appears to be a more widespread phenomenon in the animal world which has yet to be adequately explained (Kimura 1985). Some also question whether there is strong reason to believe that our present abilities are totally different in kind from those of our hominid ances-tors. The continuities in brain structure and psychological function suggest that our present cognitive make-up is the result of a long, slow process of evolution (Kimura 1985).

The **left hemisphere** is responsible for sequencing time-dependent, serial, and segmental processes. Broca's area regulates the sequence of sounds produced in speech, and an area of premotor cortex above Bro-ca's area is responsible for sequencing movements of the right hand. This raises the question of the order in which tool-use, right-handedness, and language arose in hominid evolution (Falk 1987). Hewes (1973) has suggested that hominids had a manual system of communication of some complexity, and that this gestural language not only predated vocal language, but that it is similar in its neurological foundations. There was obviously a continuity, possibly a specific motor programming system in the left hemisphere available for language because it was already present for tool manipulation. Hewes therefore suggests that cerebral laterialization, right-handedness, and gestural language preceded the development of speech. Even a gestural language would have allowed enormous survival advantages, and a silent language might have been even superior to vocal language in instances like the hunt. Early gestural language might have been limited in complexity, quite unlike the completeness of many modern created sign languages. The evolution of complex speech, as we know it, must have been a rather late development, certainly after upright walking and tool use. Homo habilis, appearing over a million years ago, not only used tools, but could shape them, indicating a high level of manual skill. There are stone tools from about 2 million years ago, and our hominid ancestors were upright walkers for at least 4 million years, meaning the arms were free for other tasks. The capacity to attach symbolic value to such manual movements must have been early and may even be reflected in the learning of sign language by modern chimps and gorillas (Kimura 1985). The capacity for making gestural movements of the arms and hands thus has been present for a long time, while speech is probably very recent.

Language may have existed in some form for maybe a million years. If so, then language would be co-extensive with Homo erectus who emerged between 1 and 1.5 million years ago, replacing the earlier Australopithecus and Homo habilis. About 300,000 years ago Homo sapiens replaced Homo erectus. Horticulture, animal domestication, and village life emerge about 10,000 years ago, and urbanization, political-economic systems, and writing arise even later. But it is language that makes possible a new kind of teamwork. Complex messages can now be transmitted, and the entire group can be kept up to date on all happenings with a minimum of effort. It could be that there were many origins or a single one, but it is certainly true that language was a real advantage in the struggle to survive, and groups without an efficient form of communiction would not have been able to compete as well. Through attrition many of those may have disappeared, but this is a history so shrouded in mystery that some scholars even forbade discussing language's origin. Many thought it empty speculation at best, and the Linguistic Society of Paris passed a resolution in 1866, and again in 1911, outlawing any papers concerned with the subject. As it was, there have been too many empty explanations which have derived human language from imitating the sounds of nature (the **ding-dong** theory), rhythmic chanting (the **yo-heave-ho** theory), or from naming other creatures from their own utterances (the **bow-wow** theory). Such explanations are not much more useful than the misguided experiments of antiquity (see Campbell and Grieve 1982 for a fascinating history of experiments initiated as royal investigations of the origin of language). For example, the Greek historian Herodotus records how the pharaoh Psammetichos gave two infants into the care of shepherds to await their first words. This, he thought, was a sure-

fire way of learning which was the first and primary language for man-
kind. Psammetichos thought it was Phrygian, because their first work
was *bekos*, ostensibly a Phrygian word--as good an explanation as *Bow-
Wow*, one supposes!

Obviously, we cannot reconstruct the primordial language like we
can reconstruct Proto-Indo-European. But we do know that the old
theories of language origins which thought of language as something
separate from humans were mistaken. The development of language is
part of the evolutionary development of the human race. It is inseparable from the other physical and mental attributes which have
evolved and now are characteristic of the human species. And this fact
has given rise to once again considering the origins of human communication and language. This time, we are armed with more fact and less
fancy. Dingwall (1988:275) notes that we are blessed with considerably newer and larger sources of evidence this time around: more fossil
evidence and better dating techniques; reconstructions of the brain and
the oral-pharyngeal tract through fossil evidence and computer modelling; biochemical evidence for species relatedness; studies of communicative and other behaviors of non-human primates, and particularly
signing and non-verbal comparative studies of human and non-human
primates; studies of the effect of isolation on the development of communicative behavior (for example, feral children); increased knowledge
of first language acquisition by children, coupled with a deeper knowledge of the complexity of linguistic structures; and finally, a better
grasp of language universals and how these may be reflected in the
development of pidgins and creoles.

Communicative Primates?

Some wonder whether some of our communicative prowess stems
exclusively from our powers as the highest rank on the phylogenetic
scale, and question whether our abilities are totally different from
those of our great-ape primate cousins. Primates are of course clever,
as work with the living apes of Africa (the gorilla, the chimpanzee, and
the pygmy chimp or *bonobo*) and Asia (the orangutan and the gibbon)
has shown us. Physical anthropologists have noted relationships in
animal structures and behaviors that are homologous for humans and
the great apes. Structures are homologous because they are inherited
from a common ancestor, and thus genetically and anatomically related
structures, and even behavioral similarities, arise from evolutionary
similarities. Evidence like manual dexterity, the expression of emotions by a particularly mobile face (Ekman 1973), radial brachiation,
and a pectoral framework adapted for swinging, suggests that apes are
more similar to man phylogenetically than any other mammal.

Primatologists put humans and great apes in the same sub-order,
Anthropoidea, and differences further distinguish the two major
branches of hominidae and pongidae. Humans alone are the surviving
species of the branch termed hominids. The split between hominids

and the closest pongid, chimpanzees, may have occurred as recently as 5 million years ago, and not 15, as many previous theories have suggested (Scovel 1988).

Primates like chimps have cognitive abilities that usually surpass those of non-primates. When Kohler was stranded in the Canary Islands during the First War, he had plenty of time to observe chimpanzee solutions to problems, like using a stick to get at out-of-reach bananas. He concluded that they displayed behaviors which were insightful or reasoned, and the more contemporary Jane Goodall reconfirms this vision of the chimpanzee as an insightful tool-user. Chimps also seem capable of symbolic capacity, and can form conceptual domains and label them with arbitrary signs (Hill 1978). They can choose between items which are same or different, and can deal with logical connectives of the *if-then* type, conjunctions like *and*, and even some logical concepts like *all, none, one, several* (Premack 1976). And they can make careful categorical distinctions, as for example, classifying the seed, stem, or peel of an apple to go with that particular fruit and no other.

But even chimpanzees, our closest cousins, do not have language. Of course, part of the question about whether primates exhibit language depends upon how we define the term *language*. Very simply, we could always define it in such a way as to keep 'them' out and 'us' in, but there is no need to do this. Teaching chimpanzees a vocal language was doomed to failure from the outset, and more success has been found in trying to teach them gestures or having them manipulate symbols on magnetic boards or rudimentary computer keyboards. These experiments employ either natural language formats like gestural languages of the Ameslan (American Sign Language) type, or artificial languages in which the chimps move or manipulate some symbols into sequences like 'sentences' (see Hill 1978 for a summary of the first decade's work on apes and language; for more recent reviews of the debate, see Parker and Gibson 1990, Gardner, Gardner and Van Cantfort 1989, and Dingwall 1988).

Manual languages, of the Ameslan sign language type, have succeeded to an upper limit of several hundred gesture 'words' with some chimps and two other primates (for a complete inventory of Washoe's and several others' signing vocabulary, see Gardner, Gardner and Nichols 1989). Washoe, the Gardners' original 'collaborator' in Project Washoe in 1966, was the first to show this symbolic ability in acquiring sign language for communication, and can even be credited with creating some word combinations (*water bird* for 'duck' and *candy drink* for 'watermelon'). Roger Fouts later took her to the Institute of Primate Studies in Oklahoma, and finally to a permanent home at Central Washington University, where continuing research with Washoe and other chimpanzees was directed at finding whether these primates would sign to communicate with one another and perhaps even pass it on to their young. And indeed, adoptee chimpanzee Loulis exhibited a number of signs that he could only have learned from surrogate mother Washoe and three other cross-fostered chimpanzees. This is the only explanation, since the 10-month-old infant chimp received absolutely no human signing for the next five years; adult chimpanzees were, of course, not bound by the rule and signed to him (Fouts, Fouts and Van Cantfort 1989). In the meantime, Project Washoe continued on in Reno with young new chimpanzees, and this time the Gardners and their human colleagues signed to one another and to the new arrivals all the time. Once introduced and learned, signing for these chimpanzees seems to be robust and self-supporting, at least to the extent that they have learned (Gardner and Gardner 1989). Chimpanzees have been observed to use signs with one another, even without humans present. And the signing is rich enough to provide 'texts' for analysis, with clarity of signing sufficient to achieve a 90% agreement by independent Ameslan observers (Fouts and Fouts 1989).

With upper limits of several hundred signs, depending on the subjects, a small number of other chimps have demonstrated these abilities, as have even a gorilla and an orangutan (for a complete inventory, see Dingwall 1988). For example, Francine Patterson has replicated the signing studies with Koko, a young female gorilla, who manages 375 signs and shows some syntactic ability. Not all are as impressed, however, with these accomplishments. H. Terrace (1980) has instead concluded that his Nim Chimpsky was imitating, rather than learning and creating, and showed little or no syntactic ability. He found Nim to be lacking in creativity and spontaneity, imitative of his teachers' signing, and highly repetitious. When Nim was moved from the Columbia University laboratory to the Oklahoma facility, however, and conversationally-oriented methods of human-chimp interaction replaced the rigors of operant conditioning, he proved to be a better conversational partner by exhibiting less expansive imitations and more turn-taking (O'Sullivan and Yeager 1989).

Other chimps have learned to manipulate plastic symbols on magnetic boards or to punch instructions onto a computer keyboard limited to a few sequences. Sarah, the Premacks' chimp, was shown to exhibit some productivity in her use of 'sentences' created by sequencing plastic symbols on a magnetic board. Lana, the Rumbaughs' main chimpanzee 'collaborator' at Emory University's Regional Primate Research Center, was also credited with creating 'sentences' by pressing buttons sequentially on a computer keyboard to make known her limited wishes about food, company, and general distraction. Her geometric symbol-using successors Sherman and Austin also showed that a large range of behaviors previously thought unique to humans can be shown for chimps, and many of these behaviors are crucial to studies in comparative intelligence theory (Hill 1978; see also Parker and Gibson 1990).

But while a certain level of cognitive ability is obviously necessary for the development of language, it is not sufficient to attain human language. The possibility of pongids acquiring a hominid capacity like language is really a question of continuity or discontinuity. Some promote a continuity between us and our early ancestors' primate communication systems (Falk 1980). Others reject the possibility of any direct continuum links outright, and still others label the search for talking animals as wrongheaded (Sebeok 1987). Much of the fascination with apes and language is tied up with the Cartesian assumption that humans are unique, one of the cornerstones of that uniqueness being language. The ape language research seems to have challenged this self-congratulatory assumption, and this may account for some of the heat in the debate. But the central issue remains: Do chimpanzees taught in these various settings have language? There is no question they are clever, but do they have language? The fact is that any and every healthy 3-year-old child has far outstripped the most clever primate in acquiring language, and without the same rigorous training regimens. And not even the most clever of primates has been seen to employ language in the creative fashion that is its most salient feature, other than a few word-combinations that leave much to the discretion of the observer.

Human brains not only increased in size before the development of language, but also differentiated in directions that we are only now coming to understand. The human brain of 1500 cc is not only larger than the 400 cc chimpanzee brain, but our brains are more asymmetrical and certainly more specialized. Human language systems also made several organizational leaps, among these the arbitrary assignment of meanings to the symbols used and the displacement of those symbols from any direct stimulus. Animal communication systems exhibit a small number of fixed vocal or gestural signals, like alarm calls, mating displays, submissive gestures, and food-related calls; each signal serves a different function and is directly tied to the stimulus which elicits its appearance. For example, primate alarm calls are given in the presence of the danger causing alarm, and family pets bark directly at the sign of an intruder, not two days later to tell their masters of the burglar. But transferred meanings are the rule in language systems, and this feature of displacement coupled with the equally important feature of arbitrariness make human language as powerful as it is (Hockett and Ascher 1964). Moreover, the fact of the levels of phonology, morphology, syntax, and discourse hierarchically building upon one another makes the system even more powerful. The communicative primates may have some ability to transfer meaning, but they only have the barest rudiments of syntax. Nor is there any metalinguistic sense of language, in the way that we humans are aware of language as language, commenting on it, correcting it, agreeing to change it or not change it, and so on.

However, there is no denying that our primate cousins have demonstrated some striking abilities which remind us of ourselves. But this is not particularly surprising if you consider that human communicative behavior is the culmination of mosaic evolution within the primate order. As Dingwall (1988:306) rightly concludes, there is no reason to claim human communicative behavior in its entirety as the unique and exclusive creation of the hominid line. Simply put, we are but one product of much that has gone on before us, and others have participated in the same general line of development that has resulted in similarities that allow us to speak of larger categories (like mammals) or more compact categories (like primates). None of their accomplishments should be particularly surprising, given the enormous genetic similarity found between humans and the great apes. If chimpanzees and humans share over nine-tenths of the DNA code, there are likely to be behavioral as well as morphological similarities. And indeed, if you construct a list of supposedly unique human behavior patterns, almost all have precursors in the behavior patterns of the great apes (see Dingwall 1988).

Biological Foundations: Contrasting Genetic and Cultural History

Eric Lenneberg (1964, 1967, 1969) must be credited for redirecting our attention back to the possibility that humans are equipped with highly specialized biological propensities for favouring and shaping speech, in the same way that our natural constitution defines the predisposition to walk or use our hands. For example, language is a form of behavior present in all cultures of the world, its onset is age-related in all cultures, and there is only one acquisition strategy for babies everywhere. And the milestones of language development correlate better with motor development than they do with chronological age. For example, at the age of 1, the child typically tries to stand, and can walk when held by one hand; in the language development side of things, the child's speech now contains syllable reduplication, as well as the first words, and evidences the understanding of some words (Lenneberg 1969). Language is based upon the same formal operating characteristics whatever its outward surface form, and these operating characteristics have been constant throughout our recorded history. It is also a form of behavior that can be impaired specifically by brain lesions which leave other mental or motor skills unaffected (Lenneberg 1969).

Lenneberg (1964) once usefully contrasted cultural and genetic history, noting that cultural history allows explanations in terms of long-range purpose and utility. Genetic history is instead an interplay between evolution as random processes and certain constraining factors. The majority of new traits have a lethal or only neutral effect. But occasionally a new trait is compatible to life and even enhances it, as happened with bill shapes for Darwin's thirteen species of finches on the Galapagos Islands. But it is too facile to 'explain' the development of such genetic traits by claiming that the 'purpose' of a large cranial vault is to house a large brain, which in turn is intended to perfect intelligence. This Calvinistic view of evolution misinterprets Darwinian notions of selective survival; a better parallel is the evolutionary 'purpose' of erosion or volcanoes in the geological evolution of the planet. Of the many new traits that may chance to appear, the great majority have a lethal effect under given environmental conditions and are thus of no consequence for evolution. But occasionally there is one that is compatible with life and will thus result in perpetuation of that characteristic in the species for some limited period of time. Which one is language? Is it a product of our genetic history or our cultural history? Lenneberg went on to examine language, commenting on which aspects we must assume to be genetically determined traits and which might be the result of cultural activity. He contrasted two types of human activities, one biologically given (walking, or bipedality), and the other a result of cultural achievement and a product of purposiveness (writing). Contrasting biologically determined with culturally determined behavior, he noted that language more often resembles the biological type, though it sometimes resembles cultural and purposive activity.

It is obvious that bipedality exhibits no intraspecies variations, nor is there a historical beginning point within the species as a species. There is evidence for an inherited predisposition and a presumption of specific organic correlates. Walking cannot be taught or learned without a biological constitution for this; the inability to walk on two feet does not arise from a deficiency in training. In contrast, writing does exhibit variations correlated with social organization, and there is only a history within the species. The earliest written records are barely 6,000 years old, taken from the records of the Sumerians of 4000 B.C. There is no evidence for an inherited predisposition, for its absence only implies a lack of training. And there is certainly no assumption of specific organic correlates. Contact with pencil and paper does not result in the acquisition of writing skills the way that exposure to spoken language results in speaking and comprehending skills.

There are no intraspecies variations for language. Despite their diversity, all languages are alike in employing the basic principles of **phonemicization** and **concatenation**. Except for true sign language which is a language in every sense of the word, human language is a vocal affair, and the sounds heard in languages are always some small subset of the total range of sounds that humans can produce. The inventory of phonemes in a language is constrained, never below a dozen and rarely above eighty or so. Among contemporary languages, Hawaiian has just over a dozen phonemic sounds, while languages like Kabardian in the Caucasus mountains boast over six dozen. Words and morphemes in all languages are constituted of a sequence of phonemes. Concatenation means the stringing of words or morphemes into more complex sequences of phrases, sentences, or discourse. No speech community has ever been described where communication is restricted to single-word discourse. Moreover, no language concatenates randomly, with any word followed by any other. This hierarchical order is the essence of syntactic structure, where a finite set of rules defines all grammatical operations in a given language. The fact that all languages are formed along strikingly similar patterns is too much to be due to chance.

Behaviors that have been important in evolution of a species are also easy to learn for species members. Successful behaviors lead to their selection and inclusion in the biological base, and over time, the behavior becomes more effective and easier to learn. Language is easy for humans to learn, but impossible for even clever primates to learn, let alone other animals. Great efforts have been made to get apes to learn language formats, but with extremely limited success, despite the fact that man and chimp share 98% of the genetic material in their nonrepeated DNA (Falk 1987).

Nowhere does the evidence take us back to language in its infancy. The changes in language that we do find, like phonetic change, occur rapidly, frequently, and continuously, but seem to follow no universal path and have a random directionality. The slow evolution of the foundational principles of language leads one to suppose that we have here the reflection of a biological matrix which forces speech to be of one and no other basic type. Genetic theory would not expect a gradual and selective process culminating in modern language, but cultural explanations would. It is true that our records and comparative reconstructions only take us back 5000 years, merely 1/10 of the age of early fossils of our direct ancestors in the Levalloiso-Mousterian culture of 50,000 years ago. Though the documented history of languages is short compared to paleontological evidence, it may not be too short to demonstrate trends in development of the principles of phonemicization/concatenation if these had a cultural history. But there is no evidence of directionality. Nor do the surface characteristics exhibit directionality other than randomness; for example, English loses its case endings, while Iroquian and Finnish add case endings.

Infant humans exhibit an innate propensity for taking in stimuli that develops automatically into language; this capacity is so deeply ingrained that language develops in varied, and even unfavourable, conditions. It is sufficient that the child grows up in an environment where it is used; language stimuli will trigger the ability to produce and understand language. Children in all languages are merely exposed to a large number of examples of how the language works, and from these examples they formulate principles with which new utterances are created that conform to the recognized rules of how that language is organized. This is remarkable, considering the limits on other cognitive and motor skills.

The development of language follows a typical natural history. Learned skills in a culturally learned sense do not usually fit into an established place in the life cycle. But language development does follow a regular schedule in the child's maturational development, appearing at a particular time and following a fixed sequence of stages. Linguistic and cultural differences have no effect on the age of onset or mastery. And language is not easily suppressed; congenitally blind children acquire it, as do children with varying degrees of input and linguistic stimulation under unfavourable conditions.

The ability to acquire language is also independent of intelligence. Children acquire language at a time when their power of reasoning is poorly developed. Except in cases of profound mental retardation, defective intelligence need not imply language deficit. Nor does the absence of language necessarily lower cognitive skills, as we have learned when deaf children that are given nonverbal tests of concept formation score as high as normal hearing peers; there are some exceptions, though, like verbally mediated over-learned concepts like the opposites in pairs like *high-low* and *up-down*.

It is as if language acquisition follows some innately mapped-in programme for behavior, the exact realization of which is dependent upon the peculiarities of the speech environment. With the lower animals we assume that their communicating traits are the result of an innate predisposition elicited by environmental circumstances; we have no reason to assume that the use of language by humans is purely an acquired behavior. Bracketing the problem of imitation per se, we might ask why the children 'imitate' in the highly characteristic way they do? It was thought that the apes that were raised in human homes failed to develop speech partly because they could not be induced to pay attention to the relevant cues in their environment. But why do all children without any special training automatically attend to these cues? No chimp or other primate has been able to learn to coordinate aspiration with the laryngeal and oral mechanisms with the speed, precision, and endurance that every child displays. It is surely due to more than just practice.

The Vocal Tract: Adaptation in the Oral and Pharyngeal Cavities

As humans began to walk with a more erect posture, the larynx was pushed down. Articulate speech is tied to the fact of the voice box having been lowered, because the vocal tract configuration now provides for a wider range of sounds. A right-angle bend in the human vocal tract makes for a long pharyngeal cavity above the resonating voice box. In fact, it is now easier to choke or drown; this configuration must have evolved for speech alone, and not for eating or breathing, for the respiratory efficiency of the adult air passage is about half that of the infant. Babies are born with the larynx or voice box high in the throat, quite close behind the tongue, allowing babies to suck milk and breathe through the nose at the same time, like so many other animals. This was also likely true for our hominid predecessors like Neanderthal.

The descent of the larynx to a position closer to the base of the throat, at the bottom of the pharyngeal tube for adults, probably took place over millions of years. From reconstructing the vocal tracts of Neanderthal from fossil remains of the skulls, Lieberman (1975) estimates that the modern right-angled shape of the supralaryngeal vocal tract appeared less than half-a-million years ago; it was not present in Australopithecus, Homo habilis, or even in Neanderthal. Early humans were better at speech than primates, but not much, because they also lacked the physical musculature necessary for it. Lieberman (1984) further speculates that because of the high laryngeal position in Neanderthal, the back of the tongue was quite immobile, limiting the production of certain speech sounds because the tongue was not free to move. Like chimps and human infants, they lacked the ability to articulate the three crucial vowels /i a u/. Chimps cannot move their tongues during a cry, whereas the human tongue is extremely agile and sounds from the vocal chords can be modulated for pitch contrasts. According to Lieberman, Neanderthal could not utter the most stable vowels /i a u/, but could make /ɪ æ u ə/; they could make labial and dental consonants but could not differentiate between orals and nasals. Very simply, Neanderthal could not articulate human speech the way we know it, since the full range of phonetic contrasts found in modern languages was simply unavailable for physical reasons. Lieberman claims that the Neanderthal did not have maximal syllable efficiency because of this lack, that they were inefficient speakers, able to transmit information at only a tenth the rate we can.

There is considerable disagreement over Lieberman's biological claims for soft tissue configuration based on skeletal fossil remains, as well as whether the La Chapelle-aux-Saints skull should be used as the Neanderthal archetype. Nor does everyone agree with Lieberman's linguistic claims as to what constitutes a necessary vowel inventory for human language to be articulated in its full richness; for example, the Caucasian language, Kabardian, has only 1 or 2 vowels, depending upon how you count, and Hawaiian has only 8 consonantal phonemes. But there is no doubt that humans have a very low positioning for the larynx, as compared to other mammals and even other primates, and that this fact is conducive to language. For example, the lower larynx allows for greater flexibility in the production of sounds because the tongue is more mobile. It also adds a third resonating chamber to the existing oral and nasal resonating cavities; with a pharyngeal cavity, we now have resonating chambers in the throat, nose, and mouth.

The Brain and Hemispheric Specialization

Tool-using and language seem to be centred on the left side of brain for most people. The left side is largely responsible for language, and the right for control of spatial judgment and the processing of non-verbal information generally. Humans have language functions lateralized to the left side of the brain, since damage to the right side of the brain does not usually result in severe language impairment. There has been a certain amount of myth-making about laterality in the popular literature of late, particularly given to separating the brain into two, the right brain and the left brain, with the left controlling logic and reasoning and the right being more creative, expressive, and intuitive (see Corballis 1980). It is true that the left brain largely houses the analytic, problem-solving, and sequential abilities essential for language processing capacities in most normal right-handed individuals; it is also true that the cognitive structure of the right hemisphere is characterized by a more holistic and global conceptual organization, and is particularly important in the understanding and communication of emotion (Tucker 1981). But there is little support for the notion of the right hemisphere having a special role in creativity, or the overly simplistic notion that there are contrasting cognitive styles to be identified with the two cerebral hemispheres (Corballis 1980). The brain is a whole brain, and the hemispheres do not function as separate halves, as separate brains; if anything, their activities are integrated and they complement one another. Very simply, one cannot develop one half of the brain, like 'pumping iron' to achieve muscle mass; both sides of the brain participate in all such cognitive activities, and both sides of the brain participate whether you analyze or create something. Although the left hemisphere is more central to matters of language processing, the right is also involved in such activities.

It is easy to see how this belief came about. The evidence shows the left to be more responsible for speech production, phonemic decoding, syntax, letter naming, perception of temporal order, and voluntary oral and manual movements, with the right more important for precise perceptual and non-verbal information processing, spatial judgment of position and orientation, perception of two- and three-dimensional shapes, faces, color, musical chords and melodies, and emotional nuances (Witelson 1987). But dichotomies like "verbal-nonverbal" or the "auditory-visual" soon proved to be inadequate for the diverse research findings. A better working hypothesis (Witelson 1987) envisions two kinds of information processing, with the type of processing, not the nature of the stimuli, as the determining factor in lateralization. Thus, the **left hemisphere** processes discrete items with reference to their temporal arrangement, while the **right hemisphere** attempts to synthesize a unified configuration, without any attention to the temporal arrangement of that information.

Aphasia may affect any of the language functions, not only speaking. Unfortunately, much of what we know about the functional organization of language in the human brain seems to come from abnormal and unfortunate circumstances. The results of stroke, accidents, and surgery have told us a great deal about specific functions of different areas of the cortex. It seems that the whole left side of the cortex is involved in language, but it is difficult to pinpoint exactly where. We are able to localize some cognitive activities like the perception of sounds and the muscular control of speech production; other functions like planning and comprehension are not so easily mapped. The classical speech areas are the cortical areas in right-handed adults which typically produce aphasic results when damage occurs. These are the left interior frontal gyrus (Broca's area), the posterior part of the superior left temporal lobe (Wernicke's area) and parts of the left parietal lobe, including especially the angular gyrus. There is some debate over the exact limits of these areas, and even over the notion of demarcated regions, but there is no question that these areas of the brain must be intact for normal linguistic functioning in most adults (Marshall 1980).

The pattern is not unique across the population, for left-handed men do not always exhibit the expected cerebral dominance for language, and there may even be some sex differences worthy of note (Marshall 1980). Where the 85% of the population is right-handed, with language functions resident in the left hemisphere, only half of the remaining 15% of left-handers show left hemisphere dominance for language. Moreover, aphasia in sinistrals, or left-handed people, following lesions to either hemisphere is less severe or more transitory. Left-handed people seem to show less severity of disorder when the speech regions are damaged, even though the left hemisphere is dominant for most left-handers. And right-handers with a strong family history of left-handedness may show better recovery patterns than those without (Geschwind 1972). Left-handedness, complete or partial, seems to imply imperfect lateralization of language to either hemisphere (Zangwill 1975).

At any rate, we do know that the right's involvement in speech diminishes during childhood and is virtually nil in right-handed adults. The patterns of language loss as a result of brain lesions led early researchers to theorize about how language functions were associated with specific areas which could be erased or affected by damage. Such studies have told us that lesions in certain areas produce aphasic disorders while others do not. An **aphasia** is a speech disorder which is the direct result of damage to the left cerebral hemisphere. But patients with aphasia may not have any impairment of general intelligence. To give a general idea of one kind of aphasia, think of the tip-of-the-tongue phenomenon--you know the word, but just can't come up with it, despite the fact you know you know the word. Only rarely does such a speech disorder occur after damage to the right hemisphere; 97 out of 100 people with permanent language disorder caused by brain lesions will have damage on the left side (Geschwind 1972).

This seemingly unilateral control of certain functions has been called **cerebral dominance**, referring to the predominant role of one hemisphere, usually the left, in governing the acquisition and use of language. It is specifically, though not uniquely, characteristic of humans, and may be linked to the evolution of handedness preference and tool-using capabilities. Handedness is obviously a reflection of cerebral asymmetry, with the asymmetry of the hands resting in the brain centers that control them, not in the hands themselves (Corballis 1980). Hand preferences do occur for chimps, monkeys, cats, even rats and mice, who show a consistent preference for one hand or paw over the other, but there seem to be as many left-handed as right-handed individuals within each species (Corballis 1980). Hand preferences for children appear toward end of the first year and beginning of the second year, but no reliable differences are associated with educational studies. There is also evidence that the anatomical basis for cerebral lateralization may have been present in Peking man and Neanderthal man, and may even be found in some primates. And we know that some bird species, like the chaffinches, canaries, and white-crowned sparrows, have singing controlled by the left side of the brain. The fact seems to be that cerebral asymmetry is not unique to humans, or even primates (Corballis 1980).

It is easy to see how the belief arose that the left hemisphere controls language, while the right would be assigned the task of perceptual processing, spatial judgment, and the task of processing non-verbal information. Not surprisingly, the easy inference from findings with the left hemisphere was that it was specialized, containing a system specialized for linguistic function (Kimura 1985). Lateral preferences in handedness in humans invited the temptation to assign the asymmetry of cerebral function to handedness, so that for a long time it was thought that the dominant hemisphere, that is, the one that results in aphasia when damaged, would be contralateral to the preferred hand. But we know now that aphasia in left-handed individuals is more frequent after left-sided than right-sided brain injury (Zangwill 1975). The majority of people, about 96% of right-handers and 70% of left-handers, have speech controlled by centers in the left hemisphere (Corballis 1980).

Early studies in the last century, by Paul Broca in the 1860s and Carl Wernicke in the 1870s, pointed to different kinds of impairment, depending upon where the lesion was located. For example, **Broca's aphasia** is characterized by slow, labored speech, misarticulations, and deletion of function words and morphological endings, leaving the impression of a telegraphic style of speech. **Wernicke's aphasia**, on the other hand, seems to have rhythm and cadence, and appears both fluent and grammatical; but upon closer examination, it is semantically empty. Damage to Broca's area produces speech which is not fluent, but which is semantically intact, while Wernicke's aphasia produces speech which is fluent, but semantically empty of content (Geschwind 1972). This simple model of language localization has proven to be overly simple, but it was useful in some general way in predicting the sites of brain lesions, given the type of language disorder (Geschwind 1972). Now the terms 'major' or 'dominant' hemisphere for the left hemisphere, and 'minor' or 'nondominant' hemisphere for the right, are no longer used so widely used, because many functions, like those of a nonverbal, perceptual nature, see the right hemisphere as dominant in the majority of individuals (Corballis 1980). There are generally discernible patterns of dissolution (Caramazza and Berndt 1978), with different parts of the brain serving different linguistic functions. But we are not as confident about localizing even what seem to be obvious aphasias, for no two aphasics are exactly alike in effect of the damage in respect to impaired language performance.

Traditional studies of aphasic language have not always told us much about normal language functions, but it is obvious that neurolinguistic findings can provide strong constraints on psycholinguistic hypotheses about language processes. For example, we know that damage to the anterior part of the dominant hemisphere will affect syntactic processing, thus allowing us to test modularity notions like whether anterior aphasics can comprehend sentences by applying lexical and heuristic mechanisms. The fact is that they can employ heuristic procedures to assign a semantic interpretation to a sentence, a finding that cannot be demonstrated with normal speaking subjects (Caramazza and Berndt 1978).

Though the details are still somewhat controversial, the production of language occurs in precentral areas of the frontal lobe and sensory functions in postcentral parietal and superior temporal fields. These specializations are not present at birth, but become gradually fixed during childhood. Thus, for adults severe left hemispheric central cortical lesions usually result in aphasia; in Luria's large-scale study (reported in Geschwind 1972), of all the patients with wounds in the primary speech areas of the left hemisphere, 97.2% were aphasic when Luria first examined them; a follow-up showed that 93.3% were still aphasic when Luria saw them later, although in most cases they were aphasic to a lesser degree. Luria also found that when the wound lay over Wernicke's or Broca's area, the result was almost always severe and permanent aphasia; when the wounds were elsewhere, aphasia was less frequent and less severe. Another report of lesions resulting in aphasia records 70%, and irreversibility for half of these (reported in Lenneberg 1969).

Anatomical asymmetries are present even before birth, but the plasticity of the two hemispheres is such that some have suggested that they are equipotential at birth. This implies a supposed equivalence of the two cerebral hemispheres for the language capacity for about the first 2 years of life, as long as language has not lateralized and come under control of one side of the brain (see Dennis and Whitaker 1977). Thus, the right hemisphere can be competent for one's entire life if the left hemispheric disturbance takes place early enough (Lenneberg 1969). The right can function vicariously for the left in the earliest years, indicating a certain plasticity of the brain in the early life. The right hemisphere may take over language development for children with left hemisphere damage, although the recovery time may differ considerably from individual to individual, and early left hemisphere damage may even result in delayed language acquisition (Schneiderman 1986). Children with the same lesions as an adult may make a much better recovery, and according to Lenneberg (1969), it is directly related to age. Under 2, such damage is no more injurious to language development than lesions to the right hemisphere; after language onset, but before 4, it may result in a transient aphasia, with language quickly re-established if the right hemisphere is intact.

Hemispherectomy parallels this general picture. The striking plasticity of the brain earlier in life is illustrated by accounts of how a damaged left hemisphere has been removed early in life, with the right hemisphere acquiring and sustaining good comprehension of language and an adequate verbal IQ (Marshall 1980).

It may be that at birth the two hemispheres are equipotential, and that the right hemisphere can take over for the left in the acquisition of language (Zangwill 1975). But the capacity of the right hemisphere to take over diminishes with age. By age 4 or 5, it is doubtful whether completely normal acquisition of language by the right hemisphere is possible (Zangwill 1975). As Dennis and Whitaker (1977) have noted, the notion of hemispheric equipotentiality does not accurately explain or predict that the two hemispheres are not equally at risk for language delay or disorder, and that they are not really equivalent substrates for language acquisition. For example, early left hemisphere damage seems to be expressed in delayed acquisition of word relationships, and the isolated right hemisphere seems to acquire aspects of auditory language less well, as for example, the ability to respond to the syntactic format of spoken utterances.

Recent evidence thus shows that neural plasticity is not without limits. The level of general cognitive functioning subsequent to brain damage is often below normal, regardless of time of onset or side of the lesion. The 'myth' that complete recovery will follow early brain damage is somewhat modified by evidence with humans and laboratory animals that exhibit some residual deficits after early brain damage (Witelson 1987). As for adults, it is well-known that the capacity of the right to take over speech functions seems to be negligible, and young war casualties have the same symptoms as old stroke patients (Lenneberg 1969).

A Critical Period for Language Acquisition?

We know that any toddler can learn any language in the world as his or her first language. We also know that children have an easier time acquiring another language before their early teens, and that for young adults, second language learning is often a frustrating academic exercise. It may be that the brain is best suited to language learning before puberty, and neurological material suggests that something happens in the brain by the early teens that changes the propensity for language acquisition. We are not sure, but it seems that this critical period coincides with the final state of brain maturity in terms of structure, function, and biochemistry, marking an end of freer regulation and locking some functions into place.

Other evidence seems to come from retarded children exhibiting mongolism. Such retarded children do acquire the basic structures of the language, though they take more time to do so than normal children. For example, mongoloid children will slowly move through stages of language development, but the rate of development will slow down and come to a standstill in the early teens. Their abilities may be arrested in the primary stages of development, which are then perpetuated for the rest of life.   Thus, even if the maturational scale is distorted by a retarding disease, the order of developmental milestones, including the onset of speech, remains invariable (Lenneberg 1967).

The notion of a critical period is a familiar one in biology, where the environment will trigger certain brain structures. This stimulation must take place during certain limited and prescribed critical periods of time, for if a particular behavior is not stimulated and responded to within a certain time frame, the behavior never fully or correctly emerges.   There has been speculation that language behavior is also subject to such a critical period (Lenneberg 1967; Scovel 1988). If language stimulation is not provided within some critical time frame, it is claimed that the ability may not emerge thereafter. A weaker version of this hypothesis would suggest that language is at least partially debilitated by a lack of appropriate stimulation.

Humans, of course, have a long nurturant period after birth, and this nurturance takes place within the care of members of the species who are all by definition language-users if they are human. It is only when this usual turn of events is disrupted by bizarre circumstances of upbringing that we have any opportunity of glimpsing whether it might be true that humans also have a critical period for language to be acquired. There is plenty of evidence of a critical period for the acquisition of spatial judgments by kittens, of following behaviors by newly-hatched ducklings, and of species birdsong by white-crowned sparrow chicks between the first 10 to 50 days of life. For example, songbirds like the male chaffinch need their species song to attract mates and stake territorial claims. They learn that birdsong by hearing adults singing that song, as well as by their own attempts to reproduce that song. The male chaffinch must hear an adult to learn that song before it becomes sexually mature in the second spring of its life; otherwise, no amount of exposure makes up for the aberrant song that develops.

It is obvious that for adults, young adults, and even late teens, the capacity to learn language varies enormously from the ability to learn language before the early teens. Very young children all learn language, but as one matures towards adulthood, this capacity seems to shut down. The ability to acquire language seems to be relatively independent of level of intelligence at early ages, whereas the ability to acquire language after a certain age is an intellectual task with an enormous range of individual variation. For very young children in the process of learning their first language, IQ simply does not control the acquisition of that first native language--that is, it is not an intellectual activity like acquiring algebra skills.

Feral Children

The most telling evidence about the critical period comes from feral children. Feral children are relatively rare, and thankfully so, for such unfortunate children brought up by bears, wolves, or whatever simply do not survive. Humans have a long gestation period, with an even longer period of nurturant caretaking; we simply are not prepared to survive in the world without the specific care of members of the same species. And one of the absolute characteristics of that older generation of caretakers is that they have language, a feature of the environment which every normal child is automatically exposed to.

Scholars have long been interested in feral or 'wild' children, because they offer an opportunity to learn about human development apart from societal input and influences. The classic case of this was the 'wild child' Victor who was 12 when found in the forest of Aveyron in southern France in 1800 (Lane 1976). There was great interest in Victor because of the Rousseaunian claim for the inherent equality of human beings, and that society effectively taught, and thereby corrupted, the noble, simple, and primitive mind. In Rousseau's time, Victor's development was of paramount interest because it afforded an opportunity to ascertain whether or not society was responsible for affecting our thought and behavioral patterns. In more modern times, of course, we have been more interested in the insights such isolated cases can provide as to the nature of language acquisition and the possibility of a critical period.

Victor was put in the charge of Dr. Jean Itard, who tried to teach the boy what he could, but finally gave up after several years. Itard left detailed records, and we know that Victor never learned to speak, never really learning to say more than several words. The problem with Victor's case, and so many other less well-recorded cases, is that we have no way of assessing his mental abilities, and whether he was in some way mentally or intellectually handicapped. Previous studies of feral children rarely cast sufficient light on the critical period issue because the documentation is either scanty or faulty, and we are never really sure if their lack of language acquisition was the result of some basic, but unrecognized and thus unreported, mental or intellectual deficiency. Unfortunately, there is the occasional modern case, which offers better evidence than what we have had to date. One of these is the case of Genie, who was not raised by wolves, but under bizarre human circumstances.

Genie

In 1970, a girl of 13 and 1/2 was brought to public attention under the name of Genie. She had been been kept in isolation from about the age of 20 months until her discovery. She was brought to UCLA to assess her language abilities, and a number of linguists were involved in trying to assess her language skills, and possibly to upgrade them (see Curtiss 1977). Thus, she was without language at a time when lateralization is normally taking place or has already taken place. Genie was certainly past the time when normal children begin to acquire their first language, and possibly at a time when certain abilities are beginning to shut down in terms of ease of acquisition and general plasticity. Genie was a severely disturbed and underdeveloped human being, given the heart-breaking story of her isolation, and she began learning her first language at about the age of 13.7. She had not been provided sufficient exposure to primary linguistic data for true language to emerge, and a number of tests in 1970 and 1971 put her at a mental age of about 2 years old. Such tests did of course underrepresent her abilities, but we at least know that she was not mentally incapacitated, and that she was at least as advanced as normal children beginning to learn language. She was showing herself to be developing cognitively and intellectually, but with a surprising scatter in her abilities. Genie continued to change and grow, and her performance on nonverbal tests of cognitive abilities slowly improved over time, though they never really approached a normal level.

As early as late 1971, she was beginning to be linguistically responsive in numerous linguistic situations, whereas up till then, she had ignored all language use around her unless addressed. Genie did indeed learn certain aspects of language after the so-called critical period, but there were also features that she could not grasp, as for example, the difference between active and passive sentences. Certain pronouns were troublesome for her in keeping their referents straight. The disjunctive *or* was particularly problematic, though the conjunctive *and* did not offer such difficulties. She could not comprehend what *or* meant, though she knew it was different from *and*, which she did control; her test responses to the conjuctive relationship with *and* were 100% correct between 1971 and 1975, while her responses to *or* were only 8.9% correct. Such examples simply underscore the fact that learning language is not a simple intellectual process.

Genie did not speak spontaneously, and was reluctant to speak unless required to do so. In fact, Curtiss' report on Genie (1977) is based upon a total output of a mere 2500 spontaneous utterances, largely telegraphic one- or two-word utterances. In sum, her passive phonology was such that she could discriminate speech sounds of English by the time that Curtiss began to test her. Her speech production was characterized by an abnormal voice quality, and her phonological system was exceptionally variable and unpredictable, so that her speech was often impossible to understand. Similar statements could be made for her morphological, syntactic, and semantic development. Her course of language acquisition in these three areas was in some respects normal, but in other respects far from normal. She was certainly not a fully competent speaker of a language, with all of the grammatical characteristics that signal a normal fluent speaker. For example, Genie's sentences continued to appear telegraphic despite other evidence that she had acquired the necessary morphology that such strings omitted. Genie seemed to understand most of what is directed to her in real-life situations, by taking advantage of environmental clues in her comprehension. But formal testing quickly revealed the deficiencies in grammar that Genie was using nonlinguistic clues to compensate for. Thus, in the final analysis, her comprehension of language was incomplete.

In respect to the critical period, Curtiss (1977) concludes that, abnormalities notwithstanding, Genie can be said to have language in its most critical and fundamental respects, though it is certainly not equivalent to normal language abilities. Thus, any strong version of the critical age hypothesis has to be dismissed, for the notion that humans cannot acquire a first language after puberty does not hold true in Genie's case. She is indeed acquiring language, or at least some aspects of it, from simply being exposed to it. But the weaker version of the critical period hypothesis cannot be dismissed, for normal language acquisition may not occur normally after the critical period has been passed. Genie's language is not the same as that of normal children, neither in the course of its development nor in terms of its absolute status as measured by the final product. She exhibits certain features that signal abnormal abilities and that we see either in distorted language development or in language breakdown. Thus, Genie's case only supports the notion of a critical period in a limited fashion, suggesting that there may be specific constraints and limitations on the nature of language acquisition outside this maturational period.

Evidence from Deaf Children

There is also some evidence from deaf children who suddenly lose their language (Lenneberg 1969). Infants coo and babble during the first 6 months of life, but congenitally deaf children cease after 6 months. Children need the stimulation of language input from the outside environment. If hearing loss occurs before language onset, their language realization is like that of the congenitally deaf. If the loss occurs after onset, say at 3 or 4, their speech deteriorates quickly. Once a child stops using language, it is difficult to maintain the skill by educational techniques. But once these children do enter schools for the deaf, their training is much more successful than that of the congenitally deaf. There is a direct relation between length of time exposed to language and proficiency seen in re-training. Sign language systems of communication can also replace the oral system best at an early age, thus fulfilling the need to communicate. And having an effective communication system like sign language often makes it easier for the deaf child to later learn another system. Sign language proponents of Ameslan suggest that it is important to exercise the language learning faculty in the crucial years. Children who can communicate with American Sign Language thus do not grow up without language, and are reasonably fluent by 3, right on the developmental schedule. Sign language is a language in every sense of the word, and not surprisingly, the language development of children who acquire sign language from birth parallels the way in which children acquire spoken languages. First 'words' appear at about the same time, as do the semantic relationships seen in the two-word stage in spoken language. Supporters claim that having a first language, even if a signed language, at least provides the deaf child with a first language which serves as basis to learn others. The expectation is that it is much easier for these children to learn English as a second language than for children in oral/ speech programs learning spoken English as a first language (see Ratner 1985/1989).

The best success of all is if one becomes deaf later in life, when language has already been established; then one already has a firm grasp of the communication system, and needs to cope primarily with the handicap of being deaf. Children with deaf parents will learn language, and so will those suffering from gross neglect. They may exhibit some delay, but it is minimal and language does emerge. Congenital blindness also has no effect, and such children will acquire language even though there are only a small fraction of words whose referents can be defined tactually. The inescapable conclusion is that language follows its own natural history, with acquisition occurring as long as the environment provides a minimum of direct interactive stimulation.

Language and the Human Species

Now that we have surveyed the biological foundations of language, we may ponder one last time, as our concluding section, the place of language in the species endowment of humankind. It is not enough to say that language originated somewhere between the separation of the hominid line from the other primates and recorded history. Human communication, as we know it today, did not suddenly arise in our ancestors by a single mutation. This complex behavior evolved gradually through a series of stages which pave the preadaptive way for more and more complex systems of mental representation. Modern scholars are equipped with more information about our past and our present than ever before, and informed speculation on how and when this all came about has begun to appear more commonly.

One of the more controversial, and thus more interesting, of these derives from Bickerton's extensive work with pidgins and creoles (Bickerton 1988, 1990). Pidgins arise when humans have no common language and yet are obliged to comunicate with one another. There must have been countless instances of this over the milennia, as speakers of mutually unintelligible languages came into contact and had to find a means to communicate with one another. But we are most acquainted with those which have arisen as a result of the period of European colonialism between the 16th and the 19th centuries. Speakers of different, often unrelated, languages were taken to faraway places like Haiti or Jamaica, under conditions of slavery; here they were forced to work closely with one another, and under masters who spoke yet other languages like French or English. Or they found themselves as indentured immigrants in places like Hawaii, where they outnumbered the plantation overseers by as much as 30 to 1, and shared their lives with fellow-workers who spoke diverse languages. Both situations exhibited rigidly stratified societies, and the contacts between the workers and the masters were even more limited than the already prohibitive numerical ratios would suggest. The result is the emergence of a language which does not really have native speakers, a contact **pidgin** used by these speakers of diverse native languages to communicate with one another. A pidgin might then become the common language of the next and ensuing generations, who use this **creole** as their first and native language thereafter. The gap between the pidgin and its nativized creole, however, is immense; where the pidgin was structureless, the creole exhibits the same range of structural types as any other natural human language. It has inevitably become a fully developed language, and will serve the community's linguistic, cultural, and intellectual needs just as adequately as any other natural language.

Bickerton has long claimed that these 'created' languages which arise from the pressure to communicate provide us with the best glimpse of the properties of universal grammar (see Bickerton 1988). Such 'catastrophically-formed' new languages, he contends, demonstrate our biologically-based ability to recreate language even where there is no shared one. They prove that the human species comes neurologically equipped to not only create new languages, but also to reconstitute language if the normal process of generation-to-generation transmission is distorted by extralinguistic forces. Even in the absence of any specific model from which the properties of language could be learned in the normal sense, humans can and will recreate language as an inevitable expression of this species-specific biological endowment.

As in much of modern theoretical linguistics, Bickerton assumes that there is a single set of universal syntactic principles. These are basic and absolute, and are given by the neurological equipment of our species. These fundamental principles of syntax, however, are filtered through an unmarked set of grammatical options by which they are realized. The principles must also be instantiated with lexical material, and these factors working together constitute the underlying essence of human language. It is this basic substrate that pidgins and creoles reflect in their incipient stages, regardless of which languages or language families have come into contact to create them. For example, such languages have characteristics like strict SVO word order, with subject and direct object marked by position. The semantics of the grammatical morphemes are relatively constant, as are their etymologies; they seem to be typically drawn from the model language in a surprisingly regular way (for example, the completive marker in the pidgin/creole is taken from a verb meaning 'to finish'). Participial forms of verbs are rarely found, and the same is true for nominalizations.

Pidgins and creoles are thus not simply reduced versions of older, established languages. Rather, their 'simplicity' is the result of human communicators falling back upon this universally-shared, neurologically-given set of syntactic principles when the model language is unavailable or unattainable through lack of contact. The lexical items are simply filled in, being taken from the imposed language or the native language(s) of the pidgin creators. There is, however, usually massive pruning of the lexical properties of the imposed model language, as well as of the native language(s), so that words in the resulting pidgin/creole continuum can be considerably different than the original ones. In contrast, the underlying substrate of syntactic principles has simply been added to in older, established languages over the years, and thereby complicated by any number of the possible morphological and lexical properties that result from historical change.

With this background, Bickerton (1990) has boldly reached out to trace what must be the evolutionary history of language, in terms of the neurological prerequisites for any species to acquire any language. Within a holistic evolutionary perspective, he notes the presence of fundamental similarities in simple conceptualization and communicative behaviors shown by our and other advanced mammal species. The antecedents of language as a representational system are to be found in the ways in which earlier and simpler species represented the world to themselves in order to respond to it appropriately. A refined representational infrastructure would have been substantially in place for the common ancestor of the great apes and humankind, and the modest successes of our contemporary primate colleagues with sign language, plastic chips, lexigrams, and computer keys simply reflect this.

For example, they automatically put elements into conceptual categories; being exposed to a banana and a sign for it, they utilize the concept of *banana* as embracing all members of the class. Yet they also exhibit an awareness of proper nouns as opposed to common nouns; *Roger* stands for the representation of a significant individual, and not for the representation of a class of objects.

In our case, Bickerton further postulates a 'protolanguage' which is intermediate between the prelinguistic state and true language. This protolanguage would have come into existence two to four million years ago, though it is likely that protolanguage did not develop until Homo erectus emerged. It is from this unstructured protolanguage that a structured system emgerged that we can call true language. This protolanguage hypothesis is consistent with a variety of findings, ranging from aphasia, the emergence of language in twins, feral children, and native sign language users in the congenitally deaf population, and of course, the emergence of the pidgin/creole continuum. Language in the human species now consists of two easily separated components, a lexical component and a syntactic component, with the lexical component having emerged first in neurologically-defined terms. In Bickerton's (1990:130) words, evolutionary development has blessed us with both "a maplike representation that uses hierarchically structured categories, and an itinerary-like representation that generates sentences (formally structured propositions) drawn from the contents of this map." Human language, then, contains both a primary representation system, as well as a secondary representation system which interacts with it. The former provides a model of the world based on sensory input, categorization, and memory, and the latter provides a model of the model whereby all this can be put into words.

The resulting system is an enormous step forward in the progressive development of increasingly more sophisticated ways of representing, and thereby knowing, the external world. Whatever the evolutionary accident that caused it, the outcome is a change, not in behavior, but in the neural organization that causes us to coordinate meaningful symbols into complex formal structures, and to do this freely and automatically. There are consequences for a species that possesses the potential for the construction of complex knowledge-systems, so much so that Bickerton feels that not only did language create our species, but it also created the world our species sees. Language frees the human species from the chokehold of immediate experience, allowing us to manipulate time and space to build complex systems that describe and perhaps even explain the world. The result has been an adaptation of a type never seen before, endowing us with powers that go beyond mere survival, but which confer upon us the stewardship of planet Earth. The biggest question now facing us is whether we will be wise enough to recapture our unity with the rest of nature, and use those powers to enrich the earth rather than dominate, and possibly destroy, it.

Summary

Language is a species-specific behavior which is part of the human genetic endowment. It is a form of behavior present in all cultures of the world, and its onset is age-related. Just as babies are born with a genetic propensity for bipedality, they are born with an instinct for language--not for any particular language, but for human language in general. Language is also a form of behavior which can be impaired specifically by brain lesions which leave other mental or motor skills unaffected. Certain physiological correlates support its presence in the human species: for example, hemispheric specialization in the brain; organs designed as much for speech as for mastication and digestion, in that a lowered larynx allows for a vocal tract configuration that provides for a wide range of sounds; a resonating quality of the mouth enhanced by its small external opening; agility of the tongue; and a relatively sensitive ear as the auditory appparatus. Given the evidence, language qualifies more as an example of a development in the genetic history of the human species that it does as cultural history.

Humans have existed for several million years. The Australopithecine hominids became distinct from other primates at least 4.5 to 5 million years ago in East Africa, but the early forms of Homo sapiens appeared only about 300, 000 years ago. Several strains evolved, so that Homo sapiens sapiens co-existed with Homo sapiens neanderthalensis over 100,000 years ago. Cro-Magnon, perhaps the best known of the Homo sapiens sapiens strain, appeared about 40,000 years ago; they may have been right-handed and cerebrally lateralized, since they have left us with traced outlines of their left hands.

In the human brain, the left hemisphere is largely responsible for language, and the right for control of spatial judgement and the processing of non-verbal information. Specifically, the left is more responsible for speech production, phonemic decoding, syntax, letter naming, perception of temporal order, and voluntary oral and manual movements; the right is more important for precise perceptual and non-verbal information processing, spatial judgment of position and orientation, perception of two- and three-dimensional shapes, faces, color, musical chords and melodies, and emotional nuances.

Right-handedness, and thus tool-using, is also usually resident in the left hemisphere, since it is responsible for sequencing time-dependent, serial, and segmental processes. Broca's area regulates the sequence of sounds produced in speech, and an area of premotor cortex above Broca's area is responsible for sequencing movements of the right hand. This suggests the inter-relatedness of tool-use, right-handedness, and language in hominid evolution. It may even be that early hominids had a manual system of gestural communication of some complexity, preceding vocal language. Similar in its neurological foundations, it would have been preadaptive in providing a motor programming system in the left hemisphere for the development of language.

Although the human brain is unique, brain asymmetry does not reflect a specialization of function exclusive to human language. Various types of brain asymmetry are present in a variety of mammals, and it also controls singing in certain birds; hemispheric asymmetry is a phenomenon in the animal world which has yet to be adequately explained. Moreover, in humans it should be remembered that the brain is a whole brain. The two hemispheres do not function as separate brains, but rather their activities are normally integrated and complementary.

The aphasic results of strokes, accidents, and surgery have told us much about specific functions for different areas of the cortex. Much of the left side of the cortex is involved in language, but it is difficult to pinpoint exactly where. We are able to localize some cognitive activities like the perception of sounds and the muscular control of speech production; other functions like planning and comprehension are not so easily mapped. The classical speech areas are the cortical areas in right-handed adults which typically produce aphasic results when damage occurs: Broca's area, Wernicke's area, and the angular gyrus. There is some debate over the exact limits of these areas, and even over the notion of demarcated regions, but there is no question that these areas of the brain must be intact for normal linguistic functioning in most adults. Broca's aphasia is characterized by slow, labored speech, misarticulations, and deletion of function words and morphological endings, leaving the impression of a telegraphic style of speech. Wernicke's aphasia, on the other hand, seems to have rhythm and cadence, and appears both fluent and grammatical, but upon closer examination, it is semantically empty. Damage to Broca's area produces speech which is not fluent, but which is semantically intact, while Wernicke's aphasia produces speech which is fluent, but semantically empty of content. Although this simple model of language localization has proven to be overly simple, it has been useful in some general way in predicting the sites of brain lesions from the type of language disorder. While studies of aphasic language do not always explain normal language functions, neurolinguistic findings do provide strong constraints on psycholinguistic hypotheses about language processes.

Some have suggested a critical period for language acquisition, sometime before the final state of brain maturity marks an end of freer regulation and locks some functions into place. The biological notion of a critical period suggests that the environment will trigger certain brain structures, and that this stimulation must take place during a prescribed period. If a particular behavior is not stimulated and responded to within that time frame, the behavior never fully or correctly emerges thereafter. Relevant evidence about the critical period comes from feral children like the 18th Century 'wolf boy', Victor, and the 20th Century sequestered child, Genie. Victor never learned to speak, learning to say no more than a few words. The problem with Victor's case, and similar poorly recorded cases, is that we have no way of assessing the child's mental and intellectual abilities. This was not true, however, in the contemporary case of Genie. Genie had been been kept in isolation from about the age of 20 months until her discovery in 1970 at the age of 13. Genie was past the time when normal children begin to acquire their first language, but she did learn certain aspects of language. There were, however, many linguistic features that she could not grasp, and although Genie can be said to have acquired language in its most critical and fundamental respects, it is certainly not equivalent to normal language abilities. Any strong version of the critical age hypothesis has to be dismissed, but the weaker version of the critical period hypothesis cannot be dismissed, for normal language acquisition may not occur normally after the critical period has been passed.

There is also some related evidence from deaf children who suddenly lose their language. If hearing loss occurs before language onset, language loss is like that of the congenitally deaf. If the loss occurs at about 3 or 4, their speech deteriorates quickly; but language training for these children is much more successful than for the congenitally deaf. There is a direct relation between length of exposure to language and the proficiency seen in re-training. Sign language systems of communication can replace the oral system best at an early age because it fulfills the human drive to communicate. Children who can communicate with a system like American Sign Language thus do not grow up without language, and are reasonably fluent by 3, right on the developmental schedule. Congenital blindness has no effect on the acquisition of language, and congenitally blind children will learn language even though only a small fraction of words have tactually defined referents. Language obviously follows its own natural history, with acquisition occurring as long as the environment provides a minimum of direct interactive stimulation.

Humans and great apes occupy the same sub-order, Anthropoidea, and differences further distinguish the two major branches of hominidae and pongidae. Humans alone are the surviving species of the branch termed hominids. Primates like chimpanzees have cognitive abilities that usually surpass those of non-primates. For example, they are capable of symbolic capacity, and can form conceptual domains and label them with arbitrary signs. Some have learned limited aspects of sign language, and once learned, they have even been observed to use signs with one another. Others have been successful with learning to manipulate some symbols into sequences on computer keyboards and plastic blackboards.

The possibility of pongids acquiring even the rudiments of a hominid capacity like language raises the question of continuity vs. discontinuity in the developmental history from early primate communication systems. While contemporary non-human primates may have some ability to transfer meaning, they only have the barest rudiments of syntax. Behaviors that have been important in evolution of a species are easy to learn for species members. Sucessful behaviors lead to their selection and inclusion in the biological base, and over time, the behavior becomes more effective and easier to learn. Language is thus easy for humans to learn, but impossible for even clever primates, despite the fact that man and chimp share 98% of the genetic material in their nonrepeated DNA.

The development of language is part of our evolutionary development, inseparable from the other physical and mental attributes which have evolved to become characteristic of the human species. Scholars are once again considering the origins of human communication and language, but armed with considerably newer and larger sources of evidence. We can call upon increased fossil evidence and better dating techniques, reconstructions of the brain and the oral-pharyngeal tract through computer modelling, biochemical evidence for species relatedness, studies of communicative and other behaviors of non-human primates, comparative studies of signing and non-verbal communication in human and non-human primates, studies of the effect of isolation on the development of communicative behavior, increased knowledge of first language acquisition by children, coupled with a deeper knowledge of the complexity of linguistic structures, and finally, a better grasp of language universals and how these may be reflected in the development of pidgins and creoles.

Human communication did not suddenly arise in our ancestors by a single mutation. This complex behavior evolved gradually through a series of preadaptive stages leading to increasingly complex systems of mental representation. A representational infrastructure must have been substantially in place for the common ancestor of the great apes and humankind, for earlier and simpler species would have represented the world to themselves in order to respond to it appropriately. Language in the human species may be said to consist of two easily separated components, a lexical component and a syntactic component, with the lexical component having emerged first in neurologically defined terms. Human language thus contains both a primary representation system, which provides a model of the world based on sensory input, categorization, and memory, as well as a secondary representation system which interacts with the first by putting it into a syntactic matrix for secondary modelling. The resulting system is a sophisticated way of representing, and thereby knowing, the external world, supporting the construction of complex knowledge-systems which describe and perhaps even explain the world.

Chapter 10

First Language Acquisition

Introductory Comments to the Study of Child Language

How does a child learn his or her first language so well in such a short time? And what is the course of language learning? Developmental psycholinguistics, the study of child language, has attempted to answer such questions over the past 30 years, and in so doing, has provided us with considerable insight into the how and why of first language acquisition. Different theoretical approaches to understanding language acquisition have each provided us with different insights, and the pace of explanatory modelling has been brisk enough to keep up with the ever-increasing amount of child language data coming in (see Bohannon and Warren-Leubecker 1985/1989 for a survey of theoretical approaches). These have ranged from the behaviorist approaches we saw in earlier chapters to more recent explanations which focus either on mechanisms of acquisition which derive from formal properties of language itself or on the social-communicative functions which language fulfills in human interaction. Both Wexler and Culicover (1980) and Pinker (1984) have been concerned with the **learnability** of formal properties of the grammar, suggesting that grammar is unlearnable through known learning principles and that it must be innately programmed. Bates and MacWhinney (1982, 1987) instead focus on the functional goals of language, suggesting that structure is driven by the communicative functions that linguistic structures must serve.

Whichever theoretical position holds sway in developmental psycholinguistics, however, the facts they must account for remain the same. No child fails to learn a native language, and it is learned largely before the age of 5. Children are not taught language in any formal way, and yet the fabric of language is already intact by the time school begins. It is amazing how each of us does it much the same way and ends with the same general abilities. But children do not wake up one day with full language capacities. Language is acquired in stages, and each stage more closely approximates adult language, so that there is a continuity which culminates in full adult competence. The stages appear to be very similar across languages, and the principles which guide the child's formulations at successive stages may well be universal. The exact ratio of *nature* to *nurture* is unknown, but both are obviously crucial to the fact of language acquisition. On the one hand, our biological heritage endows us with innate propensities that underlie language development. On the other hand, environment is equally of importance, for the child must be stimulated by linguistic input.

Physical growth and development follow temporally related maturational sequences. For example, children smile at 46 weeks after conception, or 10 weeks after birth. Certain important speech milestones are also reached in a fixed sequence and at a relatively constant chronological age. But language development correlates better with motor development than it does with chronological age, and this interaction seems a better index of maturation than age. For example, at 6 months the child can bear weight when put into a standing position while holding on to something; at about the same age, the child begins to babble with sequences like *ma, mu, da, di*. There are of course individual differences in early semantic and syntactic development (Nelson 1975), and the rate of acquiring linguistic forms and structures varies among children: for example, the age at which normal children say words ranges over as much as a year, though the age range at which they begin to combine words into sentences is narrower; children also vary as to the age when they can interpret what is said to them, particularly complex inputs. Children do differ in onset and rate of language development, but the order of stages seems to remain constant: for example, the babbling period ends somewhere around 18 months, overlapping a period of single word utterances; this is followed by a brief stage of 2-word utterances around 18 to 24 months. For average normal children, the actual divergences in rate of development are not that spectacular either.

Gathering child language data is not always an easy task, though it has been been aided by the leap from hand-written notes and diary observations to tape recorders and hand-held video recorders. Video equipment has allowed us to capture the entire context, enhancing our ability to deal with data which is complicated by the uncertain relationship between form and function. Parents, as well as researchers, often rely on context to decide what a given form meant at these successive stages. We normally assume that the child meant to communicate something, and we resort to the context to decide what it was.

We particularly need to assess the child's acquisition of communicative competence, for language is also a culturally situated social behavior. Relevant grammatical knowledge is one thing, but the child must also have appropriate strategies and skills for transacting language in the right contexts. Adult speakers exhibit both knowledge of linguistic rules and knowledge of the skills they must employ in appropriate contexts. From early on, much time is devoted to communication transactions, and the child's most stable relationships exhibit frequent exchanges (Schiefelbusch and Pickar 1984).

Comprehension vs. Production

Adults presumably possess full comprehension and production abilities, but children often have only a partial knowledge of both. Anecdotal reports usually credit young children with being able to understand more than they can produce; but they may not always show comprehension ahead of production (Clark and Hecht 1983). Logically, of course, one expects that comprehension would precede production, because to produce an utterance, one must make choices among linguistic elements, and to make these choices, one must understand them. And, indeed, some recent studies have found that children understand something of a construction before they start to produce it appropriately. For example, Clark and Barron (1988) found that children can detect ungrammatical compound nouns as 'not ok!' before they can repair them, further evidence that children's comprehension is ahead of production. From ages 3 to 6, they reject forms like *chair-duck, *wagoner-pull, *pull-wagoner, *puller-wagon; the older they get, the more ungrammatical compounds they reject. But their ability to make repairs to these ungrammatical compounds is below their comprehension ability.

When children fail to understand, they devise strategies to get by; when they lack the means to make their intentions known, they use other strategies to get the job done. Thus, it often seems that children know more than they actually do. For example, children rely on what they know about a subject, like the properties of objects, their usual roles, and the relations that usually hold between objects. Children under 2 usually put objects *in* containers and *on* surfaces, regardless of the preposition specified in task instructions. Clark and Hecht suggest that the coordination of production with comprehension is a lengthy process, demanding that children match the memory representations they have set up for production with what they have already represented for comprehension.

Linguistic Constraints and Cognitive Constraints on Language Development

The relationship between innate language strategies and overlapping cognitive strategies is not entirely clear. As Macnamara (1972) once pointed out, it is likely that the child uses meaning as a clue to language, rather than language as a clue to meaning. Obviously, without some recourse to meaning, one cannot easily discover the use of syntactic devices like word order in English to express the subject-predicate relationship in sentences like *Mommy drank the milk*. Indeed, this must also characterize the way in which young children come to understand the array of speech acts that a language makes use of. Sentence structures and speech act types are like glosses on the events around the child, who learns to match their meaning with their expression in some natural language.

Linguistic Constraints . Cross-linguistic studies in the acquisition of communicative competence over the past twenty years (see Slobin 1967) have detailed the features of language acquisition right across different languages and cultures. The focus is on universals in language development, and how the properties of a given language might influence the course of learning. A recent two-volume report on data and theoretical issues in the crosslinguistic study of language acquisition (Slobin 1985), with data from English, German, Hebrew, Japanese, Kaluli (Papua-New Guinea), Polish, French, Samoan, Turkish, and Ameslan shows that children construct grammars which have some interesting similarities. They make comparable errors, and their responses to complexities in languages are also similar, revealing a similar conceptual base.

Children seem relatively impervious to corrections by adults, and it may even be impossible to teach a child a feature of language before they would learn it themselves. The young learner benefits more from conversational interaction than by frequent adult correction of their errors (Moskowitz 1978). In fact, parents rarely correct ungrammatical sentences, but correct instead for meaning, intention, and gist. Children are actively constructing rules at each stage, and the rules increase in complexity as the child approaches adult capacities in the language. Slobin (1971, 1973, 1977) once proposed several operating principles to explain the child's predispositions to perceive speech and construct formal systems of language structure in particular ways. For example, the child seems to 'pay attention to morpheme and word order' and to 'avoid exceptions'. The actual word order does not seem to matter too much, for Slobin (1982) observes that languages of different order types do not differ too much in terms of general learnability.

When measured against the entire acquisition span, languages with varying degrees of free word order (Turkish, Russian, Finnish, and Serbo-Croatian) are learned just as completely as languages with fixed word order (English). But in the short term, different languages pose the child with different sets of formal problems to solve and learn from, for the child must discover how conceptual notions are mapped in that particular language. For example, Turkish has a regular and reliable case-inflectional system, marking the semantic roles of nouns; word order therefore does not play much of a semantic function, fulfilling pragmatic needs instead. In fact, inflections and free word order do not retard, and can even accelerate, the development of comprehension. Thus, Turkish children achieve a significant level of correct response at an earlier age than English, Italian, and Serbo-Croatian children (Slobin 1982).

As another example, Turkish and Serbo-Croatian both use inflections. But Turkish learners comprehend their inflectional cues to relational roles earlier than Slavic learners, because the languages differ as to whether their inflectional cues to the relational roles are encoded onto isolated stressed syllables. This distinction predicts the difference in learning rate. Turkish has inflectional cues which are a full syllable long, are stressed, and neither deform the phonetic structure of the root, nor contract or cliticize. The Serbo-Croatian inflectional system is fusional, and lacks the transparency of Turkish. The Turkish learner cannot make an error or overgeneralize, because there is only one possible suffix for a given relation; the Serbo-Croatian child makes errors and overgeneralizations throughout learning.

Slobin (1982) has also suggested that languages with double-cueing systems are more trouble for learners than systems with only single-cueing. Serbo-Croatian requires attention to both morphological role of inflections AND word order to recover relational roles; Turkish uses only morphological cues, with word order free. But overall, languages may not differ so much in the totality of demands placed on child learning the language. For example, the early Turkish advantage in morphology is balanced by a disadvantage in syntax; in contrast, Serbo-Croatian two-year-olds produce relative clauses with ease, suggesting they have an advantage in syntax.

Cognitive Constraints . These are obviously linguistic constraints on the sequence of acquisition which are derived from the target language, but there are also cognitive constraints on the sequence of acquisition. A form which is linguistically simple, but conceptually difficult, may emerge later. Slobin (1973, 1985) has suggested that conceptual development precedes grammatical development, and even determines the acquisition order of some grammatical forms. The mastery of a specific linguistic form is seen as a result of the cognitive complexity of the concept the form conveys, as well as its formal linguistic complexity in a structural sense. But it is cognitive development that leads the way and precedes linguistic development, for children cannot speak of isosceles triangles if they cannot conceive of them. This is the reason young children ask questions with *who, where, what* before they ask successful questions with *when, how, why.* Questions about people, places, and things are not as abstract as the concepts required for time, manner, and causality.

But the example need not be so general and just limited to content. Take, for example, the conditional *if-then* relationship which holds between two clauses in sentences like *If it is sunny on Wednesday, we'll go up to Shawnigan Lake.* It is grammatically simple in languages like English and Russian, but typically does not emerge until later because of its hypothetical nature. Although the conditional has the same grammatical structure as the simple declaratives *It is sunny* and *We'll go up to Shawnigan Lake,* it appears somewhat later. Slobin (1970) reports how Samoan and American children had difficulty in even repeating sentences with conditionals or with conjunctions involving semantically complex relations like *because, unless, whether.* Cognition is relatively independent of language, and the child is faced with the task of learning how these two representational systems map onto one another.

Child Phonology

The acquisition of phonology requires that the child must master the abstract system underlying the phonological system. But the phonetic realization of the system must also come under the child's control, as the physiological and acoustic details of speech production require coordination of a complex set of muscle movements. This is one of those instances where what a child can say is not the same as what it can process; Berko and Brown (1960) first called attention to this perception-production discrepancy in terming it the *fis phenomenon.* The child may say *fis* and is perfectly aware that it is *fish* that is intended; indeed, the child objects to adult imitations of the child's mispronuniations until the correct pronunciation is made by the adult.

Often a child in the later stages of phonological development knows that a systematic distinction exists, but is simply unable to produce it. Obviously, the 40-odd phonemic units of English do not crystallize overnight. The child goes from simplest features to the more complex in development, and phonology is no exception to this general rule. Some sounds, like /r l tʃ dʃ/, require finer coordination, in that they require a close control over the amount and time of movement. The child also learns the phonotactics of the system, ultimately avoiding that which is prohibited by the system. For example, /ŋ/ is not permitted initially in English and /h/ is not permitted finally; sequences like /pl-/ are permissible, but */pf-/ is an impossible sequence. They typically make some unpermitted sequences as they learn, as for example, *sred* for *thread*, but by 4, they are aware of which sequences are not permitted.

Speech Perception and Its Acquisition by Children

Infants are highly responsive to speech sounds even a few days after birth, for speech sounds seem to be rewarding in a way that other sounds are not. Thus, from the very beginning, children appear to discriminate speech from non-speech, and seem to pay particular attention to the human voice, as opposed to other environmental sounds. Not surprisingly, an infant is particularly sensitive to its own mother's voice, having heard it so often while still in the womb.

Eimas and his colleagues (1971, 1985) have suggested that infants perceive some sounds in a categorical way from as early as one month of age. Data suggests that infants are endowed with innate perceptual mechanisms which are attuned to the phonological characteristics of human language, preparing them for the possible linguistic categories they may find in natural languages. For example, research has shown that an infant can distinguish between two syllables differing only in voicing (/pa vs. ba/), place of articulation (/ba/ vs. /ga/), between nasal and stop consonants (/ba/ vs. /ma/), stop consonants and semivowels (/ba/ vs. /wa/), between contrasts in both voicing and place of articulation (/va/ vs. /sa/), and even contrasts in tongue height and placement (/a/ vs. /i/). But not all possible contrasts are discriminated; for example, the /sa-za/ voicing contrast is not attended to, though /pa-ba/ stop contrasts are. Infants do not have enough knowledge of the system to know that voicing is a feature, and that they are doing what adults do in making such discriminations. The suggestion is that infants may begin life with a generalized ability for categorical perception, using some system of feature detectors that pay attention to certain acoustic properties. Such properties are the ones that involve possible speech categories in human languages; thus, the effect of linguistic experience is the loss of the ability to discriminate those differences which are not phonemic in the language they acquire.

Infants exhibit a sensitivity to such categories whether or not the distinctions are important in their parent language. But the child will ultimately lose the ability to detect distinctions that do not occur in the native language. Werker and her colleagues (1981, 1984) have shown that 6- to 8-month-old infants from an English background will readily distinguish contrasts that occur in other languages. But when they are tested at the age of 12 months, they test out about the same as adult English speakers, unable to detect the contrasts which they were so sensitive to earlier on.

Werker and Tees (1984) demonstrated that infants do discriminate non-native speech sounds according to phonetic categories without prior experience, and that this ability declines within the first year of life. Earlier work (Werker, Gilbert, Humphrey and Tees 1981) had already shown that English infants 6 to 8 months old could discriminate two Hindi consonantal contrasts as well as native-speaking adults could. English-speaking adults and older children were very poor in their abilities to discriminate, but infants performed at the same discriminative level as Hindi adults. Using a head-turning measure, Werker and Tees further investigated the discriminative abilities for English infants on stop contrasts used in Thompson, an Amerindian (Salish) language of western Canada, and in Hindi, an Indo-European language from India. The Thompson contrast was the opposition of velar and uvular glottalized stops (/k'-q'/) common to Amerindian languages of the Pacific Northwest, and the Hindi one the opposition between dental and retroflex stops (/t-ʈ/), common in the languages of India. English infants aged 6 to 8 months did about as well as native speakers of those languages; the ability begins to decline, however, so that at 8 to 10 months fewer infants perceived the contrasts. By 10 to 12 months of age, the infants performed as poorly as English adults, to the degree that few infants now reached criterion on either sound contrast. Native Hindi or Thompson infants exposed to these languages continued to discriminate the relevant contrasts at 12 months of age, demonstrating that specific language experience maintains phonetic discrimination abilities for the sound contrasts a given language employs.

These results strongly suggest that infants are able to make nonnative phonetic contrasts, and are attuned to a variety of possible discriminations that natural languages might make use of, but that this early ability is lost by 10 to 12 months of age. The reason that this plasticity is lost is because the infant begins to tune out all those contrasts not used in the specific phonology of the language that is now becoming his or her native language. This is also the age when the first words are beginning to emerge in the child's language, and the acquisition of language-specific phonological contrasts is central to the acquisition of vocabulary words which contrast meanings. Language is founded on the principle of **duality**, whereby a limited set of phonemes, defined by categorical opposition, form an enormous inventory of words by being ordered in a variety of ways. But until the child reaches the stage of having to focus upon the phonological contrasts of a specific language, it would appear that he or she is endowed with an innate ability to categorically discriminate many phonetic contrasts. Such an innate ability would obviously aid the language learning task for the young child, for this predisposition to segment sounds into functionally useful categories is matched by the fact that human languages all make use of some smaller subset of phonetic contrasts as the basis of their phonological system.

Later perception of contrasts . An early detailed study of Russian children (Shvachkin 1948; cited in Garnica 1973) examined how children perceived contrasts in the acquisition of their first language. They appeared to go through systematic stages, going from the simplest to the most complex, learning to recognize Russian oppositions in nonsense monosyllables in a distinct order. They developed the ability to perceive all of the vocalic and consonantal distinctions of Russian in about 12 stages, and each child tested acquired the distinction in this order with little variation. Garnica (1973) tested Shvachkin's developmental sequence for English-speaking children, and found considerably more variation in terms of which oppositions were acquired, as well as their order. Her results cast doubt on Shvachkin's universal order in the acquisition of speech perception contrasts, suggesting that the details for each child may vary considerably. Still, there are some trends in the data, as for example, the early contrasts of sonorant vs. fricative and nasal vs. glide.

Speech Production and Its Acquisition by Children

The acquisition of phonology is largely complete by the age of 5 to 7, and not added to thereafter. One has the production of sound from the earliest days, which is similar to speech in its basic use of respiration, phonation, and articulatory channels. During their first year, infants produce a variety of sounds. The first few months sees reflexive crying and random vocalizations making room for **cooing** and **chuckling**, the vowel- and consonantal-like sounds that may be gross precursors to actual articulations. The second half of the first year sees the emergence of utterances of a repetitive type, in which V or CV syllables are repeated.

Babbling . Babbling is the first sign of structuring in the production of sounds, for it is here, at around 6 to 8 months, that a canonical pattern is often evident. It often overlaps with the production of the first words between 12 and 18 months of age, but usually decreases after the production of these first words. Typically, these syllable-like sequences (like *baba* and *mama*) exhibit some of the same constraints that the child's first words do: both babbling and first words generally begin with stops rather than fricatives; they end either with vowels or unvoiced stops; glides are more common than liquids; front consonants are more common than back consonants; and consonant clusters are virtually absent. Here the child first learns to combine phonation with articulation, thus both learning control of the respiratory system and trying out articulatory mechanisms needed for speech. The child also learns the acoustic effect of certain articulatory movements, and how to repeat those movements for the same acoustic effect.

Babbling seems to be a linguistic universal, and the babbling of infants from various linguistic communities does not seem to be easily distinguished. Thevenin et al. (1985) observe that previous experiments with infants fail to have adults recognize accurately the language background of infants from languages as different as Russian, English, and Chinese, either at the beginning of babbling (6 months) or at the end (16 months). They report no persuasive evidence that infant babbling differs because of mother tongue, at least as recognized by adults. Moreover, their own experiments with Spanish and English infants showed the same results, again at both ends of the babbling stage. Adult judges apparently cannot judge the language background significantly above chance level; it is only when longer stretches provide intonational cues that they are more successful.

There is some controversy over whether babbling is independent of the particular language or somehow statistically tied to its phonology by exhibiting the same preferences for phonetic segments and sequences found in adult speech (see Oller et al. 1976). Following Jakobson, scholars have often assumed that babbling included a random assortment of the world's speech sounds, exhibiting no relationship to the child's sounds in later meaningful speech. Jakobson believed in a strict discontinuity, discriminating between two distinct periods in vocal production: babbling and meaningful speech.

But Vihman et al. (1985) note that a growing literature points to a rejection of the discontinuity view. Oller et al. (1976) offered evidence that babbled utterances are not just random vocalizations, but show many of the same basic phonetic preferences found in later childhood pronunciations. Syllabic shapes and sound-types found in the late babbling period are also similar to those of early words. Kent and Bauer (1985) concluded that the vocalizations of 13-month-olds is continuous with both the younger babbling child and the later child in its second year. Babbling seems to follow a regular sequence of developmental stages from primarily vocalic sounds in the first few months to CV-like syllables just before the onset of speech (Stoel-Gammon and Cooper 1984). Kent and Bauer (1985) report that for 13-month-olds the most common syllable shapes are V or VV (60% of the utterances analyzed), CV (19%), and bisyllables CVCV (8%) and VCV (7%). CV syllables emerge as the dominant form in which a major phonetic contrast (C vs. V) is accomplished, and indeed, the CV syllable has assumed a privileged status in the literature. All this implies a continuity between babbling and meaningful child speech, and by implication, between babbling and phonological universals.

Articulation . At about 10 to 12 months, the child begins to copy more exactly the sounds made by adults. The emergence of the first words at 10 to 15 months is determined by the child's control of the articulatory apparatus and the ability to associate the correct labels with the appropriate objects in a symbolic fashion. The gap between child and adult pronunciation is still wide, though there may be the occasional isolated word which is perfectly pronounced. There is often more than one pronunciation of words for the same child, and of course, they vary

from child to child. Although their output varies as they make systematic approximations to adult words, children obviously can identify
words they cannot pronounce, and they can discriminate between
sounds that they are unable to produce in a contrastive sense. Thus,
although the child has the wrong phonetic output for a word, the adult
version presents no comprehension problem. By the age of 3, the
underlying representations must be much the same as the corresponding adult forms. As a result, children are considerably more accurate
at recognizing words said by unfamiliar adults than they are at hearing
other children say them. Adult pronuciations are also more accurately
recognized than even hearing a tape of their own voice saying the same
words. And any repairs are usually in the direction of the adult shape
(see Dodd 1975).

Jakobsonian Acquisition of Contrasts in Production . Jakobson's great
contribution (1941/1968) was to attempt to tie together the phonological universals of the languages of the world, how children acquire the
phonology of their first language, and even how phonological dissolution proceeds for aphasics. Instead of trying to find the sequence in
which children learn specific sounds, he focussed on the sequence in
which categories are learned. He claimed that children do not acquire
individual sounds, but that they acquire categories, and that this phonological development follows a universal order of acquisition for the
"distinctive features" that serve to contrast such categories of sounds.
Children thus gradually acquire the contrasts of adult language, not by
individual sounds, but by opposing contrasts--and thus by opposing categories. For example, when the child begins to contrast p/b, one
expects the contrast in other pairs like t/d and k/g. It is the acquisition
of the contrast that is predictable, not the acquisition of specific
sounds.
    In its time, Jakobson's theory was remarkable for its range and
daring, though he turned out to be wrong about some things like the
path of dissolution in aphasia. Jakobson postulated that certain contrasts were not only universal in being present in all languages, but
also that such universal contrasts were acquired first in a fixed order of
phonological development. His path of acquisition postulated a hierarchical development of binary distinctions, with the first three contrasts the following:

1.   oral vs. nasal, like b/m.
2.   labial vs. dental, like p/t.
3.   stop vs. fricative, like p/f.

    His data was neither experimental nor even observational; his was
a purely theoretical hypothesis based on data from diary records. As a
baseline, languages were said to have at least a pair of two-way oppositions by having a labial vs. non-labial contrast for the consonants and
a narrow vs. open contrast for the vowels. Indeed, when one looks at
the languages of the world, a two-way opposition is the minimal
requirement, although the triangular patterns of /p t k/ and /i u a/ are

more common. The only languages with a minimal two-way consonantal contrast are Hawaiian and archaic Samoan, and only the Abkhazo-Adygian languages of the North Caucasus area exhibit two vowels. The point is that all languages, whether at the top end of the range of consonantal inventory (like the Northern Caucasian languages with 70 to 80 consonants and two vowels) or at the bottom end of the consonantal inventory (like Hawaiian with its 8 consonants and 5 vowels) have these basic dimensions. Thus, all the distinctions the child learns in its native language are really subtle gradations along the two scales of sonority (the optimal vowel vs. the optimal consonant) and tonality (larger vs. smaller opening for the exiting airstream and where it is located). The child learns to make subtle gradations along the developmental scale of universal contrasts, filling in the blanks in acquiring finer and finer distinctions in the language.

The support for Jakobson's notions is mixed, but there is no doubt it was and continues to be highly influential by its theoretical claims. A major criticism is that the major orders of acquisition are violated, both in instances of children learning the same language as well as across languages. There is also counter-evidence that the presence of a contrast in a single pair of phonemes does not guarantee that the contrast will be used elsewhere in the same generalized sense. The actual acquisition sequence is thus not a successive acquisition of contrasts in the Jakobsonian sense of phonetic oppositions (see Kent and Bauer 1985 and Stoel-Gammon and Cooper 1984). It also ignores a cognitively based theory of phonological acquisition which sees the child as actively seeking and using information in solving problems (Kent and Bauer 1985). The evidence we have to date may not entirely support Jakobson's original notions, but they do allow us to make some generalizations, like the fact that vowel-consonant contrasts are the earliest, that consonant contrasts usually appear earliest in initial position, and that among these consonant contrasts the stop-fricative (/p-f/) and stop-resonant (/p-m/) are generally the earliest.

An English-speaking Child's Phonetic Inventory. At 1;6, the child might have an inventory of /i u a; p b t d f s h w y m n/ in words usually of CV or CVC syllables. Most consonants are syllable-initial. By 4, most consonants have been acquired, with the exception of several fricatives. Some initial clusters are also acquired by this age. But children commonly simplify adult speech for their own production with rules that affect entire classes of sounds. They usually shorten adult words by omitting final consonants, reducing consonant clusters, and deleting unstressed syllables. Up to the age of 2, most words are a single syllable. They also reduplicate syllables, probably to practice phonetic identity, and show certain preferences, as for example, voiced consonants initially and voiceless consonants finally. By 7, the child has mastered the missing sounds, like fricatives and affricates, and uses simplification processes far less frequently. Most words are pronounced correctly, though the longer ones are much less precise in their pronunciation (Ingram 1976).

Non-segmental Phonology

Research into non-segmental phonology like intonation, stress, rhythm, speed of speaking, and even 'voice-quality', has been less abundant. Intonation is the earliest kind of linguistic structuring in the vocalization of the child (Crystal 1973), with the emergence of such features in production as early as 6 months. Children appear to perceive intonational differences before differences in phonetic segments, discriminating intonational rise and fall contours in adult English output by 8 months. In terms of production, by 8 months one also notes an intonational rise and fall in child's output, and distinctive intonational contours can be detected in child's output. Though these early intonational patterns are not the same as fully-formed adult patterns, they may reflect their general characteristics and often signal differences in meaning.

The acquisition of Chinese tone is also accomplished early, and in a relatively short time. Li and Thompson (1977) report that the acquisition of the 4 Mandarin tones occurs well in advance of the mastery of segmentals, and within a short period of time. Just as tones are stored as part of the inherent identity of the word, so also are stress patterns in languages like German, English, and Russian. For example, the stress difference between *pErmit* and *permIt* is stored away as part of the underlying representation of these two words.

Underlying Representations

Lastly, the child must also learn that some forms vary in a regular relationship. The actual pronunciation of these morphemes is only a partial description, for such forms require a common underlying representation with rules which carry them from one form type to another. For example, the vowel shifts in word pairs like *divine/divinity, describe/description, tyrant/tyrannical* demand that the child make a distinction between phonetic representations and underlying representations which tie these morphemes together. Some, like N. Chomsky and Halle (1968) and C. Chomsky (1970) have even suggested that in English the conventional orthography may actually be doing the learning-to-read child a service by maintaining such underlying representations in the conservative orthography we employ. For example, in pairs like *musCle/muscular, siGn/signature*, the silent consonants C and G in the first member of the pair are pronounced in the second member of the pair.

The Acquisition of Morphology

Morphology involves the structural makeup of words before they become building blocks in sentences. The child must learn the part of speech classes, first noting the difference between **content words** and **function words** in the language. Content words carry lexical meanings, as do nouns, verbs, adjectives, and adverbs in English, while function words embody the grammatical machinery of the language, as do articles, conjunctions, auxiliary verbs, and prepositions in English. There are only several hundred function words in English, but they are essential to every utterance we produce.

But there is a unit smaller than the individual word, termed the **morpheme**. For example, there are only 6 words in *John's younger sisters admire his gentlemanliness*, but there are smaller recognizable units like *John, -'s, young, -er, admire, -ed*, and so on. Morphemes are the minimal units of meaning, realized phonologically by one or more **allomorphs**. Morphology is the analysis of morphemes in word-structure, traditionally broken up into the areas of inflectional and derivational morphology. A morphological construction arises by the addition of some meaningful element like a prefix, suffix, infix, or even a separate root or stem. These are added to some basic root or stem element which carries the core meaning of the resulting combination. The resulting construction is **inflectional** if the resulting word is a grammatical variant of its root (*cat>cats*), and **derivational** if the form is an entirely different word (*teach>teacher*). Morphological rules (see Derwing and Baker 1977) are the word-level rules that describe how these minimal meaning-bearing units of a language, the morphemes, are combined into larger constituents, such as stems and words.

Languages differ greatly in their morphological typology, so that some languages like English exhibit a large number of free morphemes, while some languages like Russian exhibit a high degree of affixation. English lexical morphemes are generally free; many grammatical morphemes (past tense and plural) are bound, though there are some free grammatical morphemes in English like prepositions, determiners, and the negative *not*.

Derivational vs. Inflectional Morphology

The job of **derivational morphology** is to make up new words in the language, by either compounding existing words (*door-knob*) or adding derivational prefixes (*pre-heat*) or suffixes (*heat-er*). **Inflectional morphology** operates like the function words in that they carry the grammatical relationships of the language. There are only eight inflectional morphemes in English, all suffixes: plural (*dog-s*) and possessive (*dog-'s*) on nouns; the third person singular present tense (*walk-s*), the past tense (*walk-ed*), the past participle (*walk-ed; brok-en*), the progressive (*walk-ing*) on verbs; and the comparative (*thick-er*) and superlative (*thick-est*) on adjectives.

Inflectional morphology is not inherently difficult for the child at the 2-word level. The early vs. late acquisition of inflectional morphology is determined by the typological characteristics of the adult language. Inflections are more easily acquired if, as in Turkish, they are segmentable, stressed, syllabic, and regular in their application. Thus, in Turkish, the inflectional morphology of case and verb agreement is acquired before age 2, whereas, in contrast, verb agreement is generally acquired after age 3 in less regular languages like English and Hebrew (Slobin 1982). In general, cues which are consistent in signalling particular meanings are learned first, and this general principle is true for inflectional features like case-marking right across languages (see MacWhinney 1987).

Order of Morphological Acquisition

There is a consistent order of mastery of the most common grammatical morphemes themselves, and agreement among children is very high in English. R. Brown (1973) has provided us with information regarding the acquisition of 14 frequent and easily identified morphemes, showing that children acquire them in essentially the same order. He suggests that the regular order of acquisition is dependent on the linguistic complexity of the morpheme, not its frequency of use in parental speech. His in-depth monitoring for three children showed the sequence of acquisition for these grammatical morphemes as pretty much the same: for example, the progressive form -*ing* is acquired before the past or present tense forms -*ed* and -*s*; the prepositions *in/on* are acquired before *under*; and the plural ending -*s* is acquired before the possessive ending -*'s*. Verbal constructions which include the copula verb *be* are more complex than the plural number and past tense morphemes, and thus appear even later. The plural requires a sense of number and the past tense requires a sense of earlierness, and one needs to know both number and tense to choose among the *is, are, was, were* forms of *be*.

Age is not a good indicator of language development, and so Brown proposed another metric, the Mean Length of Utterance, as a better indicator of acquisition than chronological age. Thus, as the child's MLU, or 'mean length of utterance' in morphemes, increases, their language includes more complex constructions. It is generally agreed that age is a poor independent variable for developmental work, but even substitutes like Brown's MLU to form performance groups may be too broad a metric. Different children may have different strategies, and the important question may not be how close the child is to adult norms, but what system the child is using (see Baker and Derwing 1982).

Inflectional Morphology

Inflectional morphology involves a set of grammatical variations associated with a particular part of speech, like nouns. It is usually systematic and productive. Allomorphs of an inflectional morpheme are fairly regular, that is, phonologically conditioned. For example, the regular plural is actually 3 allomorphs which appear because of phonological conditioning: /z/ appears after final voiced consonants except sibilants, /s/ after final voiceless consonants except sibilants, and /ɪz/ after final sibilants. Such allomorphs are **phonologically conditioned** by properties of the final segment of noun stem. There are also instances of **morphologically conditioned** allomorphs of morphemes, where no particular reason can be found, other than the fact that certain stems like *foot, deer, ox* require a plural which involves a vowel change (*feet*), a zero (*deer*), or an *-en* (*oxen*).

An early classic experiment (Berko 1958) in the productive use of morphological rules employed nonsense words like *wug* and *gling* to check children's abilities to produce the regular English plurals and possessives, the past tense, progressive *-ing*, and third person singular, as well as certain compounds. Children responded with more or less "correct" adult forms, except for stems ending in sibilants. If the child can supply the correct plural ending for nonsense words, then obviously the child has internalized the working system of plural allomorphs in their conditional variant forms, generalized to new cases, and selected the right form. In general, the results showed that they had mastered morphemes which had a uniform shape, like *-ing*, but had relatively more difficulty with those morphemes that had more than one shape, like present tense with its /-s, -z, -ɪz/ forms and past tense with its /-t, -d, -ɪd/ forms. Of these, the less symmetrical phonological conditions for the /-ɪz/ and /-ɪd/ allomorphs of present and past exhibited the least mastery. R. Brown's list (1973) also has *ing* learned first, long before the 3rd person singular form on verbs. Past tense is typically acquired after progressive and present tenses, because it is conceptually more difficult.

Derwing and Baker (1976, cited in Prideaux 1985) used the Berko test on children aged 3 to 9, and their order of acquisition was progressive, plural, possessive, and the third person singular present tense. The differential order of acquisition for the phonetically identical inflectional endings of plural, possessive, and third person singular present tense is worthy of note. The order in which they are acquired reflects the complexity of the different relationships the morphemes signal: the singular-plural distinction operates at the word level, the possessive relates two nouns at the phrase level, and the third person singular relates a noun and a verb at the sentence level (Moskowitz 1978).

Irregular Inflectional Morphology . Children tend to over-generalize with irregular forms, because they are making up rules which cover all instances. R. Brown (1973) notes that such overgeneralizations, as in the past tense (*eated* for *ate*), seems to last a long time. Kuczaj (1977) observed two types of such generalization for the past tense: forms like *eated*, based on the present tense, and forms like *ated*, based on the past tense. The spontaneous speech of young children shows that younger children of 3 tend to produce *eated*, while at 5 they produce more forms like *ated*. A later experiment (Kuczaj 1978) had children determine when an error was made by puppets, and found that younger children (3 and 4) accepted *eated*, children at 5 and 6 accepted both, and older (7 and 8) accepted neither. Bybee and Slobin's work (1982) with irregular verbs of the *swim/swam/swum* and *spin/spun* type showed that children, as well as adults, tended to treat 3-member verbs as if they were a 2-member paradigm when pressed for spontaneous responses.

Derivational Morphology

Derivational morphology typically causes a change in the part of speech class; for example, nominalizers convert verbs to nouns (*act>action*) or adjectives to nouns (*eager>eagerness*). Derivational morphology is less productive and less regular than inflectional morphology. Some suffixes, like *-ness*, are productive, but often it is impossible to select appropriate derivational suffixes on the basis of the stem alone, as for example, *refus-al* vs. *confus-al*. Obviously, not all derivational morphology can be treated the same way: the mental representation of some pairs is such that a single lexical item is learned plus the affixation process; others pairs are learned and stored separately; and some are open to variability among members of a linguistic community. Derwing and Baker (1974, cited in Prideaux 1985) and Derwing (1976) tested the relative productivity of 6 suffixes with children and adults. The suffixes were the agentive *-er*, instrumental *-er*, diminutive *-ie/-y*, adverbial *-ly (quickly)*, adjectival *-y (muddy)*, and some noun compounds like *birdhouse*. Not surprisingly, age correlates with productivity, but it is interesting to look at the specific affixes. The agentive *-er* was the most productive, and so also were the adjectival *-y* and noun compounds. But the morphological analysis of compound nouns is both late AND variable in the population, complementing Gleitman and Gleitman's (1970) earlier findings of adult variability in the analysis of English compound nouns. Lastly, the diminutive suffix exhibited the least productivity for all groups.

Stem Morphology

Irregularities in inflectional and derivational morphology may raise learning problems, but so also do irregular stems in some languages. For example, in English the stems of content words like nouns and verbs offer more different types of irregularity than do the inflectional and derivational affixes which are attached to them. They can be as extreme as the relationship between *go>went*, *do>did*, and *bring>brought*. Or they can retain some transparency, as in *mouse>mice* and *wife>wives*. Sometimes the traditional writing system may provide orthographic hints of an identical morphological origin in the stem, even if the pronunciation no longer does. For example, read the following pairs aloud to remind yourself of how different they sound; then note how their morphological relationship is captured by the conservative orthography in these pairs: *muscle>muscular*, *meter>metric*, and *ignite>ignition*.

Child Syntax

Many studies have treated the child as speaking an "exotic" language at each of the developmental stages, with the emphasis on writing a grammar of what the child says. This approach to describing the child's grammar does not attempt to impose the grammatical rules of well-formed adult grammar on the child's utterances at the various stages. Instead, these grammars account for what the child is actually saying, and what its rules produce. In so doing, the analyst is able to portray growth and syntactic development by showing the changes in successive grammars associated with each of those stages. For other developmental psycholinguists, continuity is the key issue, and they believe that child language data is best described in relation to the fully-formed target language of adults. Both positions have their advantages, but both must account for the following structural properties of child syntax at various points in the acquisition process.

Early Syntax

Early syntactic development is typically analyzed into three stages: the holophrastic stage, the two-word stage, and the hierarchical stage.

The One-Word or Holophrastic Stage. Holophrases are one-word sentences that contain what adults would express in a whole sentence, for example, *milk* meaning "I want some milk". The maximum sentence length is a single word and coincides with the emergence of the first words at about 12 months. These early words are typically concrete nouns and verbs, with the more abstract adjectives appearing later.

Two-Word Stage. Between 18 and 24 months of age, we see the first evidence of juxtaposition of words, with the typical utterance two or three words in length. Here the child experiments with the possible semantic-syntactic relationships to be found between objects, like actor-action (*dog run*), action-object (*love dog*), possessor-possessed (*my dog*).

Early 2-word syntactic analysis in the 1960s concentrated simply on the formal structure of the utterances, noting their possible arrangements. The word classes in such simple syntax appeared to be of two types, and Braine (1963) christened them **pivot** and **open**. A few words appeared to be used as pivot or fixing points around which the sentences seemed to be organized, occurring in the same position in every sentence, rarely used alone. To these were attached other words which seemed to belong to a larger class of words, words which could also be used on their own. For example, the pivot word *it* might have open words like *have, want, eat, drink* attached to it in sentences like *have it, want it, eat it, drink it,* and so forth. Indeed, in some ways the pivot/open distinction was reminiscent of the distinction between content words and function words in adult syntax, and some speculated that such classes might be the precursors of how grammatical classes were beginning to form.

But increased attention to the role of meaning de-emphasized the centrality of syntactic form in language acquisition. For example, Bloom (1970) began assessing the meaning of what young children intend to communicate and noted that the same utterance can have different meanings within different contexts. For example, *mommy sock* could mean either Mommy is putting the sock on the child, or it could mean that the sock belongs to Mommy. She noted at least 5 relations for noun-noun combinations:

1.   conjunction: 'block, dolly'
2.   attribution: 'party hat'
3.   genitive: 'daddy hat'
4.   subject-locative: 'sweater chair'
5.   subject-object: 'mommy book'

Very simply, one must pay attention to the rich semantic interpretations that such two-word sentences may convey. The problem with just a formal analysis of two-word sentences is that it does not take into account the child's semantic knowledge. Like the problem of mental representations for words in phonology, the child knows the semantic difference between *mommy sock/possessor object* and *mommy sock/ agent object*, but is limited by the available grammatical machinery to express this richer semantic knowledge.

Noting the typical range of expressions in the two-word stage, some suggested that there might be universals at this stage of grammatical development by children (Slobin 1970). The semantic relations realized in these early utterances seem to be much the same in languages as different as German, Russian, English, Finnish, Luo in Kenya, and Samoan, and the utterances read like direct translations of one another. Not all types of semantic relationships appear commonly in such lists, however, and some are rare or missing (Bowerman 1975):

1.   action-location: Kendall's 'sit bed'
2.   indirect objects: 'give mommy'
3.   adverbs: 'push hard'
4.   predicate nominatives: 'mommy [is a] lady', 'ball [is a] toy'
5.   instruments: 'eat spoon'

The first two-word combinations are not an abrupt development, because children exhibit a period in which they use successive single words in 'vertical constructions'. Single-word sentences are simply not enough to convey their thoughts, so they begin stringing single words together in a chain of **vertical constructions** to logically sequence their thoughts (Scollon 1976). Ninio and Snow (1988) also show that many gambits in one-word stage express particular speech acts, and that much of the simple syntax in early word combinations reflects the speech act performed by the utterance.

Hierarchical Stage. Once the child starts stringing words together, the hierarchical relationships among items in a sentence emerges, and it no longer matters whether sentences are three, six, or eighteen words long. For example, a sentence like *this my doggie* exhibits the noun phrases *my doggie*, the two members of which share a close internal relationship which sets them off hierarchically from the other words *this*. Word order also has some salience as an early sort of syntactic rule for children. All languages seem to use order in some way or another, and it is not surprising to see order rules emerge early, for they offer a way of elaborating upon the information contained in the words themselves. In a language like English, many grammatical relations are shown by a fixed word order, though case-inflected languages like Latin use order much less.

Sentences at this stage appeared to early analysts to be reduced in much the same way that adults reduce their sentences for telegraphic transmission, where words cost money. Adults typically leave out words that do not contribute to the intelligibility of a message in a way that justifies their cost, namely, items like articles, prepositions, auxiliary verbs, the inflections on nouns and verbs, and so forth. But unlike telegrams, we cannot guarantee that the reason certain words were eliminated was because they could not be justified in terms of their cognitive cost. Children's sentences often drop out the function words and grammatical morphemes, leaving the content words. Though there is a **telegraphic** quality to such utterances, they do demonstrate that the child already grasps the basic structure of sentence formation. The telegraphic characterization, however, is not useful except as a loose concept, because it is too negative in focussing on what is missing from the child's language, rather than what is present.

Later Syntax: Acquiring Transformational Rules

The course of later syntactic development is largely a matter of learning to produce and comprehend the major transformations of the language, like questions, negatives, and passives, as well as how to control complex sentences with more than one clause. More recent linguistic formulations in Chomsky's Government and Binding model focus on the child's search for the specific 'parameter settings' in the language, but the notion of sentence alternations is still a useful concept in explaining the transitional growth from simple sentences to more complex syntactic constructions. In general, linguistically complex sentences require more in both comprehension and production than do simple sentences, and thus, these are learned later.

Questions and Negatives . English, like all languages, has two kinds of questions. For example, we can ask whether *John can swim* by keeping the same order, but changing the intonation, as in *John can swim?*. A more common way of producing a yes/no question in English, however, is to reverse the auxiliary verb or the *be* verb form, as in *Can John swim?* and *Is John a student?*. In contrast to these yes/no questions, wh-questions ask for specific information, and any constituent of the sentence may be questioned. Wh-words like *what* signal that the answer desired is a noun phrase, *where* elicits an answer with a prepositional phrase or a place name, and so on. The distinguishing characteristic of such questions is that an auxiliary verb precedes the subject noun phrase. If more than one auxiliary is present in the corresponding declarative sentence, only the first auxiliary of the verb phrase is inverted with the subject, and it is always the first auxiliary that carries any marking for tense and number. For example, consider the following sentence pairs:

1.   Rover is guarding the doghouse > Is Rover guarding the doghouse?
2.   Rover has chewed that bone to a frazzle > Has Rover chewed that bone to a frazzle?
3.   Rover can catch that frisbee in mid-air > Can Rover catch that frisbee in mid-air?

This inversion of the first auxiliary (which may be a form of *be, have,* or a modal verb like *can* or *will*) and the subject is the basic **question transformation**. In sentences without an auxiliary, a different process occurs; consider *He knows how to swim > Does he know how to swim?*. The **do-insertion transformation** provides the auxiliary verb *do* for the number and tense that were moved by the question transformation.

Questions first appear in child speech with a gross distinction between a falling intonation for declaratives and a rising intonation for interrogatives. Later, the distinguishing characteristic of question words in wh-questions is added; and still later the process of inversion for questions with auxiliaries or *be* as the main verb appears, as does the inversion of the *do* auxiliary for other verbs of the intransitive, transitive, and copulative categories. Thus, for a brief period one has questions which have the correct wh-words, but which do not have the correct inversion, as in *What he can ride?*.

The **do-insertion transformation** is also used in forming negative sentences. At first, the child simply adds *no* or *not* to the whole sentence to make it negative, as in *No my Teddy*. Then the child learns to insert the negative inside the sentence, next to the adjective or verb, as in *This no good* and *This no work*. Later, the negative element is attached to just that element that is inverted with the subject in questions. For example, compare *John can swim > John can't swim* and *He knows how to swim > He doesn't know how to swim*.

Passives . Most transitive sentences have a passive form, and the passive can have a truncated version. Simple active structures are acquired earlier than the more complex passive structures, but truncates appear before full passives in child speech. They are also used more frequently and are processed more easily than full passives, suggesting that they are unrelated structures in child syntax at this stage.

1. Active: The hunters killed the deer.
2. Passive: The deer were killed by the hunters.
3. Truncated passive: The deer were killed.

Children typically do not understand passives until age 4 or 5, or even later. Even at 2 or 3, children have no trouble with *The candy is eaten by the girl*, because of the implausibility of an interpretation of the candy eating the girl. But in reversible sentences which allow for either event to be equally likely, as for example *The cow is kicked by the horse*, three and four year-olds assume the first noun is the agent. Thus, for them, the cow is the one who does the kicking. Children place considerable reliance on word order, and their attention to this word order principle leads them to ignore the actual sentence structure. Passives are an example of this phenomenon in English; similarly, German children may ignore case endings, like dative or accusative, on articles, treating the first noun in a sentence as if it were the subject. Later, when the exact interaction between morphological affixes and syntactic ordering rules are worked out, such sentences no longer pose a processing problem.

By 5, children understand action verb sentences like *The mouse was bitten by the squirrel*, but may still fail with non-action verb sentences like *The man was remembered by the boy* (see Maratsos, Kuczaj, Fox and Chalkley 1979). Comprehension, however, is much improved in sentences like *The frog was frightened by the princess* if the object is made the focus of attention, as when Frog is the hero of a story.

Compound and Complex Sentences . True relative clauses are not common in children's speech until after school age, and children of 3 are poor at conveying relationships between parts of a story. They often speak in single sentences or link them with *and*, without any real ordering of events. Sentential coordination with additive conjunctions like *and* appear early, but disjunctives with *or* are more cognitively more difficult. Compare, for example, sentences like *I will move this truck and you move that bulldozer* and *You dig that sand or I will bring the bulldozer*.

Smith and van Kleeck (1986) examined the interaction between sentence complexity and performance by measuring how tasks like toy moving and imitation were affected by complex structures like the following.

1. John called Mary before Bill invited Sue.
2. John called Mary before inviting Sue.
3. John called Mary before Sue.

The first sentence requires no interpretive rule besides standard tense and aspect rules; the second requires that the empty PRO category (*John-i called Mary before PRO-i inviting Sue*) be interpreted; the third requires that two empty PRO categories (*John-i called-j Mary before PRO-i PRO-j Sue*) be interpreted, plus a syntactic ambiguity. They conclude that the relation between complexity and performance depends upon the requirements of the performance. There is no simple 1-to-1 relation, but rather, linguistic factors affecting performance are task-dependent. For their children from 3;6 to 6;0, sentences like (3) that were high in interpretive complexity were the most difficult in the toy-moving task, but easiest in the imitation task. And vice versa, sentences like (1) that were low in complexity were easiest in the toy-moving task, and hardest in the imitation task.

Children at 3 also do not understand the true meaning of some conjunctions, and assume that the order in which a sentence mentions events is the way the real events occur. This works for sentences like (1-2), but not (3-4).

1. After you clean your teeth, brush your hair.
2. Clean your teeth before you brush your hair.
3. Before you clean your teeth, brush your hair.
4. Clean your teeth after you brush your hair.

Syntactic Development after Age Five

While the five-year-old can carry on a syntactically correct conversation, considerable development in syntax and other aspects of language still occurs after this age. For example, the complex rules which are required to accurately produce relative clauses continue to develop. The replacement of the minimal distance principle with underlying representations containing gaps and fillers continues to develop after the age of 5 and right up until at least 10 (see Clifton and Frazier 1989 for an example of adult processing). Until that happens, children do not correctly comprehend sentences involving *ask, tell, promise* and use a **minimal distance principle** until they are about eight years old. This principle simply assumes that the noun phrase preceding the predicate is its subject, and children systematically realize that there are exceptions to this rule in stages (C. Chomsky 1969). For example, in sentences like *John wanted Bill to leave*, it is Bill who does the leaving; but in *John promised Bill to leave*, it is John who does the leaving. In the case of *want*, the strategy works, but in the case of *promise*, the child's strategic principle of minimal distance is misleading. *Bill* may be the noun phrase immediately preceding the verb *to leave*, but it is not its subject.

C. Chomsky (1969) has also examined the comprehension of sentences in which the surface structure subject is not the deep structure subject by asking children *Is this doll easy to see or hard to see?* in the context of a blindfolded doll. Her results showed that five-year olds interpret the sentence to mean that the doll was the subject of the infinitive; *the doll is hard to see* was interpreted to mean that the doll had a hard time seeing because it was blindfolded. By 9, children correctly interpret the question. Kess and Hoppe (1983a) noted the ability to disambiguate sentences varied not only by individual but by age group right up through the ages of 9, 11, and 13. It is obvious that some syntactic abilities take longer to mature, and some aspects of linguistic structure are being developed and elaborated upon after 5 and right up until 10 or 12.

The Acquisition of Semantics

The Child's Vocabulary

Semantics is an even more complicated system than phonology or syntax, and it is a system that we keep adding to throughout our entire lives. The meaning of early words is often different when matched with adult glosses, and will often change again before it reaches that stage. The first 50 words usually includes things the child can act on, some things that can act of themselves, and a few large objects which simply exist in the environment. Thus, one typically gets words like *socks* more often than *refrigerator* (Nelson 1973). A child often knows 1000 words by the age of 3, and may have mastered over 10,000 by the age of 6. Conservative estimates suggest that at this age the rate of acquisition for words may be as high as 20 words a day (Johnson-Laird 1987). By contrast, the communicative chimpanzee Washoe had only learned 34 signs after 21 months of training, and a total of 160 signs after 4 years. None of us reach the full 450,000 inventory of the 1961 *Webster's Third International Dictionary*, and the child's 10,000 is very respectable when compared with the total of 35,000 words used by the erudite Robert Browning in his entire career.

The child's acquisition of vocabulary advances so rapidly that it is impossible to keep an accurate count. Vocabulary counts are not as useful as they look, for they are subject to the vagaries of sampling. Recognition vocabulary is always higher, and the child's passive vocabulary is only partially reflected in counts of what a child has actually produced. Such inventories tell us little about semantic development, except to remind us of the exponential growth of vocabulary. For example, some have claimed that all early words are context-bound rather than referential, that is, produced only in specific situations or contexts. Bloom (1973) noticed that her nine-month-old daughter began to use *car* only while looking out the window at cars moving in street below. But Harris et al. (1988) have shown that although many early words are context-bound, a significant number are also referential. They also found that there was a relationship between the child's early use of words and the mother's use of these same words in her speech to the child.

Semantic Systems

But vocabulary is only the tip of the iceberg. What we really need to understand is the semantic system that individual words find themselves a part of. The semantic system is the knowledge of individual lexical items that speakers must have to understand sentences and to relate them to knowledge of the world. The child's semantic system is often incomplete, and the use of a word does not guarantee the adult meaning for that word. We have already seen it necessary to contrast form and function on other levels like syntax, and semantics is no exception to this general rule. For example, one of my daughter's earliest words was *bird*, but she used it not only for birds, but also for the squeaky noise that Windex makes in cleaning windows; my son at first extended *pea* to cover small, round edibles like grapes. The young child must learn the correct, relevant, and useful labels for items, usually based on finer specifications.

Semantic Feature Hypothesis

One approach, termed the **Semantic Feature Hypothesis** by E. Clark (1973b) has attempted to describe this phenomenon. The child acquires meanings of words by adding specific semantic features, with more general features acquired before specific ones. Although the child uses identifiable words, they exhibit an incomplete mastery of the semantic features which constitute the word. The child's semantic categories are typically larger than the categories used by adults, since only one or two features are criterial. For example, the feature of *four-legged* might be over-extended from its original referent *doggie* to cover dogs, horses, cows, sheep, and cats, until successive features narrow the category down. Those first semantic features are derived from the child's perceptions, like movement, shape, size, sound, taste, and texture. Not all perceptual features serve as criterial features for early semantic categories, however, and color is a notable exception to the list. Clark has suggested this **overextension** may be a universal of development during the one-word and two-word stages, a time when we see rapid vocabulary growth. Overextensions allow the child to build large semantic categories by overlooking dissimilarities between objects, drawing attention to similarity along some specific dimension.

Underextension may also occur, when words are used for a narrower range of objects or events. The label is not applied when it should be, as for example, when the child insists on labelling a button-up sweater a *shirt*, instead of recognizing its membership in the sweater category. The Semantic Feature Hypothesis has been criticized by some for failing to account for overlap or underextension, for it seems that the underlying principle here is very much the same. Others, like Nelson (1974), stress functional characteristics instead of perceptual features as the major determinant of early word use. She argues that children do not start out analyzing objects into perceptual features like 'round' or 'four-legged', then using such components as a basis for classifying those objects. Children experience objects as wholes, and attend to the dynamic relationships and actions that they can enter into. Objects are regarded as similar not because they look similar but because they act or can be acted upon in the same way.

Polar Opposites, Positive/Negative Pairs, and Marked/Unmarked Pairs

Children appear to confuse the meaning of word pairs which are closely related by being opposite poles along a single dimension. They tend to use the positive form or the unmarked form of such word pairs, and generally comprehend the unmarked member of the pair first; children thus even seem to treat some antonyms as if they were synonyms, and the marked member is often interpreted as having the meaning of the unmarked member. For example, in word pairs like *more/less, big/little, tall/short*, the meaning of one of the pair is often extended to cover both words, and it is the unmarked or positive form which does this.

Our attention was first called to this phenomenon by Donaldson and Balfour's (1968) discovery that 3-year-olds often treat *less* as if it meant *more*. When given the task of hanging mock apples on cardboard apple trees, many children could not differentiate *less* from *more*. They appeared to act as if they did not know the meaning of *less*, or as if they thought the meaning was synonymous with *more*. Palermo (1973) replicated the experiment with nursery school four-year-olds, for both discrete object comparisons (apples on plywood tree) and continuous substances (water in glasses). Even some seven-year-olds were still confused. Children who did not know the *more/less* difference gave similar values on a complementary Semantic Differential test.

Donaldson and Wales (1970) later reported how children comprehended comparative and superlative forms of the dimensional adjectives *big/wee, long/short, thick/thin, high/low, tall/short, fat/thin*. Scots children responded correctly more often with the positive adjective; for example, comprehension was better with *bigger/biggest* than with *wee-er/wee-est*. E. Clark (1972) demonstrated that 4- and 5-year-olds show a general trend of development where global terms like *big* are extended to refer to other dimensions like those covered by *tall* or *fat*. Thus, *big* is treated as a synonym for many unmarked adjectives like *high, tall, long, wide, thick, old*, while *small* is treated as a synonym for many marked adjectives like *short, thin, low, young, shallow*. Less complex terms seem to be learned first, with a distinct order of acquisition based on their relative complexity of meaning; for example, *big-small* before *long-short* before *thick-thin*. This order of difficulty reflects both frequency and the psychological primacy of the dimension named. We talk more about height and length than width or thickness of objects, and *big/little* is more general in referring to size along any dimension.

Many papers published in the 1970s supported the compositional view of development in a wide variety of semantic domains. But there is conflicting evidence for spatial adjectives (Carey 1982). And parents use *more* with greater frequency than they use *less*. Some child-adult contrasts are unique as well. Kuczaj and Lederberg (1977) showed that the child first interprets *old* as *big* or *tall* and *young* as *small* or *short*, probably because of adult phrases like *when you're older* used interchangeably with *when you're bigger*. There are also objections that the Semantic Feature Hypothesis may have been too specific by claiming that there is a universal unmarked preference (Eilers, Oller and Ellington 1974).

Carey (1978) suggests that there are other factors at work; for example, children may have a response bias toward addition. Using a nonsense word *tiv*, children were instructed to make it so that there was *tiv/more/less* water in a glass. Even without knowing the meaning of *tiv*, children easily generate responses which show a response bias toward adding, even when there is a demonstration by finger adjustment as to what to do. Carey concludes that there is no point in the development of *less* when it is not in some opposition with *more*. We have seen other instances of such bias, as for example, E. Clark's (1973a) report that when a child is requested to place object A with respect to object B, the NON-linguistic bias is to place the object A *in*, otherwise *on*, and only as a last resort *under* object B. There are obviously non-linguistic strategies at work here, which determine the order of acquisition for some forms and thus may influence the responses to tasks which elicit responses to such forms.

Carey (1982) concludes that the Semantic Feature Hypothesis has not stood the test of time, and that it is no longer widely held that overgeneralizations provide evidence for incomplete lexical entries. The overgeneralizations made in production are denied in comprehension, and probably simply reflect stretching a limited vocabulary. Rescorla (1980) found that only a third of the first 75 words acquired by children were ever over-extended. Rescorla also suggests that normal extension and over-extension are two aspects of the same basic process, a difference in quality, not kind. But there is still striking consistency across children in the types of extensions they make, suggesting that the process is central to categorization and concept formation.

On the matter of bias, Donaldson and McGarrigle (1973) provide evidence that other confounding factors influence the child's interpretation of how statements are evaluated. Changes in the properties of the referent which are irrelevant to adults may produce changes in children's judgments. For example, there is something compelling about 'fullness', in that it may override other criteria in influencing the truth values assigned. When objects like cars were enclosed in containers like garages, children responded differently than when there were no garages. Manipulating 9 cars and 10 garages, the children were questioned about settings with the garages in position around the cars and with the garages absent. Asked which had *more*, children choose a smaller subset when the garages were around the cars. They did so because the smaller subset was full, in a 1-to-1 correspondence between garages and cars; their answer suggested strategies like *There's more on that shelf cuz there's enough to go in there*. In sum, these results are similar to the conservation tasks in that a judgment is elicited about some state of affairs, and then some change is introduced which is essentially irrelevant. The judgment is elicited once again, and a surprising number of children then change their judgments in the face of seemingly irrelevant changes. Lexical or syntactic rules cannot explain the phenomenon, but local criteria may assign truth values when the linguistic rules are vague to the child. There may be a hierarchical ordering of such rules, as for example, fullness taking preference over length as a criterial feature, then length over density, and so forth. Thus, more cars are said to exist in the garage structure when the garage structure is full, even though they are lesser in number. But the fact of there being more cars is evaluated correctly row when the garages are not there.

Word Associations and Grammatical Relations

With age, the tendency of pre-school children to give lengthy responses diminishes, and school children will give single-word associations in free association tests. Before 8, children give more responses from other syntactic classes, like *eat-food, chair-sit, boy-run, send-letter*. Later, adult preferences for responses for the same part of speech class emerge, responses like *table-chair, boy-girl, send-mail, fat-heavy*. Brown and Berko (1960) had considerable early impact in suggesting a relationship between children's word associations and the acquisition of syntax, with the change in responses a consequence of organizing the vocabulary into the syntactic classes called parts of speech.

Nelson (1977) has questioned the simplicity of this explanation. It is true that adults tend to give predominantly paradigmatic responses, while children tend to syntagmatic responses, and that the shift from younger to older responses seems to occur within the 5 to 9 age range. Other qualitative shifts occur in this period, both in the linguistic and cognitive domains; for example, Piagetian pre-operational thought shifts to logical concrete operations. The question is whether the shift in word associations reflects a general cognitive re-organization or whether it is strictly a linguistic re-organization. Nelson concludes that, on basis of both adult and child data, the frequency of paradigmatic vs. syntagmatic responses is conditioned by form class, frequency, and by the particular characteristics of the words sampled. The syntagmatic-to-paradigmatic shift is most dramatically observed for high-frequency adjectives; nouns tend to be paradigmatic at all ages; and verbs tend to be strongly syntagmatic throughout development. Instructions have an effect too, for giving noun-noun examples in the instructions greatly increases noun responses for all subjects. Similarly, asking college students to respond with the first 'thing' they think of, provides more image than verbal responses. Younger children have difficulty with word association tasks, because it is not a meaningful task for them; but by 8 or 9, children have acquired a 'task mode', which is available when confronted with the word association task. Perhaps the shift in response types that is observed reflects the child's changing ability to deal with non-meaningful verbal tasks, coupled with changes in the availability of hierarchical conceptual relationships.

Learning the Meaning of New Words through Verbal Context

Nouns, verbs, and interjections are very common as early words, as measured by the adult's part of speech classification for the same words. This may reflect the frequency of such forms in the adult speech directed at children, and perhaps the frequency of use in itself is a reflection of semantic importance. The child may learn the meaning of these new words by having the adult name and define them for the child, or by 'fast mapping' (Carey 1978). Here the child quickly hypothesizes about the meaning of a word, because contextual contrast rapidly narrows down the meaning. For example, in *Bring me the beige one, not the blue one, beige* has to be a color word referring to the property of an object in the environment (see Carey and Bartlett 1978). Context contrasts a novel term with a well-known one, thus providing an enormous amount of information (see Heibeck and Markman 1987).

Adults do often name objects for children, but much learning comes from overheard speech as well. New words are introduced in sentences so that the syntax identifies the part of speech the word belongs to. If *car* is a noun, one can anticipate many of the acceptable uses, and exclude the unacceptable uses. The chances are also that the noun is a concrete item, for children's nouns often have the concrete characteristics of size, shape and visual contour. Verbs are usually actions, typically human or animal movements. R. Brown (1957) has observed that the nouns and verbs of children are more consistent with traditional classroom definitions based on semantic values.

The part of speech membership of a new word is in turn a clue to its meaning type, for children exploit syntactic context in learning words and word meaning. R. Brown (1957) showed a picture of a strange action on a strange container filled with strange stuff. Preschool children indicated the action when asked to show *sebbing*, the container when asked to show *a seb* and the stuff when asked to show *some seb*. Katz, Baker and Macnamara (1974) showed that 18-month-old girls knew the difference between proper and common nouns. When introduced to a doll named *Dax*, they reserved that name for that doll alone; when other girls were introduced to the doll as *a dax*, they applied the noun to other dolls because of the determiner. Taylor and Gelman (1988) also found children use form class to figure out new meanings. Children of 2 learned either *a zav* or *a zav one*, and were asked to select a named toy from an array. A sentence like *Can you point to a zav?* allowed them to use form class to guide their search for meaning. They also found children expect words to be nonsynonymous. When an object was unfamiliar, they readily interpreted a new noun as naming a category of similar objects; but when an object was well-known and already had a name (like *dog*), a new word was used only to refer to the named object as if it were a special proper noun. Previous studies had already shown that children assume new nouns refer to novel or previously unnamed objects; for example, if child is presented with a brush, a fork, a crayon, and a plastic keychain attachment with no previous name, the keychain attachment will be given if asked for *the dax*.

Markman and Wachtel (1988) suggest that children assume that words tend to be mutually exclusive, employing the simple strategy of mapping novel labels onto novel objects. This matches Slobin's (1973, 1977) operating principle that children expect language organization to be clearly and overtly marked. Although formulated for morphemes in a sentence, it can be applied to mutual exclusivity of category terms, with a category referred to by only one term. Pinker's (1984) uniqueness principle also works similarly. The child can acquire grammatical rules in the absence of negative feedback, because if faced with a set of alternative structures which fulfill the same function, the child assumes that only one is correct. Taylor and Gelman's (1988) results support these notions, because here the novel noun given to a familiar object is used to refer only to the named object. When children hear someone label an object, they normally assume that the label refers to the object taken as an exemplar of a taxonomic category. *Dog* does not refer to brown, furry, or a dog chewing on a bone. The label is not taken to refer to the object as a specific individual (*Rover*) or to one of its parts, its attributes, or its relation to other objects. The child normally takes it as the label of an object category (*dog*). The presence of a novel word causes children to first seek taxonomic rather than thematic relations (Markman and Wachtel 1988).

Creating New Verbs from Nouns. Vocabulary about actions lags behind that of objects, so children create new verbs for particular actions from the nouns for the entities involved in the actions they wish to talk about (E. Clark 1982). Any noun denoting a concrete entity can be used as a verb for talking about the state, process, or activity associated with that activity. They have learned the conventions for innovation, but there is often no adult model for the specific word they have created. Adults do often make verbs out of nouns (*denominal verbs*), but children apply their rule too generally, so that *sweep* replaces *broom*, *drive>car*, *fly>airplane*, *shoot>gun*. E. Clark found that the overall patterns of innovation were the same in English, French, and German, with the largest categories of denominal verbs being the following:

1. Instrument verbs: denominal verbs whose parent nouns denote the instrument used in the activity. Adult 'She wedged the door open'. Child 'Won't you hatchet this?' (asking for some sticks to be chopped).

2. Locatum verbs: denominal verbs whose parent nouns denote an object that is placed somewhere. Adult 'He plastered the ceiling.' Child 'Will you chocolate my milk?'; 'Mummy trousers me' (talking about getting dressed).

3. Verbs of characteristic activity: denominal verbs which denote the characteristic activity done by or to the particular entity denoted by the parent

noun of the verb. Adult examples are rare or non-existent, except for weather verbs like 'It's raining' or 'It's snowing'. Children's examples: Act of, as in 'The buzzer is buzzering'. 'It's trucking' (watching a truck pass by); Act done to, as in 'I'm souping' (eating soup). 'Will you nut these?', (bringing mother walnuts to crack).

Adjectives . Adjectives are used by adults in a variety of functions (Nelson 1976):

1.   Describe something: 'Chrissy is a beautiful child'.
2.   Specify which of a number of alternatives is being referred to: 'It was the tall blond man who pulled the gun'.
3.   Sub-classify: 'Dan bought an electric typewriter'.

But there is a differential frequency at different developmental levels. Predicate adjectives like *Broken; It's broken* appear at the one-word stage, but attributives develop later, and then predominate, either as a mode of classification or to subdivide a prior class. Descriptive properties are used, primarily size and some color terms, with size the preferred mode of distinguishing at 2. By 2;6, the child can use adjectives to comment on transient states of objects by using a predicate adjective, can distinguish among objects by size or color, and classify objects according to possession or use.

Semantic Networks

Societies contrast what is considered significant, and the culture is portrayed in its ethnolinguistic paradigms. Certain of these structures, like kin systems, pronouns, space, and time, are learned relatively early. The names provided by parents anticipate this functional structure of the child entering the adult world; things are so named as to categorize them in a maximally useful way. For example, there is no need to distinguish between breeds of *dog*, for they are the same in terms of how the child is expected to behave toward them and vice versa; *animal* is too general, because behaviors that are appropriate to dogs are not appropriate for snakes, horses, and raccoons. *Flowers* is a term at the appropriate level and is used because they are to be sniffed and enjoyed, but not eaten or stomped on; there is no need to distinguish *tulips* and *roses*. R. Brown (1958b) termed this the **level of usual utility**, since the most useful name is given according to how things are categorized for the community's linguistic purposes, without being too specific or too general.

Categorization by Children

Categories are basic to human cognition, allowing children to extend their knowledge beyond the obvious by making inferences beyond mere surface appearances (Gelman 1988). Children develop a number of important cognitive abilities at 1;6, like object permanence and means-end understanding; they also begin to categorize objects in new ways at this age (Gopnik and Meltzoff 1987). Disappearance words like *gone* now appear in order to match object-permanence abilities, just as success-failure words like *there, uh-oh* match means-end achievements. The sudden burst of naming that occurs around 1;6 is paralleled in the flurry of categorization that is taking place, and early semantic development may be shaped by the child's specific cognitive concerns. Very simply, some of the child's emerging vocabulary is a direct reflection of what he or she is cognitively preoccupied with at that stage.

Gelman (1988) reminds us that many categories have a theoretical basis and incorporate more than just intuitive surface similarities. We can deliberately overlook salient properties such as color, shape, and size to form theory-based categories; for example, a legless lizard is not a snake. Most have held that young children cannot do this, and that they are instead misled by appearances, that they have a strong bias to concrete, obvious perceptual characteristics, as opposed to more conceptual or abstract qualities. But more recent studies have shown that children appreciate that categories go beyond the obvious. Gelman and Markman (1987) show that children readily draw inductive inferences from one object to another in the same category, even when such inferences conflict with outward appearances. For example, 4-year-olds learned that a fish like a large gray shark breathes underwater; they were then asked whether a small, green tropical fish or a large, gray dolphin breathes underwater. Realizing that members of the same category share important behaviors and structures, regardless of appearance, they reported that sharks and tropical fish breathe alike because both are fish; they in fact denied that sharks and dolphins breathe alike because they are not both fish.

Gelman and Watson O'Reilly (1988) tested pre-schoolers and second graders on their understanding that members of a category have similar internal parts, and report that children at both ages draw many inferences concerning the internal structure of objects. Gelman (1988) reports that children can readily form stable categories which extend beyond superficial features, because they accept category labels in which category membership and outward appearance do not perfectly coincide. Children often assert that all members of a basic-level category share the same internal structure, and younger children are even more likely to assume this. When asked *Do you think that all dogs/spiders/vacuums/dolls have the same kind of stuff inside?*, they assume that category labels are the key to uncovering deeper similarities among objects and even report that all category members have the same internal structure.

Children are, however, slow to acquire superordinate terms and seem to misunderstand those that they do use. Nelson (1988) claims that it is the hierarchical relationship among terms that poses problems for the child, not the logic of class inclusion, nor a problem of abstracting similarity relations. After all, superordinate categories are not 'natural kinds'; superordinate terms are defined in the language and not in the world. Superordinate terms dominate other terms, and the taxonomic relation is a relation among other words. There is no animal that includes dogs/horses/tigers/rhinos, all of which are natural classes; there is only a language term *animal* which stands in an abstract hierarchically inclusive relationship to these terms. This hierarchy creates the taxonomy, for there is no natural taxonomy. The taxonomies in a community are constructed by the language community, and have to be acquired anew by each child.

Discourse

Discourse to Children

Language socialization begins with the first social contact during infancy (see Schieffelin and Ochs 1986). There is a continuity between pre-linguistic communication and linguistic communication in the social competence that the baby develops in first interactions with the mother. Snow (1976) suggests that the earliest interactions are conversational in nature, with the mother using a conversational model that has both turns and the reciprocal exchange of information. Much of the content is related to the baby, its activities or focus of attention, and much speech is directed towards eliciting responses from the baby. At 0;3, burps, smiles, and vocalizations are all responded to as if they were directly interpretable. By 0;7, babies are more active partners, and the mother only responds to high-quality vocalizations like elaborate and lengthy babbling sequences. At 1;0, mothers may expand or explain the babble, implicitly accepting it as an attempt at a word, and by 1;6, the child often takes turns, with most unit-types consisting of a word. Even if the mother has nothing to say, she at least responds by repeating the word, insisting on the politeness formula of responding with a turn, even if empty. Snow suggests that a conversational model helps explain these striking aspects of early mother-child interaction, as well providing a reason for the high frequency of questions, tag-questions, and post-completers like *hmmm?*. They are essentially devices for passing turns to the baby conversational partner.

Language is functionally interactive, and children can only learn language by speaking and being spoken to. For example, children of bilingual immigrant parents often do not learn the parents' language if it is only overheard; nor will hearing children of deaf parents learn a language from the television. It must be used to communicate with others in the child's environment, and this must be an active and inter-active process (Ervin-Tripp 1971). Transformational grammar and the emphasis on innate universal principles as the basis for language acquisition temporarily devalued the contribution of parental input. The assumption was that children heard only random, often ungrammatical, samples of adult utterances. But studies in the 1970s demonstrated that sentences addressed to children are usually grammatical, and quite lacking in hesitations, false starts, errors, and phonological or grammatical deviations. Adults, and even older children, were shown to modify discourse directed at children, often employing a distinct speech register (variously labelled as **caretaker speech**, **child-directed speech**, and even **motherese**), characterized by simplified vocabulary, phonological simplification of some words, higher pitch and exaggerated intonations, and short, simple sentences.

Baby Talk . A very special, but limited, instance of caretaker speech is known as **baby talk**. It is that special subset of the language which a group regards as appropriate for use only to small children, occasionally favorite pets. The style is not presented to other adults, except in marked situations like sarcasm, satire, or poignant speech. In its use with very young children, it may exhibit a limited suppletive lexical set, phonological substitution or simplification, and morphological devices like diminutives, reduplication, or special affixation. Any of these may be absent, and all may occur in any combination or proportion, with different languages favoring one device over another. For example, in English one commonly finds a simplified or diminutivized vocabulary for terms relating to food, toys, animals, and body functions, as well as phonological simplification expressed by reduplication of syllables (*wawa, choochoo, booboo, tumtum*) and reduction of consonant clusters (*tummy, side< slide*). There is a folk wisdom shared by adults in some communities that baby talk is easier for children to use, that baby talk is a tuitional paradigm, presumably easier for the child to imitate and thus learn. Other language communities exhibit negative attitudes toward baby talk, considering it to more typically a female activity, slightly silly, or undignified to use outside of settings where very young children are present. Among English speakers, it is not uncommon to find those who claim that using baby talk past a certain point is detrimental to the child's language development, though there is no evidence for this piece of folklore.

Baby talk may only fulfill a pseudo-function in linguistic terms, in that it is not as much a learning protocol as it is a marker of affection and caring (see Kess and Kess 1986). This function is supported by the finding that babies typically prefer voices that employ baby talk characteristics. And it is complemented by similar solicitous styles; for example, Levin, Snow and Lee (1984) have found a **nurturant talk** register, aimed at children who are sick, uncomfortable, in hospital, and in need of special nurturance. This style is characteristic of speech to distressed children of all ages studied (up to 9) by male and female caregivers, and though identifiably different from baby talk, it shares some of the same goals.

Caretaker Speech: How Do Adults Talk to Children? . Speech to children is highly repetitive, containing both paraphrases and expansions of deleted material. In one sample addressed to a 2-year-old, about 40% of the utterances were repeated, with the general syntactic form retained. Input tends to be feedback productive, since it contains many imperatives and questions, with a much higher percentage of these than to adults. Some studies have also shown that middle-class mothers increase syntactic complexity with children between 2 and 3, so that input maintains a consistent relation to the child's interpretive skills (Ervin-Tripp 1971). Discourse directed at children attempts to maintain their attention and ensure their understanding. Adults thus use considerable repetition to very young children, but less redundancy as they grow older. Snow (1972) found greater sentence complexity for 10-year-olds than for two-year-olds in English, and reports (Snow et al. 1976) the same findings for Dutch children, with no differences for mothers from different social classes.

In general, the verbal interaction patterns between parents and children increase in difficulty with the language skills of the child. Adults are always monitoring the child's degree of attention and understanding, and adjust the features of their speech to maintain responsiveness at optimal levels. Even women with little experience with young children modified their speech when preparing tapes for two-year-olds, and although they modified their speech less, the differences were significant (Snow 1972). Even children as young as 4;0 produce many of the same modifications when addressing two-year-olds (Snow 1976).

The Motherese Controversy . There seems little doubt that simplification may facilitate the acquisition of language, but the question is whether simplification is essential for language learning to occur. The design features of mother-child discourse suggested that **motherese** might be a simplified teaching language. But a re-evaluation of the current status of the Motherese Hypothesis finds that most effects of the mother on the child's language growth are restricted to a very young age group. Increased complexity of maternal speech is positively correlated with language growth in this age range only (Gleitman, Newport and Gleitman 1984). Affirming that general properties of maternal speech explain the learning sequence may be too much like saying the obvious fact that French children learn French and English children learn English from their caretakers. We should instead be aware that the child is selective in what is used from the environment provided, as well as selective about when in the course of acquisition it is to be used; for example, child learns the functors *the/and/-ed* late, even though these are the most frequent items in the mother's speech. In the end, it may be that restrictive and non-obvious predispositions about information-handling and language itself may explain language-learning better than transparent inductions from the input corpus.

The extent of simplification in maternal speech should not be overestimated either, for the mother's speech is still more complex than any child's speech. And some properties of adult speech to children has to do with what the adult is trying to accomplish. For example, care-takers may be trying to manage or direct a child's behavior, and so the discourse is filled with questions like *Who left their muddy boots in the bathtub?* and imperatives like *Turn down the TV!*. Children them-selves talk about what they already know, particularly about things in their immediate environment like toys, people and pets, and routines of the day. In fact, maternal utterances to very young children also talk about things and events that are in view, not about absent puppies or past birthday parties (see Gleitman et al. 1984). Some discourse rou-tines, like greetings, seasonal or holiday formulas, and polite expres-sions like 'the magic word' *please*, are explicitly taught by parents. So are some aspects of pragmatic behavior, like turn-taking, interruptions, volume, speaking with the mouth full, and so forth (Berko Gleason 1987). In actively teaching such skills, the parent at some points does aid the child to become an acceptable conversationalist.

A major assumption in acquisition theories has been that adults ignore children's speech errors, that it is really the truth of the child's contribution that matters, not its form. Since the primary concern is the ability to communicate, even blatant grammatical errors go uncor-rected as long as they are true. The classic source for this assumption, Brown and Hanlon (1970), examined parental responses to four syntac-tic rules, and found that parents did not overtly correct grammatical mistakes, but corrected for semantic errors like a 'red' chair called 'blue'. But children may indeed be sensitive to differential adult behaviors that follow language errors. Bohannon and Stanowicz (1988) examined childrens' errors in syntax, phonology, and semantics, and found that all adults, male or female and even non-parents, respond differentially to children's mistakes. Adults generally were more likely to request clarification of, or repeat, with changes, sentences containing syntactic or phonological errors. Adults were also more likely to use the correct syntactic or phonological form in a following sentence if the child's sentence contained only one syntactic or phonological error, but did not do this when multiple errors appeared. Almost 70% of child's errors do escape adult comment, and though the reported rates of dif-ferential feedback may seem low, the cumulative effect of corrections over a child's entire language learning career would contain millions of such corrective exchanges.

Discourse by Children: Communicative and Pragmatic Functions

Pragmatics refers to the rules for using language in context, and the communicative functions of early child discourse has been the focus of much research recently. There is much to be learned, even after the basic structures have been mastered. The child must learn how to choose the right linguistic structure for the speech activity the child wishes to achieve. Mastery of the forms is no guarantee that they will be deployed appropriately, and the child is faced with the task of coor-dinating illocutionary force with the range of direct and indirect speech acts available in the language. As if this were not enough, the child must also fit them into a constellation of styles and registers that are appropriate to different listeners and different situations. Some have charted a theoretical framework of speech acts as a useful way of analyzing these developments in early child language. For example, Dale (1980) has proposed a coding system for the number of pragmatic functions, and Dale, Cook and Goldstein (1981) provide evidence that the range of pragmatic functions expressed grows steadily, though without any consistent sequence, during the 1-word and 2-word phases.

Children's knowledge may also be revealed in their actual pragmatic practices, as well as in metapragmatic comments which indicate the status of their knowledge of such rules. Becker (1988) reports that 4-, 5-, and 6-year-olds can judge the appropriateness of affirmative requests like *Can you shut the door?* and even negatively worded requests like *Can't you answer the phone?*. Only 6-year-olds understand *Must you play the piano?*. Children of 4 can judge which of two requests are nicer or bossier, but children of 8 are both likely to judge indirect requests as appropriate and to explain their judgments. Generally, by 7 children are already able to explain their judgments of the appropriateness of utterances expressing thanks, warnings, congratulations, and other speech acts.

In general, by the time children go to school in this culture, we expect them to be linguistically aware of politeness routines. But even pre-schoolers exhibit some metapragmatic knowledge, though the subtlety of childrens' judgments, as well as the richness of their explanations, increases during the elementary school years. Becker has examined their spontaneous metapragmatic comments, observing that preschoolers can display quite sophisticated metapragmatic knowledge. They make explicit comments about repairing or maintaining the ongoing conversation, comments about intended listeners, manner of responding, and taking turns. They even use language for social manipulation; for example, a father interrupting a four-year-old's conversation may receive *I was talking to Mommy. You shouldn't interrupt. That's the rule, Daddy.* The rules may even be used to the child's own advantage. For example, children are taught to respond promptly when spoken to, but not when the mouth is full; but when the literalist child does not wish to reply, it may claim that the mouth is full, even extending this to filling the mouth with air and puffing out the cheeks to make the point.

In concluding, we should note that these are not just 'cute' behaviors. In fact, these strategies are all precursors of how the developing child is learning to employ language to establish and maintain relationships and to get things done. The remainder of his or her adult social life will rely heavily on how well these 'rules of the road' have been learned. The communicative and pragmatic functions are not just a decorative overlay on the basic linguistic structures; instead, they constitute the essential purpose of language that the child has been aiming at all this time.

Metalinguistic Abilities: What Do Children Know about What They Know?

Metalinguistic abilities refers to the fact that language is not only used by humans, but that we also know about the rules by which this is done and can even comment on them. It is not limited to just identifying linguistic units (phrases, words, syllables, sounds), providing definitions, or explaining why certain sentences are possible and why others are not. Metalinguistic skills also mean a general awareness of language, as in monitoring one's ongoing utterances and, if necessary, repairing one's own speech. Children also engage in the conscious practice of sounds, words, and sentences, role-playing and "doing the voices" for different roles, and even adjusting one's speech to the sociolinguistic characteristics of the listener.

Commenting on the correctness of one's utterances and that of others suggests a certain metalinguistic maturity. These abilities appear relatively late in development, and signify the speaker's knowledge of and ability to reflect upon the rules that are being followed or violated. Children of 5, 6, and 7 possess metalinguistic abilities to some degree, in that they can contemplate the structure of the language. They exhibit other metacognitive abilities during this period as well, like storing material for later retrieval in intentional learning tasks and realizing that something has been recollected. Adult-like performance on linguistic tasks emerge at this time, as does the ability to explain judgments of space and number. These are matched by abstract knowledge about levels of language structure like phonology and syntax; for example, the child can now recognize paraphrases and reject deviant, though meaningful, sentences on the syntactic level. Children also engage in a fair amount of **word play** and verbal nonsense, making up words and rhymes, and constructing monologues and even dialogues which display considerable insight into what is to be said and why.

There are of course individual differences in linguistic creativity, and metalinguistic abilities are no exception. Gleitman and Gleitman (1970) found this for adults in their study of paraphrase, and there is no reason to expect children to be any different in their metalinguistic skills. Using compounds like *black bird-house vs. black-bird house*, they found considerable individual differences in paraphrase abilities for adults, along educational lines. The most educated group, Ph.D. professionals, were biased to attend to **surface** syntactic properties, while the other group, clerical workers, would attend to the plausible semantic interpretations of the separate words. The same is true for children, such that one will also find differences among individuals.

Metalinguistic abilities, unlike normal language activities, appear late; they develop over the middle and late childhood years and on into adulthood. The late acquisition of metalinguistic abilities also implies large individual differences. In general, classificatory judgments for deeper, more meaningful, or more global properties appear earlier than for more surface structural properties. That is, children at the age of 5 can be taught the difference between the concept of a word or sentence with little difficulty. But the conceptual differences between word, syllable, and sound are much finer, and more difficult to convey to young children. Children of 5 or 6 have difficulty segmenting speech into words, more difficulty segmenting words into syllables, and the most difficulty at segmenting words or syllables into phonemes. The lower the level of linguistic representation called for, the more difficult the task for young children. Linguistic units at higher levels are easier to access, while lower-level syntactical or phonological units are more difficult to recognize and manipulate even for adults. Performance here is highly variable, for not all language users are good language analysts. Children can detect violations in phonology, morphology, syntax, and semantics before they can explain them. There are also developmental differences within each linguistic domain; in morphology, for example, awareness of tense and plural rules precedes awareness of derivational rules. In general, then, the late appearance of a metalinguistic skill in children is mirrored by the task's degree of difficulty for and extent of individual variation in adults. And the degree of difficulty of making judgments is a function of the type of language level involved.

One example of metalinguistic abilities is the capacity to recognize ambiguity, and either resolve it or appreciate its contribution to making some utterances funny. Hirsh-Pasek, Gleitman and Gleitman (1978) examined children's judgments concerning ambiguity, and found large and consistent differences in performance on metalinguistic tasks like joke interpretation. The ability to explain ambiguity emerges much later than the ability to detect it; 6-year-olds and 7-year-olds rarely provide adequate responses, while 10-year-olds and 11-year-olds do. In Gleitman et al.'s study, the adequacy of children's responses was clearly related to verbal talent as measured grossly in terms of reading skill, with poor readers performing about a year behind good readers. Very simply, even metalinguistic abilities that we take quite for granted in children, like the appreciation and explanation of verbal humour like jokes, emerge somewhat later and with differential performance capabilities.

Summary

Developmental psycholinguistics is the study of child language, and focusses on how the child learns his or her first language. Our biological heritage endows us with innate propensities that underlie language development, but the environment must provide linguistic input for the child to be stimulated. Children are not taught language in any formal way, and yet the fabric of language is already intact by the time school begins. Language is acquired in stages, with each stage more closely approximating adult language. While there are individual differences in onset and rate of language development, the order of stages seems to remain constant.

Different languages pose the child with varying sets of formal problems to solve and learn from, and the child must discover how conceptual notions are mapped in that particular language. There are linguistic constraints on the sequence of acquisition which are derived from the target language, as well as cognitive constraints on the sequence of acquisition. A form which is linguistically simple, but conceptually difficult, may emerge later.

Research suggests that infants perceive some sounds in a categorical way from as early as one month of age. Human infants may be endowed with innate perceptual mechanisms which are attuned to the phonological characteristics of language, preparing them for the possible contrasts they may find in natural languages. They can discriminate between certain phonetic categories without prior experience, but this ability is lost by 10 or 12 months of age. The reason is found in the emergence of the first vocabulary words in what is becoming their first language. That native language will use its own limited set of phonemic contrasts to form an inventory of words.

The acquisition of phonology requires that the child master the abstract system underlying the phonological system, as well as the physiological details of speech production and the acoustic details of speech perception. In both production and perception, children appear to go through systematic stages, going from the simplest to the most complex. The child also learns the phonotactics of the system, learning to discriminate between possible and impossible sequences in the language. The acquisition of phonology is largely complete by the age of 5 to 7, and is not added to thereafter.

In learning morphology, the child must learn the part of speech classes, and the way in which they operate as either content words or function words in the language. Content words, like nouns, verbs, adjectives, and adverbs in English, carry lexical meanings; function words, like articles, conjunctions, auxiliary verbs, and prepositions in English, embody the grammatical machinery of the language.

Languages differ greatly in their morphological typology, so that some languages like English exhibit a large number of free morphemes, while some languages like Russian exhibit a high degree of inflectional affixation. Inflectional morphology operates like the function words in that it carries the grammatical relationships of the language. Derivational morphology, on the other hand, makes up new words in the language, by either compounding existing words or adding derivational affixes. There seems to be a consistent order of mastery for the most common grammatical morphemes, and agreement among children is very high in English. The order of acquisition is dependent on the linguistic complexity of the morpheme, not its frequency of use in parental speech.

The earliest syntax at the holophrastic stage exhibits a maximum sentence length of a single word. This stage coincides with the emergence of the first words at about 12 months. Between 18 and 24 months of age, the first evidence of juxtaposition of words emerges, with the typical utterance two or three words in length. Here the child experiments with the possible semantic-syntactic relationships to be found between objects, and the semantic relations realized in these early utterances seem to be much the same in different languages. In the next stage, hierarchical relationships among lexical items in the sentence emerge, along the basic structural lines of sentence formation in adult language. Children's sentences at this stage often keep the content words, and drop out the function words and grammatical morphemes, thus giving a telegraphic quality to such utterances.

The course of later syntactic development is largely a matter of learning to produce and comprehend the major transformations of the language, like questions, negatives, and passives, as well as how to control compound and complex sentences with more than one clause. Some syntactic abilities take even longer to mature, and structural complexities like the replacement of the minimal distance principle with underlying representations containing gaps and fillers are being developed and elaborated upon after 5 and right up until at least 10.

Semantics is an equally complicated system which we keep adding to throughout our entire lives. The rate of acquisition for words in the early years may be anywhere from 2 to 20 words a day. Recognition vocabulary is always higher, and the child's passive vocabulary is only partially reflected in counts of what a child has actually produced. A child often knows 1000 words by the age of 3, and may have mastered over 10,000 by the age of 6.

Although the child uses identifiable words, they often exhibit an incomplete mastery of the semantic range for the word. The child's semantic categories are typically larger than the categories used by adults, and some have suggested that the child acquires meanings for words by adding specific semantic features. General features are acquired before specific ones, and such overextensions allow the child to build large semantic categories by overlooking dissimilarities between objects and drawing attention to similarity along some specific dimension. Underextension may also occur, however, and words may be used for a narrower range of objects or events. Children also appear to confuse the meaning of word pairs which are closely related by being opposite poles along a single dimension. They tend to use the positive form or the unmarked form of such word pairs, with the unmarked member of the pair comprehended first. They even seem to treat some antonyms as if they were synonyms, and the marked member is often interpreted as having the meaning of the unmarked member. But there are also other factors at work, as for example, response biases toward certain objects or activities.

Categories are basic to human cognition, and children extend their knowledge beyond the obvious by making inferences beyond mere surface appearances. But taxonomies in a community are constructed by the language community, and have to be acquired anew by each child. The sudden burst of naming that occurs around 1;6 is paralleled in the flurry of categorization that is taking place, and early semantic development may be shaped by the child's specific cognitive concerns. Children also develop other important cognitive abilities at this age, like object permanence and means-end understanding, and the child's emerging vocabulary often reflects what he or she is cognitively preoccupied with at that stage.

Pre-school children tend to give lengthy responses, but school children will give single-word associations in free association tests. Adults tend to give predominantly paradigmatic responses, while children tend to syntagmatic responses, with a shift to paradigmatic responses occurring within the 5 to 9 age-range. The frequency of paradigmatic vs. syntagmatic responses, however, is conditioned by form class, frequency, and by the particular characteristics of the words sampled. The syntagmatic-to-paradigmatic shift is most dramatically observed for high-frequency adjectives; nouns tend to be paradigmatic at all ages; and verbs tend to be strongly syntagmatic throughout development.

Language socialization begins with the first social contact during infancy, and the earliest interactions are conversational in nature. Mothers use a conversational model that has both turns and the reciprocal exchange of information. Much of the content is related to the baby, its activities or focus of attention, and much speech is directed towards eliciting responses from the baby. Later, caretaker speech addressed to young children is usually grammatical, usually lacking in hesitations, false starts, errors, and phonological or grammatical deviations. Adults, and even older children, thus seem to modify discourse directed at children, often employing a distinct speech register, characterized by simplified vocabulary, phonological simplification of some words, higher pitch and exaggerated intonations, and short, simple sentences. Discourse directed at children uses these features to maintain their attention and ensure their understanding.

Early discourse by children shows that they are beginning to be aware of the communicative and pragmatic rules for using language in context. The child must now learn how to choose the right linguistic structure for the speech activity he or she wishes to achieve. Mastery of forms is no guarantee that they will be deployed appropriately, and the child is faced with the task of coordinating illocutionary force and speech acts, as well as the constellation of styles and registers that are appropriate to different listeners and different situations.

Metalinguistic skills imply a general awareness of language, so that the child exhibits knowledge of and ability to reflect upon the rules that are being followed or violated. Metalinguistic abilities, unlike normal language activities, appear late; they develop over the middle and late childhood years and on into adulthood. The late acquisition of metalinguistic abilities also implies large individual differences. In general, classificatory judgments for more meaningful or more global properties appear earlier than for more surface structural properties.

References

Andrews, S. 1986. "Morphological Influences on Lexical Access: Lexical or nonlexical effects". *Journal of Memory and Language* 25.726-740.

Aronoff, M. 1982. "Potential Words, Actual Words, Productivity, and Frequency". *Preprints of the Plenary Session Papers, XIIIth International Congress of Linguists*, 141-148. Tokyo.

Austin, J. L. 1962. *How to Do Things with Words*. New York: Oxford Univ. Press.

Baker, W. J. & B. L. Derwing. 1982. "Response Coincidence Analysis as Evidence for Language Acquisition Strategies". *Applied Psycholinguistics* 3.193-221.

Bartlett, F. C. 1932. *Remembering*. Cambridge: Cambridge Univ. Press.

Bates, E. & B. MacWhinney. 1982. "Functionalist Approaches to Grammar". *Language Acquisition: The state of the art* ed. by E. Wanner & L. R. Gleitman, 173-218. Cambridge: Cambridge Univ. Press.

Bates, E. & B. MacWhinney. 1987. "Competition, Variation, and Language Learning". *Mechanisms of Language Acquisition* ed. by B. MacWhinney, 157-194. Hillsdale, NJ: Erlbaum.

Becker, J. A. 1988. "I Can't Talk, I'm Dead: Preschoolers' spontaneous metapragmatic comments". *Discourse Processes* 11.457-468.

Begg, I. & A. Paivio. 1968. "Concreteness and Imagery in Sentence Meaning". *Journal of Verbal Learning and Verbal Behavior* 8.21-27.

Belmore, S. M., J. M. Yates, D. R. Bellack, S. N. Jones, & S. E. Rosequist. 1982. "Drawing Inferences from Concrete and Abstract Sentences". *Journal of Verbal Learning and Verbal Behavior* 21.338-351.

Benedict, R. F. 1946. *The Chrysanthemum and the Sword: Patterns of Japanese culture*. Boston: Houghton Mifflin Company.

Berko, J. 1958. "The Child's Learning of English Morphology". *Word* 14.150-177.

Berko, J. & R. Brown. 1960. "Psycholinguistic research methods". *Handbook of Research Methods in Child Development* ed. by P. H. Mussen, 517-577. New York: John Wiley & Sons.

Berlin, B. 1978. "Ethnobiological Classification". *Cognition and Categorization* ed. by E. Rosch & B. Lloyd, 9-26. Hillsdale, NJ: Lawrence Erlbaum Associates.

Berlin, B. & P. Kay. 1969. *Basic Color Terms*. Berkeley: Univ. of California Press.

Berwick, R. C. & A. S. Weinberg. 1985. "The Psychological Relevance of Transformational Grammar: A reply to Stabler". *Cognition* 19.193-204.

Bever, T. G. 1970. "The Cognitive Basis for Linguistic Structures". *Cognition and the Development of Language* ed. by J. R. Hayes, 279-362. New York: John Wiley & Sons.

Bever, T. G. 1971. "The Integrated Study of Language". *Biological and Social Factors in Psycholinguistics* ed. by J. Morton, 158-209. London: Logos Press.

Bever, T. G., M. F. Garrett & R. Hurtig. 1973. "The Interaction of Perpectual Processes and Ambiguous Sentences". *Memory and Cognition* 1.277-286.

Bickerton, D. 1988. "Creole Languages and the Bioprogram". *Linguistics: The Cambridge survey* ed. by F. J. Newmeyer, vol. II (*Linguistic Theory: Extensions and implications*), 268-284. Cambridge: Cambridge Univ. Press.

Bickerton, D. 1990. *Language & Species*. Chicago: Univ. of Chicago Press.

Birdwhistell, R. L. 1970. *Kinesics and Context*. Philadelphia: Univ. of Pennsylvania Press.

Blake, B. J. 1990. *Relational Grammar*. London: Croom Helm.

Blakemore, D. 1988. "The Organization of Discourse". *Linguistics: The Cambridge survey.* ed. by F. J. Newmeyer, vol. IV (*Language: The socio-cultural context*), 229-250. Cambridge: Cambridge Univ. Press.

Bloom, L. 1970. *Language Development: Form and function in developing grammars.* Cambridge, MA: MIT Press.

Bloom, L. 1973. *One Word at a Time.* The Hague: Mouton.

Bloomfield, L. 1914. *An Introduction to the Study of Language.* New York: Holt.

Bloomfield, L. 1933. *Language.* New York: Holt.

Blumenthal, A. 1970. *Language and Psychology: Historical Aspects of Psycholinguistics.* New York: John Wiley & Sons.

Blumenthal, A. 1974. "An Historical View of Psycholinguistics". *Current Trends in Linguistics* ed. by T. A. Sebeok, vol.12, 1105-1135. The Hague: Mouton.

Blumenthal, A. 1987. "The Emergence of Psycholinguistics". *Synthese* 7.313-323.

Bock, M. 1978. "Levels of Processing of Normal and Ambiguous Sentences in Different Contexts". *Journal of Psychological Research* 40.37-51.

Bohannon, J. N. & L. Stanowicz. 1988. "The Issue of Negative Evidence: Adult responses to children's language errors". *Developmental Psychology* 24.684-689.

Bohannon, J. N. & A. Warren-Leubecker. 1985. "Theoretical Approaches to Language Acquisition". *The Development of Language* ed. by J. B. Gleason, 167-224. Columbus: Merrill Publishing. (2nd ed., 1989.)

Bolinger, D. L. 1965. *Forms of English: Accent, Morpheme, Order.* Cambridge, MA: Harvard Univ. Press.

Bower, G. H. & R. K. Cirilo. 1985. "Cognitive Psychology and Text Processing". *Handbook of Discourse Analysis* ed. by T. A. van Dijk, vol.1 (*Disciplines of Discourse*), 71-105. Orlando: Academic Press.

Bowerman, M. F. 1975. "Cross-linguistic Similarities at two Stages of Syntactic Development". *Foundations of Language Development* ed. by E. H. Lenneberg & E. Lenneberg, 267-282. New York: Academic Press.

Boyce, S., C. P. Browman & L. Goldstein. 1987. "Lexical Organization and Welsh Consonant Mutations". *Journal of Memory and Language* 26.419-452.

Braine, M. D. S. 1963. "The Ontogeny of English Phrase Structure: The first phase". *Language* 39.1-13.

Bransford, J. D., J. R. Barclay & J. J. Franks. 1972. "Sentence Memory: A constructive versus interpretive approach". *Cognitive Psychology* 3.193-209.

Bransford, J. D. & J. J. Franks. 1971. "The Abstraction of Linguistic Ideas". *Cognitive Psychology* 2.331-350.

Bransford, J. D. & M. K. Johnson. 1973. "Considerations of Some Problems Comprehension". *Visual Information Processing* ed. by W. G. Chase, 383-438. New York: Academic Press.

Bresnan, J. 1978. "A Realistic Transformational Grammar". *Linguistic Theory and Psychological Reality* ed. by M. Halle, J. Bresnan & G. Miller, 1-59. Cambridge, MA: MIT Press.

Bresnan, J. 1981. "An Approach to Universal Grammar and Mental Representation". *Cognition* 10.39-52.

Bresnan, J., ed. 1982. *The Mental Representation of Grammatical Relations.* Cambridge, MA: MIT Press.

Bresnan, J. & R. M. Kaplan. 1982. "Introduction: Grammars as mental representations of language". *The Mental Representation of Grammatical Relations* ed. by J. Bresnan, xvii-lii. Cambridge, MA: MIT Press.

Broadbent, D. E. 1962. "Attention and the Perception of Speech". *Scientific American* 206.143-151.

Broadbent, D. E. 1984. "Mental Models". *Quarterly Journal of Experimental Psychology* 36.673-68.

Brown, C. H. 1977. "Folk Botanical Life-forms: Their universality and growth". *American Anthropologist* 79.317-342.

Brown, C. H. 1979. "Folk Zoological Life-forms: Their universality and growth". *American Anthropologist* 81.791-817.

Brown, C. H. 1982. "Folk Zoological Life-forms and Linguistic Marking". *Journal of Ethnobiology* 2.95-112.

Brown, C. H. 1984. *Language and Living Things: Uniformities in folk classification and naming*. New Brunswick, NJ: Rutgers Univ. Press.

Brown, C. H. 1986. "The Growth of Ethnobiological Nomenclature". *Current Anthropology* 27.1-19.

Brown, C. H. & S. R. Witkowski. 1980. "Language Universals". *Toward Explaining Human Culture: A critical review of the findings worldwide cross-cultural research* ed. by D. Levinson Ed., 359-384. Chicago: HRAF Press.

Brown, R. 1957. "Linguistic Determinism and the Part of Speech". *Journal of Abnormal and Social Psychology* 55.1-5.

Brown, R. 1958a. *Words and Things*. Glencoe, IL: Free Press.

Brown, R. 1958b. "How Shall a Thing Be Called?". *Psychological Review* 65.14-21.

Brown, R. 1973. *A First Language: The early stages*. Cambridge, MA: Harvard Univ. Press.

Brown, R. 1976. "Reference: In memorial tribute to Eric Lenneberg". *Cognition* 4.125-153.

Brown, R. & J. Berko. 1960. "Word Association and the Acquisition of Grammar". *Child Development* 31.1-14.

Brown, R. & C. Hanlon. 1970. "Derivational Complexity and the Order of Acquisition in Child Speech". *Psycholinguistics* ed. by R. Brown, 155-207. New York: Free Press.

Brown, R. & E. H. Lenneberg. 1954. "A Study in Language and Cognition". *Journal of Abnormal and Social Psychology* 49.454-462.

Brown, R. & D. McNeill. 1966. "The 'Tip of the Tongue' Phenomenon". *Journal of Verbal Learning and Verbal Behavior* 5.325-337.

Butterworth, B. & S. Whittaker. 1980. "Peggy Babcock's Relatives". *Tutorials in Motor Behavior* ed. by G. E. Stelmach & J. Requin, 647-656. Amsterdam: North-Holland.

Bybee, J. L. 1985. *Morphology: A study of the relation between meaning and form*. Amsterdam: John Benjamins B.V.

Bybee, J. L. & C. L. Moder. 1983. "Morphological Classes as Natural Categories". *Language* 59.251-270.

Bybee, J. L. & D. I. Slobin. 1982. "Rules and Schemas in the Development and Use of the English Past Tense". *Language* 58.265-289.

Cairns, H. S. 1973. "Effects of Bias on Processing and Reprocessing of Lexically Ambiguous Sentences". *Journal of Experimental Psychology* 97.337-343.

Cairns, H. S. & J. D. Kamerman. 1975. "Lexical Information Processing during Sentence Comprehension". *Journal of Verbal Learning and Verbal Behavior* 14.170-179.

Cairns, H. S. & J. Ryan Hsu. 1980. "Effects of Prior Context on Lexical Access during Sentence Comprehension: A replication and reinterpretation". *Journal of Psycholinguistic Research* 9.319-326.

Campbell, R. N. & R. Grieve. 1982. "Royal Investigations of the Origin of Language". *Historiographica Linguistica* 9.43-74.

Caramazza, A. & R. S. Berndt. 1978. "Semantic and Syntactic Processes in Aphasia: A review of the literature". *Psychological Bulletin* 85.898-918.

Caramazza, A., A. Laudanna & C. Romani. 1988. "Lexical Access and Inflectional Morphology". *Cognition* 28.297-332.

Carey, P. W., J. Mehler & T. G. Bever. 1970a. "Judging the Veracity of Ambiguous Sentences". *Journal of Verbal Learning and Verbal Behavior* 9.243-254.

Carey, P. W., J. Mehler & T. G. Bever. 1970b. "When Do we Compute All the Interpretations of an Ambiguous Sentence?". *Advances in Psycholinguistics* ed. by G. B. Flores d'Arcais & W. J. M. Levelt, 61-75. Amsterdam: North-Holland Publishing Company.

Carey, S. 1978. "Less May Never Mean More". *Recent Advances in the Psychology of Language* ed. by R. N. Campbell and P. T. Smith, 109-132. New York: Plenum Press.

Carey, S. 1978. "The Child as Word Learner". *Linguistic Theory and Psychological Reality* ed. by M. Halle, J. Bresnan & G. Miller, 264-293. Cambridge, MA: MIT Press.

Carey, S. 1982. "Semantic Development: The state of the art". *Language Acquisition: The state of the art* ed. by E. Wanner & L. R. Gleitman, 348-389. Cambridge: Cambridge Univ. Press.

Carey, S. & E. Bartlett. 1978. "Acquiring a Single New Word". *Papers and Reports on Child Language Development* 15.17-29.

Carlson, G. N. & M. K. Tanenhaus, eds. 1989a. *Linguistic Structure in Language Processing*. Dordrecht: Kluwer Academic Publishers.

Carlson, G. N. & M. K. Tanenhaus. 1989b. "Introduction". *Linguistic structure in language processing* ed. by G. N. Carlson & M. K. Tanenhaus, 1-26. Dordrecht: Kluwer Academic Publishers.

Carmichael, L., H. P. Hogan & A. A. Walter. 1932. "An Experimental Study of the Effect of Language on the Reproduction of Visually Perceived Forms". *Journal of Experimental Psychology* 15.73-86.

Carpenter, P. A. & M. Just. 1975. "Sentence Comprehension: A psycholinguistic processing model of verification". *Psychological Review* 82.45-73.

Carroll, J. B. 1963. *The Study of Language: A survey of linguistics and related disciplines in America*. Cambridge, MA: Harvard Univ. Press.

Carroll, J. B. & J. B. Casagrande. 1958. "The Function of Language Classifications in Behavior". *Readings in Social Psychology* ed. by E. E. Maccoby, T. M. Newcomb & E. L. Hartley, 18-32. New York: Holt, Rinehart & Winston.

Carston, R. 1988. "Language and Cognition". *Linguistics: The Cambridge survey* ed. by F. J. Newmeyer, vol. III (*Language: Psychological and biological aspects*), 38-68. Cambridge: Cambridge Univ. Press.

Chafe, W. L. 1970. *Meaning and the Structure of Language*. Chicago: Univ. of Chicago Press.

Charrow, R. P. & V. R. Charrow. 1979. "Making Legal Language Understandable: A psycholinguistic study of jury instructions". *Columbia Law Review* 79.1306-1374.

Charrow, V. R. 1982. "Linguistic Theory and the Study of Legal and Bureaucratic Language". *Exceptional Language and Linguistics* ed. by L. K. Obler & L. Menn, 81-101. New York: Academic Press.

Charrow V. R. & M. K. Erhardt. 1986. *Clear and Effective Legal Writing*. Boston: Little, Brown & Company.

Cherry, E. C. 1953. "On the Recognition of Speech with One, and with Two Ears". *Journal of the Acoustical Society of America* 25.975-979.

Cherry, C. 1957. *On Human Communication*. Cambridge, MA: MIT Press. (2nd ed., 1966.)

Chomsky, C. 1969. *The Acquisition of Syntax in Children from 5 to 10*. Cambridge, MA: MIT Press.

Chomsky, C. 1970. "Reading, Writing, and Phonology". *Harvard Educational Review* 40.287-309.

Chomsky, N. 1957. *Syntactic Structures*. The Hague: Mouton.

Chomsky, N. 1959. Review of Skinner (1957). *Language* 35.26-58.

Chomsky, N. 1965. *Aspects of the Theory of Syntax*. Cambridge, MA: MIT Press.

Chomsky, N. 1968. *Language and Mind*. New York: Harcourt Brace.

Chomsky, N. 1971. "Deep Structure, Surface Structure, and Semantic Interpretation". *Semantics: An interdisciplinary reader in philosophy, linguistics, and psychology* ed. by D. D. Steinberg & L. A. Jakobovits, 183-216. New York: Cambridge Univ. Press.

Chomsky, N. 1975a. *Reflections on Language*. New York: Pantheon/Random House.

Chomsky, N. 1975b. *The Logical Structure of Linguistic Theory*. New York: Plenum.

Chomsky, N. 1981. *Lectures on Government and Binding*. Dordrecht: Foris Publications.

Chomsky, N. 1982. *Some Concepts and Consequences of the Theory of Government and Binding*. Cambridge, MA: MIT Press.

Chomsky, N. & M. Halle. 1968. *The Sound Pattern of English*. New York: Harper & Row.

Clark, E. 1972. "On the Child's Acquisition of Antonyms in Two Semantic Fields". *Journal of Verbal Learning and Verbal Behavior* 11.750-758.

Clark, E. 1973a. "Non-linguistic Strategies and the Acquisition of Word Meaning". *Cognition* 2.161-182.

Clark, E. 1973b. "What's in a Word: On the child's acquisition of semantics in his first language". *Cognitive Development and the Acquisition of Language* ed. by T. E. Moore, 65-110. New York: Academic Press.

Clark, E. 1982. "The Young Word Maker: A case study of innovation in the child's lexicon". *Language Acquisition: The state of the art* ed. by E. Wanner & L. R. Gleitman, 390-425. Cambridge: Cambridge Univ. Press.

Clark, E. & B. J. S. Barron. 1988. "A Thrower-button or a Button-thrower? Children's judgements of grammatical and ungrammatical compound nouns". *Linguistics* 26.3-19.

Clark, E. & B. F. Hecht. 1983. "Comprehension, Production, and Language Acquisition". *Annual Review of Psychology* 34.325-349.

Clark, H. H. 1969. "Linguistic Processes in Deductive Reasoning". *Psychological Review* 76.387-404.

Clark, H. H. 1974. "Semantics and Comprehension". *Current Trends in Linguistics* ed. by T. A. Sebeok, vol.12, 1291-1498. The Hague: Mouton.

Clark, H. H. 1979. "Responding to Indirect Speech Acts". *Cognitive Psychology* 11.430-477.

Clark, H. H. & S. K. Card. 1969. "The Role of Semantics in Remembering Comparative Sentences". *Journal of Experimental Psychology* 82.545-552.

Clark, H. H. & W. G. Chase. 1972. "On the Process of Comparing Sentences against Pictures". *Cognitive Psychology* 3.472-517.

Clark, H. H. & E. V. Clark. 1968. "Semantic Distinctions and Memory for Complex Sentences". *Quarterly Journal of Experimental Psychology* 20.129-138.

Clark, H. H. & E. V. Clark. 1977. *Psychology and Language: An introduction to psycholinguistics*. New York: Harcourt Brace Jovanovich.

Clark, H. H. & P. Lucy. 1975. "Understanding What is Meant from What is Said: A study in conversationally conveyed requests". *Journal of Verbal Learning and Verbal Behavior* 14.56-72.

Clifton, C. & L. Frazier. 1989. "Comprehending sentences with long-distance dependencies". *Linguistic structure in language processing* ed. by G. N. Carlson & M. K. Tanenhaus, 273-318. Dordrecht: Kluwer Academic Publishers.

Clifton, C. & P. Odom. 1966. "Similarity Relations among Certain English Constructions". *Psychological Monographs* 80:5.1-35.

Collins, A. M. & E. F. Loftus. 1975. "A Spreading-activation Theory of semantic processing". *Psychological Review* 82.407-428.

Collins, A. M. & M. R. Quillian. 1969. "Retrieval Time from Semantic Memory". *Journal of Verbal Learning and Verbal Behavior* 8.240-247.

Comrie, B. 1981. *Language Universals and Language Typology: Syntax and morphology*. Oxford: Basil Blackwell.

Conrad, C. 1974. "Context in Sentence Comprehension: A study of the subjective lexicon". *Memory and Cognition* 2.130-138.

Corballis, M. C. 1980. "Laterality and Myth". *American Psychologist* 35.284-295.

Crain, S. & M. Steedman. 1985. "On not Being Led up the Garden Path: The use of context by the psychological syntax processor". *Natural Language Parsing* ed. by D. R. Dowty, L. Karttunen & A. M. Zwicky, 320-358. Cambridge: Cambridge Univ. Press.

Crystal, D. 1973. "Non-segmental Phonology in Language Acquisition: A review of the issues". *Lingua* 32.1-45.

Curtiss, S. 1977. *Genie: A psycholinguistic study of a modern-day 'wild child'*. New York: Academic Press.

Cutler, A. 1981. "The Reliability of Speech Error Data". *Linguistics* 9.561-582.

Cutler, A. 1989. "Auditory Lexical Access: Where do we start?". *Lexical Representation and Process* ed. by W. Marslen-Wilson, pp. 342-356. Cambridge, MA: MIT Press.

Cutler, A., S. Butterfield & J. N. Williams. 1987. "The Perceptual Integrity of Syllabic Onsets". *Journal of Memory and Language* 26.406-418.

Dale, P. S. 1980. "Is Early Pragmatic Development Measurable?". *Journal of Child Language* 7.1-11.

Dale, P. S., N. L. Cook & H. Goldstein. 1981. "Pragmatics and Symbolic Play: A study in language and cognitive development". *Child Language--An International Perspective* ed. by P. S. Dale & D. Ingram, 151-173. Baltimore: University Park Press.

Danks, J. & S. Glucksberg. 1980. "Experimental Psycholinguistics". *Annual Review of Psychology* 31.391-417.

Derbyshire, D. C. & G. K. Pullum. 1981. "Object-initial Languages". *International Journal of American Linguistics* 47.192-214.

Dauer, R. M. 1983. "Stress-timing and Syllable-timing Reanalyzed". *Journal of Phonetics* 11.51-62.

Davis, R. 1961. "The Fitness of Names to Drawings: A cross-cultural study in Tanganyika". *British Journal of Psychology* 52.259-268.

Deese, J. 1965. *The Structure of Associations in Language and Thought*. Baltimore: Johns Hopkins Univ. Press.

Deese, J. 1962. "On the Structure of Associative Meaning". *Psychological Review* 69.161-175.

Dell, G. S. 1988. "The Retrieval of Phonological Forms in Production: Tests of predictions from a connectionist model". *Journal of Memory and Language* 27.124-142.

Dennis, M. & H. A. Whitaker. 1977. "Hemispheric Equipotentiality and Language Acquisition". *Language Development and Neurological Theory* ed. by S. J. Segalowitz & F. A. Gruber, 93-106. New York: Academic Press.

Derwing, B. L. 1976. "Morpheme Recognition and the Learning of Rules for Derivational Morphology". *Canadian Journal of Linguistics* 21.38-66.

Derwing, B. L. & W. J. Baker. 1974. *Rule Learning and the English Inflections*. Final Report to the Canada Council, File #S73-0387.

Derwing, B. L. & W. J. Baker. 1976. *On the Learning of English Morphologicical Rules*. Final Report to the Canada Council, File #S73-0387.

Derwing, B. L. & W. J. Baker. 1977. "The Psychological Basis for Morphological Rules". *Language Learning and Thought* ed. by J. Macnamara, 85-110. New York: Academic Press.

Diehl, R. L., K. R. Kluender, D. J. Foss, E. M. Parker & M. A. Gernsbacher. 1987. "Vowels as Islands of Reliability". *Journal of Memory and Language* 26.564-573.

Dingwall, W. O. 1988. "The Evolution of Human Communicative Behavior". *Linguistics: The Cambridge survey* ed. by F. J. Newmeyer, vol. III (*Language: Psychological and biological aspects*), 274-313. Cambridge: Cambridge Univ. Press.

Dixon, P. 1987. "The Processing of Organizational and Component Step Information in Written Directions". *Journal of Memory and Language* 26.24-35.

Dodd, B. 1975. "Children's Understanding of their own Phonological Forms". *Quarterly Journal of Experimental Psychology* 27.165-172.

Donaldson, M. & G. Balfour. 1968. "Less Is More: A study of language comprehension in children". *British Journal of Psychology* 59.461-472.

Donaldson, M. & J. McGarrigle. 1973. "Some Clues to the Nature of Semantic Development". *Journal of Child Language* 1.185-194.

Donaldson, M. & R. J. Wales. 1970. "On the Acquisition of Some Relational Terms". *Cognition and the Development of Language* ed. by J.R. Hayes, 235-268. New York: John Wiley & Sons.

Dowty, D., R. E. Wall & S. Peters. 1981. *Introduction to Montague Semantics*. Dordrecht: Reidel.

DuBois, J. W. 1974. "Syntax in Mid-sentence". *Berkeley Studies in Syntax and Semantics* 1.1-25.

Duncan, S. 1969. "Nonverbal Communication". *Psychological Bulletin* 72.118-147.

Duncan, S. 1972. "Some Signals and Rules for Taking Speaking Turns in Conversations". *Journal of Personality and Social Psychology* 23.283-292.

Duncan, S. & D. W. Fiske. 1985. *Interaction Structure and Strategy*. Cambridge: Cambridge Univ. Press.

Eilers, R. E., D. K. Oller & J. Ellington. 1974. "The Acquisition of Word-meaning for Dimensional Adjectives: The long and short of it". *Journal of Child Language* 1.195-204.

Eimas, P. D. 1963. "The Relation between Identification and Discrimination along Speech and Non-speech Continua". *Language and Speech* 6.206-217.

Eimas, P. D. 1985. "Perception of Speech in Early Infancy". *Scientific American* 252.46-52.

Eimas, P. D., E. R. Sigueland, P. Jusczyk & J. Vigorito. 1971. "Speech Perception in Infants". *Science* 171.303-306.

Ekman, P., ed. 1973. *Darwin and Facial Expression: A century of research in review.* New York: Academic Press.

Emmorey, K. D. & V. A. Fromkin. 1988. "The Mental Lexicon". *Linguistics: The Cambridge survey* ed. by F. J. Newmeyer, vol. III (*Language: Psychological and biological aspects*), 124-149. Cambridge: Cambridge Univ. Press.

Enc, M. 1988. "The Syntax-Semantics Interface". *Linguistics: The Cambridge survey* ed. by F. J. Newmeyer, vol. I (*Linguistic Theory: Foundations*), 239-254. Cambridge: Cambridge Univ. Press.

Ervin-Tripp, S. 1971. "An Overview of Theories of Grammatical Development". *The Ontogenesis of Grammar* ed. by D. Slobin, 189-215. New York: Academic Press.

Ervin-Tripp, S. & D. I. Slobin. 1966. "Psycholinguistics". *Annual Review of Psychology* 17.435-474.

Evans, J. 1972. "Reasoning with Negatives". *British Journal of Psychology* 63.213-219.

Falk, D. 1980. "Language, Handedness, and Primate Brains: Did the australopithecines sign?". *American Anthropologist* 82.72-78.

Falk, D. 1987. "Hominid Paleoneurology". *Annual Review of Anthropology* 16.13-30.

Fay, D. & A. Cutler. 1977. "Malapropisms and the Structure of the Mental Lexicon". *Linguistic Inquiry* 8.505-520.

Feldman, L. B. & C. A. Fowler. 1987. "The Inflected Noun System in Serbo-Croatian: Lexical representation of morphological structure". *Memory and Cognition* 15.1-12.

Felker, D., ed. 1980. *Document Designers: A review of the relevant research.* Washington, D.C.: American Institutes for Research.

Felker, D. et al. 1981. *Guidelines for Document Designers.* Washington, D.C.: American Institutes for Research.

Ferreira, F. & C. Clifton. 1986. "The Independence of Syntactic Processing". *Journal of Memory and Language* 25.348-368.

Fillenbaum, S. 1966. "Memory for Gist: Some relevant variables". *Language and Speech* 9.217-227.

Fillenbaum, S. 1971a. "Psycholinguistics". *Annual Review of Psychology* 22.251-308.

Fillenbaum, S. 1971b. "On Coping with Ordered and Unordered Conjunctive Sentences". *Journal of Experimental Psychology* 87.93-98.

Fillenbaum, S. 1974a. "Pragmatic Normalization: Further results for some conjunctive and disjunctive sentences". *Journal of Experimental Psychology* 102.574-578.

Fillenbaum, S. 1974b. "Or: Some uses". *Journal of Experimental Psychology* 103.913-921.

Fillenbaum, S. & A. Rapoport. 1971. *Structures in the Subjective Lexicon.* New York: Academic Press.

Fillmore, C. 1968. "The Case for Case". *Universals in Linguistic Theory* ed. by E. Bach & R. T. Harms, 1-90. New York: Holt, Rinehart & Winston.

Fillmore, C. 1977. "The Case for Case Reopened". *Syntax and Semantics: Grammatical relations* ed. by P. Cole & J. Sadock, 59-81. New York: Academic Press.

Fodor, J. A. 1966. "How to Learn to Talk: some simple ways". *The Genesis of Language: A psycholinguistic approach* ed. by F. G. Smith & G. A. Miller, 105-128. Cambridge, MA: MIT Press.

Fodor, J. A. 1983. *Modularity of Mind*. Cambridge, MA: MIT Press.

Fodor, J. A., T. Bever & M. F. Garrett. 1974. *The Psychology of Language: An introduction to psycholinguistics and generative grammar*. New York: McGraw-Hill.

Fodor, J. A. & M. F. Garrett. 1967. "Some Syntactic Determinants of Sentential Complexity". *Perception and Psychophysics* 2.289-296.

Fodor, J. D. 1977. *Semantics: Theories of meaning in generative grammar*. New York: Thomas Y. Crowell Company.

Fodor, J. D. 1988. "On Modularity in Syntactic Processing". *Journal of Psycholinguistic Research* 17.125-167.

Forster, K. I. & L. A. Ryder. 1971. "Perceiving the Structure and Meaning of Sentences". *Journal of Verbal Learning and Verbal Behavior* 10.285-296.

Foss, D. J. 1970. "Some Effects of Ambiguity upon Sentence Comprehension". *Journal of Verbal Learning and Verbal Behavior* 9.699-706.

Foss, D. J. 1988. "Experimental Psycholinguistics". *Annual Review of Psychology* 39.309-348.

Foss, D. J., T. Bever & M. Silver. 1968. "The Comprehension and Verification of Ambiguous Sentences". *Perception and Psychophysics* 4.304-306.

Foss, D. J. & C. M. Jenkins. 1973. "Some Effects of Context on the Comprehension of Ambiguous Sentences". *Journal of Verbal Learning and Verbal Behavior* 12.577-589.

Fouts, R. S. & D. H. Fouts. 1989. "Loulis in Conversation with Cross-fostered Chimpanzees". *Teaching Sign Language to Chimpanzees* ed. by R. A. Gardner, B. T. Gardner & T. E. Van Cantfort, 293-307. Buffalo: SUNY Press.

Fouts, R. S., D. H. Fouts & T. E. Van Cantfort. 1989. "The Infant Loulis Learns Signs from Cross-fostered Chimpanzees". *Teaching Sign Language to Chimpanzees* ed. by R. A. Gardner, B. T. Gardner & T. E. Van Cantfort, 280-292. Buffalo: SUNY Press.

Fowler, C. A. 1986. "An Event Approach to the Study of Speech Perception from a Direct-realist Perspective". *Journal of Phonetics* 14.3-28.

Fowler, C. A. & J. Housum. 1987. "Talkers' Signalling of 'New' and 'Old' Words in Speech and Listeners' Perception and Use of the Distinction". *Journal of Memory and Language* 26.489-504.

Fowler, C. A., S. E. Napps & L. Feldman. 1985. "Relations among Regular and Irregular Morphologically Related Words in the Lexicon as Revealed by Repetition Priming". *Memory and Cognition* 13.241-255.

Frauenhelder, U. H. & L. K. Tyler. 1987. "The Process of Word Recognition: An introduction". *Cognition* 25.135-155.

Frawley, W. 1987. Review article of van Dijk (1985). *Language* 63.361-397.

Frazier, L. 1989. "Against Lexical Generation of Syntax". *Lexical Representation and Process* ed. by W. Marslen-Wilson, 505-528. Cambridge, MA: MIT Press.

Frazier, L. & K. Rayner. 1982. "Making and Correcting Errors during Sentence Comprehension: Eye movements in the analysis of structurally ambiguous sentences". *Cognitive Psychology* 14.178-210.

Frazier, L. & K. Rayner. 1987. "Resolution of Syntactic Category Ambiguities: Eye movements in parsing lexically ambiguous sentences". *Journal of Memory and Language* 26.505-526.

Frege, G. 1952. "On Sense and Reference". *Translations from the Philosophical Writings of Gottlob Frege* ed. by P. Geach & M. Black, 56-78. Oxford: Basil Blackwell. (2nd ed., 1960).

Fries, C. C. 1952. *The Structure of English: An introduction to the construction of English sentences.* New York: Harcourt, World & Brace.

Fries, C. C. 1954. "Meaning and Linguistic Analysis". *Language* 30.57-68.

Fromkin, V. A. 1971. "The Non-anomalous Nature of Anomalous Utterances". *Language* 47.27-52.

Fromkin, V. A., ed. 1973. *Speech Errors as Linguistic Evidence.* The Hague: Mouton.

Furth, H. G. 1966. *Thinking without Language.* New York: Free Press.

Gardner, B. T., R. A. Gardner & S. G. Nichols. 1989. "The Shapes and Uses of Signs in a Cross-fostering Laboratory". *Teaching Sign Language to Chimpanzees* ed. by R. A. Gardner, B. T. Gardner & T. E. Van Cantfort, 55-180. Buffalo: SUNY Press.

Gardner, R. A. & B. T. Gardner. 1989. "A Cross-fostering Laboratory". *Teaching Sign Language to Chimpanzees* ed. by R. A. Gardner, B. T. Gardner & T. E. Van Cantfort, 1-28. Buffalo: SUNY Press.

Gardner, R. A., B. T. Gardner & T. E. Van Cantfort, eds. 1989. *Teaching Sign Language to Chimpanzees.* Buffalo: SUNY Press.

Garnham, A. 1982. "Testing Psychological Theories about Inference Making". *Memory and Cognition* 10.341-349.

Garnham, A. 1985. *Psycholinguistics: Central issues.* London: Methuen.

Garnica, O. K. 1973. "The Development of Phonemic Speech Perception". *Cognitive Development and the Acquisition of Language* ed. by T. E. Moore, 216-222. New York: Academic Press.

Garrett, M. F. 1970. "Does Ambiguity Complicate the Perception of Sentences?". *Advances in Psycholinguistics* ed. by G. B. Flores d'Arcais & W. J. M. Levelt, 48-60. Amsterdam: North-Holland Publishing Company.

Garrett, M. F. 1975. "The Analysis of Sentence Production". *The Psychology of Learning and Motivation* ed. by G. H. Bower, 133-177. New York: Academic Press.

Garrett, M. F. 1980. "Levels of Processing in Sentence Production". *Language Production* ed. by B. Butterworth, 177-220. New York: Academic Press.

Garrett, M. F. 1988. "Processes in Language Production". *Linguistics: The Cambridge survey* ed. by F. J. Newmeyer, vol. III (*Language: Psychological and biological aspects*), 69-96. Cambridge: Cambridge Univ. Press.

Garrett, M. F., T. Bever & J. A. Fodor. 1966. "The Active Use of Grammar in Speech Perception". *Perception and Psychophysics* 1.30-32.

Gazdar, G., E. Klein, G. Pullum & I. Sag. 1985. *Generalized Phrase Structure Grammar.* Cambridge, MA: Harvard Univ. Press.

Gee, J. P. & F. Grosjean. 1984. "Empirical Evidence for Narrative Structure". *Cognitive Science* 8.59-85.

Gelman, S. A. 1988. "Children's Expectations Concerning Natural Kind Categories". *Human Development* 31.28-34.

Gelman, S. A. & E. M. Markman. 1987. "Young Children's Inductions from Natural Kinds: The role of categories and appearances". *Child Development* 58.1532-1541.

Gelman, S. A. & A. Watson O'Reilly. 1988. "Children's Inductive Inferences within Superordinate Categories: The role of language and category structure". *Child Development* 59.876-887.

Geschwind, N. 1972. "Language and the Brain". *Scientific American* 226.76-84.
Gibbs, R. W. 1979. "Contextual Effects in Understanding Indirect Requests". *Discourse Processes* 2.1-10.
Gibbs, R. W. 1981. "Your Wish Is My Command: Convention and context in interpreting indirect requests". *Journal of Verbal Learning and Verbal Behavior* 20.431-444.
Gibbs, R. W. 1987. "Mutual Knowledge and the Psychology of Conversational Inference". *Journal of Pragmatics* 11.561-588.
Givon, T. 1978. "Negation in Language: Pragmatics, function, ontology". *Syntax and Semantics: Pragmatics* ed. by P. Cole, 69-112. New York: Academic Press.
Gleason, J. Berko. 1987. "Language and Psychological Development". *Papers and Reports on Child Language Development* 26.1-17.
Gleitman, L. R. & H. Gleitman. 1970. *Phrase and Paraphrase*. New York: W. W. Norton.
Gleitman, L. R., E. L. Newport & H. Gleitman. 1984. "The Current Status of the Motherese Hypothesis". *Journal of Child Language* 11.43-79.
Glenberg, A. M., M. Meyer & K. Lindem. 1987. "Mental Models Contribute to Foregrounding during Text Comprehension". *Journal of Memory and Language* 26.69-83.
Glucksberg, S., P. Gildea & H. B. Bookin. 1982. "On Understanding Non-literal Speech: Can people ignore metaphors?". *Journal of Verbal Learning and Verbal Behavior* 21.85-98.
Goffman, E. 1976. "Replies and Responses". *Language in Society* 5.257-313.
Goldman-Eisler, F. 1968. *Psycholinguistics: Experiments in spontaneous speech*. New York: Academic Press.
Goldman-Eisler, F. & M. Cohen. 1970. "Is N, P, PN Difficulty a Valid Criterion of Transformational Operations?". *Journal of Verbal Learning and Verbal Behavior* 9.161-166.
Gopnik, A. & A. Meltzoff. 1987. "The Development of Categorization in the Second Year and its Relation to Other Cognitive and Linguistic Developments". *Child Development* 58.1528-1531.
Gordon, P. C. & D. E. Meyer. 1984. "Perceptual-motor Processing of Phonetic Features in Speech". *Journal of Experimental Psychology: Human Perception and Performance* 10.153-178.
Gough, P. B. 1965. "Grammatical Transformations and Speed of Understanding". *Journal of Verbal Learning and Verbal Behavior* 4.107-111.
Gough, P. B. 1966. "The Verification of Sentences: The effects of delay of evidence and sentence length". *Journal of Verbal Learning and Verbal Behavior* 5.492-496.
Greenberg, J. H., ed. 1963. *Universals of Language*. Cambridge, MA: MIT Press. (2nd ed., 1966.)
Greenberg, J. H. 1968. *Anthropological Linguistics*. New York: Random House.
Greenberg, J. H. 1975. "Research on Language Universals". *Annual Review of Anthropology* 4.75-94.
Greenberg, J. H., ed. 1978. *Universals of Language*. Vol.1-4. Stanford: Stanford Univ. Press.
Greene, J. O. & J. N. Cappella. 1986. "Cognition and Talk: The relationship of semantic units to temporal patterns of fluency in spontaneous speech". *Language and Speech* 29.141-157.

Grice, H. P. 1975. "Logic and Conversation". *Syntax and Semantics: Speech acts* ed. by P. Cole & J. L. Morgan, 41-58. New York: Academic Press.

Grosjean, F. & J. P. Gee. 1987. "Prosodic Structure and Spoken Word Recognition". *Cognition* 25.135-155.

Grosjean, F., L. Grosjean & H. Lane. 1979. "The Patterns of Silence: Performance structures in sentence production". *Cognitive Psychology* 11.58-81.

Grosz, B. J. & C. Sidner. 1986. "Attention, Intentions, and the Structure of Discourse". *Computational Linguistics* 12.175-204.

Hakes, D. T. 1972. "Effects of Reducing Complement Constructions on Sentence Comprehension". *Journal of Verbal Learning and Verbal Behavior* 11.278-286.

Hakes, D. T. & H. S. Cairns. 1970. "Sentence Comprehension and Relative Pronouns". *Perception and Psychophysics* 8.5-8.

Halle, M., J. Bresnan & G. A. Miller, eds. 1978. *Linguistic Theory and Psychological Reality*. Cambridge, MA: MIT Press.

Hankamer, J. 1989. "Morphological Processing and the Lexicon". *Lexical Representation and Process* ed. by W. Marslen-Wilson, 392-408. Cambridge, MA: MIT Press.

Harris, M., M. Barrett, D. Jones & S. Brookes. 1988. "Linguistic Input and Early Word Meaning". *Journal of Child Language* 15.77-94.

Haviland, S. E. & H. H. Clark. 1974. "What's New? Acquiring New Information as a Process in Comprehension". *Journal of Verbal Learning and Verbal Behavior* 13.512-521.

Heibeck, T. H. & E. M. Markman. 1987. "Word Learning in Children: An examination of fast mapping". *Child Development* 58.1021-1034.

Heider, E. Rosch. 1972. "Universals in Color Naming and Memory". *Journal of Experimental Psychology* 93.10-21.

Henderson, L. 1985. "Towards a Psychology of Morphemes". *Progress in the Psychology of Language* ed. by A. W. Ellis, 15-72. Hillsdale, NJ: Lawrence Erlbaum Associates.

Henderson, L. 1989. "On Mental Representation of Morphology and its Diagnosis by Measures of Visual Access Speed". *Lexical Representation and Process* ed. by W. Marslen-Wilson, 357-391. Cambridge, MA: MIT Press.

Henle, P., ed. 1958. *Language, Thought, and Culture*. Ann Arbor: Univ. of Michigan Press.

Herriot, P. 1969. "The Comprehension of Active and Passive Sentences as a Function of Pragmatic Expectations". *Journal of Verbal Learning and Verbal Behavior* 8.166-169.

Herskovits, M. J. 1950. *Man and his Works*. New York: Knopf.

Hewes, G. W. 1973. "Primate Communication and the Gestural Origin of Language". *Current Anthropology* 14.5-32.

Heynick, F. 1983. "From Einstein to Whorf: Space, time, matter, and reference frames in physical and linguistic relativity". *Semiotica* 45.35-64.

Hill, J. H. 1978. "Apes and Language". *Annual Review of Anthropology* 7.89-112.

Hill, J. H. 1988. "Language, Culture, and World-View". *Linguistics: The Cambridge survey* ed. by F. J. Newmeyer, vol. IV (*Language: The socio-cultural context*), 14-36. Cambridge: Cambridge Univ. Press.

Hirsh-Pasek, K., L. R. Gleitman & H. Gleitman. 1978. "What Did the Brain Say to the Mind? A study of the detection and report of ambiguity by young children". *The Child's Conception of Language* ed. by A. Sinclair, R. J. Jarvella & W. J. M. Levelt, pp. 97-132. Berlin: Springer-Verlag.

Hirst, G. 1987. *Semantic Interpretation and the Resolution of Ambiguity*. Cambridge: Cambridge Univ. Press.

Hjelmquist, E. 1984. "Memory for Conversations". *Discourse Processes* 7.321-336.

Hockett, C. F. 1963. "The Problem of Universals in Language". *Universals of Language* ed. by J. Greenberg, pp. 1-29. Cambridge, MA: MIT Press. (2nd ed., 1966.)

Hockett, C. F. & R. Ascher. 1964. "The Human Revolution". *Current Anthropology* 5.135-168.

Hoffman, R. R. & R. P. Honeck. 1980. "A Peacock Looks at its Legs: Cognitive science and figurative language". *Cognition and figurative language* ed. by R. P. Honeck & R. R. Hoffman, 3-24. Hillsdale, NJ: Erlbaum.

Hogaboam, T. W. & C. A. Perfetti. 1975. "Lexical Ambiguity and Sentence Comprehension". *Journal of Verbal Learning and Verbal Behavior* 14.265-274.

Holland, M. K. & M. Wertheimer. 1964. "Some Physiognomic Aspects of Naming, or Maluma and Takete Revisited". *Perceptual and Motor Skills* 19.111-117.

Holmes, V. M., R. Arwas & M. F. Garrett. 1977. "Prior Context and the Perception of Lexically Ambiguous Sentences". *Memory and Cognition* 5.103-110.

Hoppe, R. A. & J. F. Kess. 1986. "Biasing Thematic Contexts for Ambiguous Sentences in a Dichotic Listening Experiment". *Journal of Psycholinguistic Research* 15:3.225-241.

Hormann, H. 1971. *Psycholinguistics: An introduction to research and theory*. New York: Springer-Verlag. (2nd revised ed., 1979.)

Hornby, P. A. 1972. "The Psychological Subject and Predicate". *Cognitive Psychology* 3.632-642.

Householder, F. W. 1961. "On Linguistic Primes". *Psycholinguistics: A book of readings* ed. by S. Saporta, 15-25. New York: Holt, Rinehart & Winston.

Hymes, D. Ed. 1964. *Language in Culture and Society: A reader in linguistics and anthropology*. New York: Harper & Row.

Ingram, D. 1976. "Current Issues in Child Phonology". *Normal and Deficient Child Language* ed. by D. M. Morehead & A. E. Morehead, 3-27. Baltimore: University Park Press.

Jackendoff, R. 1972. *Semantic Interpretation in Generative Grammar*. Cambridge, MA: MIT Press.

Jackendoff, R. 1977. *X-Bar Syntax: A study of phrase structure*. Cambridge, MA: MIT Press.

Jackendoff, R. 1983. *Semantics and Cognition*. Cambridge, MA: MIT Press.

Jaeger, J. J. 1984. "Assessing the Psychological Status of the Vowel Shift Rule". *Journal of Psycholinguistic Research* 13.13-36.

Jakobson, R. 1941. *Kindersprache, Aphasie, und allgemeine Lautgesetze*. Uppsala Universitets Aarsskrift. (Translated as *Child Language, Aphasia, and Phonological Universals*. 1968. The Hague: Mouton.

James, D. 1974. *The Syntax and Semantics of Some English Interjections. University of Michigan Papers in Linguistics*. 1:3.

Jenkins, J. J., W. A. Russell & G. J. Suci. 1958. "An Atlas of Semantic Profiles for 360 Words". *American Journal of Psychology* 71.688-699.

Jespersen, O. 1922. *Language: Its nature, development, and origin*. New York: Holt.

Johnson, M. K., J. D. Bransford & S. Solomon. 1973. "Memory for Tacit Implications of Sentences". *Journal of Experimental Psychology* 98.203-205.

Johnson, N. 1965. "The Psychological Reality of Phrase Structure Rules". *Journal of Verbal Learning and Verbal Behavior* 4.469-475.

Johnson, N. 1966. "On the Relationship between Sentence Structure and the Latency in Generating the Sentence". *Journal of Verbal Learning and Verbal Behavior* 5.375-380.

Johnson-Laird, P. N. 1974. "Experimental Psycholinguistics". *Annual Review of Psychology* 25.135-160.

Johnson-Laird, P. N. 1980. "Mental Models in Cognitive Science". *Cognitive Science* 4.71-115.

Johnson-Laird, P. N. 1981. "Mental Models of Meaning". *Elements of Discourse Understanding* ed. by A. K. Joshi, B. L. Webber & I. Sag, 106-126. Cambridge: Cambridge Univ. Press.

Johnson-Laird, P. N. 1983. *Mental Models*. Cambridge, MA: Harvard Univ. Press.

Johnson-Laird, P. N. 1986. "Reasoning without Logic". *Reasoning and Discourse Processes* ed. by T. Myers, K. Brown & B. McGonigle, 13-50. London: Academic Press.

Johnson-Laird, P. N. 1987. "The Mental Representation of the Meaning of Words". *Cognition* 25.189-211.

Johnson-Laird, P. N. & J. M. Tridgell. 1972. "When Negation Is Easier than Affirmation". *Quarterly Journal of Experimental Psychology* 24.87-91.

Jorgensen, C. C. & W. Kintsch. 1973. "The Role of Imagery in the Evaluation of Sentences". *Cognitive Psychology* 4.110-116.

Jusczyk, P. W. & J. Bertoncini. 1988. "Viewing the Development of Speech Perception as an Innately Guided Learning Process". *Language and Speech* 31.217-237.

Just, M. A. & H. H. Clark. 1973. "Drawing Inferences for the Presuppositions and Implications of Affirmative and Negative Sentences". *Journal of Verbal Learning and Verbal Behavior* 12.21-31.

Kaplan, R. M. & J. Bresnan. 1982. "Lexical-functional Grammar: A formal system for grammatical representation". *The Mental Representation of Grammatical Relations* ed. by J. Bresnan, 173-281. Cambridge, MA: MIT Press.

Kasher, A. 1985. "Philosophy and Discourse Analysis". *Handbook of Discourse Analysis* ed. by T. A. van Dijk, vol. 1 (*Disciplines of discourse*), 231-248. Orlando: Academic Press.

Katz, B., G. Baker & J. Macnamara. 1974. "What's in a Name? On the child's acquisition of proper and common nouns". *Child Development* 45.269-273.

Katz, J. J. 1966. *The Philosophy of Language*. New York: Harper & Row.

Katz, J. J. & J. A. Fodor. 1963. "The Structure of a Semantic Theory". *Language* 39.170-210.

Katz, J. J. & P. Postal. 1964. *An Integrated Theory of Linguistic Descriptions*. Cambridge, MA: MIT Press.

Katz, L., S. Boyce, L. Goldstein & G. Lukatela, G. 1987. "Grammatical Information Effects in Auditory Word Recognition". *Cognition* 25.235-263.

Kay, P. 1975. "Synchronic Variability and Diachronic Change in Basic Color Terms". *Language in Society* 4.257-270.

Kay, P. & W. Kempton. 1984. "What is the Sapir-Whorf Hypothesis?". *American Anthropologist* 86.65-79.

Kay, P. & C. K. McDaniel. 1978. "The Linguistic Significance of the Meanings of Basic Color Terms". *Language* 54.610-646.

Kearney, M. 1984. *World View*. Novato: Chandler & Sharp.

Keenan, J. M., B. MacWhinney & D. Mayhew. 1977. "Pragmatics in Memory: A study of natural conversation". *Journal of Verbal Learning and Verbal Behavior* 16.549-560.

Keller, E. 1981. "Gambits: Conversational strategy signals". *Conversational Routine* ed. by F. Coulmas, 93-114. The Hague: Mouton.

Kemper, S. & D. Thissen. 1981. "Memory for the Dimensions of Requests". *Journal of Verbal Learning and Verbal Behavior* 20.552-563.

Kent, R. D. & H. R. Bauer. 1985. "Vocalizations of One-year-olds". *Journal of Child Language* 12.491-526.

Kess, J. F. 1976a. Review of Fodor, Bever & Garrett (1974). *Canadian Journal of Linguistics* 21.126-131.

Kess, J. F. 1976b. "Reversing Directions in Psycholinguistics". *Language Sciences* 42.1-5.

Kess, J. F. 1976c. *Psycholinguistics: Introductory perspectives.* New York: Academic Press.

Kess, J. F. 1979. "A Psycholinguistic Frame of Reference for Focus and Topic in Philippine Languages". *Proceedings of the Second International Conference on Austronesian Linguistics* ed. by S. A. Wurm & L. Carrington, fasc.1 (*Western Austronesian*), 443-461. (*Pacific Linguistics.* Series C-61.)

Kess, J. F. 1981. Review of Halle, Bresnan & Miller (1978). *Language Sciences* 3.193-200.

Kess, J. F. 1982. "Theme versus Context". *Journal of the Atlantic Provinces Linguistic Association* 4.54-62.

Kess, J. F. 1983. "The Wundtian Origins of Early Bloomfieldian Psycholinguistics". Introduction to *An Introduction to the Study of Language.* (= *Classics in Psycholinguistics,* 3.) by Leonard Bloomfield, xvii-xxxviii. Amsterdam & Philadelphia: John Benjamins.

Kess, J. F. 1985. *Psycholinguistic Principles Applicable to the Formulation of Jury Instructions: An annotated bibliography.* Toronto: Canadian Law Information Council.

Kess, J. F. 1986. Review article of van Dijk (1985). *Canadian Journal of Linguistics* 31.386-396.

Kess, J. F. 1989. "The Structuring of Inferential Processes in Oral Documentation". *Thinking across Cultures* ed. by D. M. Topping, D. C. Crowell & V. N. Kobayashi, 135-146. Hillsdale, NJ: Lawrence Erlbaum Associates.

Kess, J. F. 1990. "On the Developing History of Psycholinguistics". *Language Sciences* 13:1.1-20.

Kess, J. F. 1991a. Review of Carlson & Tanenhaus (1989a). *Language* 67.3.

Kess, J. F. 1991b. Review of Marslen-Wilson (1989a). *Language* 67.4.

Kess, J. F. & R. A. Hoppe. 1981a. *Ambiguity in Psycholinguistics.* Amsterdam: John Benjamins.

Kess, J. F. & R. A. Hoppe. 1981b. "The Effect of Bias on Ambiguity Detection in the Presence of Context". *International Journal of Psycholinguistics* 8.137-152.

Kess, J. F. & R. A. Hoppe. 1983a. "Individual Differences and Metalinguistic Abilities". *Canadian Journal of Linguistics* 28.47-53.

Kess, J. F. & R. A. Hoppe. 1983b. "The Interaction of Bias and Context in Ambiguity Detection". *Proceedings of the XIIIth International Congress of Linguists* ed. by S. Hattori & K. Inoue, 776-778. Tokyo.

Kess, J. F. & R. A. Hoppe. 1985. "Bias, Individual Differences, and Shared Knowledge in Ambiguity". *Journal of Pragmatics* 9.21-39.

Kess, J. F. & R. A. Hoppe. 1989. "Pragmatic Constraints on Ambiguous Text". *Pragmatics at Issue: Selected papers from the 1987 International Pragmatics Conference,* Part II. Amsterdam: John Benjamins B.V.

Kess, J. F. & A. C. Kess. 1986. "On Nootka Baby Talk". *International Journal of American Linguistics* 52.201-211.

Kim, K. O. 1977. "Sound Symbolism in Korean". *Journal of Linguistics* 13.67-75.

Kimura, D. 1985. "The Origin of Human Communication". *Cognitive Science Memorandum No. 19*, Centre for Cognitive Science, Univ. of Western Ontario.

Kintsch, W., ed. 1974. *The Representation of Meaning in Memory*. Hillsdale, NJ: Lawrence Erlbaum Associates.

Kintsch, W. 1977. "On Comprehending Stories". *Cognitive Processes in Comprehension* ed. by M. A. Just & P. Carpenter, 32-62. Hillsdale, NJ: Lawrence Erlbaum Associates.

Kintsch, W. & G. Glass. 1974. "Effects of Propositional Structure upon Sentence Recall". *The Representation of Meaning in Memory* ed. by W. Kintsch, 140-150. Hillsdale, NJ: Lawrence Erlbaum Associates.

Kintsch, W. & J. M. Keenan. 1973. "Reading Rate and Retention as a Function of the Number of Propositions in the Base Structure of Sentences". *Cognitive Psychology* 5.257-274.

Kintsch, W. & T. A. van Dijk. 1978. "Toward a Model of Text Comprehension and Production". *Psychological Review* 85.363-394.

Kohn, S. E., A. Wingfield, L. Menn, H. Goodglass, J. B. Gleason & M. Hyde. 1987. "Lexical Retrieval: The tip-of-the-tongue phenomenon". *Applied Psycholinguistics* 8.245-266.

Koivukari, A. M. 1987. "Question Level and Cognitive Processing: Psycholinguistic dimensions of questions and answers". *Applied Psycholinguistics* 8.101-120.

Krauthamer, H. 1981. "The Prediction of Passive Occurrence". *Linguistics* 19:307-324.

Kuczaj, S. A. 1977. "The Acquisition of Regular and Irregular Past Tense Forms". *Journal of Verbal Learning and Verbal Behavior* 16.589-600.

Kuczaj, S. A. 1978. "Children's Judgement of Grammatical and Ungrammatical Past Tense Forms". *Child Development* 49.319-326.

Kuczaj, S. A. & A. R. Lederberg. 1977. "Height, Age, and Function: Differing influences on children's comprehension of 'younger' and 'older'". *Journal of Child Language* 4.395-416.

Kuhn, T. S. 1962. *The Structure of Scientific Revolutions*. Chicago: Univ. of Chicago Press. (2nd ed., 1970.)

Kurtzman, H. S. 1985. *Studies in Syntactic Ambiguity Resolution*. Bloomington: Indiana Univ. Linguistics Club.

Lackner, J. R. & M. F. Garrett. 1972. "Resolving Ambiguity: Effects of biasing context in the unattended ear". *Cognition* 1.359-372.

Ladefoged, P., J. De Clerk, M. Lindau & G. Papcun. 1972. "An Auditory-motor Theory of Speech Production". *U.C.L.A. Working Papers in Linguistics* 22.48-75.

Ladusaw, W. A. 1988. "Semantic Theory". *Linguistics: The Cambridge survey* ed. by F. J. Newmeyer, vol. I (*Linguistic Theory: Foundations*), 89-112. Cambridge: Cambridge Univ. Press.

Lakoff, G. 1971. "On Generative Semantics". *Semantics: An interdisciplinary reader in philosophy, linguistics, and psychology* ed. by D. D. Steinberg & L. A. Jakobovits, 232-296. New York: Cambridge Univ. Press.

Lakoff, G. 1987. *Women, Fire, and Dangerous Things: What categories reveal about the mind*. Chicago: Univ. of Chicago Press.

Lakoff, G. & M. Johnson. 1980. *Metaphors we Live by*. Chicago: Univ. of Chicago Press.

Lakoff, R. 1973. "The Logic of Politeness". *Papers from the Ninth Regional Meeting of the Chicago Linguistic Society* ed. by C. Corum et al., 292-305. Chicago: Chicago Linguistic Society.

Lane, H. 1976. *The Wild Boy of Aveyron*. Cambridge, MA: Harvard Univ. Press.

Langacker, R. W. 1986. "An Introduction to Cognitive Grammar". *Cognitive Science* 10.1-40.

Langacker, R. W. 1987. *Foundations of Cognitive Grammar*. Stanford: Stanford Univ. Press.

Langendoen, D. T. 1969. *The Study of Syntax: The generative-transformational approach to the structure of American English*. New York: Holt, Rinehart & Winston.

Lashley, K. S. 1951. "The Problem of Serial Order in Behavior". *Cerebral Mechanisms in Behavior* ed. by L. A. Jeffress, 112-136. New York: John Wiley & Sons.

Leech, G. N. 1977. "Language and Tact". *L. A. U. T.* Paper No. 46. (Trier.)

Lees, R. B. 1957. Review of Chomsky (1957). *Language* 33.375-408.

Lenneberg, E. H. 1964. "The Capacity for Language Acquisition". *The Structure of Language* ed. by J. A. Fodor & J. J. Katz, 579-603. Englewood Cliffs, NJ: Prentice-Hall.

Lenneberg, E. H. 1967. *Biological Foundations of Language*. New York: John Wiley & Sons.

Lenneberg, E. H. 1969. "On Explaining Language". *Science* 164.635-643.

Lenneberg, E. H. & J. R. Roberts. 1956. "The Language of Experience: A study in methodology". *International Journal of American Linguistics*, Memoir No. 13.

Levelt, W. J. M. 1983. "Monitoring and Self-repair in Speech". *Cognition* 14.41-104.

Levin, H., C. Snow & K. Lee. 1984. "Nurturant Talk to Children". *Language and Speech* 27.147-162.

Li, C. N. & S. A. Thompson. 1977. "The Acquisition of Tone in Mandarin-speaking Children". *Journal of Child Language* 4.185-199.

Liberman, A. M. 1970. "The Grammars of Speech and Language". *Cognitive Psychology* 1.301-323.

Liberman, A. M., F. S. Cooper, D. P. Shankweiler & M. G. Studdert-Kennedy. 1967. " Perception of the Speech Code". *Psychological Review* 74.431-461.

Liberman, A. M. & I. G. Mattingly. 1985. "The Motor Theory of Speech Perception Revisited". *Cognition* 21.1-36.

Lieberman, P. 1975. *On the Origins of Language*. New York: Macmillan.

Lieberman, P. 1984. *On Biology and Evolution of Language*. Cambridge, MA: Harvard Univ. Press.

Lightfoot, D. 1982. *The Language Lottery: Toward a biology of grammars*. Cambridge, MA: MIT Press.

Lima, S. D. 1987. "Morphological Analysis in Sentence Reading". *Journal of Memory and Language* 26.84-99.

Linebarger, M. C. 1989. "Neuropsychological Evidence for Linguistic Modularity". *Linguistic Structure in Language Processing* ed. by G. N. Carlson & M. K. Tanenhaus. Dordrecht: Kluwer Academic Publishers. pp. 197-238.

Loftus, E. F. & J. C. Palmer. 1974. "Reconstruction of Automobile Destruction: An example of the interaction between language and memory". *Journal of Verbal Learning and Verbal Behavior* 13.585-589.

Loftus, G. R. & E. F. Loftus. 1976. *Human Memory: The processing of information.* Hillsdale, NJ: Lawrence Erlbaum Associates.

Lounsbury, F. G. 1956. "A Semantic Analysis of the Pawnee Kinship Usage". *Language* 32.158-194.

Lucy, J. A. & J. V. Wertsch. 1987. "Vygotsky and Whorf: A comparative analysis". *Social and Functional Approaches to Language and Thought* ed. by M. Hickmann, 67-86. Orlando: Academic Press.

Lukatela, G., B. Gligorjevic, A. Kostic & M. T. Turvey. 1980. "Representation of Inflected Nouns in the Internal Lexicon". *Memory and Cognition* 8.415-423.

Lupker, S. J. 1984. "Semantic Priming without Association: A second look". *Journal of Verbal Learning and Verbal Behavior* 23.709-733.

Luria, A. R. 1976. *Cognitive Development.* Cambridge, MA: Harvard Univ. Press.

MacKay, D. G. 1966. "To End Ambiguous Sentences". *Perception and Psychophysics* 1.426-436.

MacKay, D. G. 1972. "The Structure of Words and Syllables: Evidence from errors in speech". *Cognitive Psychology* 3.210-227.

MacKay, D. G. 1978. "Derivational Rules and the Internal Lexicon". *Journal of Verbal Learning and Verbal Behavior* 17.61-71.

MacKay, D. G. 1979. "Lexical Insertion, Inflection, and Derivation: Creative processes in word production". *Journal of Psycholinguistic Research* 8.477-498.

MacKay, D. G. & T. G. Bever. 1967. "In Search of Ambiguity". *Perception and Psychophysics* 2.103-200.

Maclay, H. 1958. "An Experimental Study of Language and Non-linguistic Behavior". *Southwestern Journal of Anthropology* 14.220-229.

Maclay, H. 1973. "Linguistics and Psycholinguistics". *Issues in Linguistics* ed. by B. Kachru, 569-587. Urbana: Univ. of Illinois Press.

Maclay, H. & C. E. Osgood. 1959. "Hesitation Phenomena in Spontaneous English Speech". *Word* 15.19-44.

Macnamara, J. 1972. "Cognitive Basis of Language Learning in Infants". *Psychological Review* 79.1-13.

B. MacWhinney. 1987. "The Competition Model". *Mechanisms of Language Acquisition* ed. by B. MacWhinney, 249-308. Hillsdale, NJ: Erlbaum.

Malt, B. C. & E. E. Smith. 1984. "Correlated Properties in Natural Categories". *Journal of Verbal Learning and Verbal Behavior* 23.250-269.

Mandler, J. M. 1984. *Stories, Scripts, and Scenes: Aspects of schema theory.* Hillsdale, NJ: Lawrence Erlbaum Associates.

Mandler, J. M. 1986. "On the Comprehension of Temporal Order". *Language and Cognitive Processes* 1.309-320.

Mandler, J. M. & M. S. Goodman. 1982. "On the Psychological Validity of Story Structure". *Journal of Verbal Learning and Verbal Behavior* 21.507-523.

Manes, J. & N. Wolfson. 1981. "The Compliment Formula". *Conversational Routine* ed. by F. Coulmas, 115-132. The Hague: Mouton.

Maratsos, M. P., S. A. Kuczaj, D. E. C. Fox & M. A. Chalkley. 1979. "Some Empirical Studies in the Acquisition of Transformational Relations: Passives, Negatives, and the Past Tense". *Children's Language and Communication* ed. by W. A. Collins, 1-45. Hillsdale, NJ: Lawrence Erlbaum Associates.

Markman, E. M. & G. F. Wachtel. 1988. "Children's Use of Mutual Exclusivity to Constrain the Meanings of Words". *Cognitive Psychology* 20.121-157.

Marschark, M. 1985. "Imagery and Organization in the Recall of Prose". *Journal of Memory and Language* 24.734-745.

Marschark, M., C. L. Richman, J. C. Yuille & R. R. Hunt. 1987. "The Role of Imagery in Memory: On shared and distinctive information". *Psychological Bulletin* 102.28-41.

Marshall, J. C. 1980. "On the Biology of Language Acquisition". *Biological Studies of Mental Processes* ed. by D. Caplan, 106-148. Cambridge, MA: MIT Press.

Marslen-Wilson, W., ed. 1989a. *Lexical Representation and Process*. Cambridge, MA: MIT Press.

Marslen-Wilson, W. 1989b. "Access and Integration: Projecting sound onto meaning". *Lexical Representation and Process* ed. by W. Marslen-Wilson, 3-24. Cambridge, MA: MIT Press.

McCauley, R. N. 1987. "The Not so Happy Story of the Marriage of Linguistics and Psychology or Why Linguistics Has Discouraged Psychology's Recent Advances". *Synthese* 72.341-353.

McCawley, J. D. 1970. "Semantic Components in Complex Verbs". Calgary: Univ. of Calgary Symposium on Trends in Linguistics.

McCawley, J. D. 1973. *Grammar and Meaning*. Tokyo: Taishukan.

McCawley, J. D. 1982. *Thirty Million Theories of Grammar*. London: Croom Helm.

McCloskey, M. 1980. "The Stimulus Familiarity Problem in Semantic Memory Research". *Journal of Verbal Learning and Verbal Behavior* 19.485-502.

McGonigle, B. & M. Chalmers. 1986. "Representations and Strategies during Inference". *Reasoning and Discourse Processes* T. Myers, K. Brown & B. McGonigle, 141-164. London: Academic Press.

McKoon, G. & R. Ratcliff. 1981. "The Comprehension Processes and Memory Structures Involved in Instrumental Inference". *Journal of Verbal Learning and Verbal Behavior* 20.671-682.

McNeill, D. 1964. "Developmental Psycholinguistics". *New Directions in the Study of Language* ed. by E. H. Lenneberg, 15-84. Cambridge, MA: MIT Press.

McNeill, D. 1970. *The Acquisition of Language*. New York: Harper.

Mehler, J., J. Segui & P. Carey. 1978. "Tails of Words: Monitoring ambiguity". *Journal of Verbal Learning and Verbal Behavior* 17.29-35.

Mervis, C. B. & E. M. Roth. 1981. "The Internal Structure of Basic and Non-basic Color Categories". *Language* 57.384-405.

Meyer, D. E. & P. C. Gordon. 1984. "Dependencies between Rapid Speech Perception and Production: Evidence for a shared sensory-motor voicing mechanism". *Attention and Performance X* ed. by H. Bouma & D. G. Bouwhuis, 265-377. Hillsdale, NJ: Lawrence Erlbaum Associates.

Meyer, D. E. & P. C. Gordon. 1985. "Speech Production: Motor programming of phonetic features". *Journal of Memory and Language* 24.3-26.

Miller, G. A. 1956. "The Magical Number Seven, Plus or Minus Two: Some limits on our capacity for processing information". *Psychological Review* 63.81-97.

Miller, G. A. 1962. "Some Psychological Studies of Grammar". *American Psychologist* 17.748-762.

Miller, G. A. 1964a. "The Psycholinguists". *Encounter* 23.29-37.

Miller, G. A. 1964b. "Language and Psychology". *New Directions in the Study of Language* ed. by E. H. Lenneberg, 89-108. Cambridge, MA: MIT Press.

Miller, G. A. 1967. "Psycholinguistic Approaches to the Study of Communication". *Journeys in Science* ed. by D. L. Arm, 22-73. Albuquerque: Univ. of New Mexico Press.

Miller, G. A., G. Heise & W. Lichten. 1951. "The Intelligibility of Speech as a Function of the Context of the Test Materials". *Journal of Experimental Psychology* 41.329-335.

Miller, G. A. & S. Isard. 1963. "Some Perceptual Consequences of Linguistic Rules". *Journal of Verbal Learning and Verbal Behavior* 2.217-228.

Miller, G. A. & P. N. Johnson-Laird. 1976. *Perception and Language.* Cambridge: Cambridge Univ. Press.

Miller, G. A. & P. E. Nicely. 1955. "Analysis of Perceptual Confusions among some English Consonants". *Journal of the Acoustical Society of America* 27.338-353.

Mines, M. A., B. F. Hanson & J. E. Shoup. 1978. "Frequency of Occurrence of Phonemes in Conversational English". *Language and Speech* 21.221-241.

Moeser, S. D. 1974. "Memory for Meaning and Wording in Concrete and Abstract Sentences". *Journal of Verbal Learning and Verbal Behavior* 13.682-697.

Moore, T. 1986. "Reasoning and Inference in Logic and in Language". *Reasoning and Discourse Processes* ed. by T. Myers, K. Brown & B. McGonigle, 51-66. London: Academic Press.

Morgan, J. L. 1982. "Discourse Theory and the Independence of Sentence Grammar". *Analyzing Discourse: Text and talk* ed. by D. Tannen, 198-204. Washington, D.C.: Georgetown Univ. Press.

Morris, C. W. 1938. "Foundations of the Theory of Signs". *International Encyclopedia of Unified Science* 12.77-137.

Morrow, D. G. 1986. "Grammatical Morphemes and Conceptual Structure in Discourse Processing". *Cognitive Science* 10.423-455.

Morton, J. 1979. "Word Recognition". *Psycholinguistics 2: Structure and process* ed. by J. Morton & J. C. Marshall, 107-156. Cambridge, MA: MIT Press.

Moskowitz, B. A. 1973. "On the Status of Vowel Shift in English". *Cognitive Development and the Acquisition of Language* ed. by T. E. Moore, 223-260. New York: Academic Press.

Moskowitz, B. A. 1978. "The Acquisition of Language". *Scientific American* 239.92-108.

Motley, M. T. 1985. "Slips of the Tongue". *Scientific American* 253.116-126.

Neisser, U. 1967. *Cognitive Psychology.* New York: Appleton.

Nelson, K. 1973. "Structure and Strategy in Learning to Talk". *Monographs of the Society for Research in Child Development* 38:149.1-135.

Nelson, K. 1974. "Concept, Word, and Sentence: Inter-relations in Acquisition and Development". *Psychological Review* 81.267-285.

Nelson, K. 1975. "Individual Differences in Early Semantic and Syntactic Development". *Annals of the New York Academy of Sciences* 263.132-139.

Nelson, K. 1976. "Some Attributes of Adjectives Used by Young Children". *Cognition* 4.13-30.

Nelson, K. 1977. "The Syntagmatic-paradigmatic Shift Revisited: A review of research and theory". *Psychological Bulletin* 84.93-116.

Nelson, K. 1988. "Where do Taxonomic Categories Come From?". *Human Development* 31.3-10.

Newman, J. E. & G. S. Dell. 1978. "The Phonological Nature of Phoneme Monitoring: A critique of some ambiguity studies". *Journal of Verbal Learning and Verbal Behavior* 17.359-374.

Newmeyer, F. J. 1980. *Linguistic theory in America: The first quarter-century of transformational generative grammar.* New York: Academic Press. (2nd revised ed., 1986.)

Nichols, J. 1971. "Diminutive Consonant Symbolism in Western North America". *Language* 47.826-849.

Ninio, A. & C. E. Snow. 1988. "Language Acquisition through Language Use: The functional sources of children's early utterances". *Categories and Processes in Language Acquisition* ed. by Y. Levy, I. M. Schlesinger & M. D. S. Braine, 11-30. Hillsdale, NJ: Lawrence Erlbaum Associates.

Norris, D. & A. Cutler. 1988. "The Relative Accessibility of Phonemes and Syllables". *Perception and Psychophysics* 43.541-550.

Oden, G. C. 1978. "Semantic Constraints and Judged Preference for Interpretations of Ambiguous Sentences". *Memory and Cognition* 6.26-37.

Oden, G. C. 1987. "Concept, Knowledge, and Thought". *Annual Review of Psychology* 38.203-227.

Ogden, C. K. & I. A. Richards. 1923. *The Meaning of Meaning.* London: Routledge & Kegan Paul.

Oller, D. K., L. A. Wieman, W. J. Doyle & C. Ross. 1976. "Infant Babbling and Speech". *Journal of Child Language* 3.1-11.

Olson, D. R. & N. Filby. 1972. "On the Comprehension of Active and Passive Sentences". *Cognitive Psychology* 3.361-381.

Olson, D. R., N. Torrance & A. Hildyard, eds. 1985. *Literacy, Language and Learning: The nature and consequences of reading and writing.* Cambridge: Cambridge Univ. Press.

Olson, J. N. & D. G. MacKay. 1974. "Completion and Verification of Ambiguous Sentences". *Journal of Verbal Learning and Verbal Behavior* 13.457-470.

Ong, W. J. 1982. *Orality versus Literacy: The technologizing of the word.* New York: Methuen.

Onifer, W. & D. A. Swinney. 1981. "Accessing Lexical Ambiguities during Sentence Comprehension: Effects of frequency of meaning and contextual bias". *Memory and Cognition* 9.225-236.

Ortony, A. 1979. "Beyond Literal Similarity". *Psychological Review* 86.161-180.

Ortony, A., R. J. Vondruska, M. A. Foss & L. E. Jones. 1985. "Salience, Similes, and the Assymetry of Similarity". *Journal of Memory and Language* 24.569-594.

Osgood, C. E. 1964. "Semantic Differential Technique in the Comparative Study of Cultures". *American Anthropologist* 66.171-200.

Osgood, C. E. & T. A. Sebeok. 1954. *Psycholinguistics: A survey of theory and research problems.* Indiana Univ. Publications in Anthropology and Linguistics, Memoir 10.

Osgood, C. E., G. Suci & P. Tannenbaum. 1957. *The Measurement of Meaning.* Urbana: Univ. of Illinois Press.

O'Sullivan, C. & C. P. Yeager. 1989. "Communicative Context and Linguistic Competence: The effects of social setting on a chimpanzee's conversational skill". *Teaching Sign Language to Chimpanzees* ed. by R. A. Gardner, B. T. Gardner & T. E. Van Cantfort, 269-279. Buffalo: SUNY Press.

Paivio, A. 1971. *Imagery and Verbal Processes.* Toronto: Holt, Rinehart & Winston.

Paivio, A. 1986. *Mental Representations: A dual coding approach.* Oxford: Oxford Univ. Press.

Palermo, D. S. 1973. "More about Less: A study of language comprehension". *Journal of Verbal Learning and Verbal Behavior* 12.211-221.

Parker, S. & K. Gibson, eds. 1990. *"Language" and Intelligence in Monkeys and Apes: Comparative developmental perspectives.* Cambridge: Cambridge Univ. Press.

Pereira, F. C. 1985. "A New Characterization of Attachment Preferences". *Natural Language Parsing* ed. by D. R. Dowty, L. Karttunen & A. M. Zwicky, 307-319. Cambridge: Cambridge Univ. Press.

Perfetti, C. A. 1972. "Psychosemantics: Some cognitive aspects of structural meaning". *Psychological Bulletin* 78.241-259.

Perfetti, C. A., S. Beverly, L. Bell, K. Rodgers & R. Faux. 1987. "Comprehending Newspaper Headlines". *Journal of Memory and Language* 26.692-713.

Perfetti, C. A. & D. Goodman. 1970. "Semantic Constraints on the Decoding of Ambiguous Words". *Journal of Experimental Psychology* 86.420-427.

Perlmutter, D. 1980. "Relational Grammar". *Syntax and Semantics 13: Current approaches to syntax* ed. by E. Moravcsik & J. Wirth, 195-229. New York: Academic Press.

Perrig, W. & W. Kintsch. 1985. "Propositional and Situational Representations of Text". *Journal of Memory and Language* 24.503-518.

Piaget, J. 1979. "Relations between Psychology and Other Sciences". *Annual Review of Psychology* 30.1-8.

Piaget, J. & B. Inhelder. 1958. *The Growth of Logical Thinking from Childhood to Adolescence*. New York: Basic Books.

Piaget, J. & B. Inhelder. 1969. *The Psychology of the Child*. London: Routledge.

Pike, K. L. 1964. "Towards a Theory of the Structure of Human Behavior". *Language in Culture and Society: A reader in linguistics and anthropology* ed. by D. Hymes, 54-62. New York: Harper & Row.

Pike, K. L. 1967. *Language in Relation to a Unified Theory of the Structure of Human Behavior*. The Hague: Mouton. (2nd ed.)

Pinker, S. 1984. *Language Learnability and Language Development*. Cambridge, MA: Harvard Univ. Press.

Pisoni, D. B. 1985. "Speech Perception: Some new directions in research and theory". *Journal of the Acoustical Society of America* 78.381-388.

Pitts, M. K., M. K. Smith & H. R. Pollio. 1982. "An Evaluation of Three Different Theories of Metaphor Production through the Use of an Intentional Category Mistake Procedure". *Journal of Psycholinguistic Research* 114.347-368.

Pollack, I. & J. M. Pickett. 1964. "Intelligibility of Excerpts from Fluent Speech: Auditory versus structural content". *Journal of Verbal Learning and Verbal Behavior* 3.79-84.

Pollio, H. R., J. M. Barlow, H. J. Fine & M. R. Pollio. 1977. *Psychology and the Poetics of Growth: Figurative language in psychology, psychotherapy, and education*. Hillsdale, NJ: Erlbaum.

Premack, D. 1976. *Intelligence in Ape and Man*. Hillsdale, NJ: Lawrence Erlbaum Associates.

Prideaux, G. D., ed. 1979. *Perspectives in Experimental Linguistics*. Amsterdam: John Benjamins B.V.

Prideaux, G. D. 1985. *Psycholinguistics: The experimental study of language*. New York: Guilford Press.

Prideaux, G. D., B. Derwing & W. J. Baker, eds. 1980. *Experimental Linguistics: Integration of theories and applications*. Ghent: E. Story-Scientia.

Pritchett, B. L. 1988. "Garden Path Phenomena and the Grammatical Basis of Language Processing". *Language* 64.539-576.

Rakerd, B. & R. R. Verbrugge. 1987. "Evidence that the Dynamic Information for Vowels Is Talker Independent in Form". *Journal of Memory and Language* 26.558-563.

Randall, J. H. 1980. "-*ity*: A study in word formation restrictions". *Journal of Psycholinguistic Research* 9.523-534.

Ratner, N. B. 1985. "Atypical Language Development". *The Development of Language* ed. by J. B. Gleason, 369-406. Columbus: Merrill. (2nd ed., 1989.)

Rayner, K., M. Carlson & L. Frazier. 1983. "The Interaction of Syntax and Semantics during Sentence Processing: Eye movements in the analysis of semantically biased sentences". *Journal of Verbal Learning and Verbal Behavior* 22.358-374.

Reber, A. S. 1973. "On Psycho-linguistic Paradigms". *Journal of Psycholinguistic Research* 2.289-319.

Reber, A. S. 1987. "The Rise and Surprisingly Rapid Fall of Psycholinguistics". *Synthese* 72.325-339.

Reiser, B. J. & J. B. Black. 1982. "Processing and Structural Models of Comprehension". *Text* 2.225-252.

Repp, B. H. 1988. "Integration and Segregation in Speech Perception". *Language and Speech* 31.239-271.

Rescorla, L. A. 1980. "Overextension in Early Language Development". *Journal of Child Language* 7.321-335.

Rieber, R. W. & G. Voyat. 1981. "An Overview of the Controversial Issues in the Psychology of Language and Thought". *Journal of Psycholinguistic Research* 10.341-361.

Rips, L. J., E. J. Shoben & E. E. Smith. 1973. "Semantic Distance and the Verification of Semantic Relations". *Journal of Verbal Learning and Verbal Behavior* 12.1-20.

Rosch, E. 1973. "On the Internal Structure of Perceptual and Semantic Categories". *Cognitive Development and the Acquisition of Language* ed. by T. E. Moore, 111-144. New York: Academic Press.

Rosch, E. 1975. "Cognitive Representations of Semantic Categories". *Journal of Experimental Psychology* 104.192-233.

Rosch, E. 1978. "Principles of Categorization". *Cognition and Categorization* ed. by E. Rosch & B. Lloyd, 27-48. Hillsdale, NJ: Lawrence Erlbaum Associates.

Rosch, E. & C. B. Mervis. 1975. "Family Resemblances: Studies in the internal structure of categories". *Cognitive Psychology* 7.573-605.

Roth, E. M. & C. B. Mervis. 1983. "Fuzzy Set Theory and Class Inclusion Relations in Semantic Categories". *Journal of Verbal Learning and Verbal Behavior* 22.509-525.

Rubenstein, H. & M. Aborn. 1960. "Psycholinguistics". *Annual Review of Psychology* 11.129-322.

Sachs, J. S. 1967. "Recognition Memory for Syntactic and Semantic Aspects of Connected Discourse". *Perception and Psychophysics* 2.437-442.

Sacks, H., E. A. Schegloff & G. Jefferson. 1974. "A Simplest Systematics for the Organization of Turn-taking for Conversation". *Language* 50.696-735.

Samuel, A. G. 1981. "Phonemic Restoration: Insights from a new methodology". *Journal of Experimental Psychology: General* 110.474-494.

Samuel, A. G. 1987. "Lexical Uniqueness Effects on Phonemic Restoration". *Journal of Memory and Language* 26.36-56.

Saporta, S., ed. 1961. *Psycholinguistics: A book of readings*. New York: Holt, Rinehart & Winston.

Savin, H. B. & T. G. Bever. 1970. "The Non-perceptual Reality of the Phoneme". *Journal of Verbal Learning and Verbal Behavior* 9.295-302.

Schank, R. 1980. "Language and Memory". *Cognitive Science* 4.243-284.

Schank, R. 1982. *Dynamic Memory*. Cambridge: Cambridge Univ. Press.

Schank, R. & R. P. Abelson. 1977. *Scripts, Plans, Goals, and Understanding*. Hillsdale, NJ: Lawrence Erlbaum Associates.

Schank, R. & M. Burstein. 1985. "Artificial Intelligence: Modelling memory for language understanding". *Handbook of Discourse Analysis* ed. by T. A. van Dijk, vol.1 (*Disciplines of discourse*), 145-166. Orlando: Academic Press.

Schegloff, E. A. 1968. "Sequencing in Conversational Closings". *American Anthropologist* 70.1075-1095.

Schegloff, E. A. & H. Sacks. 1973. "Opening up Closings". *Semiotica* 8.289-327.

Schiefelbusch, R. L. & J. Pickar. 1984. *The Acquisition of Communicative Competence*. Baltimore: University Park Press.

Schieffelin, B. & E. Ochs. 1986. "Language Socialization". *Annual Review of Anthropology* 15.163-191.

Schiffrin, D. 1988. "Conversation Analysis". *Linguistics: The Cambridge survey* ed. by F. J. Newmeyer, vol. IV (*Language: The socio-cultural context*), 251-276. Cambridge: Cambridge Univ. Press.

Schmidt, R. & J. F. Kess. 1986. *Television Advertising and Televangelism: Discourse analysis of persuasive language*. Amsterdam: John Benjamins.

Schneiderman, E. I. 1986. "Leaning to the Right: Some thoughts on hemisphere involvement in language acquisition". *Language Processing in Bilinguals: Psycholinguistic and neuropsychological perspectives* ed. by J. Vaid, 233-251. Hilldales, NJ: Lawrence Erlbaum Associates.

Schvaneveldt, R. W., D. E. Meyer & C. A. Becker. 1976. "Lexical Ambiguity, Semantic Context, and Visual Recognition". *Journal of Experimental Psychology: Human Perception and Performance* 22.243-256.

Scollon, R. 1976. *Conversations with a One-year-old: A case study of the developmental foundation of syntax*. Honolulu: Univ. of Hawaii Press.

Scovel, T. 1988. *A Time to Speak: A psycholinguistic inquiry into the critical period for human speech*. New York: Newbury House/Harper & Row.

Searle, J. R. 1969. *Speech Acts*. London: Cambridge Univ. Press.

Searle, J. R. 1975. "Indirect Speech Acts". *Syntax and Semantics: Speech acts* ed. by P. Cole & J. L. Morgan, 59-82. New York: Academic Press.

Searle, J. R. 1976. "A Classification of Illocutionary Acts". *Language in Society* 5.1-23.

Searle, J. R. 1977. "A Classification of Illocutionary Acts". *Proceedings of the Texas Conference on Performatives, Presuppositions, and Implicatures* ed. by A. Rogers, B. Wall & J. P. Murphy, 27-45. Arlington: Center for Applied Linguistics.

Sebeok, T. A., ed. 1974. *Current Trends in Linguistics* Vol. 12. The Hague: Mouton.

Sebeok, T. A. 1987. "Toward a Natural History of Language". *Semiotica* 65.343-358.

Seidenberg, M. S., M. K. Tanenhaus, J. M. Leiman & M. Bienkowski, 1982. "Automatic Access of the Meanings of Ambiguous Words in Context: Some limitations of knowledge-based processing". *Cognitive Psychology* 14.489-537.

Seidenberg, M. S., G. A. Waters, M. Sanders & P. Langer, 1984. "Pre- and Postlexical Loci of Contextual Effects and Word Recognition". *Memory and Cognition* 12.315-328.

Sells, P. 1985. *Lectures on Contemporary Syntactic Theories: An introduction to government-binding theory, generalized phrase structure grammar, and lexical-functional grammar*. Stanford: Center for the Study of Language and Information.

Sharkey, N. E. & A. J. C. Sharkey. 1987. "What Is the Point of Integration? The loci of knowledge-based facilitation in sentence processing". *Journal of Memory and Language* 26.255-276.

Shannon, C. E. & W. Weaver. 1949. *The Mathematical Theory of Communication.* Urbana: Univ. of Illinois Press.

Shuy, R. W. & D. L. Larkin. 1978. "Linguistic Considerations of the Simplification/ Clarification of Insurance Policy Language". *Discourse Processes* 1.305-321.

Shvachkin, N. K. 1948. "Razvitiye Fonematicheskogo Vospriyatiya Rechi v Rannem Vozraste". ["The Development of Phonemic Awareness of Speech in Early Childhood".] *Izvestiya Akademii Pedagogicheskih Nauk RSFSR* 13.101-132.

Simpson, G. B. 1981. "Meaning Dominance and Semantic Context in the Processing of Lexical Ambiguity". *Journal of Verbal Learning and Verbal Behavior* 20.120-136.

Sinclair, H. 1975. "The Role of Cognitive Structures in Language Acquisition". *Foundations of Language Development* ed. by E. H. Lenneberg & E. Lenneberg, vol.1, 223-237. New York: Academic Press.

Skinner, B. F. 1957. *Verbal Behavior.* New York: Appleton.

Slobin, D. I. 1963. *Grammatical Transformations in Childhood and Adulthood.* Unpublished doctoral dissertation, Harvard Univ..

Slobin, D. I. 1966. "Grammatical Transformations in Childhood and Adulthood". *Journal of Verbal Learning and Verbal Behavior* 5.219-227.

Slobin, D. I. 1967. *A Field Manual for Cross-cultural Study of the Acquisition of Communicative Competence.* Berkeley: Univ. of California Press.

Slobin, D. I. 1968. "Recall of Full and Truncated Passive Sentences in Connected Discourse". *Journal of Verbal Learning and Verbal Behavior* 7.876-881.

Slobin, D. I. 1970. "Universals of Grammatical Development in Children". *Advances in Psycholinguistic Research* ed. by G. B. Flores d'Arcais & W. J. M. Levelt, 174-186. Amsterdam: North-Holland.

Slobin, D. I. 1971. "Developmental Psycholinguistics". *A Survey of Linguistic Science* ed. by W. O. Dingwall, 267-316. College Park: Univ. of Maryland Press.

Slobin, D. I. 1973. "Cognitive Prerequisites for the Development of Grammar". *Studies of Child Language Development* ed. by C. A. Ferguson & D. I. Slobin, 175-208. New York: Holt, Rinehart & Winston.

Slobin, D. I. 1977. "Language Change in Childhood and in History". *Language Learning and Thought* ed. by J. Macnamara, 185-214. New York: Academic Press.

Slobin, D. I. 1982. "Universal and Particular in the Acquisition of Language". *Language Acquisition: State of the art* ed. by E. Wanner & L. Gleitman, 128-170. Cambridge: Cambridge Univ. Press.

Slobin, D. I., ed. 1985. *The Crosslinguistic Study of Language Acquisition.* 2 Volumes. Hillsdale, NJ: Lawrence Erlbaum Associates.

Smith, C. S. & A. van Kleeck. 1986. "Linguistic Complexity and Performance". *Journal of Child Language* 13.389-408.

Smith, E. E., E. J. Shoben & L. J. Rips. 1974. "Structure and Process in Semantic Memory: A featural model for semantic decisions". *Psychological Review* 81.214-241.

Smith, F. G. & G. A. Miller, eds. 1966. *The Genesis of Language: A psycholinguistic approach.* Cambridge, MA: MIT Press.

Smith, M. K., H. R. Pollio & M. K. Pitts. 1981. "Metaphor as Intellectual History: Conceptual categories underlying figurative usage in American English from 1676-1975". *Linguistics* 19.911-935.

Snider, J. & C. E. Osgood. 1968. *Semantic Differential Technique: A sourcebook*. Chicago: Aldine Press.

Snow, C. E. 1972. "Mothers' Speech to Children Learning Language". *Child Development* 43.549-565.

Snow, C. E. 1976. "The Development of Conversation between Mothers and Babies". *Journal of Child Language* 4.1-22.

Snow, C. E., A. Arlman-Rupp, Y. Hassing, J. Jobse, J. Joosten & J. Vorster. 1976. "Mother's Speech in Three Social Classes". *Journal of Psycholinguistic Research* 5:1.1-20.

Stanners, R. F., J. J. Neiser, W. P. Hernon & R. Hall. 1979. "Memory Representation for Morphologically Related Words". *Journal of Verbal Learning and Verbal Behavior* 18.399-412.

Steinberg, D. D. 1982. *Psycholinguistics: Language, mind, and world*. New York: Longman.

Stevens, K. N. 1972. "Segments, Features, and Analysis by Synthesis". *Language by Ear and by Eye* ed. by J. F. Kavanaugh & I. G. Mattingly, 47-52. Cambridge, MA: MIT Press.

Stillings, N. A., M. H. Feinstein, J. L. Garfield, E. L. Rissland, D. A. Rosenbaum, S. E. Weisler & L. Baker-Ward. 1987. *Cognitive Science: An introduction*. Cambridge, MA: MIT Press.

Stoel-Gammon, C. & J. A. Cooper. 1984. "Patterns of Early Lexical and Phonological Development". *Journal of Child Language* 11.247-271.

Stubbs, M. 1983. *Discourse Analysis*. Chicago: Univ. of Chicago Press.

Studdert-Kennedy, M. 1974. "The Perception of Speech". *Current Trends in Linguistics* ed. by T. A. Sebeok, vol.12, 15-48. The Hague: Mouton.

Studdert-Kennedy, M. 1976. "Speech Perception". *Contemporary Issues in Experimental Phonetics* ed. by N. J. Lass, 243-293. Springfield, IL: Charles C. Thomas.

Swinney, D. A. 1979. "Lexical Access during Sentence Comprehension: (Re)Consideration of context effects". *Journal of Verbal Learning and Verbal Behavior* 18.645-659.

Swinney, D. A. & D. T. Hakes. 1976. "Effects of Prior Context upon Lexical Access during Sentence Comprehension". *Journal of Verbal Learning and Verbal Behavior* 15.681-689.

Tannenbaum, P. H. & F. Williams. 1968. "Generation of Active and Passive Sentences as a Function of Subject or Object of Focus". *Journal of Verbal Learning and Verbal Behavior* 7.246-250.

Tanenhaus, M. K. & G. N. Carlson. 1989. "Lexical Structure and Language Comprehension". *Lexical Representation and Process* ed. by W. Marslen-Wilson, 529-561. Cambridge, MA: MIT Press.

Tanenhaus, M. K. & S. Donnenworth-Nolan. 1984. "Syntactic Context and Lexical Ambiguity". *Quarterly Journal of Experimental Psychology* 36A.649-661.

Tanenhaus, M. K., J. M. Leiman & M. S. Seidenberg. 1979. "Evidence for Multiple Stages in the Processing of Ambiguous Words in Syntactic Contexts". *Journal of Verbal Learning and Verbal Behavior* 18.427-440.

Taylor, I. K. 1969. "Content and Structure in Sentence Production". *Journal of Verbal Learning and Verbal Behavior* 8.170-175.

Taylor, I. K. & M. M. Taylor. 1962. "Phonetic Symbolism in Four Unrelated Languages". *Canadian Journal of Psychology* 16.344-356.

Taylor, I. K. & M. M. Taylor. 1965. "Another Look at Phonetic Symbolism". *Psychological Bulletin* 64.413-427.

Taylor, M. & S. A. Gelman. 1988. "Adjectives and Nouns: Children's strategies for learning new words". *Child Development* 59.411-419.

Terrace, H. S. 1980. *Nim: A chimpanzee who learned sign language.* New York: Knopf.

Thevenin, D. M., R. E. Eilers, D. K. Oller & L. Lavoie. 1985. "Where's the Drift in Babbling Drift? A cross-linguistic study". *Applied Psycholinguistics* 6.3-15.

Thorndyke, P. W. 1976. "The Role of Inferences in Discourse Comprehension". *Journal of Verbal Learning and Verbal Behavior* 15.437-446.

Thorndyke, P. W. 1977. "Cognitive Structures in Comprehension and Memory of Narrative Discourse". *Cognitive Psychology* 9.77-110.

Tucker, D. M. 1981. "Lateral Brain Function, Emotion, and Conceptualization". *Psychological Bulletin* 89.19-46.

Tyler, L. K. 1989. "The Role of Lexical Representations in Language Comprehension". *Lexical Representation and Process* ed. by W. Marslen-Wilson, 439-462. Cambridge, MA: MIT Press.

Tyler, L. K. & W. Marslen-Wilson. 1977. "The On-line Effects of Semantic Context on Syntactic Processing". *Journal of Verbal Learning and Verbal Behavior* 16.683-692.

Ullman, S. 1966. "Semantic Universals". *Universals of Language* ed. by J. Greenberg, 172-207. Cambridge: MIT Press.

van den Broek, P. 1988. "The Effects of Causal Relations and Hierarchical Position on the Importance of Story Statements". *Journal of Memory and Language* 27.1-22.

van Dijk, T. A. 1977a. *Text and Context: Explorations in the semantics and pragmatics of discourse.* London: Longman.

van Dijk, T. A. 1977b. "Context and Cognition: Knowledge frames and speech act comprehension". *Journal of Pragmatics* 1.211-232.

van Dijk, T. A. 1979. "Relevance Assignment in Discourse Comprehension". *Discourse Processes* 2.113-126.

van Dijk, T. A., ed. 1985. *Handbook of Discourse Analysis.* Vol.1 (*Disciplines of Discourse*); vol.2 (*Dimensions of Discourse*); vol.3 (*Discourse and Dialogue*); vol.4 (*Discourse Analysis in Society*). Orlando: Academic Press.

van Dijk, T. A. & W. Kintsch. 1983. *Strategies of Discourse Comprehension.* New York: Academic Press.

Vihman, M. M., M. A. Macken, R. Miller, H. Simmons & J. Miller, 1985. "From Babbling to Speech: A re-assessment of the continuity issue". *Language* 61.397-445.

Vuchinich, S. 1977. "Elements of Cohesion between Turns in Ordinary Conversation". *Semiotica* 20.229-257.

Vygotsky, L. S. 1962. *Thought and Language.* Cambridge, MA: MIT Press.

Walker, C. H. & F. R. Yekovich. 1987. "Activation and Use of Script-based Antecedents in Anaphoric Reference Effects". *Journal of Memory and Language* 26.673-691.

Warren, R. M. 1970. "Perceptual Restoration of Missing Speech Sounds". *Science* 167.392-393.

Warren, R. M. & C. J. Obusek. 1971. "Speech Perception and Phonemic Restorations". *Perception and Psychophysics* 9.358-363.

Warren, R. M. & G. L. Sherman. 1974. "Phonemic Restorations Based on Subsequent Context". *Perception and Psychophysics* 16.150-156.
Warren, R. M. & R. P. Warren. 1970. "Auditory Illusions and Confusions". *Scientific American* 223.30-36.
Wason, P. 1961. "Response to Affirmative and Negative Binary Statements". *British Journal of Psychology* 52.133-142.
Wason, P. 1965. "The Contexts of Plausible Denial". *Journal of Verbal Learning and Verbal Behavior* 4.7-11.
Watson, J. B. 1919. *Psychology from the Standpoint of a Behaviorist*. Philadelpia: Lippincott. (2nd ed., 1924.)
Watson, J. B. 1924. *Behaviorism*. New York: C. C. Norton.
Werker, J. F., J. H. Gilbert, K. Humphrey & R. C. Tees. 1981. "Developmental Aspects of Cross-language Speech Perception". *Child Development* 52.349-355.
Werker, J. F. & R. C. Tees. 1984. "Cross-language Speech Perception: Evidence for perceptual reorganization during the first year of life". *Infant Behavior and Development* 7.49-63.
Wertsch, J. V. 1986. *Vygotsky and the Social Formation of Mind*. Cambridge, MA: Harvard Univ. Press.
West, C. 1984. *Routine Complications: Troubles with talk between doctors and patients*. Bloomington: Indiana Univ. Press.
Wexler, K. & P. Culicover. 1980. *Formal Principles of Language Acquisition*. Cambridge, MA: MIT Press.
Whorf, B. L. 1956. *Language, Thought, & Reality: Selected writings of Benjamin Lee Whorf*. Edited by J. B. Carroll. Cambridge, MA: MIT Press.
Whorf, B. L. 1964. "A Linguistic Consideration of Thinking in Primitive Communities". *Language in Culture and Society* ed. by D. Hymes, 129-141. New York: Harper & Row.
Wickelgren, W. A. 1966. "Distinctive Features and Errors in Short-term Memory for English Consonants". *Journal of the Acoustical Society of America* 39.388-398.
Wierzbicka, A. 1986. "A Semantic Metalanguage for the Description and Comparison of Illocutionary Meanings". *Journal of Pragmatics* 10.67-107.
Wilks, Y. 1986. "Relevance and Beliefs". *Reasoning and Discourse Processes* ed. by T. Myers, K. Brown & B. McGonigle, 265-290. London: Academic Press.
Wilson, D. & D. Sperber. 1986. "Inference and Implicature in Utterance Interpretation". *Reasoning and Discourse Processes* ed. by T. Myers, K. Brown & B. McGonigle, 241-264. London: Academic Press.
Winograd, T. 1972. "Understanding natural language". *Cognitive Psychology* 3.1-191.
Winograd, T. 1983. "Viewing Language as a Knowledge-based Process". *Language as a Cognitive Process* ed. by T. Winograd, vol.1 (*Syntax*), 1-34. Reading, MA: Addison-Wesley.
Witelson, S. F. 1987. "Neurobiological Aspects of Language in Children". *Child Development* 58.653-688.
Witkowski, S. R. & C. H. Brown. 1978. "Lexical Universals". *Annual Review of Anthropology* 7.427-451.
Wright, P. 1972. "Some Observations on How People Answer Questions about Sentences". *Journal of Verbal Learning and Verbal Behavior* 11.188-195.
Wunderlich, D. 1980. "Methodological Remarks on Speech Act Theory". *Speech Act Theory and Pragmatics* ed. by J. R. Searle, F. Kiefer & M. Bierwisch, 291-312. Dordrecht: D. Reidel.

Yekovich, F. R. & P. W. Thorndyke. 1981. "An Evaluation of Alternative Functional Models of Narrative Schema". *Journal of Verbal Learning and Verbal Behavior* 20.454-469.

Yeni-Komshian, G. H., J. E. Kavanagh & C. A. Ferguson, eds. 1980. *Child Phonology*. Vol.1 (*Production*); vol.2 (*Perception*). New York: Academic Press.

Zangwill, O. L. 1975. "The Ontogeny of Cerebral Dominance in Man". *Foundations of Language Development* ed. by E. H. Lenneberg & E. Lenneberg, 137-147. New York: Academic Press.

Zipf, G. K. 1949. *Human Behavior and the Principle of Least Effort*. Cambridge, MA: Addison-Wesley.

Index

In the CURRENT ISSUES IN LINGUISTIC THEORY (CILT) series (Series Editor: E.F. Konrad Koerner) the following volumes have been published thus far, and will be published during 1991:

1. KOERNER, E.F. Konrad (ed.): *The Transformational-Generative Paradigm and Modern Linguistic Theory*. Amsterdam, 1975.
2. WEIDERT, Alfons: *Componential Analysis of Lushai Phonology*. Amsterdam, 1975.
3. MAHER, J. Peter: *Papers on Language Theory and History I: Creation and Tradition in Language*. Foreword by Raimo Anttila. Amsterdam, 1977.
4. HOPPER, Paul J. (ed.): *Studies in Descriptive and Historical Linguistics: Festschrift for Winfred P. Lehmann*. Amsterdam, 1977. Out of print.
5. ITKONEN, Esa: *Grammatical Theory and Metascience: A critical investigation into the methodological and philosophical foundations of 'autonomous' linguistics*. Amsterdam, 1978.
6. ANTTILA, Raimo: *Historical and Comparative Linguistics*. Amsterdam/Philadelphia, 1989.
7. MEISEL, Jürgen M. & Martin D. PAM (eds): *Linear Order and Generative Theory*. Amsterdam, 1979.
8. WILBUR, Terence H.: *Prolegomena to a Grammar of Basque*. Amsterdam, 1979.
9. HOLLIEN, Harry & Patricia (eds): *Current Issues in the Phonetic Sciences, Proceedings of the IPS-77 Congress, Miami Beach, Fla., 17-19 December 1977*. Amsterdam, 1979. 2 vols.
10. PRIDEAUX, Gary (ed.): *Perspectives in Experimental Linguistics. Papers from the University of Alberta Conference on Experimental Linguistics, Edmonton, 13-14 Oct. 1978*. Amsterdam, 1979.
11. BROGYANYI, Bela (ed.): *Studies in Diachronic, Synchronic, and Typological Linguistics: Festschrift for Oswald Szemerényi on the Occasion of his 65th Birthday*. Amsterdam, 1980.
12. FISIAK, Jacek (ed.): *Theoretical Issues in Contrastive Linguistics*. Amsterdam, 1980.
13. MAHER, J. Peter with coll. of Allan R. Bomhard & E.F. Konrad Koerner (ed.): *Papers from the Third International Conference on Historical Linguistics, Hamburg, August 22-26, 1977*. Amsterdam, 1982.
14. TRAUGOTT, Elizabeth C., Rebecca LaBRUM, Susan SHEPHERD (eds): *Papers from the Fourth International Conference on Historical Linguistics, Stanford, March 26-30, 1980*. Amsterdam, 1980.
15. ANDERSON, John (ed.): *Language Form and Linguistic Variation. Papers dedicated to Angus McIntosh*. Amsterdam, 1982.
16. ARBEITMAN, Yoël & Allan R. BOMHARD (eds): *Bono Homini Donum: Essays in Historical Linguistics, in Memory of J. Alexander Kerns*. Amsterdam, 1981.
17. LIEB, Hans-Heinrich: *Integrational Linguistics*. 6 volumes. Amsterdam, 1984-1986. Vol. I available; Vol. 2-6 n.y.p.
18. IZZO, Herbert J. (ed.): *Italic and Romance. Linguistic Studies in Honor of Ernst Pulgram*. Amsterdam, 1980.
19. RAMAT, Paolo et al. (eds): *Linguistic Reconstruction and Indo-European Syntax. Proceedings of the Coll. of the 'Indogermanische Gesellschaft' Univ. of Pavia, 6-7 Sept. 1979*. Amsterdam, 1980.
20. NORRICK, Neal R.: *Semiotic Principles in Semantic Theory*. Amsterdam, 1981.
21. AHLQVIST, Anders (ed.): *Papers from the Fifth International Conference on Historical Linguistics, Galway, April 6-10, 1981*. Amsterdam, 1982.

22. UNTERMANN, Jürgen & Bela BROGYANYI (eds): *Das Germanische und die Rekonstruktion der Indogermanische Grundsprache.* Akten, Proceedings from the Colloquium of the Indogermanische Gesellschaft, Freiburg, 26-27 February 1981. Amsterdam, 1984.
23. DANIELSEN, Niels: *Papers in Theoretical Linguistics.* Amsterdam, n.y.p.
24. LEHMANN, Winfred P. & Yakov MALKIEL (eds): *Perspectives on Historical Linguistics. Papers from a conference held at the meeting of the Language Theory Division, Modern Language Ass., San Francisco, 27-30 December 1979.* Amsterdam, 1982.
25. ANDERSEN, Paul Kent: *Word Order Typology and Comparative Constructions.* Amsterdam, 1983.
26. BALDI, Philip (ed.) *Papers from the XIIth Linguistic Symposium on Romance Languages, University Park, April 1-3, 1982.* Amsterdam, 1984.
27. BOMHARD, Alan: *Toward Proto-Nostratic.* Amsterdam, 1984.
28. BYNON, James: *Current Progress in Afroasiatic Linguistics: Papers of the Third International Hamito-Semitic Congress, London, 1978.* Amsterdam, 1984.
29. PAPROTTÉ, Wolf & René DIRVEN (eds): *The Ubiquity of Metaphor: Metaphor in Language and Thought.* Amsterdam, 1985.
30. HALL, Robert A., Jr.: *Proto-Romance Morphology.* Amsterdam, 1984.
31. GUILLAUME, Gustave: *Foundations for a Science of Language.* Translated and with an introd. by Walter Hirtle and John Hewson. Amsterdam, 1984.
32. COPELAND, James E. (ed.): *New Directions in Linguistics and Semiotics.* Houston/ Amsterdam, 1984. No rights for US/Can. *Customers from USA and Canada: please order from Rice University.*
33. VERSTEEGH, Kees: *Pidginization and Creolization: The Case of Arabic.* Amsterdam, 1984.
34. FISIAK, Jacek (ed.): *Papers from the VIth International Conference on Historical Linguistics, Poznan, 22-26 August 1983.* Amsterdam, 1985.
35. COLLINGE, N.E.: *The Laws of Indo-European.* Amsterdam, 1985.
36. KING, Larry D. & Catherine A. MALEY (eds): *Selected Papers from the XIIIth Linguistics Symposium on Romance Languages.* Amsterdam, 1985.
37. GRIFFEN, T.D.: *Aspects of Dynamic Phonology.* Amsterdam, 1985.
38. BROGYANYI, Bela & Thomas KRÖMMELBEIN (eds): *Germanic Dialects: Linguistic and Philological Investigations.* Amsterdam, 1986.
39. BENSON, James D., Michael J. CUMMINGS & William S. GREAVES (eds): *Linguistics in a Systemic Perspective.* Amsterdam, 1988.
40. FRIES, Peter Howard and Nancy (eds): *Toward an Understanding of Language: Charles C. Fries in Perspective.* Amsterdam, 1985.
41. EATON, Roger, et al. (eds): *Papers from the 4th International Conference on English Historical Linguistics.* Amsterdam, 1985.
42. MAKKAI, Adam & Alan K. MELBY (eds): *Linguistics and Philosophy. Essays in honor of Rulon S. Wells.* Amsterdam, 1985.
43. AKAMATSU, Tsutomu: *The Theory of Neutralization and the Archiphoneme in Functional Phonology.* Amsterdam, 1988.
44. JUNGRAITHMAYR, Herrmann & Walter W. MUELLER (eds): *Proceedings of the 4th International Hamito-Semitic Congress.* Amsterdam, 1987.
45. KOOPMAN, W.F., F.C. VAN DER LEEK, O. FISCHER & R. EATON (eds): *Explanation and Linguistic Change.* Amsterdam, 1987.

46. PRIDEAUX, Gary D., and William J. BAKER: *Strategies and Structures: The Processing of Relative Clauses*. Amsterdam, 1986.
47. LEHMANN, Winfred P.: *Language Typology 1985. Papers from the Linguistic Typology Symposium, Moscow, 9-13 Dec. 1985*. Amsterdam, 1986.
48. RAMAT, Anna Giacalone (ed.): *Proceedings of the VII International Conference on Historical Linguistics, Pavia 9-13 September 1985*. Amsterdam, 1987.
49. WAUGH, Linda R. & Stephen RUDY (eds): *New Vistas in Grammar: Invariance and Variation*. Amsterdam/Philadelphia, 1991.
50. RUDZKA-OSTYN, Brygida (ed.): *Topics in Cognitive Linguistics*. Amsterdam/Philadelphia, 1988.
51. CHATTERJEE, Ranjit: *Aspect and Meaning in Slavic and Indic*. Amsterdam/Philadelphia, 1988.
52. FASOLD, Ralph & Deborah SCHIFFRIN (eds): *Language Change and Variation*. Amsterdam/Philadelphia, 1989.
53. SANKOFF, David (ed.): *Diversity and Diachrony*. Amsterdam, 1986.
54. WEIDERT, Alfons: *Tibeto-Burman Tonology. A Comparative Analysis*. Amsterdam, 1987.
55. HALL, Robert A. Jr.: *Linguistics and Pseudo-Linguistics*. Amsterdam, 1987.
56. HOCKETT, Charles F.: *Refurbishing our Foundations. Elementary Linguistics from an Advanced Point of View*. Amsterdam, 1987.
57. BUBENIK, Vít: *Hellenistic and Roman Greece as a Sociolinguistic Area*. Amsterdam/Philadelphia, 1989.
58. ARBEITMAN, Yoël L.: *FUCUS. A Semitic/Afrasian Gathering in Remembrance of Albert Ehrman*. Amsterdam/Philadelphia, 1988.
59. VOORST, Jan van: *Event Structure*. Amsterdam/Philadelphia, 1988.
60. KIRSCHNER, Carl and Janet DECESARIS (eds): *Studies in Romance Linguistics*. Amsterdam/Philadelphia, 1989.
61. CORRIGAN, Roberta, Fred ECKMAN and Michael NOONAN (eds): *Linguistic Categorization*. Amsterdam/Philadelphia, 1989.
62. FRAJZYNGIER, Zygmunt (ed.): *Current Progress in Chadic Linguistics*. Amsterdam/Philadelphia, 1989.
63. EID, Mushira (ed.): *Perspectives on Arabic Linguistics I. Papers from the First Annual Symposium on Arabic Linguistics*. Amsterdam/Philadelphia, 1990.
64. BROGYANYI, Bela (ed.): *Essays in Linguistics. Offered in honor of Oswald Szemerényi on the occasion of his 75th birthday*. Amsterdam/Philadelphia, n.y.p.
65. ADAMSON, Sylvia, Vivien A. LAW, Nigel VINCENT and Susan WRIGHT (eds): *Papers from the 5th International Conference of English Historical Linguistics*. Amsterdam/Philadelphia, 1990.
66. ANDERSEN, Henning and Konrad KOERNER (eds): *Historical Linguistics 1987. Papers from the 8th International Conference on Historical Linguistics, Lille, August 30-September 4, 1987*. Amsterdam/Philadelphia, 1990.
67. LEHMANN, Winfred (ed.): *Language Typology 1987. Systematic Balance in Language. Papers from the Linguistic Typology Symposium, Berkeley, 1-3 December 1987*. Amsterdam/Philadelphia, 1990.
68. BALL, Martin, James FIFE, Erich POPPE and Jenny ROWLAND (eds): *Celtic Linguistics / Ieithyddiaeth Geltaidd. Readings in the Brythonic Languages. Festschrift for T. Arwyn Watkins*. Amsterdam/Philadelphia, 1990.

69. WANNER, Dieter and Douglas A. KIBBEE (eds): *New Analyses in Romance Linguistics. Papers from the XVIII Linguistic Symposium on Romance Languages, Urbana-Champaign, April 7-9, 1988.* Amsterdam/Philadelphia, 1991.
70. JENSEN, John T.: *Morphology. Word Structure in Generative Grammar.* Amsterdam/Philadelphia, 1990.
71. O'GRADY, WILLIAM: *Categories and Case. The sentence structure of Korean.* Amsterdam/Philadelphia, 1991.
72. EID, Mushira and John McCARTHY (eds): *Perspectives on Arabic Linguistics II Papers from the Second Annual Symposium on Arabic Linguistics.* Amsterdam/Philadelphia, 1990.
73. STAMENOV, Maxim (ed.): *Current Advances in Semantic Theory.* Amsterdam/Philadelphia, n.y.p.
74. LAEUFER, Christiane and Terrell A. MORGAN (eds): *Theoretical Analyses in Romance Linguistics.* Amsterdam/Philadelphia, n.y.p.
75. DROSTE, Flip G. and John E. JOSEPH (eds): *Linguistic Theory and Grammatical Description.* Amsterdam/Philadelphia, 1991.
76. WICKENS, Mark A.: *Grammatical Number in English Nouns.* Amsterdam/Philadelphia, 1991.
77. BOLTZ, William G. and Michael C. SHAPIRO (eds): *Studies in the Historical Phonology of Asian Languages.* Amsterdam/Philadelphia, 1991. n.y.p.
78. KAC, Michael: *Grammars and Grammaticality.* Amsterdam/Philadelphia, 1991. n.y.p.
79. ANTONSEN, Elmer H. and Hans Henrich HOCK (eds): *STÆFCRÆFT: Studies in Germanic Linguistics.* Amsterdam/Philadelphia, 1991.
80. COMRIE, Bernard and Mushira EID (eds): *Perspectives on Arabic Linguistics III.* Amsterdam/Philadelphia, 1991.
81. LEHMANN, Winfred P. & H.J. HEWITT (eds): *Language Typology 1988. Typological Models in Reconstruction.* Amsterdam/Philadelphia, 1991.
82. VAN VALIN, Robert D. (ed.): *Advances in Role and Reference Grammar.* Amsterdam/Philadelphia, n.y.p.
83. FIFE, James & Erich POPPE (eds): *Studies in Brythonic Word Order.* Amsterdam/Philadelphia, 1991.
84. DAVIS, Garry W. & Gregory K. IVERSON (eds): *Explanation in Historical Linguistics.* Amsterdam/Philadelphia, n.y.p.
85. BROSELOW, Ellen, Mushira EID & John McCARTHY (eds): *Perspectives on Arabic Linguistics IV.* Amsterdam/Philadelphia, n.y.p.
86. KESS, Joseph L.: *Psycholinguistics. Psychology, Linguistics, and the Study of Natural Language.* Amsterdam/Philadelphia, 1992.